Noun + Verb Compounding in Western Romance

Kathryn Klingebiel

UNIVERSITY OF CALIFORNIA PRESS

Berkeley • Los Angeles • London

UNIVERSITY OF CALIFORNIA PRESS
BERKELEY AND LOS ANGELES, CALIFORNIA

340295   UNIVERSITY OF CALIFORNIA PRESS, LTD.
LONDON, ENGLAND

ISBN: 0-520-09729-7
LIBRARY OF CONGRESS CATALOG CARD NUMBER: 88-32406

Library of Congress Cataloging-in-Publication Data

Klingebiel, Kathryn
    Noun + verb compounding in Western romance / Kathryn Klingebiel.
        p.   cm. — (University of California publications in
linguistics; v. 113)
    Rev. ed. of the author's thesis (doctoral—University of
California, 1985) with the title: Romance reflexes of the Latin
compositional type manūtenēre.
    Bibliography: p.
    Includes indexes.
    ISBN 0-520-09729-7
    1. Romance languages—word formation. 2. Romance languages—
compound words. 3. Romance languages—Noun. 4. Romance languages—
Verb. 5. Latin language—Influence on Romance. I. Title.
II. Title: Noun plus verb compounding in Western romance.
III. Series.
PC103.K55   1989
440—dc19   88-32406
                                                       CIP

NOUN + VERB COMPOUNDING
IN WESTERN ROMANCE

To Yakov Malkiel

Contents

Preface

This monograph represents a revised, slightly expanded version of my doctoral thesis, "Romance Reflexes of the Latin Compositional Type *manūtenēre*" (University of California, Berkeley, 1985), directed by Professor Yakov Malkiel. Thanks are due to the many teachers, colleagues, friends, and family members who offered me an uncommon measure of support at the dissertation stage, as well as to those who have been instrumental in the processes of revision and final preparation. My son Chris made the printing possible. I would like to express my gratitude to Armin Schwegler, Al Muth, and Anne Flexer, for their help in preparing the revised Appendices. Special thanks go to Professors Yakov Malkiel, Jerry R. Craddock, and Ruggero Stefanini, as well as to Professor Gary Holland for his generous help with the reworking of Chapter 2, the responsibility for which remains mine alone. The remainder of the text has benefitted enormously from a final rereading by Professor Malkiel, to whom it is my privilege and great pleasure to dedicate this work.

Abbreviations

Linguistic Abbreviations

1. *Languages and Areas*: Cl. = Classical; Med. = Medieval;
   O = Old; M(id.) = Middle; Mod. = Modern

Amer.	American Spanish
Andal.	Andalucia
Anj.	Anjou
A.-Norm.	Anglo-Norman
Arag.	Aragonese
Ast.	Asturian
Auv.	Auvergnat
Aveyr.	Aveyron (Auvergne)
B.-Alpes	Basses-Alpes
Béar.	Béarnais
Belg.	Belgium, Belgian
Boul.	Boulogne (Pas-de-Calais)
Bourg.	Bourgogne
Bret.	Breton
Brit.	British
Cast.	Castilian
Castr.	Castres (Tarn)
Cat.	Catalan
Cév.	Cévennes
Champ.	Champagne
Dauph.	Dauphiné
Eng.	English
Engad.	Engadine
Fr.	French
FrComté	Franche-Comté
Fr-Pr.	Franco-Provençal
Frk.	Frankish
Gasc.	Gascon

Gir.	Gironde
Gm.	German
Gmc.	Germanic
Gk.	Greek
Guy.	Guyenne
H.-Alpes	Hautes-Alpes
HG	High German
IE	Indo-European
It.	Italian
L.	Latin
Lang.	Languedoc
Lim.	Limousin
Logud.	Logudorese
Mars.	Marseille
Mex.	Mexican Spanish
Morv.	Morvan
Mos.	Moselle
Moz.	Mozarabic
Narb.	Narbonne
Nav.	Navarrese
Norm.	Normandy
Occ.	Occitan
Périg.	Périgord
Pic.	Picard
PIE	Proto-Indo-European
Poit.	Poitou
Pr.	Provence, Provençal
PRom.	Proto-Romance
Ptg.	Portuguese
Puiss.	Puisserguier (Hérault)
Pyr.	Pyrenees
Quer.	Quercy
RLs	Romance languages
Rouerg.	Rouergue (Auvergne)
Rum.	Rumanian
Skt.	Sanskrit
Sp.	Spanish
Suisse Rom.	Suisse Romande
Toul.	Toulouse
Val.	Valais
Vaud.	Vaudois
Viv.	Vivarais
VL.	Vulgar Latin
Wall.	Walloon

2. Terms

Adj	adjective
Adv	adverb
arch.	archaic

archeol.	archeology
archit.	architecture
Art	article
att.	attested
augm.	augmentative
bot.	botanical
colloq.	colloquial
Compl	complement
culin.	culinary
cult.	cultismo (learnèd formation)
denom.	denominal
der.	derivative
dial.	dialect
Dir	Direct
dm	determinatum
dt	determinans
eccles.	ecclesiastical
f.	feminine
fig.	figurative
freq.	frequentative
Genit	genitive
hap.	hapax legomenon
hort.	horticultural
impt.	imperative
Ind	indirect
Inf	infinitive
Instr	instrumental
intr.	intransitive
m. or masc.	masculine
mil.	military
N	noun
naut.	nautical
n.d.	no date
n.g.	no gloss
nom.	nominal
n.p.	no place
Num	numeral
O or Obj	object
obl.	oblique
onom.	onomatopoeic
ornith.	ornithological
pass.	passive
PersPn	personal pronoun
pl.	plural
Pn	pronoun
Prep	preposition
Pres	present
Ptc	participle
refl.	reflexive

std.	standard
S or Subj	subject
synon.	synonym(s)
tech.	technical
TG	transformational-generative [grammar]
V	verb
var.	variant
WO	word order

Bibliographic Abbreviations

Acad 1970, *Acad* 1984   *Diccionario de la lengua española*. Real Academia Española.

AD   *Traité de la formation des mots composés dans la langue française* Darmesteter 1894.

AH   *Léxico del . . . Siglo de Oro* Alonso Hernández 1976.

AlemB   *Tratado de la formación de palabras en la lengua castellana* Alemany Bolufer 1920.

ALG   *Atlas linguistique et ethnographique de la Gascogne* Séguy 1954–73.

Alibert   *Gramatica occitana segon los parlars lengadocians* Alibert 1976.

AM   *Diccionari català-valencià-balear* Alcover-Moll 1930–62.

A.-Norm. Dict   *Anglo-Norman Dictionary* Stone–Rothwell–Reid 1977–81.

Archives Gironde   *Archives historiques de la Gironde*, ed. E. Abbadie 1902.

AThomas 1898   "Les Noms composés et la dérivation en français et en provençal" Thomas 1898.

BDE[LC]   *Breve diccionario etimológico de la lengua castellana* Corominas 1961.

BFE   *Boletín de Filología Española*. Madrid.

BH   *Bulletin Hispanique*. Bordeaux.

BM   *Gramàtica catalana* Badia Margarit 1962.

BSGers   *Bulletin de la Société Archéologique, Historique, Littéraire et Scientifique du Gers*. Auch.

BSLP   *Bulletin de la Société de Linguistique de Paris*. Paris.

B-W   *Dictionnaire étymologique de la langue française* Bloch–Wartburg 1968.

DAG   *Dictionnaire onomasiologique de l'ancien gascon* Baldinger 1975a.

DAO   *Dictionnaire onomasiologique de l'ancien occitan* Baldinger 1975b.

DCE[LC]   *Diccionario crítico etimológico de la lengua castellana* Corominas 1954–57.

DECC   *Diccionari etimològic i complementari de la llengua catalana* Corominas 1980–.

Dicc 1982   *Diccionari de la llengua catalana* 1982.

Dicc Vox 1983   *Diccionari manual castellà-català, català-castellà*.

Dictionnaire général   *Dictionnaire général de la langue française* Darmesteter 1932.

DuC   *Glossarium Mediae et Infimae Latinitatis* Du Cange 1845.

EDAF   Nuevo Diccionario General Español-Inglés EDAF 1977.

FEW   Französisches etymologisches Wörterbuch Wartburg 1922–.

GdeD 1985   *Diccionario etimológico español e hispánico* Garcia de Diego 1985.

GMLCat   Glossarium Mediae Latinitatis Cataloniae 1960–79.

God   *Dictionnaire de l'ancienne langue française* Godefroy 1880–92.

God *Lex   Lexique de l'ancien français* Godefroy 1901.

GRS   Grammatik der romanischen Sprachen Vol. 2 Meyer-Lübke 1895.

HR   Hispanic Review. Philadelphia.

JA   *Grammaire de l'ancien provençal* Anglade 1921.

JR   *Grammaire [h]istorique des parlers provençaux modernes* Ronjat 1937.

KN   *Grammaire historique de la langue française* Nyrop 1924.

LA   *Dictionnaire occitan-français d'après les parlers languedociens* Alibert 1977.

LeG   Le Gascon Rohlfs 1977.

L-S   *A Latin Dictionary* Lewis–Short 1969.

M   *Lou Tresor dóu Felibrige* Mistral 1932.

MLN   Modern Language Notes. Baltimore.

MR   Medioevo Romanzo. Naples.

MzP   *Manual de gramática histórica española* Menéndez Pidal 1941.

NGML   Novum Glossarium Mediae Latinitatis Blatt 1957–.

PA   *Nuevo diccionario etimológico aragonés* Pardo Asso 1938.

Pal   *Dictionnaire du béarnais et du gascon modernes* Palay 1980.

PF   *Diccionari general de la llengua catalana* Fabra 1966.

Rayn   *Lexique roman* Raynouard 1838–44.

REW   Romanisches etymologisches Wörterbuch Meyer-Lübke 1930–35.

RF   Romanische Forschungen. Frankfort on the Main.

RFE   Revista de Filología Española. Madrid.

RLiR   Revue de Linguistique Romane. Lyon and Paris.

Ro   Romania. Paris.

RPh   Romance Philology. Berkeley and Los Angeles.

RR   Romanic Revue. New York.

RRL   Revue Roumaine de Linguistique. Bucharest.

SCL   Studii şi Cercetări Lingvistice. Bucharest.

T-L   *Altfranzösisches Wörterbuch.* Tobler–Lommatzsch.

TLF   Trésor de la langue française 1977–86.

TLL   Travaux de Linguistique et de Littérature. Strasbourg.

Tresor   Tresor de la llengua, de les tradicions i de la cultura popular de la Catalunya Griera 1935–47.

UCPL   University of California Publications in Linguistics. Berkeley and Los Angeles.

VR   *Vox Romanica*. Bern.
XdeF   *Lou pichot trésor* Xavier de Fourvières 1973.
ZPhon   *Zeitschrift für Phonetik, Sprachwissenschaft und Kommunikationsforschung.*
       Berlin.
ZRPh   *Zeitschrift für romanische Philologie*. Halle, then Tübingen.

INTRODUCTION

INTRODUCTORY REMARKS

Reflexes and analogs of Med.L. *manūtenēre* arose from verb-final Latin syntax, yet today have become morphologically distinguishable compounds through changes in basic word order. This monograph traces the rise and development of N[oun] + V[erb] compound formations, e.g., Fr. *maintenir* (12th c.) 'to defend, protect'; (Mod.) 'to maintain, keep', in four major Romance languages. Since the early 1960s, increasing attention has been paid to word formation in general, and in particular to composition—or compounding, as it is more frequently called nowadays.

My exploratory research into Romance compounding uncovered one type particularly deserving of full-length study, the N + V pattern, abundantly attested in Occitan and Catalan, although virtually absent from standard Northern French and Spanish. A corpus culled from these four Western Romance [1] languages offers ample scope and diversity for comparative and diachronic study of this compound pattern. Inclusion of Catalan (sometimes grouped with Occitan into Occitano-Romance) provides not only the link between Gallo- and Hispano-Romance, but also the eastern analog of Gascon (itself particularly active in N + V compounding among the Occitan dialects). The various dialects of Occitan, including Gascon, are taken here as parts of a linguistic whole. Similarly, the French *patois* must be understood as part and parcel of northern Gallo-Romance, which is certainly broader than the standard

---

[1]"Western Romance" as used here refers to Gallo-Romance (French and Occitan) and Hispano-Romance (Catalan, Spanish, but not Portuguese); this is a geographical, not a chronological, distinction within the Romance continuum.

literary dialect based on *francien*. Brief mention is made of other Romance languages in which the N + V pattern is or has been extant.

Compound verbs constitute the major component of each Western Romance N + V corpus. By supplementing compound verbs with similarly structured adjectives and nouns, the problem of establishing absolute priorities is relegated to secondary place. In very general terms, infinitives consisting of nominal and verbal elements fall into a useful hierarchy of four types, illustrated here with French and Spanish:

    (i) Fr. *eau donner*
    (ii) Fr. *maintenir*
    (iii) Sp. *man(i)festar*
    (iv) Sp. *manumitir*

Type (i), (18th c.) *eau donner* 'to soak before adding indigo' (step in dying process), a "locution verbale" structurally almost equivalent to *tenir tête* 'to keep up with', invites comparison with the remainder, which are written as one word. Type (iv) embraces crass Latinisms, e.g., *manumitir*, denom. *manufacturer*, harkening back directly to Latin structure and lexicon. They are flanked by a substantial number of partially or wholly vernacular counterparts, e.g., OFr. *manumetre, mainmetre*, OPr. *mafa(i)t* (MANŪ FACTUS; no corresponding verb is available). While Neo-Graeco-Latin compounds formed with stems or composition vowels—cf. Fr. *télévision* or Sp. *pediluvio* 'foot-bath'—are peripheral to this monograph, the increasing popularity of either type since the Middle Ages may have played some part in the development of vernacular N + V compounds: witness attested wavering between compounds formed with a thematic vowel and those lacking such a vowel, e.g., Sp. (17th c.) *maniatar*, (18th c.) *manatar*; Sp. *mantener, manutener*. Type (i) represents one potential source of Romance N + V compounding, just as Cl.L. *manū tenēre* 'to have personal knowledge of' relates to Med.L. *manūtenēre* 'to defend = hold with/ by the hand'; types (iii) and (iv) provide additional evidence, but the focus here will be on type (ii), *maintenir* and its like, in which independently identifiable lexemes are compounded without recourse to phonetic or morphological readjustment, to Graeco-Latin patterns, or to direct loan translation (calquing).

Since N + V structure involves more than *manūtenēre*, compounds having nouns or adjectives as their second constituent have been included in the discussion of both medieval/Renaissance and also modern N + V corpuses. This makes possible the illustration of analogical influences that have contributed to the success and propagation of its reflexes, and its developments.

Fr. *maintenir* and its congeners have been variously labeled and analyzed, most convincingly by Jules Ronjat in his historical grammar of the Mod. Occitan dialects (1937, repr. 1980) (see Chapter 1). It is true, nonetheless, that several frequently cited examples of N + V compounding continue to be incorrectly identified in the literature; e.g., *arc-bouter* 'to support with a flying buttress' (which Darmesteter

[1894:164] identified as a denominal from *arcboutant* 'flying buttress') still figures as an example of N + V in Giurescu (1975) and Thiele (1981). The archaic, allegedly nonproductive status of N + V compounds has probably worked against full-scale investigation of this type; even recent studies of V + N compounds (e.g., Fr. *porte-feuille* 'wallet', *lave-vaisselle* 'dishwasher'; see, e.g., Bierbach [1982] and [1983]) have failed to appreciate the potential benefits of overt comparison and contrast with N + V. [2]

French leans heavily on V + N, to the virtual exclusion of its converse. Occitan dialects, including Gascon, lean just as heavily on V + N, but to this day N + V

---

[2]Among its manifestations in Romance, the N + V pattern has furnished a few V + N compounds by apparent reversal of elements, e.g., Cat. *lloctinent/tinentlloc* (both 14th c.); Cat. (14th c.) *camalliga*/(16th c.) *lligacama*; Sp. (11th c.) *misacantano/* Andal.–Mex. (from 16th–17th c.?) *cantamisano* 'priest'; Occ. *a palavira/a vira-palados* 'in profusion', lit. 'by the shovelful'; Occ. (14th c.) *manobra* 'manual labor, worker'/ Old Occ. *obre-mâ* 'worker'; Poit. *mau-faisant/faisantmau* 'mischievous, harmful'. Cf. Klingebiel, "New Compounds from the Old: An Unexpected Source of Verb + Noun Compounds in Romance", *Proceedings of the Fourteenth Annual Meeting of the Berkeley Linguistics Society* (Berkeley, Calif., 1988), 88-99.

It should be noted that the internal (= syntactic) relation between nominal and verbal elements in either type is unaltered by a reversal of word order. There are other essential similarities. The exocentric nature of V + N compounds (Fr. *lave-vaisselle* 'x [which] washes the dishes') and of adjectival compounds such as Fr. *bouche-bée* 'openmouthed' (= 'x with mouth opened wide') equally applies to N + V Pres Ptc: Sp. *misacantano* 'x who sings the mass', and to N + V Past Ptc: Occ./ Cat. *solabatut* 'footsore' = 'x [whose] sole [is] beaten', or 'x is beaten in the sole'. In the case of a transitive N + V compound verb, two direct objects occasionally emerge without being necessarily present in the speaker's consciousness, e.g., Gasc. *que la m'ha capbirade* '(a new lover) turned her away from me'. Such cases offer tangible proof that compounding proceeds at differing levels of predication. A dual (or triple) predication underlies any compound; it is frequently impossible to capture unequivocally the initial relationship. Underlying Cat. *lligacama, camalliga* is a noun in direct-object relation to its verb. It is less clear what motivates Occ.–Sp. *pelmudar*: (i) *la pel muda* 'the skin changes', or (ii) *[x] muda la pel* 'someone changes skin'. Fr. *tournesol*, Occ. *virasolelh*, It. *girasole* 'sunflower', lit. 'turn' + 'sun', may represent (i) an indirect object, 'turn to the sun', as Alibert argued (1976:394); or, conceivably, (ii) a vocative ('turn, [o] Sun'). Speakers of a language, however, have no trouble both producing and decoding compounds based on such hazy relationships.

Where a nominal and a verbal element are present, for example, in a primary predication, either N + V or V + N surface word order could theoretically be realized if both patterns were available to the speaker at a given moment. The disposition of elements might even accord primarily with need, following a kind of natural word order. If a nominal compound was needed, for example, V + N would prevail, since final N confers an essentially nominal value on the whole; conversely, were the final element a V, the resultant compound would acquire a preeminently verbal value.

remains a viable, even if marginal, type. A rapid search through the standard dictionary of Béarnais and Gascon (Palay [1980]) casts off numerous pairs such as Gasc. *a passe-bie* 'on the way' (*bie* < VĬA); and *bie-passà* 'to exceed, transcend the limits', 'outrepasser'. Each vernacular corpus consists of items available in glossaries and dictionaries. The actual degree of lexicalization of these items resists attempts at specification, and in fact must be considered tangential to the creative potential demonstrated by the N + V pattern. The majority of N + V compound examples presented below appear to be words of local provenance, many of which fail to spread widely, according to available evidence, and may well disappear within a relatively short period of the time. N + V compounds appear so frequently (albeit without mention of date or source) in Palay's dictionary of Gascon, for example, that one wonders whether the lexicographer has not taken liberties. Yet if a single speaker/writer of a language invents a form in a moment of need, that form has all the validity of his or her competence; in a dictionary-based study of compounding such as this, lexicographic listing is the ultimate validation. [3]

---

[3]Occasional comments from the *FEW* and *DECC* throw light on my material. In the latter, Corominas qualifies, e.g., *corferir* 'to afflict, cause pain', *corfondre* 'to become confused, feel faint' as literary, and as archaic *colltrencar* 'to dislocate or break the back of the neck'. In discussing *escarapelar*, which he traced to CARPĔRE, the same scholar elsewhere (*DCE*, s.v. "cara") comments: "Claro que luego se entendió como compuesto de *cara* + *pelar*, pero no es de creer que sea ésta la etimología verdadera, pues esta clase de formación sería extraordinaria en castellano." Other analyses in the *DCE* consistently support this point of view, at the expense of acknowledging genuine, if limited, occurrences of N + V compounding in Spanish. The newer *DECC* fails to expand upon the surprising vitality of Catalan N + V compounding in relation to Spanish, despite more explicit awareness of the nominal value accruing to *cap* 'head, end' in Cat. *capllevar* (*DECC*, s.v. "lleu"—see Appendix C for full citation). Evidence from the *FEW* has occasionally been slighted in the *DCE* and *DECC*, to unfortunate effect: *FEW* XI, s.v. "sanguis" cites several cognates of Cat. *sang-foniment*, *-fús* from Anglo-Norman, Old Provençal, and southern Occitan which seem to support Alcover-Moll's conjectured **sanguifŭndĕre* rather than an explanation based on reinterpreted SUB- (*DECC*, s.v. "fondre"). Neither of these two Hispano-Romance dictionaries does anything to correct an apparently long-standing tradition of analyzing ALL first elements in non-simplex words as prefixes.

I have sought to palliate the vagaries of dictionary practices by examining many of the *FEW* lexicographic sources, as well as the *FEW* itself. To these have been added a considerable supplement of post-1969 reference books (including dictionaries) for Occitan; these appear as a Bibliographic Supplement to Klingebiel (1986*b*). My research has also turned up results differing—although not significantly—from those of the twenty-four volumes of the *FEW*: some examples absent there, and some that I would not have otherwise found. Inconsistencies of ana-lysis, e.g., double listings and hesitations, in the *FEW* also came to light. I note: (i) Lim. *banlevar* 'to upset, turn over' attributed to both **bank-* (I, 60a) and **banks* (I,

"Compound" is used here to refer to a lexeme consisting of two (or more) identifiably independent lexemes or lexical units. In the Appendices, each compound is analyzed into its constituents, which are separately glossed (see the latter half of this Introduction for a fuller description of the corpus and appendices). Taxonomic analysis in the Appendices is based on constituent parts of speech. Taxonomies, however, have no power to illuminate the varied sources of N + V compounding in Western Romance: (i) direct inheritance from spoken Latin; (ii) loan translations from Latin or Greek; (iii) back-formation; (iv) remodeling of existing compounds; and (v) independent creation of compounds. Finally, (vi) the corpus of N + V nouns is augmented by a small number of conversions from infinitival formations.

Both (iv) and (v) are admittedly analogical processes, (iv) characterized by Marouzeau as "analogie assimilatrice," by which associated types are made more similar, and (v) as "analogie créatrice," resulting in the appearance of a new word (1961:18–19). This latter process, in turn, applies in several recognizable cases: reinforcement of simplex verbs, e.g., dial. Fr. *peaumuer* 'to molt', as against std. Fr. *muer* idem; and creation of new words by chaining, or "enchaînement associatif" (a convenient term found in Séguy [1953]): either constituent of a compound can be subject to paradigmatic replacement by other elements in a given (semantic) series, even when the result is superficially absurd (**chante-pierre* lit. 'where the stone sings' or 'song of the stone', on the model of *chante-loup* 'where the wolf sings', 'song of the wolf', and so on). However, "enchaînement associatif" cannot fully suffice to explain another group of compounds which seemingly spring into existence from nowhere, e.g., Gasc. *causse-ha* 'to knit socks', Arag. *mancuspir* 'to spit into one's hands and rub them together before taking hold of a tool'. This type of compound has English counterparts, e.g. (20th c.), *to bulb-snatch*, which have been called "inversions [of corresponding syntactic phrases, e.g., *to snatch bulbs*] with back-formation as back-ground influence" (Pennanen 1966:117). In his full-length study of English back-formations, Pennanen somewhat qualifies the term "inversions" by admitting that *to bulb-snatch*, etc., may represent back-formations from imperfectly recorded agent or action nouns, e.g., **bulb-snatcher, *-snatching*. In my view, both verbs can be considered true compounds in the absence of direct, attested lexical support.

Only a finely focused examination of all these sources will suffice to explain the proliferation of N + V in post-medieval Occitan and Catalan, as against French and Spanish. The medieval corpus of N + V compounds in all four target languages arose, unexceptionally, as a function of internal diachronic evolution from Latin to

---

238a); (ii) Fr. Norm. *embaufumer* 'to stink out'/Reims *embaufumé* 'ill' attributed to both *fumus* (II, 856a) and *buff-, puff-* (I, 596b); (iii) dial. Fr. *bourrenflé* 'swollen' attributed to either *bod-* (I, 422) or *burra*, through *bourrer* 'to stuff' (*inflare*, IV, 675b).

Romance; yet, in its contrast with literary French and Spanish, the modern Occitano-Romance situation emerges as a function of analogical factors, particularly relative freedom from the strictures of a forbiddingly codified literary language. For the key to exploitation of the N + V pattern, the most satisfactory approach remains the multiple, combining internal (principally syntax and semantics) and external (particularly analogy) factors.

My research was conducted with the following questions in mind: What favors the appearance or survival of certain compound types, and their spread, in any given language? Subsidiarily, can compounds be considered as relics of older syntactic patterns? How does the Latin status of N + V contrast and compare with the pattern in medieval and modern Romance? How do medieval and modern examples of the *manūtenēre, maintenir, mantener* type differ? Why does this type flourish today in Occitan (particularly Gascon) and Catalan, as against French and Spanish? Concurrently, what semantic fields are favored for this type at either stage of the four target languages? To these questions the following chapters should supply answers that will complement the predominantly synchronic studies of compounding, both Romance and general, of the last quarter-century.

THE CORPUS AND APPENDICES

In Chapter 3, each vernacular corpus runs through the 16th century; in Chapter 4, through the 20th century. The Old French period is generally considered, with Tobler and Lommatzsch, to have ended ca. 1350; if a middle period is to be distinguished for Occitan, Old Provençal would also run through ca. 1350, while Old Spanish and Old Catalan continue until 1479 (the date of the accession of Ferdinand and Isabella, when the Catalan language was officially abandoned for Spanish). Although its classical period ended with the taking of Monségur in 1244, literary Old Provençal continued in use well into the 15th century; according to the *FEW* (s.v. "manumittere"), Old Gascon extended at least through 1440. By the 16th century, Med. Latin had disappeared everywhere in Western Europe, and vernacular SVO structures had been generalized, leaving only a residue of frozen OV phrases (Fr. *sans coup férir* 'without striking a blow').

Constituents of the *manūtenēre* type during both the medieval and modern periods include:

> N + V: Fr. *maintenir*; OBéar. *carn-bedar* 'Lent' (lit. 'flesh' + 'to prohibit');
> Béar. *causse-ha* 'to knit socks'

N + V Pres Ptc: OFr. *nientdisant* 'insignificant', 'of which one can say naught'; OFr. *painquerant* 'seeking [gifts of] bread'; Béar. *gay-hasén* (adj.) 'pleasing' (lit. 'joy' + 'making')

N + V Past Ptc: OFr. *champcheü* (adj.) 'fallen on the battlefield'; OSp. *mampuesta* (nom.) 'protection'; Béar.–Cat. *cap-pelat* 'bald'; Arag. *botinchau* 'swollen' (+ INFLĀTU[M])

These constituents could combine into the following parts of speech having N + V structure:

V: (infinitives, verbal periphrases, and parasynthetics: [4] Fr. *maintenir*; OFr. *amentevoir* 'to remember'; Béar. *ha la camalliga* 'to trip someone'; Béar. *acabourrá/encabourrí* 'to get stubborn' (cf. Gasc. *cap-bourrùt* 'stubborn')

N: OBéar. *carn-bedar* 'Lent' (verbal form lacking); Béar. *co-heride* 'heartache'; Sp. *misacantano* 'priest'

Adj: OFr. *champcheü* 'fallen on the battlefield'; Béar. *gay-hasén* 'pleasing'

Adv. Phrase: OSp. *a manteniente* 'forcefully'; OFr. *en manaye* 'abundantly' (< MANŪ ADIŪTU[M]); Béar. *a palafica* 'abundantly', *a la mâ-taste* 'by hand'

In Chapters 3 and 4, each corpus is arranged into twenty informal semantic fields. Continued exploitation of the N + V pattern has always depended particularly upon semantic notions. In the medieval period there was important support drawn from still-viable OV syntactic structures; in the modern period as well, close investigation of the semantic fields into which these compounds fall is vital to an understanding of continued vitality of N + V after the disappearance of Latin in the very late medieval period of each vernacular.

Chapter 3 opens with a section devoted to Latin borrowings of all periods. These compounds are defined by their formal characteristics: lack of syncope, of lenition, or of other signs of vernacular phonetic evolution—i.e., by their minimal adjustment to Romance phonology and morphology. Med. Latin is included with Romance in the semantic fields detailed in Chapter 3, section 2; the substantial Med. Latin corpus offers evidence of an identifiable N + V pattern in which those processes visible in the vernacular corpuses, and partially if not wholly at the Cl. Latin level, are also operative (section 3).

Following the onomasiological presentation of N + V compounds, [5] both of these

---

[4]"Parasynthetic," admittedly not the best of labels, is used to denote verbs carrying both prefix and suffix.

[5]Several non–N + V formations are included for additional illustration. Occitan compounds with adv. *for-*, Gasc. *horo-* (cf. well-known Fr. *forsené*, It. *forsennato*, etc. 'deranged, out [*hors*] of one's mind [*sens* 'senses'] < L. *foris*, *foras* 'out of doors,

chapters provide statistical breakdowns of nominal and verbal elements in the four Romance corpuses. Section 5 of Chapter 3 reviews syntactic and semantic supports for the vernacular N + V pattern; section 6 presents evidence of short-lived artistic experimentation with classical nominal-adjectival models, but few instances of new infinitival N + V compounds except as reinterpretations of expressive V + V formations (Fr. *culbuter*, from *culer* 'to strike on the butt' + *buter* 'to strike', through nom. *culbute* 'tumble') or as denominals. The final section of Chapter 4 analyzes the modern corpus as a whole, throwing into sharp focus the relative richness of N + V in Occitano-Romance, and the renewed vitality of this pattern since the 19th century.

In a few instances punctuation has been regularized, e.g., Palay's *capseca's* 'to dry from the top' is given here as *capseca-s*. Although I have chosen to list normalized spellings from Alibert (1977) ahead of other regional Occitan variants, no attempt has been made to normalize the spelling of any entry.

Appendices A–E present alphabetized corpuses of N + V compounds: French (App. A), Occitan (App. B), Catalan (App. C), Spanish (App. D), and Medieval Latin (App. E). The diachronic Romance corpuses contain wholly and partly vernacular compounds, including borrowings and loan translations. Specified are: century of first attestation, wherever available; glosses; etymological notes, where necessary; sources; and analysis into compound constituents, also glossed separately. Within the main body of each corpus are included a number of nouns of prefixal origin but which have shifted to N + V format through the influence of related compounds and/or syntactic structures (OFr. *colporter, portacol, porter a col*); similarly, the N + V corpuses contain nouns and adjectives with N + V Past Ptc (actually N + Adj) structure flanked by attested infinitives (OPr.–OCat.–OSp. *manl[l]euta, manl[l]evar*; OCat. *sangfús, sangfondre*) or by fixed expressions (OFr. *foimenti, mentir sa foi*); and N + Adj compounds unaccompanied by inflected verbs but in which the determiner precedes the determined element, e.g., OFr. *champcheü* 'fallen on the battlefield', OCat. *terra-batut* 'fallen on bad times', OSp. *barbiponiente* 'starting to grow a beard'. Included as well are fairly extensive listings of derivatives from N + V compounds, including denominal verbs whose second element fails to correspond to an unbound lexeme (OCat. *manlleutar*, OSp. *salpresar*).

---

beyond' + Med.L. **sennatus*) typify the diversity of Adv + V compounds, in supplementing the following categories:

    [A. Animals] *fornisà*, Gasc. *horonià*, etc., 'to leave the nest' (of birds)

    [B. Plants] Gasc. *horecréche* 'to send out shoots beyond original vine', 'pousser à
        côté du pied-mère'

    [K. Technical] OPr. *forget* 'awning', 'avant-toit', Occ. *forojit*, Béar. *horojit*, Occ.
        foro-teit 'overhang of a roof', 'stillicide'

Adv + V compounds have not been included in this investigation; they are numerous enough to merit separate study.

After each Romance N + V corpus, a category titled "Other Compound Structures Approximating N + V" includes (i) de-adjectival verbs from N + Adj (Occ. *acabourrá, encabourrí,* from *capbourrut*), from Adj + N (Fr. *faufiler*), or from V + V (Fr. *peslemesler,* after differentiation of *mesle-mesle*); (ii) N + N compounds (Fr. [16th c.] *saugrenu* lit. 'salt-grained'); (iii) N + Adj compounds in which determiner follows the determined element; (iv) Adv + V and V + V compounds that mimic N + V (OFr. *ferlier, jointenant; houcepignier, culbuter*). Included as well are suffixal derivatives that have undergone reinterpretation into N + V format (Fr. *vermoulu*). Finally, under "Dubious" are grouped: (a) compound verbs resulting from a cross between two verbs (Sp. *escamondar, [es]camochar*); (b) apparent compounds whose first element strongly suggests a prefix (Occ. *se pelleba*); (c) apparent compounds with an opaque element (Fr. *vertaper,* Gasc. *amourlica,* Lim. *s'emarlica,* Cat. *carnxancar-se*); and (d) etymologically debatable forms (OPr. *mantuzar,* Sp. *carcomer, mastronzar*).

The Med. Latin corpus (App. E) is grouped by nominal element, in the absence of noun and verb indexes. Vowel length in Med. Latin has been omitted. Compounds in Appendix E have been taken from a number of standard Med. Latin dictionaries and glossaries, where their inclusion does not necessarily imply a judgment as to ultimate origin, e.g., *fidementūtus,* OFr. *foimenti,* OPr. *fementit,* and so on. My research into British post-Classical Latin, in conjunction with Forcellini and the modern successors of Du Cange, concentrated only on N + V compounding but demonstrated even in that single domain the European continuity of Med. Latin. Borrowing between Med. Latin and the vernaculars was a constant process, a sort of osmosis, its very frequency rendering problematic the identification of ultimate provenance. Neither the logical relation between constituents nor the semantic nature of the first element suffices to determine the relative anteriority of any Med. Latin compound vis-à-vis Med. Romance. Not even Du Cange's dating of A.D. 794 for *fidementūtus* allows us to rule out absolutely the possibility of borrowing from early Romance rather than the reverse. In a few cases, the sources and the direction of borrowing are clear—e.g., Cl.L. *manūmittĕre* as the model of Med. Latin and Romance—or are generally agreed upon—e.g., Med.L. *dēmanūtenēre* underlying OCat. *desmantenir* 'to abandon' (*GMLCat,* s.v. "demanutenere"); and, inversely, OFr. *mainbournie* > Med.L. *manuburnia* (*NGML,* s.v. "manuburnia"). In general, however, I have refrained from specifying the exact avenue of borrowing, or from identifying Latinized Romance compounds amid the Med. Latin corpus. This file is partially cross-referenced to the vernaculars through the expedient of enclosing forms in double brackets; cross-referencing has been restricted to word groups with reflexes of a mixed nature, neither fully vernacular nor fully learnèd, or to cases of loan translation.

Med. Latin compound constituents are available only within the corpus itself (App. E). Each Romance corpus, in contrast, is followed by separate indexes of nominal, then verbal, elements, which are meant to facilitate the analysis of shared forms as well as of innovations. Nominal, verbal, and adverbial compounds with identical first and second elements are listed only once, e.g., OPr. *captenir* and its deverbal, *captenh*, count as a single instance of *cap + tenir*. In these N + V lists, opaque and transparent compounds are treated alike, with their constituents identified in modern vernacular form wherever possible—capitals have been used only in the absence of a satisfactory Romance form belonging to the language in question. Although several years in the making, each corpus must be taken as representative rather than rigorously exhaustive, since it has not been possible to consult all currently available sources and since new materials will surely continue to appear.

1

PREVIOUS STUDIES OF N + V
IN WESTERN ROMANCE

The examination of N + V compounds in Romance has previously been attempted from both morphological and syntactic points of view, yet with no real thoroughness; Benveniste (1966) makes the most recent call for a new comparative investigation in his study of French compounds with a verbal element, e.g., *porte-monnaie* 'coin-purse' beside *maintenir*. [1] Bierbach's 3500 French listings testify to the vast productivity of the V + N pattern (1982, 1983). What of its converse? N + V compounds, whether functioning as nouns, adjectives, or adverbs, are plentifully available to illustrate that compositional pattern, but successive descriptions in the literature—their documentation spotty, even inaccurate—have unfortunately tended to be derivative, leaning heavily on earlier sources without independent evaluation (e.g., Tollemache 1945), and confusing the N + V type with V + V (e.g., Darmesteter 1894), N + Adj (e.g., Meyer-Lübke 1895), and Adj + V compounds (e.g., Nyrop 1908). Among the monographs and articles to be reviewed in this chapter, relatively few of the standard works of comparative Romance linguistics have made any significant contribution to the topic of this investigation.

---

[1] "Compound noun" here and below refers to a compound endowed with the morphological shape of a noun, e.g., *artifex, manœuvre*; or, secondarily, one which functions like a noun, e.g., nominalized infin. Béar. *carn-bedar* 'Lent'. By the same token, "compound verb" refers to a (generally) fully inflected verb, listed in the infinitive, e.g., *manūtenēre, maintenir*. This nomenclature differs in general from Indo-Europeanist use of the terms, e.g., Benveniste (1966), where "composé verbal" (i.e., containing a verbal element) applies both to nom. V + N, e.g., *porte-monnaie*, and verbal N + V (*maintenir*). Ronjat's "phrase nominale" and "phrase verbale" (1980:§738) echo 19th-c. comparatist terminology; his labels refer respectively to nominal sentences and to clauses containing a finite verb, while "compound noun" and "compound verb" as I use these terms refer to resultant parts of speech.

11

The study of N + V compounds must begin with a careful review of representative previous treatments. The majority of these are descriptive taxonomies, which undeniably can be useful, particularly for comparison, but lack explanations of development. At best, they only hint at the how and the why of compounding. An approach through transformational-generative grammar, e.g., Giurescu (1975), is unable to account on the synchronic plane for the varying morphological shapes of several compounds all predicated on a single underlying syntactic structure. While Giurescu's individual studies of Italian (1965, 1968), Portuguese (1973), and Spanish (1972) provide fresh data, her broader-gauged inquiry (1975) into Romance compounding has gone virtually unnoticed, presumably because it was based on a strictly syntactic approach to word formation which was discarded in certain quarters before the monograph even came to be published. Giurescu's approach ultimately tells us nothing new about V + N nor, more to the point here, about N + V. More typical yet is the single paragraph in Thiele 1981, falling at the end of a modest monograph devoted to Mod. French word formation. Both of these figure below; the search begins, however, with Arsène Darmesteter and will remain for the most part within the bounds of traditional rather than state-of-the-art linguistic analyses.

Foremost among the standard treatments has been Arsène Darmesteter's *Traité de la formation des mots composés* (1874, 2d ed. 1894, repr. 1967), whose strengths—no less than weaknesses—have had lasting influence on the analysis of French composition. In French, indeed in Romance, compounding occurs with words rather than themes, as it did in the IE dialects. The author's distinction of Romance compounds into true compounds, including N + V, vs. juxtaposed formations ("juxtaposés") is based on ellipsis, which results from composition rather than defining or causing that process. At the Latin stage, N + V compounds, e.g., Cl.L. *manūmittĕre* 'to emancipate', Med.L. *manūtenēre*, represented "juxtaposés" as against their true compound status in Romance, e.g., Fr. *maintenir*. According to Darmesteter, N + V is rare in modern-day French, although Spanish and Occitan retain many more examples.

Darmesteter's analytic distinction between "juxtaposés" and true compounds echoes in different garb the 19th-c. comparatist's proper/improper dichotomy, so-called proper compounds lacking inflection on all non-final segments. For Darmesteter, juxtaposed forms coalesce from ordinary syntactic phrases, e.g., Med.L. *manūtenēre* 'to defend, protect by the hand (= power)'; Fr. *vinaigre* 'vinegar' ← *vin aigre* 'sour wine'. In the true compound, on the other hand, essential syntactic elements are missing, e.g., *arrière-cour* 'back yard' ← *cour [qui est] arrière* 'yard that is in back'.

Despite the success of his approach, Darmesteter's dichotomy contains inherent contradictions which critics, Nyrop (1908:§555, particularly subsection 1) among the earliest, have not hesitated to point out. Meyer-Lübke (1895:§542) disagreed with Darmesteter's classification of *pourboire*. A compound like *pourboire* 'tip' arises from an actually occurring syntactic phrase, making it a "juxtaposé" on formal grounds, whereas Darmesteter had classified it (1894:146) as a true compound, presumably on the basis of its exocentric nature, *pourboire* 'x [which is] for [a] drink'.

There is evidence that Darmesteter came to feel uncomfortable with his analytic approach. In the *Traité*, only a "juxtaposé" owes its existence to frequency, while a true compound is born the moment its constituents are set next to each other; in *De la création actuelle des mots nouveaux* three years later (1877), Darmesteter qualified *des yeux tabac d'Espagne* as "un apposé en voie de formation—un demi-composé" (82). Darmesteter's shifting grasp of the very nature of composition itself, as well as the occasional confusion of syntactic and logical criteria (insofar as there is ellipsis in *pourboire*, it is logical rather than syntactic) made imperative a comparison of the two editions of his *Traité* (Klingebiel 1983). Upon close examination they show relatively few significant differences, certainly fewer than Gaston Paris would have the reader of the revised second edition believe. Bierbach (1982:10*n*4) detects no significant difference in the treatment of V + N compounds in the 1894 edition; as regards N + V compounds, there is no change whatsoever in the 1894 version.

It should be noted that Darmesteter's colleague Louis-Francis Meunier refused to subscribe to the same terminology. Meunier's analysis of syntactic composition in the classical languages was thoroughly known to Darmesteter, who eventually prepared the younger man's work for posthumous publication (1872). Meunier reasoned that a single label, "compound," should suffice for forms that arise by coalescence of a syntagm or phrase into a new lexical unit, whether or not there is syntactic ellipsis. [2]

Darmesteter's analysis of Fr. *maintenir* 'to defend, protect, maintain' and its analogs in the *Traité* (1894:161–67) is fairly extensive. While *maintenir*, etc., are true compounds in French, the corresponding Latin formations were still "juxtaposés" showing no syntactic ellipsis. Darmesteter cites *manūmittĕre* 'to emancipate', *animadvertĕre* 'to consider, notice' (= *anim[um] advertĕre*), *aurōclāvātus* 'gold-nailed',

---

[2]I have had occasion elsewhere (Klingebiel 1983) to mention the two scholars' difference of opinion regarding the analysis of V + N compounds, such as *porte-glaive* 'sword-bearing'. Darmesteter's "juxtaposé"/"true compound" dichotomy sought to go beyond both the comparatists' "proper"/"improper" labels and also Meunier's "syntactic"/"asyntactic" tags, determined by the presence or absence of normal syntactic agreement. Meunier's primary criterion for analysis led him to call *porte-glaive* 'sword-bearing' (*un chevalier porte-glaive*) syntactic in the singular but asyntactic in the plural (*des chevaliers porte-glaive*, not **portent-glaive*). Darmesteter rejected such incongruity, analyzing both singular and plural forms as true compounds concealing an ellipsis ('knight [who] bears [a] sword').

crŭcifĭgĕre 'to crucify', *manūpretium* 'wages'. He sees fit to include nominal and adjectival formations as well as compound verbs. Although his analytical distinction between compounds and "juxtaposés" is ultimately based on syntax, he refrains from explicitly mentioning the role of diachronic word-order change as a factor in the shift from syntactic juxtaposition to morphological composition.

The section devoted to *maintenir*, etc. (under the rubric "Verbes composés d'un substantif régime et d'un verbe"), treats consecutively: (I.1) verbs; (I.2) participles and adjectives; and (II) a series of verbs ending in *-fier*, compounded from Adj + FACĔRE 'to make, do' or from -*(I)FĬCĀRE (based on cognate -FIC-). In Section I.1, Proto-Romance compound formation ("la formation romane"), e.g., *manœuvrer* 'to maneuver', *mentevoir* 'to remember, notice', *boursouf(f)ler* 'to swell', is contrasted with compounds of chronologically French creation: older *cloufichier/cloufire* 'to drive in a nail, crucify', *ferarmer* and more recent *billebarrer* 'to be striped', *blanc-poudrer* 'to be white with powder', *bouleverser* 'to upset, turn over', *cailleboter* 'to coagulate', *chantourner* 'to cut out along a given pattern', *champlever* 'to remove material around a pattern', *chavirer* 'to capsize', *colporter* 'to peddle', *culbuter* 'to tumble', *morfondre* (Mod.) 'to mope, fret', *pelleverser* 'to shovel'. Section I.2 presents a series of participles and adjectives in which the N has an ablative function (material or instrument): *vermoulu* 'worm-eaten', *saugrenu* 'preposterous', *crouste-levé* 'with separated crust' (of bread), *lettre-féru* 'learnèd', perhaps also *blanc-signé* 'signature to a blank document'. In *lieutenant* and *foimenti* 'traitor', both examples still representing syntactic "juxtaposés," the N has accusative function. *Arc-bouter* is excluded from N + V formations on semantic grounds: it cannot represent **bouter avec un arc*, but, rather, 'to support with an *arc-boutant*' (N + Adj + *-er*).

According to Section II, Latin, unlike Greek, could derive verbs directly from adj. N + V compounds, e.g., *magnificus* 'splendid' (radical *magni-fic-* + adj. ending *-us*). Originally causative *magnificus* served as the basis for *magnificāre* 'to esteem highly', and so on; eventually, the lack of transparency of -*(i)ficāre* led to its use as a verbal derivative, e.g., OFr. *-efier*, later *-ifier* (cf. Fr. *pacifier* 'to pacify', not **pacifiquer*). Similarly, L. LIQU-E-FACĔRE yielded *liquéfier* 'to liquify', not **liquefaire* (1894:167); of the verbs in -FACĔRE, only CAL(E)FA(CĔ)RE (PRom. *calfare*, Fr. *chauffer*, etc., 'to heat') stands apart in the evolution of its verbal element. [3]

Darmesteter's classic work, available today in reprint, continues to exert influence, just as it provides valuable comparative data. Citing Italian, Spanish, Portuguese, and

---

[3]Compounds in -FACĔRE and *-FĬCĀRE survived (or were developed) particularly in Old Judeo-Romance, where their expressive character neatly translated the flavor of certain causative biblical Hebrew verbs. See, e.g., D. S. Blondheim, *Poèmes judéo-français du moyen âge* (Paris: Champion, 1927); Raphael Levy, *Trésor de la langue des juifs français au moyen âge* (Austin: U. of Texas Press, 1964).

Provençal examples, Darmesteter points out that in these languages, unlike French, the first (= determining) element can function as the complement of a N or Adj as well as of a V (1894:164). Moreover, since Italian, Spanish, and Portuguese have vocalic noun endings, the notion of theme seems more likely to survive or be reinstated; hence the appearance of compositional *-i-* in, e.g., It. *capitombolare* 'to tumble', (ornith.) *codirosso* 'songbird with a red tail', Sp. *maniobrar* 'to maneuver, work with the hands', *boquiancho* 'wide-mouthed'.

Darmesteter's analysis hinges neither on absolute numbers nor on incidence of examples; he makes no statements about productivity. The Romanist must regret that N + V compounding in the *Traité* has not been accorded a more truly pan-Romance focus. Among N + V compounds outside French, Darmesteter mentions the earliest formations parallel to *maintenir* (OPr.–Cat.–OSp. *manl[l]evar* 'to borrow, bail out' and OPr.–OCat.–OSp. *captener* 'to govern, support, defend') only in connection with Spanish and again without explicit comment. According to later sources, Fr. *mainlevée* 'withdrawal, release of mortgage' (listed as *main levée* under N + Adj "juxtaposés" in the *Traité*, without gloss or discussion) is attested for the first time in the 14th century and survives today as a legal term, 'withdrawal, release (of a mortgage, etc.)'; no reflexes of CAPUT TENĒRE have found their way into Mod. French, although the *FEW* does list OFr. *chatien* 'aide', as well as MFr.-Pr. (16th c.) *chateni* 'to stop a bull or ram by the horns'.

The *Dictionnaire général de la langue française*, compiled by Darmesteter with Hatzfeld and Thomas ([1889–1901] 1932:86–87, "Composition du type *colporter*") essentially echoes Darmesteter's approach in his *Traité*. In addition to the examples listed above, one finds *court-mancher* 'to prepare a shoulder of lamb' and *houspiller* 'to scold'. Once again, there is a statement to the effect that the Romance pattern has a Latin origin, although at present "*maintenir* ne peut s'expliquer par la syntaxe française," since the noun has become a sort of theme "dont le verbe seul détermine le rôle dans la composition."

In his *Grammatik der romanischen Sprachen*, vol. 2, *Formenlehre* (1895:§594), Meyer-Lübke arrives at several divergent conclusions. Unlike Darmesteter, he considers juxtaposed forms like L. *manūtenēre*, Fr. *manœuvrer*, nom. Fr. *pourboire* 'tip', Sp. *manlevar*, etc. to be true compounds, although arising from an actually occurring syntactic phrase. Meyer-Lübke distinguishes between two chronological strata, more recent N Dir Obj + V, e.g., Fr. *bouleverser*, Sp. *maniatar*, as against pre-Romance N + V, e.g., *maintenir*, *manœuvrer*. For Meyer-Lübke, the greater or lesser relative age of the latter two examples evidently determined the phonetic shape of their nominal elements. MANU developed under atonic stress in *manœuvrer*, which would presumably be older, since the actual process of consolidation into a compound predated Old French; in more recent *maintenir*, where either constituent retained individual stress, nom. MANU- would show tonic development (Cl.L. *a* + nasal consonant > *ai*).

Further development of the *maintenir, manœuvrer* type led to the formation of OFr. *ferarmer* 'to cover oneself in armor', *fervestir* idem, *ferlier* 'to attach tightly', *cloufichier* 'to drive in a nail, crucify', *ramentevoir* 'to remember'; Mod.Fr. *billebarrer* 'to be striped', *colporter* 'to peddle', *culbuter* 'to tumble', *chantourner* 'to cut out along a given pattern', *champlever* 'to remove material around a pattern', MFr. *peslemesler* 'to mix', *saupoudrer* 'to sprinkle (with salt)'; Cat. *ullpenre* 'to bewitch'; Sp. *captener* 'to protect' (modeled on *mantener*), *mampresar* 'to catch horses'. (Henceforth, glosses will be limited to items occurring for the first time.)

Meyer-Lübke is apparently willing to include some indirect consideration of reversibility, in V + N–structured *tourneboeler* 'to tumble' ('turn' + OFr. *boele* 'bowel' + *-er*). While admitting several V Pres Ptc constructions, e.g., Fr. *arcboutant*, to the N + V category under scrutiny, he strictly excludes denominal verbs, e.g., *faufiler* (Adj + N + *-er*) and *tournevirer* 'to spin around' (V + V + *-er*), since compounding had taken place in the formation of the noun rather than the verb. To §594 should be added the slender evidence from §556, conjoining (a) N + V Ptc, e.g., It. *cap-aguto* 'sharpened'; and (b) N + Adj, e.g., OFr. *champcheü, ferarmé* '(armored) warrior', *fervesti* 'armor-clad', and *foimenti* 'traitor'.

Overall, the debt to Darmesteter is considerable. Meyer-Lübke agrees with Darmesteter's contention that verbal *manœuvrer* was primary, nom. *manœuvre* secondary. Although the French scholar argues that "le sens s'y prête mieux," Med. Latin evidence suggests that nom. MANŪŎPERA was indeed the source of the verbal derivation, rather than vice versa; see also *FEW* VI/1, s.v. "manuopera". The inclusion of Catalan evidence is opportune, but some departures from the *Traité* are infelicitous: Meyer-Lübke fails to heed Darmesteter's careful exclusion of *arc-bouter*, with its N + Adj + *-er* structure (*arc-bout[ant]* + *-er*), and the Swiss scholar's listing of *pêlemêler* proves unfounded, as is his inclusion of *tourneboeler*, with its patent V + N + *-er* structure. Modern analysis no longer groups *ferlier* (Adj + V, cf. OWall. *ferm lier*, A.-Norm. *ferlier* 'to bind tightly'; see *FEW*, s.v. "firmus") with *ferarmer, -vêtir* (N + V).

Volume 3 of Nyrop's classic *Grammaire historique de la langue française* (1908:§569) offers but a summary discussion of two N + V combinations: (a) N Dir Obj, "très rare," e.g., *lieutenant, foimenti* 'traitor'; (b) N Ind Obj, properly Latin rather than Romance, e.g., *mentevoir* 'to remember'. Nyrop's summary list, including a handful of examples appearing by analogy as late as the 18th century, is presented alphabetically: *billebarrer, blanc-poudré, bouleverser, cailleboter, chantourner,* Gallo-Rom. *cloufichier,* OFr. *cloufire,* Mod.Fr. *colporter, culbuter,* OFr. *ferarmer, ferlier, fernoer* 'to tie up tightly', *fervestir, maintenir, morfondre, saupoudrer, vermoulu.* He carries Meyer-Lübke's erroneous *ferlier* one step further in adding *ferno(u)er*. The Danish scholar rejects Darmesteter's "composé"/ "juxtaposé"dichotomy, since ellipsis is no more than a grammarian's afterthought (Lloyd 1964:754). Nyrop bases his own compound analysis on the distinction between coordination (in, e.g., *vinaigre*, *arrière-cour*) and subordination (e.g., *chef-d'œuvre*, *porte-monnaie*); whatever its initial impetus, the compositional process must be considered unitary.

In contrast to the foregoing studies of literary French, a tantalizing paragraph buried in an early glossary of Picard not only informs readers that Picard is richer in compounds than French but also provides a substantial list of formations in *-fiker* (*ficher* 'to fix [to], put') (Corblet [1851, repr. 1978:30]). N + V compounds among these (also available below in Appendix A) include: Pic. *bornifiker* 'to slap in the face'; *corni-*, *cornu-fiker* 'to butt with a horn'; *décafiker* 'to husk, hull (nuts and fruits)'; *détafiker* 'to displace, detach'; *(s')estafiker* 'to settle into one spot'; and *harlifiker* 'to beat with a *hart* (band, binder for a bundle of twigs)'. Of all those listed by Corblet, one compound alone, *cafiker* 'to wriggle', has found its way into *FEW*, s.v. "figicare"; one other, *s'estafiquer* (*-fiker*), figures in a note under "stare". [4]

Edward L. Adams' *Word-Formation in Provençal* (1913), from a Harvard dissertation directed by Charles Grandgent, also gains partial distance from Darmesteter in its treatment of compounds (550ff.). Adams handles composition after affixation (with parasynthetics included), grouping compounds by (i) resulting part of speech; and (ii) constituent. Listed (571–73) as N + V combinations are *calpisar* 'to crush underfoot', *capvirar* 'to turn one's head, tumble', *manlevar*, *mansaizir* 'to give s.th. to s.o.', *mantener*, *marfondre* 'to catch cold' (of horses), *mentaver* (*mentaure*) 'to mention, remember', *prestlevar* 'to lend, borrow', *salpicar* 'to spread with ashes', *vianar* 'to travel'; **cambaterrar*, found in Raynouard only as *cambaterrat* 'dismounted', is relegated to a note, in which Adams expresses misgivings about the wisdom of its inclusion.

Adams (566) lists four nouns, actually substantivized adjectives, formed from N + V Pres Ptc: *benstenen* 'heir' ('property-holding'), *logatenen* 'deputy' ('place-holding'), *mantenen* 'balustrade', *viandan* 'wayfarer'; he then goes on (568) to analyze a long list of compound adjectives consisting mostly of N + V Ptc, e.g., *captrencat* 'having one's head cut off', *fervestit*. He makes explicit the parallel with N + Adj adjectives, both types being apparently exocentric (adj. *captrencat* 'having a head that has been cut off') rather than endocentric (nom. *captrencat* 'a head that has been cut off'). Passing mention is made of the similarity of these adjectives to N +

---

[4]Other compounds in Corblet's list include Pic. *affiker* 'to strike'; *bernifiker* 'to besmear with dung'; *s'estrafiker* 'to turn sideways'; *effiker* 'to fray, taper'; *erfiker* 'to replace'; *intamfiker* 'to stand upright'; *infiker* 'to put into'; *rinfiker* 'to put back'; *surfiker* 'to put on'.

V compound verbs (OFr. *fervestir*). Among suffixal hybrids, Adams (581–82) cites adj. *mesacantan* 'priest'; *cambaterrat*, identified as past ptc. of unattested *cambaterrar; and adv. *mantenemen* 'now', *mentagudament* 'especially', both with suffixal *-men[t]*.

Old Provençal—or at least the troubadours' version of it—evidently made no extensive use of these forms; in Levy's *Supplement*, which included inter alia Bible translations and administrative/legal documents, forms beyond the strictly literary were made available to Adams, e.g., OPr. (15th c.) *mansaizir*. Adams also adduced N + V materials absent from Darmesteter or Meyer-Lübke, e.g., *capvirar*, yet his conclusions are insufficient to account for the 25 compound verbs which research for this monograph has yielded. Take, e.g., his claim that the noun "in the words of this kind" was never the object of the verb "as it was in the *nouns* composed of these two parts." While *manlevar* may have arisen from *ā manū levāre* 'to remove with the hand (= power)' rather than *manu(m) levāre* 'to raise the hand', other medieval Occitan examples provide unassailable proof of direct-object function in their nom. constituent: OPr. *caravirar* 'to change political party', OGasc. *capbira* 'to train oxen to pull either to right or to left', *coo-transi* [*sic*] 'to pierce the heart'.

In his grammar of Old Provençal, Joseph Anglade (1921; repr. 1977:397, under the rubric "Noms composés d'un nom et d'un verbe") cites *capvirar*, *mentaver/mentaure*, and *vian(d)ar*. Forms are listed by part of speech, then by constituent. Compound adjectives include N + V Past Ptc–structured *fementit* 'traitor', *fervestit*, and *capcaudat* (a metrical term also assigned to the N + Adj pattern). No nominal forms are listed; *mantener* and *captener* are mentioned among verb paradigms as compounds of *tener*, but not specifically brought into Anglade's discussion of compound words except in connection with "parasynthetic" *mantenedor*, *captenemen*, *captenensa*.

Among the modern Occitan dialects, Gascon outranks its eastern and northern sister languages in overall exploitation of the pattern. Yet in Rohlfs 1977, compounding has been relegated to the final paragraph (§571) of his substantial monograph entirely devoted to Gascon. In addition to his own extensive field notes, Rohlfs' sources include Palay's dictionary (1932–34; 3d ed. 1980) and, in the revised 3d ed. of *Le Gascon* (1977), the *ALG*. The author contents himself with pointing out the frequency of compounds with N Compl + V structure, particularly N Dir Obj + V, as well as the relatively high occurrence of compound verbs, e.g., *coulou-muda* [*sic*] 'to change color', *cap-mounta* 'to raise the head'. N + V is characterized as "tout à fait vivant en gascon," although admittedly rare in French. Similarly structured adjectives (both N + Adj, e.g., *nasi-lounc* 'long-nosed', and also N + V Ptc, e.g., *gay-hasén*) occur, as do nouns, e.g., *cordoulou̇* 'heartbreak'. Several Western Romance parallels are cited, French for the N Compl verbs, Spanish (including *alicortado* 'wounded', etc., with link vowel *-i-*) and Aragonese for adjectives.

Rohlfs' treatment has the advantage of encompassing several resultant parts of speech, although he makes no comment on the possible links between them. No historical perspective is offered, leaving unexplicated the contrast between the antiquity of the adj. N + Adj type and the relative newness of the N + V compounds. Attentive reading discloses that the logical relation between constituents, rather than between the resulting parts of speech, constitutes the compositional principle on which the paragraph hinges. In the unrelated section §547, Rohlfs discusses emphatic structures such as left-extraposition; these hardly qualify as a satisfactory explanation for N + V vogue. No types beyond N + V appear in §571, despite its claim to handling composition in Gascon.

Of all the previous studies surveyed here, Ronjat 1937 (repr. 1980) most fully documents and discusses N + V compound structures. Within the confines of a massive historical grammar of the Occitan dialects, Ronjat considers (1980, III:477–82) some 30 verbs, as well as certain related nominal forms with N + V structure, grouped according to function of the nominal element. Ronjat opens his discussion of compound nouns (§§732ff.) by noting his debt to Charles Bally in observing the Romance preference for derivation rather than compounding, a predilection which seems to tally with a trend toward obliqueness and exclusiveness ("notation") rather than transparency ("explication"). [5]

Not confined to a simple taxonomic listing, Ronjat's analysis of compound nouns mixes factors of historical phonology and morphology with analogy, word order, case relations, and semantic conditioning. Nominal compounds preserve (a) lexemes otherwise fallen into desuetude (DIĒS 'day', Pr. *dilun* 'Monday'); (b) reflexes of Latin 3d-declension adjectives that have eluded an analogical shift to the 1st/2d declensions (FORTIS 'strong', Pr. *aigo-fort* 'etching', lit. 'strong water'; PENDĒNS 'hanging', Pr. *a l'aigue-pendent* 'on the slope'); (c) other archaic nominal-verbal elements; and (d) vestiges of the Latin composition vowel -*i*-, (bot.) *cabrifuelh* 'privet, honeysuckle' alone surviving directly from Latin. Specifically, §734, subsection i, surveys parts-of-speech constituents of: iteratives, copulatives, Noun + Adj/Genit [t + t', determinatum + determinans], and the inverse [t' + t]; subsection ii examines case relations; and subsection iii gives syntactico-semantic categories, combining examples of hypostasis and Darmesteter's syntactic ellipsis. Hypostasis is defined [§717] as transposition of one syntactic category to another, e.g., Fr. *un caractère enfant* 'a childish character'. The term "hypostasis" is used to designate the suppression of an element that speaker and hearer fail to think of simultaneously, whereas, thanks to

---

[5]In §717*n*1, Ronjat cites personal communications from Bally, as well as notes from the Swiss scholar's University of Geneva lectures, as the source for several of his own key paragraphs on Occitan compounding, including §§738–39 on N + V verbs.

context, mutual comprehension is not threatened by ellipsis. Noteworthy in subsection iv is the analyst's willingness to consider the reversibility of N + V (or Compl + V) and V + N (or V + Compl), e.g., *arré-bau* and *bau-arré* 'good-for-nothing', Fr. *vaurien*, since in grammar function overrides word order. Subsection v focuses on nouns formed from verbal elements, e.g., *viro-passo* 'somersault', and subsection vi looks at multipartite compounds comprising whole phrases and sentences, e.g., toponymic Pr. *Benlivèn*, lit. 'on y vient facilement'. Next, §735 rapidly surveys inflection and gender; §736, plural formation. Ronjat's section on verbs (§§737–39) invokes the four functions outlined in §734, iv: subject; direct object; essential complement, i.e., material or tool; plus adverbial complement. A handful of examples with N + V Past Ptc structure brings us full circle back to the nominal starting point.

In §738, Ronjat seeks to ascertain possible syntactic sources for these N + V formations: could verb-final position in subordinate clauses account for N Dir Obj and N adv. Compl, under §734 iv? OPr. *per pels partir* 'in order to part the hair' might underlie *pelpartidura* 'part [in hair]'. Ronjat prefers this filiation to a direct carryover from the sparse Latin examples. He advances a double hypothesis: for nouns with subject and instrumental function (ultimately traceable to N Subj), he posits hypostasis of whole sentences; but for verbs, hypostasis of nominal sentences structured N + V Past Ptc. Such a reconstruction has the advantage of accounting for both transitive and intransitive values of the resultant compound verb. It offers as well a neat explanation of V + N and N + V ordering in compound nouns and corresponding verbs: V impt. + N order would on the whole be obligatory, while the N generally preceded other forms of the V at an early date. Several examples of compound verbs structured V + N [t + t'], e.g., *batecoura* 'to have heart palpitations' are unmasked as denominals from V + N structures, e.g, *bate-cor* 'palpitation'; other so-called exceptions can be explained as V + V copulatives and their denominals, e.g., Fr. *culbute* → *culbuter* 'to tumble', Pr. *viropass(r)* 'to tumble'.

In summary, Ronjat's alternative explanations (which are not based on noun function within the pattern) include:

   a. survival from VL;
   b. formation at a time when the infinitive was final in subordinate clauses
      (e.g., OPr. *per pels partir* → *pelpartidura*);
   c. hypostasis of whole sentences (e.g., OPr. *la pels muda* 'la peau change' →
      pelmudar 'molt', to which might be added *x la pel muda* 's.o. changes
      skin'), from what Ronjat called "la phrase verbale";
   d. hypostasis of N + Past Ptc (e.g., Occ. *sang-begut* 'numbed (with cold, etc.)',
      lit. 'le sang [est] bu' → *sang-beure* 'désirer, convoiter'), from a "phrase
      nominale."

As if to complement this pioneering work, a rapid glance at the first normalized grammar of Mod. Occitan yields additional examples of the N + V type. According to Alibert (1976:396), the nominal element functions alternatively as direct object (*cambalevar* 'to trip s.o.'), or as indirect object (*salpicar*). Although a generous 18 examples are cited, the analysis remains atomistic, drawing no parallels between categories of compounds. Two types of secondary derivation also come up for mention: parasynthetics, and "mots ibrids," from compound + suffix, e.g., *capvirament* 'dizzy spell' from *capvirar*.

Occitan itself is complemented by evidence from representative Spanish and Catalan treatments. Menéndez Pidal's *Manual* (§127 "Composición propiamente dicha") lists only isolated *mantener*, *manfestar* 'to reveal, make public' (mod. *manifestar*), *facerir* 'to wrong, offend' (Mod. *zaherir* 'to reproach, criticize' ← *faz ferir* 'to strike one's face'), *maniatar* 'to manacle', *alicortar* 'to cut the wings off, wound', *perniquebrar* 'to break one's legs'. *Mantener* is found to have no compound value, i.e., it is no longer transparent. This meager harvest is supplemented only by Latin examples built on -FACĔRE, -*FĪCĀRE, which Romance has not imitated. José Alemany Bolufer's survey of Spanish word formation is considerably more informative, identifying under N + V (1920:171–72) a good number of verbs, plus a sprinkling of nouns, although it does mix vernacular forms with Latinisms. The corpus is subdivided according to noun function within the compound: N Dir Obj (OSp. *fazferir*, *escamondar* 'to prune a tree', *pelechar* 'to molt', *reivindicar* 'to claim one's rights', *misacantano*); and N obl (*mamparar*, *mampresar*, *mantornar* 'to plow a second time', *mantener*, *manutener* 'to maintain, support', *manuscribir* 'to write by hand' [← *manuscrito*], *mampuesto* 'rubble, rough stone', *sietelevar* 'to raise by seven [in a card game]').

For Catalan, Antoni Badía Margarit's *Gramática Catalana*, II (1962:§352) offers back-to-back analyses of V + N and N + V, the latter encompassing *sangglaçar-se* 'to take fright', *sangcremar-se* 'to become impatient', *colltòrcer* 'to twist one's neck', *ullprendre*, *capficar* 'to vex', *aiguabarrejar-se* 'to merge' (of two or more rivers), *pelltrencar-se* 'to excoriate', *capalçar* 'to raise the head or end', *capgirar* 'to turn upside down, upset', followed by nom.-adj. examples: *fefaent* 'authentic', *missacantant* 'priest', *terratinent* 'landowner', *lloctinent* 'lieutenant', *vianant* 'traveler, pilgrim', *llampferit* 'struck by lightning'. Supplementing this array with the more recent list found in Ruaix (1979:79), one can add *camatrencar-se* 'to break one's legs' (of an animal), *tallgirar-se* 'to become dull' (of a knifeblade), *capserrar* (no gloss available), *peucalcigar* 'to trample under foot', *coresforçar-se* 'to make an effort'. Against Spanish and French, the much higher productivity of this pattern in Occitano-Romance begins to emerge in sharp relief.

Finally, let us take a brief look at a transformational-generative treatment of Romance N + V infinitives (Giurescu 1975), which had the misfortune to appear after Chomsky's lexicalist stance (1970) had knocked out the monograph's underpinnings. In chapter 3, §7.1, devoted to compound constituents, L. *manūmittĕre* ranks as a model for later Romance examples, all of them synthemes with inseparable constituents, e.g., It. *barcamenare* (refl.) 'to get along, manage', Fr. *arc-bouter*, *champlever*, and Sp. *perniquebrar*. The following chapter, limited to deep structures of currently productive compounding patterns, entirely omits the N + V type. An examination of N + V Pres Ptc adjectives (chap. 3, §3.6, e.g., Fr. *arc-rampant* 'rampant arch', Sp. *lugarteniente*) leads to the conclusion that the lack of a formally distinct pres. ptc. in Rumanian must preclude any representation in that language; chapter 4, §2.4, mentions *lugarteniente* without illustration. Unfortunately, the perfunctory treatment of these forms is unenlightening on any level. Giurescu's examples are poorly chosen—denom. Fr. *arc-bouter* 'to buttress' is unsuitable on any account, as is *arc-rampant*—with the result that they offer no clear picture of the scope of N + V compounding in cognate languages.

At this point, a handful of comments from the *FEW* may be adduced to enhance this investigation of N + V compounds, and of N + Adj adjectives as well, since they represent an important source of back-formations (see below, Chapters 3 and 4). For Wartburg and his associates, the function of nom. *mor(r)-*'snout' in the compound *morfondre* 'to catch cold', (Mod.) 'to mope, fret' (*FEW* III, s.v. "fundere") remains elusive, because *mor-* can be identified alternately as (a) an accusative (cf. *pelmudar* 'to molt', lit. 'to change skin'); (b) a locative (cf. *kaplumat* 'bald', lit. 'shorn on the head'); or (c) an ablative (cf. *palabira* 'to turn with a shovel'). Apropos of *palfer* 'iron-shod stick' (*FEW* VII, s.v. "palus"), four relations can be posited between constituents: (i) N + N (*fer*); (ii) N + Adj (FERREUS); (iii) N + *de* + N; (iv) N + V Past Ptc (FERRĀTUS). On a smaller scale, Bloch–Wartburg has this to say about *maintenir*: "L'existence de ce composé dans les langues romanes, sauf en roumain (it. *mantenere*, esp./apr. *mantener*), prouve qu'il date de l'époque latine." [6]

On the whole, Romanists have concerned themselves with taxonomic analysis of resultant parts of speech, of constituent parts of speech, and of case relations; diachronic discussion has generally centered on whether N + V involves a Latin or a Romance pattern, and, if the latter holds, whether a juxtaposed or an elliptically compounded form is at issue. There is considerably more to concern us: one needs to know more about Latin composition itself, as well as something about IE

---

[6]A possible Rumanian example may be available, if we accept Diez' listing of Rum. *mun-tui*, (Mod.) *mîntui* (1887, s.v. "mantenere," contrasting with *men-tui* in the 1st ed.), which he derived from MANŪ TUĒRĪ 'hand' (= power) + 'protect, defend'; modern dictionaries, however, agree in showing a Hungarian origin for this verb.

compounding with nominal and verbal elements. Valuable genetic and typological insights have been provided in two key articles.

"Convergences typologiques" (Benveniste 1966; repr. 1974) examines N + V infinitives from the chosen point of view, contrasting a French corpus, which the author felt to be exhaustive, with tantalizing glimpses of several Amerindian languages in which the pattern is productive as well, including members of the Uto-Aztec family (Aztec, Paiute, Shoshone) as well as Iroquois and Takelma. Frequently the form of the N is slightly reduced, showing a tendency to prefixal status; but invariably its function is instrumental. For Benveniste, this type of verbal compounding is anomalous with respect to IE, despite parallel constructions with past participle in Sanskrit, German, or English, e.g., *devá-datta* 'god-given', *gottgesandt* 'god-sent', *handwoven*. In his 1930 description of Southern Paiute, Sapir analyzed similar nominal elements as instrumental prefixes: "They are on the whole specialized forms of incorporated nouns with instrumental function." In Whorf's treatment of an Aztec dialect (1946), they were labeled "modifiers" of the V, since the verb, when transitive, can still take an independent direct object. Benveniste's conclusion: "Cette création romane que nous considérons en français, bien qu'elle se soit épuisée assez vite, demeure comme le témoignage d'une innovation typologique de grande portée générale" (112).

The French examples (drawn for the most part from Darmesteter–Hatzfeld's *Dictionnaire général*) are structured exclusively N Instr + V: *bouleverser, chantourner, chavirer, colporter, culbuter, maintenir, manœuvrer, morfondre, saupoudrer*, plus nominal derivatives *vermoulu, saugrenu*, and *saupiquet* 'spicy sauce or stew'. To these Benveniste adds a number of older formations, from the productive period of the pattern: *billebarrer, blanc-poudré*, OFr. *chanfreindre* 'to bevel', *cloufichier, ferarmer, ferlier, fervestir, pelleverser*. In the Amerindian examples cited, the N is a full-fledged instrumental prefix, e.g., Paiute *ma(n)-* 'hand' ([1966] 1974:108).

In his discussion of Tübatulabal *hani-hal-* 'to visit', Benveniste glosses the elements as 'maison' + 's'asseoir', adding 'to house-sit' almost as an afterthought to the French gloss. Now English, while lacking **handweave*, does have a considerable number of N + V compound verbs sharing pertinent features with noun incorporations such as *hani-hal-*, e.g., back-formed *baby-sit, house-sit*, and analogically created *baby-squat, baby-tend, bulb-snatch*, either type occurring with accusative as well as oblique function (see Pennanen [1966] for fuller discussion of both types; see Mithun [1984] for a recent synopsis of noun incorporation). Modern Romance examples not dependent on direct lexical supports (back-formation, calquing, etc.) also demonstrate both these functions: Gasc. *causse-ha* 'sock' + 'make', *sou-coélhe* 'sun' + 'harvest', Arag. *mancuspir* 'hand' + 'spit', as do N + V deriving from other sources. Where Bloch–Wartburg identify a continuation of Latin in *maintenir* and its congeners,

Benveniste sees, rather, a Romance innovation. Against the genetically accountable rise and propagation of N + V across medieval Romance stand its occurrences among unrelated languages of North America, as well as its manifestations in spoken registers of modern-day Romance. In this valuable article one misses explicit extension of the discussion to Romance N functions other than oblique, since N Dir Obj and even N Subj have existed and continue to exist in the Gallo- and Hispano-Romance languages surveyed here. Extension of Benveniste's monochromatic discussion to this latter possibility in both Romance and Uto-Aztecan would have been typologically revealing, as would some mention of other Romance languages. We can only regret the inadequate documentation which led Benveniste to speak precipitously of the pattern's demise in Romance.

"Convergences typologiques" was the immediate inspiration for Kuryłowicz 1976, coming near the end of a brilliant career. Fr. *maintenir* is examined within the context of syntactic change and word-order typology; to illustrate the shift from syntax to morphology, Kuryłowicz glances at the possible accusative value of nominal elements before concluding that compound structures (like idioms and set phrases) often reflect archaic syntactic patterns. Kuryłowicz differentiates a Proto-Romance morphological stratum in which the ablative gradually yielded ground to prepositional constructions, from a more recent stratum in which the N could function as an accusative. The instrumental type originally dates back to the earlier stratum (which, according to Meyer-Lübke [*GRS* §594] may well have been pre–Proto-Romance, i.e., actually Cl. Latin). *Manūtenēre* and its analogs might have spawned meanings not transparently analyzable by speakers as, e.g., *cum manū tenēre, in manū tenēre*; thanks to these semantic variants, the morphological pattern survived in the face of ongoing syntactic development and the switch to prepositional phrases.

A similar process is posited for structures of the more recent type [N Dir Obj + V]; here, however, OV word order rather than inflection is preserved. For Kuryłowicz, in either case semantic fusion is responsible for morphological fusion and for the perpetuation of the N + V pattern. The author's slightly qualified general conclusion: "on peut se demander si ce n'est pas en général le cas, que historiquement toute composition provient en dernière ligne de constructions syntaxiques tombées en désuétude par suite de renouvellements morphologiques" (165).

Romance is contrasted diachronically with other members of the Indo-European family. The morphological impetus for, e.g., Sanskrit, Greek, and Germanic compositional patterns is not word order, but the gradual replacement of thematic first elements, survivors of "un état de langue dépourvu de désinences" (165), by inflected forms, leaving so-called thematic compounds in the historical languages. Indo-European nominal flexion must at one time have consisted of a simple opposition of nom.-acc./oblique themes, replaced by postposed desinences, and in a yet later period, by prepositional forms. Indo-European and Romance compound patterns thus emerge as having separate but parallel origins in (i) changes in diachronic syntax and in (ii) a shift of the encoding procedure for grammatical information.

The Romance materials sketched in by Benveniste are somewhat augmented by Kuryłowicz, who cites *maintenir, manœuvrer, morfondre, pêle-mêle, saupoudrer,* and *vermoulu,* all with instrumental value; also added in a footnote are: *billebarrer, blanc-poudrer, cloufichier, ferarmer, ferlier, fervestir, pelleverser, saupiquet* 'spicy sauce or stew'. Unfortunately, full identification of sources is neglected. In another footnote, Kuryłowicz takes issue with John Orr's (1951) attempt to explain away some of these forms as analogical reformations, e.g., *vermoulu* as a reinterpretation of OFr. *verm-elu, -elé* 'wormy'. Citing *amentevoir* and *viandante* as illustrations of two additional noninstrumental functions of the ablative, Kuryłowicz stumbles slightly over Occ.–Cat.–Sp. *vian(d)ant,* since as early as the *REW* OPr.–OSp. *vian(d)ar (via + an[d]ar)* was recognized as a popular reinterpretation of simplex VIĀNS, -NTIS (present participle of a lost verb VIĀRE). He goes beyond Benveniste in listing N Dir Obj + V examples, among them: (i) Fr. *chavirer* (glossed with Pr. *capvirar* (N Dir Obj + V), as against Darmesteter's 'virer de tête'; [7] (ii) Sp. *perniquebrar, maniatar;* and (iii) Sp. *carcomer* 'to be worm-eaten', presented as a straightforward development of *CARNEM COMĔDĔRE (a derivation traceable to Diez but which has since been considerably refined in favor of CARIĒS; see *DCE[LC],* s.v. "carcoma").

It is regrettable that the *FEW* was not called into service for an updated discussion of, e.g., *ferlier* and *culbuter,* the former currently regarded as an Adj + V construction, the latter recognized as a tautological V + V compound of the kind so highly prized in the 15th and 16th centuries. Once again, despite the interest of this article for students of compounding, a debt to Darmesteter and Meyer-Lübke is obvious, as is the need for an eventual setting-aside of compounds which arise through reinterpretation, e.g., *colporter (FEW* II, s.v. "comportare"), or forms that continue to be offered erroneously as evidence of N + V, e.g., *arc-bouter, culbuter, ferlier, pêle-mêle, vermoulu.*

In a single paragraph devoted to verbal N + V compounds in Mod. French, Thiele (1981) errs in many of the same ways as his eminent predecessors, repeating (and in some instances even compounding) errors long left uncorrected in the

---

[7]Since Benveniste had included this verb in his original N Instr list, one wonders whether the structure of French itself does not lead to such contradictions. Does *virer de tête* represent 'to turn the head' or 'for the head to turn'? In Fr. *chavirer,* Pr. *capvirar,* the N is arguably N Dir Obj or perhaps even N Subj. If N Instr, it should yield 'to turn by means of the head', which seems unlikely.

literature: Why indeed should *arc-bouter* still be cited as N + V? Why has *colporter* not been identified as the analogical reformation it is known to be?

Of the above descriptions, those contributed by Romanists appear to be on much the firmer ground where Romance material has been handled. Traditional explanation as exemplified by Ronjat has much to offer, if only because it is not overly concerned with any one type of formal or semantic analytic criteria. Ronjat's arguments are syntactically based, as are Kuryłowicz'; the great Occitanist, in explicitly identifying a multiplicity of sources for N + V, paved the way for thorough investigation in a manner since unrivalled. Rohlfs' description—analysis would be too technical a label—disappoints by its incomplete, almost desultory nature. In similar fashion, Benveniste's article is unsatisfactory in its use of Romance as incompletely digested illustrative material for general linguistic conclusions, rather than in and for itself. Despite the passage of more than half a century, Benveniste was content to base a short study on selected nuggets of (borrowed) information without illuminating anything beyond the most obvious corner of the field staked out. Without significant enlargement, nothing like Benveniste's or Kuryłowicz' mixed bag of a corpus could yield any consistent analysis of N + V. One is left, after reading the last two articles, with the overall feeling of having caught a pair of eminent Indo-Europeanists on somewhat ill-advised forays into Romance, during which valid and potentially important general points are made despite inadequate use of the Romance materials chosen to illustrate them.

On the positive side, Menéndez Pidal (1941) and Thiele (1981) are entirely correct in pointing out that the modern speaker is no longer aware of the bipartite compound nature of *maintenir*. Nyrop found no new lexicalized examples in literary French after the 18th century, but evidence from the northern Gallo-Rom. dialects (to be examined in Chapters 3 and 4) suggests that the pattern as an active derivational reality may not be wholly defunct. If the various inconsistencies uncovered above are to be eliminated, what is needed is a detailed investigation of this Romance type based on a substantial (if less than exhaustive) corpus—one that will uncover the exciting diachronic and comparative possibilities of N + V compounding.

THE INDO-EUROPEAN BACKGROUND
OF MANŪTENĒRE

Manūtenēre (attested ca. A.D. 800), with an instrumental determinans (*manū* 'by the hand = power'), is prefigured by a number of Latin N + V compound formations having diverse origins: Inherited compounds with uninflected nominal members, e.g., Cl.L. *crēdĕre* 'to trust' (from **crĕd-dĕre*, lit. 'to place one's trust' < IE **krĕd-* + **dhē-*); calques of Greek models, e.g., Late L. *genuflectĕre*, either a calque of deadjectival Gk. *gonuklineîn* 'to bend the knee, kneel' (from *gonuklinḗs* 'kneeling, on bended knee'), or, less likely, from L. *genuflexiō*, itself a calque of Gk. *gonuklisía* (Benveniste [1966] 1974:105); and back-formations from nominal or adjectival compounds, e.g., Cl.L. *manūmittĕre* 'to set free, release from one's power', cf. *manū missus* 'emancipated'. By the time *manūtenēre* is attested, increased evidence of Latin N + V compound verbs, adjectives, and nouns allows identification of analogical influences such as chaining (Séguy's [1953] "enchaînement associatif"), e.g., (9th c.) *caput tenēre* = *manūtenēre*. [1] Still other compounds, including (late 2d-c.) *fidĕicommittĕre*, *fidĕi committĕre* 'to entrust s.th. to s.o.'s good faith' ← *fidēs* 'trust' + *committĕre* 'to command; designate', and *manūtenēre* itself, appear to have coalesced directly from verb-final syntactic phrases, in the absence of direct lexical supports.

The background of a Romance and Medieval Latin N + V pattern is here documented through a brief survey of certain compound types in Sanskrit and Greek, both languages having luxuriant compositional traditions, and of the less copious Cl. Latin evidence, particularly those compounds in which *manus* occurs as first constituent. The view of Indo-European composition presented below is based mainly

---

[1] Graphic representation as one or two units—*manū mittĕre* or *manūmittĕre*—need not necessarily correspond to any notion of compoundedness in Latin (Buck 1933; repr. 1969:353), since written conventions fluctuated. Even today, graphy is no reliable guide in the study of compounds.

on work by W. P. Lehmann and T. Burrow (for Sanskrit); Karl Brugmann, Albert Debrunner, and Ernst Risch (for Greek); Carl D. Buck (for Greek and Latin); and Françoise Bader (for Latin). Latin's verb-final structure notwithstanding, no argument will be advanced here for a direct dependence of N + V compounding on syntax. While compound structures often reflect earlier syntactic patterns (Kuryłowicz [1976]), the role played by analogy, both in the remodeling of existing compounds and in the creation of novel formations, must not be underestimated. Analogy and natural ordering as well have played significant roles in the history of N + V in Romance, as in its parent language. [2]

While constituent order in compounds definitely corresponds, at the original level, to prevailing syntactic patterns, the formal nature of those constituents may provide additional evidence of syntactic evolution: witness the loss of most suffixal nominal inflection in the shift from Latin to Romance. Lehmann discusses the varying shapes of compound constituents in the context of syntactic change: "Thematic forms of noun stems and derived forms of verbal roots are used, as in Skt. *devá-kṛta* 'made by the gods'. Such extended constituents become more and more prominent, and eventually are characteristic elements of compounds" (1974:82).

Following Brugmann–Delbrück (1891), initial elements of the N + V compounds examined in this chapter will be shown to comprise (i) nominal roots; (ii) thematic stems; and (iii) case-marked (hence, syntactically independent but still subject to univerbation) lexemes. Verbal elements include: (iv) roots; (v) derived forms congealed as bound morphemes; and (vi) syntactically independent lexemes. The structure of *manūtenēre, maintenir,* most closely resembles a combination of (iii) + (vi), with the difference that, in the latter verb, *main-* lacks case-marking. Given the loss of nominal inflection in Mod. French, save marking for plural and occasionally gender, such a description cannot be said to contradict Darmesteter's evaluation of N + V as "la seule formation de composé en français où la notion de thème apparaisse" (1894:161). Whether taken as theme or as lexeme, Fr. *main-* is morphologically transparent, as was the nominal element of *manūtenēre,* and of *manūmittĕre* before it. Despite the 1300-year difference in their first attestations, *manūmittĕre* and *maintenir* both represent similarly structured, synchronically analyzable compounds. The very fact of their transparency argues for a certain degree of productivity at each stage; judging from the appearance of 20th-c. compounds such as Gasc. *causse-ha* 'to knit socks' (lit. 'sock' + 'make'), the N + V pattern, still

---

[2]Benveniste's characterization of N + V compound verbs as "non-Indo-European" ([1966] 1974:107) provided little more than a strong pivot on which to introduce his corpus of Amerindian N + V verbs.

characterized by analyzable elements, is extant today in Western Romance, despite declarations to the contrary by several generations of Romanists.

While it has been argued that lack of inflection on nominal elements in early stem compounds, e.g., L. *crēdĕre*, reflects their general age (or the relative age of the type in general), neither presence nor absence of nominal inflection affects comprehensibility. Explicit marking of the logical relation between N and V is unnecessary to the comprehensibility of a compound, at least in part because compounds may mean something different from the sum of their parts. Logical relations are unspecified in *crēdĕre*, lit. 'trust' + 'place', and unspecified as well in Romance N + V compounds, e.g., Fr. (12th c.) *maintenir* lit. 'hand' + 'hold', Occ.– Cat. (14th c.) *cama[l]liga* 'garter', lit. 'leg' + 'bind' (with its converse, OPr. *liacamba*, Cat. [16th c.] *lligacama* 'bind' + 'leg').

Logical relations between N and V in compounds can be partially, if not wholly, inferred from the lexical properties of the given verb, e.g., in L. *crēdĕre*, transitive *-dĕre* (< IE **dhē-* 'place') implies a N Dir Obj function for *crĕd-* 'trust'. In seeking to make explicit the parallel between syntactic relationships in compounds of attested Indo-European dialects and overall syntactic functions of PIE roots (as typical of the language ca. 3000 B.C.), Lehmann (1974) enumerates a list of possible relations between nominal and verbal elements of Vedic Sanskrit synthetic compounds (ca. 1200–800 B.C.): target, receptor, instrument/means, time, source, place, manner, agent—in short, the entire range of sentence relations. The vast majority of Vedic synthetic compounds, i.e., compounds in which one member is used in an inflectional form which it could not assume when used alone, shows a target relationship (= verb and its object, e.g., *agnídh-* 'priest', lit. 'fire-kindler') between unmarked forms of N and V (77–78; Lehmann's hyphenation is given): [3]

---

[3]In nominal first elements of Greek synthetic compounds, Debrunner (1917:34) identified the following cases:
   N nominative: *hektḗ-moros* 'having one-sixth as its share'
   N genitive: *diós-dotos* 'god-given'
   N dative: *arēí-philos* 'beloved by (lit. 'dear to') Ares'
   N accusative: *karē-komóōntes* 'long-haired, with hair on the head'
   N locative: *aerí-oikos* 'having its house in the air'.
Latin examples from Juret (1937:68) and Stolz–Leumann (1977:§336 1a, 2a, 3, 4) show the nominal element functioning as:
   N nominative: *sēstertius* 'two and a half' ← *sēmis* 'half' + *tertius* 'third'
   N genitive: *lēgislātor* ← *lēx* 'law' + *lātor* 'proposer'
   N accusative:
      (+ verb root) *artifex* 'artist' ← *ars* 'work of art' + *fac(ĕre)* 'to make'
      (+ *-o-* stem) *sacri-legus* 'stealing sacred things' ← *sacer* 'sacred' + *legĕre* 'to gather, pick up'

N target + V: *agnídh-* 'priest' ← *agni* 'fire' + *idh* 'kindle'
N receptor + V: *devahédana* 'angering the gods' ← *deva* 'god' + *heḍana*
    'angering'
N instrument/means + V: *ádrijūta* 'speeded by the stones' ← *adri* 'pressing
    stone' + *jūta* 'impelled'
N time + V: *ṛtajá* 'born at the right time' ← *ṛta* 'cosmic order' + *ja* 'born'
N source + V: *anhomuc* 'freeing from trouble' ← *anhas* 'difficulty' + *muc*
    'free'
N place + V: *dru←ad* 'sitting in a tree' ← *dru* 'tree' + *sad* 'sit'
N manner + V: *īśānakṛt* 'acting like a ruler' ← *īśāna* 'ruling' + *kṛt* 'making'
N agent + V: *tvá-datta* 'given by you' ← *tvá* 'you' + *datta* 'given'

In Pāṇini's grammar, rules for proper compounds establish relations between members which may or may not be manifest in their physical shape (Staal 1966:171). Morphological segregation into "proper" and "improper" categories—the forebears of Darmesteter's "composé"/"juxtaposé" dichotomy—results in the virtual exclusion from that grammar of improper compounds having an inflected first member; such flectional compounds were not rare, merely less frequent than their proper counterparts. [4]

Pāṇini's chief types of proper Sanskrit compounds are: (a) the determinatives, or *tatpurusha* (lit. 'the man is that'); (b) possessive *bahuvrihi* (lit. 'having much rice'); (c) iterative *amredita* ('repetitions'); and (d) coordinating *dvandva* ('two [and] two').

    (+ masc. *-a-* stem) *agricola* 'tiller of the field' ← *ager* 'field' + *col(ĕre)*
    'to cultivate'
    (+ ptc.) *arci-tenēns* 'holding a bow' ← *arcus* 'bow' + *tenēns* 'holding'
N ablative/instrumental *manūmissiō* 'setting free' ← *manus* 'hand' + *missiō*
    'sending away'
    (+ verbal derivative) *vēli-volans* 'flying with sails' ← *vēlum* 'sail' + *volāns*
    'flying'

[4]There is no justification, in descriptive linguistics, for dividing compounds into so-called proper and improper categories, despite the taxonomic usefulness of such labels. Salus (1965) reaches a similar conclusion in his study of Indo-European nominal compounding. What emerges clearly from Salus' article, despite its various infelicities (particularly, an excessive reliance on secondhand materials), is a striking divergence among the dialects in respect both of the types of compounds favored in any given period, and of the innovations peculiar to each dialect. Tocharian, which exhibited no flectional types, had so-called group inflection (in which a phrase was inflectionally marked only on the last member): e.g., *a kuklas yukas oṅkälmāsyo* 'with carts, horses, and elephants' (each member having the form of the oblique pl. but only the last carrying the instrumental suffix *-yo*. Certain Germanic dialects have the ability (shared with Celtic) to string together long combinations of independent morphemes. Salus' conclusion: The presence of flectional compounding among the IE dialects was virtually uniform, hence the unsuitability of the proper/improper dichotomy.

Tatpurusha compounds fall into several subclasses, among which are (i) numeral determinatives, or *dvigu*; and (ii) so-called attributive (or appositive) *karmadharaya*, also called descriptive determinatives, in which the first element (N in apposition, Num, Adj, Adv) is predicated on the latter (always N) and describes it, e.g., Skt. *nīlotpalam* '[variety of] blue lotus' (cf. the corresponding syntactic group *nīlam utpalam* 'a blue lotus'). In another subtype, (iii) dependent determinatives, the second element is a verbal adjective or a verbal action noun, e.g., *devāhūti* 'invocation of the gods' (*deva* 'god' + *hūti* 'invocation'), and *kumbhakāra* 'pot-maker' (*kumbha* 'pot' + *kṛ* 'make'), in which *-kāra* has been analyzed broadly as a nonfinite verbal form, and specifically as agentive 'maker'.

The distinguishing characteristic of dependent *tatpurusha* compounds lies in the syntactic relationship between their constituents: the first member (N genitive, dative, ablative, locative, instrumental, accusative) is syntactically dependent on the second (N or V): Skt. *devátta* (or *devádatta*) 'given by the gods', similarly Gk. *theódotos*, Fr. *Dieudonné*. When new accentual patterns eradicated former distinctions between possessive *bahuvrihi* (e.g., adj. Vedic *rája-putra* 'having a king as son') and determinative *tatpurusha* (e.g., nom. Cl.Skt. *rāja-putrá* 'king's son'), the two types could occasionally be confused, e.g., ambiguous Gk. *eupátōr*, respectively 'having a noble father' (*bahuvrihi*) and 'a noble father' (*tatpurusha*).

Manūtenēre and other N + V compounds examined here represent the *tatpurusha* type, or at least demonstrate a similar syntactic dependence. The ulterior shift from IE/Latin SOV ordering to Romance SVO ordering has posed no threat to the survival of *manūtenēre* and its reflexes, or to continued occurrences of N + V compounding in Western Romance, as witnessed by the enhanced vitality of this pattern in the last two centuries. In early Romance examples Benveniste (1966) argues unequivocally for an oblique relationship (neither nominative nor accusative) between determining nominal constituent and following verbal determinatum.[5] Early Romance N + V compounds are divided between verbs, nouns, and adjectives, including several cases in which primary nominal or verbal shape is disputed in the literature, e.g., OFr. *manœuvre, manœuvrer*.[6] Nominal N + V still occurs in modern

---

[5]The concept of a *casus obliquus* to this day resists any single clear-cut definition. In contrast to Benveniste (1966) and Kuryłowicz (1976), Pāṇini's grammar of Sanskrit includes the accusative among the oblique cases; "oblique" is taken here too as non-nominative, a distinction particularly apt in Western Romance, where nominal declension resolved itself into nominative vs. all other cases, before the ultimate loss of case marking by the 13th and 14th centuries. As a label, N Compl (see Ronjat 1937 [1980]:§734) is more suitable than N obl., since *complement* may, yet need not obligatorily, include direct object function.

[6]*REW* (3d ed.) takes **manūŏperāre* as the etymon, as does Darmesteter; the *FEW* listing under *manūŏpera* gives us at a glance the preferable view.

Romance (as it did earlier among the IE dialects) where no compound verbs are known to exist, e.g., Cat. *aigualleix, aigualeixos* 'alluvium' (lit. 'deposited by water'), *feina-fuig* 'lazy' (lit. 'work' + 'flee'), in the absence of **aigualleixar, *feina-fugir*; cf. Eng. *potmaker* but not **to pot-make*. Romance nominal compounds of this type are flanked by another, much more frequent type, adjectival N + V Ptc (= N + Adj) formations, e.g., Fr. *bouche-bée*, OPr. *golabadat* 'open-mouthed' (lit. 'mouth opened wide'), existing in the absence of verbal **bouche-bayer* 'to open one's mouth'. Both nominal and adjectival patterns, which Marchand characterized as "double-stressed synthetics" in English (e.g., *potmaker, hand-made*; see 1969 §2.1.4), provide potential bases for derived verbs in Western Romance, as in English (*to baby-sit*, etc.; see Pennanen [1966]): Cat. *aiguabarreig* 'confluence' (of two rivers), denom. *aigua-barrejar-se* (*DECC* "aigua", I:95b, N → V); Cat. *cappelat* 'bald', infin. *cappelar* 'to lose one's hair'. Lacking recognition as yet are the instances of true N + V compositional activity also to be found in Western Romance, e.g., Gasc. *causse-ha* ('sock' + 'make'), Arag. *mancuspir* ('hand' + 'spit'), neither calques, reinterpretations, nor back-formations. N + V compounding need not correlate with unmarked word order; novel compounds of this type appear to represent, rather, a renewal of synthetic word formation in Western Romance.

Nominal members of compounds in early Sanskrit carried no inflection. *Bahuvrihis* retained their original characteristics during and after the brief period of productivity of flectional compounds. In Vedic there appeared a handful of inflected *tatpurusha*, whose first member kept a genitive ending, e.g., *aṃhasaspati* = an intercalary month ← *aṃhasas* 'distress' + *pati* 'lord'; later this inflected type yielded to proper *tatpurusha* (Burrow 1965:211).[7] Burrow, like Lehmann, finds a chronological progression from bound stem form to greater formal independence in other *tatpurusha* having a verbal adjective as second member, e.g., *hastá-kṛta* 'hand' + 'made' (213), and cf. *devá-kṛta* 'made by the gods', both with passive past participle of *kṛ* 'to make'.

Foreshadowing Burrow's (1965) and Lehmann's (1974) arguments for the chronological spread of inflected nominal and verbal constituents in Sanskrit, Brugmann–Delbrück identified similar expansion in Greek: from nominal roots to thematic forms (supra (ii)), from verb roots (iv) to derived forms (v), hence from adjective to participle (vi) (1891:§144), and from nomen agentis (v) to infinitive [vi] (§156). Such a development was possible because the second constituent—whether

---

[7]Subsequent return to so-called proper *tatpurusha* in Sanskrit appears loosely to parallel the resurgence of Classical nominal compounding in Romance, e.g., *television* (lit. 'distance' + 'seeing'); *manicure* ('hand' + 'care'); *ventriloquist* (actually known in the trade as *belly-talker*); and adjectival compounds with Graeco-Latin linking vowels (Fr. *gréco-latin*).

root or nomen actionis—had the meaning of a participle, active or passive (Risch 1974:176). Active meanings can be identified in very early examples: Skt. *vājam-bharā-ḥ* 'prize-bearing' (← inflected *vājam* 'prize' + *bhara* 'bear'), Gk. *aethlo-phóros* idem. Benveniste (1966) supplies: *gonukleneîn* 'to bend the knee' (← adj. *gonuklinés* 'kneeling, with bended knee'), *gonupeteîn* 'to fall on the knee' (← *gonupetés* 'falling to the knee'), and *oikophoreîn* (← *oikophorós* 'bearing one's house').[8] Verbal *karatomeîn* 'to behead' coexisted with adjectives having both active value (paroxytonic *kara-tómos* 'beheading', lit. 'head-cutting') and passive value (proparoxytonic *kará-tomos* 'beheaded', according to Debrunner 1917: 36*n*1).[9] The participial second constituent, like a nomen agentis, could govern a case, i.e., it was assimilated to the characteristics and construction of a verb (Brugmann 1891:§156). Among verbal determinatives, Brugmann includes both *philó-xenos* 'loving a stranger, hospitable' (*phílos* 'loving' + *xénos* 'stranger, host') and *psycho-pompós* 'conductor of souls'; compounds in *-tēs* could be interpreted as nominal (= agentive) or adjectival, e.g., *su-bótēs* 'swineherd', 'herding swine'; *hipp-ēlátēs* 'driver of horses', 'driving horses'. The potential verbal force of *-ēlátēs* 'driving' manifests itself in *hipp-ēlateîn* 'to ride, drive' (Debrunner 1917:§97).

In Latin, the spread of compounds with an inflected first member has been represented as a late development, an innovation of the historical period (Buck [1933] 1969:§521); compounds at that time began to arise directly from syntactic structures, e.g., from prepositional phrases (*obvius* 'in the way') or syntactic groups (*anim[um] advertĕre* 'to notice', lit. 'to turn one's attention'). Buck distinguishes "formal" Greek and Latin composition (through coalescence of a word group, or juxtaposition, e.g., L. *animadvertĕre*) from the older type of stem composition, e.g., *crēdĕre* (§515).

Additional evidence of continued expansion in Latin nominal constituents is provided in Françoise Bader's definitive analysis of Latin nominal compounds (1962). The earliest stratum of Latin composition, according to Bader (6), predated both the rise of flexions and also the ensuing separation of nouns and verbs, e.g., *crēdĕre* 'to trust' (**crĕd-dĕre* 'to place one's trust'). In Bader's second stage, nomina agentis (verbal determinatives, e.g., L. *agricola* 'tiller [← *colĕre* 'to cultivate'] of the field', were formed on verbal second constituents, while *bahuvrihis* appeared with nominal second members. Both types had adjectival value. Finally, in the third period, there

---

[8]Liddell & Scott lists no infin. **oiko-phoreîn* after the adjective. On the other hand, verbal *kara-dokeîn* 'to be attentive, wait for the outcome of' exists in the absence of an attested **kara-dókos* (Debrunner 1917:36*n*1).

[9]Proparoxytonic *kará-tomos*, which both Debrunner (1917:36*n*1) and Liddell & Scott (877b) gloss as 'beheaded', can perhaps be paraphrased as 'one who has a head-cutting'.

appeared, with fully transparent second constituents: (i) nonderived nominal compounds, e.g., *agricultor, altitonāns* 'high-thundering'; and (ii) inflected compound verbs, often chronologically preceded by participial forms, e.g., *belligerāns*, then *belligerāre* 'to wage war'.

Classical Latin was conspicuously archaic in its compositional practices. Latin did show certain innovating tendencies, according to Bader, in the creation of V + N Obj compounds, say, *flexanimus* 'touching, affecting'; such compounds are occasionally found in Sanskrit and OHG, where they again rank as innovations.[10] Cl. Latin, which had a much poorer range of literary compound patterns than Cl. Sanskrit, stands scholars in good stead as a witness to IE itself (1962:§514), as does Hittite. The older types of derived compounds predominated in religion and law; newer nonderived forms were relegated to less noble domains, such as botany, zoology, veterinary medicine, grammar, military and commercial writings, and inscriptions and glosses (§392). Not surprisingly, these were the types most characteristic of the spoken language—and the ones best attested in the RLs today.

Bader's basic definition of an IE compound in the first stage of composition—with an inflectionally unspecified nominal first member followed by a head constituent having verbal value—remains relevant to Latin and Romance N + V combinations:

> la définition des composés comme reliquats des plus anciens syntagmes comprenant un déterminé (à valeur verbale et en deuxième place) et un déterminant (au cas indéfini et en première place) ne vaut pas pour les composés de langues d'une typologie différente de celles des langues indo-européennes (§508).

The very earliest compounds corresponded to a period in which verbal and nominal forms were not yet distinguished, when inflections were still unavailable to make explicit the syntactic relationships between the elements of a group or phrase (§507). Eventually, according to Bader, adjectival compounds found themselves in competition with new syntactic combinations, both nominal and verbal—in the latter case, relative clauses or participial clauses (§510).

---

[10]The forebear of the Romance languages had only begun to exploit VO compound structures: (i) iteratives or *amreditas* (e.g., *feriferux* ← *ferus* 'wild'); (ii) coordinatives or *dvandvas* (*hircocervus* ← *hircus* 'he-goat' + *cervus* 'stag', *dulcamāris*); (iii) V + N compound type (e.g., *flexanimus* 'touching'); (iv) Prep + N (e.g., *exlex* 'lawless'); and perhaps (v) N + Adj (e.g., *equifer* 'wild horse', and structurally similar *bahuvrihi*, e.g., *animaequus* 'even-tempered'). Of the above, only the first two—and scholars still disagree as to whether they were VO-ordered—appear in Sanskrit analyses. Bader considers that any Latin compound whose first member governed its second (= VO type) owes its existence to Greek influence. In addition to (i–v) above, she lists other unusual first elements in calques: (vi) Adv (*sempervīvus* 'eternal') and (vii) Pn (*sibiplacentia* 'self-assured') (1962:§399).

In the morphology and syntax of Latin, the verb grew ever more important, and compound verbs correspondingly exerted greater influence on nominal compounds; among the IE dialects, Latin is known for its vigorous verbal syntax and its less-than-vigorous tradition of nominal composition. As Latin gradually abandoned synthetic IE nominal compound types, syntactic compounding, or juxtaposition, became increasingly frequent. There was some adjustment of OV to VO types: among verbal expressions, *ŏpus est* yielded to *est ŏpus*, itself confirmed by Lerch and Jud as the etymon of OFr. *est-ovoir, -evoir, -avoir,* Engad. *stuvair,* etc., 'to be obligatory, must'. [11] But few of the synthetic nominal compounds mentioned in this chapter survived widely into Romance: e.g., ARTIFEX > OIt. *artefe, artefice;* AURIFEX 'goldsmith' > It. *órafo,* AURIFICE(M) > It. *orefice,* OSp. *orebze* (Mod.Sp. *platero de oro* 'goldsmith'), etc. Of L. *cordolium* 'heartache, grief', *cor coctiōne(m)* 'heartburn', *cor *ārsiōne(m)* idem, *cor pŭlsiōne(m)* 'heartbeat', and their analogs, only scattered traces remain. [12]

In Latin synthetic compounds, a linking vowel ("Fugenvokal") generally preceded consonant-initial second constituents. The compositional vowel most typical of Latin was *-i-* (from stems in *-o-, -io-,* and *-i-* itself). Occasionally the link was missing, by syncope: *manceps, mānsuētus, prīnceps.* Other phonetic processes affected stems: (a) syncope: *au-spex [-spec-s]* 'bird-seer' from **avi-spec-; iūdic-* 'judge, law-sayer' (from **ioues-dic-,* Stolz–Leumann [1926–28] 1977:§334 1.c); (b) reduction: *homi-cīda* 'man-slayer' (on *homin-,* perhaps after *pari-cīda,* §334 1.b); (c) assimilation (*malluviae* 'basin for washing the hands', from **man-lov-,* §334 1.c); and (d) other types of blurring (*cordolium* 'heartache' ← **cordi-dolium,* perhaps by haplology, §334 1.c).

---

[11]See *REW* §6079 for other forms of *est ŏpus,* which survives in arch. Eng. *estovers* 'necessaries allowed by law'. The Latin phrase was studied in Eugen Lerch, "Altfranzösisch *estuet (est ŏpus),* die Lautgesetze und der Bedeutungswandel," *RF* 55 (1941), 337–75; Jakob Jud, "Altfrz. *estuet;* bündnerrom. *stuver, stuvair*", *VR* 9 (1946–47), 29–56. It has recently been reexamined in a paper by Yakov Malkiel, "The Romance Vicissitudes of Latin *opus est:* Jakob Jud's Reconstruction Reconsidered", *Classica et Mediaevalia* 38 (1987), 189–202.

[12]Action nouns such as L. *cordolium, stillicidium* 'dripping water' admit of more than one analysis. Bader champions one possibility, N Subj + V = 'the heart burns'; a more convincing approach can be found in N Genit + N, or, as Malkiel puts it (1958:204), "concrete N + abstract N," e.g., COR *ĀRSIŌNE > Sp. *corazón,* Poit. *cœurasson* 'heart[burn]'. See Antoine Thomas, "Notes étymologiques et lexicographiques: *cœurasson* (Poitou)," *Ro* 38 (1909), 374–75. Although N + N was generally supplanted in Romance by V + N, e.g., Fr. *crève-cœur,* further examples of the former include: COR CŎCTIONE > OFr. *kurceuson* 'itching', dial. Fr. *corcusson, cœurcueilson,* Rouerg. *courcouysson* 'heartburn, itching'; COR PŬLSUS > OFr. *cuerpous* 'heartbeat', COR PŬLSIŌNE > Occ. (Toul) *courpouissou* 'shortness of breath'. Reflexes of CORDOLIUM (OSp. *cordojo,* OFr. *cordoeil, -dueil,* OPr. *corduelh,* Occ. *cor-doulou[r],* Cat. *cordol* 'compassion, mal au cœur') could eventually give rise to denominal verbs, e.g., Occ. *còr-dòldre* 'to be heartsore'.

As an initial constituent of Latin compounds, *manus* could be subjected to unusual phonetic evolution. The short *-u-* of *manufestus* 'palpable, manifestly betraying, clear' appeared phonetically dubious to Ernout–Meillet (1979:590); this adjective was remodeled to *manifestus* in Imperial Latin, giving rise to *manifestāre* 'to reveal'. [13] *Mandō, -āre* 'to commit to the charge of' was also troublesome for Ernout–Meillet because of its stress pattern—**mandĕre* was to be expected from *manum dăre*, but *mandō, -ĕre* 'to chew' had already occupied the slot. *Mānsuēscĕre* 'to become tame, to tame' appeared late, its original athematic second element *(mān)-suēs* remodeled to *-suētus* before the derivation of the infinitive. *Masturbāre* has long been assumed to contain *manu(m)* (but see D. Q. Adams [1985]); its second element also remains problematic. Bader deems this verb obscure (1962:§305) but records two possible solutions: **man-stuprāre* 'manu stuprum perpetrare', from *turbāre*, or **man-sturbāre*, as a by-form of *turbāre*; the verb itself gave rise to agentive *masturbātor*. Against these phonetic difficulties stand unexceptional *manceps* 'purchaser' and *mancipium* 'taking possession of', from which *mancipāre* arose through the intermediary of a verbal syntagm such as we find in Paulus ex Festo: "*manceps* dictus quod manucapiatur" (Ernout–Meillet 1979:381b). Cl. Latin *malluviae* 'water or basin for washing hands', as well as *pelluviae* 'basin for washing the feet', resurfaced in Med. Latin with a linking vowel (*maniluvium, pediluvium*). Next to *mantēl(i)um* 'towel, [table]cloth' (having a verbal second element, *telum* < TERG- 'wipe') there appeared Med.L. (7th c.) *manūtergium* 'towel'.

The appearance of *manūtenēre* is prefigured in the relative chronology of pairs such as *agricola*[14]/*agricultor*, *sacerdōs*/*sacrifex*, *altitonus*/*altitonāns*, *-pos*/*-potēns*,

---

[13]The explanation of *manifestus* through **manū festus* is not unanimously accepted (Bader 1962:§315).

[14]In an article on the Latin type *agricola*, Saussure (1909) pays tribute to Louis Havet's reconstruction of **aes-tŭmā* 'bronze-cutter', 'coupe-bronze' (← *aes* 'bronze' + *tŭmā* 'cut'), underlying L. *aestumāre* 'to appraise, value'. Saussure posits a primitive IE archetype for structurally similar nom. *agricola* 'field-tiller' and fellow 1st-declension masculine nouns in *-a*, e.g., *indigena* 'native' (*indus* 'in' + *genu[m]* 'born'), *pār[r]icīda* 'parent-murderer' (← *patr-* 'father' + *caed-* 'kill'), etc. The nominal first element of *agricola* was shared by remodeled *agricultor*; the earlier form *sacerdōs* differs sharply from later *sacru-*, *sacri-fex*, *sacrilegus* (Brugmann–Delbrück 1891:§33). For the **aestŭmā, agricola* type, therefore, Saussure rejects analogical influence from the Greek type *oikodomḗ*, as well as Brugmann's conjecture of denominal derivation from a primary feminine action noun (cf. *agri-cultūra* 'agriculture' = 'field' + 'cultivating'). Malkiel referred to both Saussure and Havet in his etymological excursus on Hisp. *tomar* (1976:116 and *n*d), arguing that the originally commercial value of L. *aestim-/aestum-āre* facilitated the ancients' nonetymological identification in this verb of *aes* 'copper, bronze, money, etc.' + *ti-/ tu-māre*.

-ficus/-ficāns, malluviae/maniluvium, pelluviae/pediluvium. The latter member of each pair, whether nominal or verbal element, gained in transparency, if not necessarily in phonic substance or syntactic independence. Enhanced morphological transparency also translates to greater synchronic productivity, as is clear from an examination of the fate of L. *-fex* 'maker, doer'; beyond *artifex, aurifex,* and *sacrifex,* a total of some 50 compounds can be adduced. [15] As regards, e.g., *sacerdōs/sacrifex,* one may argue remodeling or replacement, since the members of this pair were synonymous— perhaps the only link between them a semantic one. [16]

During the Classical period, the second constituent of certain synthetics had already come to be paralleled by more transparent forms—, e.g., *-pos/-potēns* and *-ficus/-ficāns,* even in the absence of a corresponding verb, as seems to have been the case with *belliger* 'warlike'/*belligerāns,* predating *belligerāre* 'to wage war'. Compounds with *-gerāns* were formed analogically on denominatives in *-ger,* before the appearance of *gerāre* (Bader 1962:§301). Cf. also *arcitenēns* 'holding a bow' (from *arcu-*). Agentives in *-tor,* paralleling Gk. *-tēr, -tōr,* e.g., *soliversor* (from *solum vertĕre* 'to

---

[15]The following list of some 50 compounds in *-fex* 'maker, doer' has been compiled from a number of sources, principally Du Cange and Per Sigurd Baecklund, *Die lateinischen Bildungen auf -fex und -ficus* (Uppsala: K. W. Appelbergs Boktryckeri, 1914):
aedifex 'builder, architect'; *aerifex* 'bronzesmith'; *archipontifex* 'highest priest, archbishop'; *argentifex* 'silversmith'; *armifex* 'arms-maker'; *artifex* 'artist; author, maker', (Med.) 'skilled craftsman'; *aurifex* 'goldsmith'; *calcifex* 'lime-maker'; *cantrifex* 'maker of tin tankards'; *carnifex, carnufex* 'executioner, slayer; butcher'; *cerifex* 'wax-maker, chandler'; *clauifex* 'nail-, key-maker'; *coartifex* 'co-worker?'; *concarnifex* 'co-executioner?'; *contifex* 'centipes'; *coopifex* 'co-worker?'; *c(h)ordifex* 'rope-maker, one who restrings chairs'; *corifex* 'currier', 'courroier'; *dapifex* 'cook; seneschal, intendant'; *funifex* 'rope-maker'; *lanifex* 'clothier' (lit. 'wool-maker'); *linifex* 'flaxmaker, one who makes or works with linen'; *manifex*; *manuartifex* 'handcraftsman'; *maurifex* = *mūrifex*; *medifex*; *mellifex* 'honey-maker, beekeeper'; *mortifex*; *mūnifex* 'one who performs service, is on duty' (of soldiers), also 'qui fait des présents'; *mūrifex* 'wall-maker?'; *nāuifex* 'shipmaker'; *offex* 'hinderer, dissuader'; *opifex* (Cl.) 'worker, maker, framer, fabricator', (Med.) 'surgeon'; *organifex* 'instrument-maker', 'facteur d'orgues'; *panifex* 'baker'; *pannifex* 'cloth-maker, -merchant'; *pellifex* 'tanner, one who prepares or sells skins'; *pontifex* 'high priest, bishop'; **postifex*; *praefex* (Med.) 'author, instigator (of a crime)'; *rētifex* 'fisherman, net-maker'; *sacrifex* 'priest'; *sīgnifex* (Cl.) 'maker of statues or images'; *stannifex* 'tinsmith'; *stupifex*; *t(h)urifex* 'priest'; *turrifex* 'jailer?'; *uenēfex* 'poison-maker?', 'poisoner?'; *uestifex* 'tailor, garment-maker'; *uitrifex* 'glazier'. To these perhaps should be added OFr.-Pr. *carbon-fadere, charbofaziera* 'charcoal-maker, -merchant' (*Girart de Roussillon*), OGasc. *fort[s]-fasedor* 'wrongdoer'.

[16]Use of the terms "remodeling" and "replacement" must remain contingent upon the extent to which the link between older and newer constituents proved synchronically analyzable; either term will be used here and throughout subject to that qualification.

change one's country, go into exile'), sprang into existence (§335). The oldest of the adjectival compounds in *-ficus* were deverbal, e.g., *dēlēnificus* 'charming' (cf. *dēlēnīre* 'to charm'). These in turn made possible the coining of factitive verbs in *-facĕre* (e.g., *calefacĕre* 'to make warm') and *-ficāre*, which was to evolve into a common verbal formative in Romance after signal success in Christian Latin. Last in the progression of types came nonderived adjectives in *-ficus* based on predicate adjectives, e.g., *laetificus* 'pleasing' (*laetus* 'cheerful') → *laetificāre* 'to gladden', *magnificus* 'splendid' (*magnus* 'great') → *magnificāre* 'to esteem highly' (§260). The chronology of their attestation does not always support claims for a neat chronological progression: while *belligerāns* predates *belligerāre*, *laetificāns* is found in Plautus before the appearance of *laetificus*. Nonderived OV-ordered nominal synthetics, e.g., *-ficus*, *-ficāns*, *-gerāns*, illustrate a stage intermediate between hereditary IE types and the compounds of a language such as French, in which both constituents represent independent lexemes (§392).

During the transition to Romance, all the distinguishing characteristics of IE compounds—their original form, function, and use—were lost or profoundly modified:

> Par une série de bouleversements successifs, toutes les particularités des composés hérités de l'indo-européen se trouvent éliminées en roman, quant à la forme, la fonction (puisqu'un simple ne change plus de valeur à son entrée en composition, et que la fonction du composé dépend uniquement de celle du simple), et l'emploi (en dehors des calques de composés latins effectués lors de la Renaissance, les composés ont proportionnellement moins d'emplois poétiques en français qu'en latin, mais dans le langage parlé sont moins nombreux en latin qu'en français—cela est lié à leur caractère de nom en français, d'adjectif en latin). (Bader 1962:§393)

In recapitulation, a range of Cl. Latin verbs with N + V structure, showing varying degrees of morphological cohesion and transparency, arose from the following sources.

(i) From the combination of two stems, e.g., *crēdĕre* (**crĕd-dĕre*, cf. Skt. *śrad-dhá́-*, bipartite *śrad dadhāmi* 'I place my trust in s.o.' ← *śrad-* 'trust' + *dhá́-* 'place'); post-Cl. *flammigāre* 'to emit flames' (*flamma* 'flame' + *agĕre* 'to make'); *lītigāre* 'to dispute, quarrel' (*līs, lītis* 'lawsuit' + *agĕre*); *mandāre* 'to entrust to s.o.' (lit. 'to put in s.o.'s hands'); *nāvigāre* 'to sail' (**nāv-* 'ship' + *agĕre* 'to drive').

(ii) Nominals, e.g., *manceps/mancipium* → *man-cipāre*; *vindex* 'protector' (with an obscure first element) → *vindicāre* 'to assert a claim'; *iūdex* → *iūdicāre* 'to be a judge, to judge'; *manifestus -āre*, *mānsuētus* → *mānsuēscĕre* 'to tame, become tame'.

(iii) Formal coalescence of OV verbal syntagmata, e.g., *anim[um]-advertĕre* 'to consider, notice'; [17] *cūr[am]-agĕre* 'to pay attention to'; *os-citāre* 'to gape, yawn' (Stolz–Leumann [1926–28] 1977:§418); *tergiversārī* 'to make excuses, practice evasion' (cf. *tergum vertĕre* 'to turn the back'); *vēn[um]-īre* 'to go on sale, put up or expose for sale'; perhaps *vēndĕre* 'to put on sale' (specifically of slaves) ← *vēnum, vēnī* 'sale' + *dăre* 'to give' (Ernout–Meillet 1979:1086).

Finally, (iv) syntagmata demonstrating semantic isolation but not necessarily morphological coalescence, e.g., *manū mittĕre, manūmittĕre* 'to set free'; *fidĕ(i) committĕre* 'to entrust s.th. to s.o.'s good faith'; *mĕnte habēre* 'to remember, mention, notice', flanked by *mĕnte tenēre* 'to know', *memoriā tenēre* 'to remember'. [18]

In later Latin, juxtaposed or syntactic compounds increased in frequency. Scattered signs of their coming were already visible in the Golden Age, e.g., *manū missus*, source of *manūmittĕre* and *manūmissor*; *tergi-versārī, -versātiō* occur in Cicero (Ernout–Meillet, s.v. "tergum"), *tergiversātor* clearly follows (mid-2d c. A.D.). Calques on Greek begin to appear, e.g., *genuflectĕre*, still unusual in the post-Classical language (Bader 1962:§487). But Late Latin legal and religious coinings, e.g., *manūmittĕre, genuflectĕre, fidĕicommissum* (cf. *fidĕ(i) committĕre*), *fidĕ(i)iubēre, fidĕiussor* (← *fidĕ[i] iubēre*), *fidĕ(i)promissor, fidedictor*, are all harbingers of the eventual appearance of compound *manūtenēre*.

Classical *manū tenēre* 'to have tangible evidence or personal knowledge of, know for certain' (cf. It. *avere in mano*) is a fixed expression, its nominal constituent, e.g., "cum indicia mortis se comperisse manifesto et manu tenere dicere" (Cicero *Brutus*) still independent enough to allow, not of interruption, but of pluralization, with a slight shift in meaning (*manibus tenērī* 'to be certain'), and even of coupling with another body part: e.g., "sed oculis et manibus teneretur" (Cicero *Pro Cluentio*). By

---

[17]Constituent order in the fixed phrase *animum advertĕre*, its N Dir Obj + V relationship remaining constant after coalescence to *animadvertō, -ĕre*, has been characterized by J. N. Adams ("A Typological Approach to Latin Word Order," *Indogermanische Forschungen* 81 [1976], 70–99, at p. 92) as rare already during the historical period of Latin. Adams demonstrates that, by the time of Plautus, undeniable (typological) VO features were present in informal spoken Latin. Despite these features, the Classical literary dialect maintained object + verb ordering as a marked device long after the shift to VO.

[18]A number of partially opaque Latin compound verbs were reduced to opaque Romance simplexes, e.g., MANDĀRE (Fr. *mander*, Sp. *mandar* 'to entrust with, to send'); VENDĔRE (Fr. *vendre*, Sp. *vender*, etc.); *credere* (Fr. *croire*, Sp. *creer*, etc.). Opaque Fr. *chauffer*, OPr. *calfar*, etc., descend from L. CALFA[CĔ]RE. Reflexes of -FICUS, -FICĀNS yielded suffixal -*(I)FICĀRE > Fr. -*ifier*, Sp. -*iguar*, etc., all destined for considerable productivity in Romance, particularly in Judeo-Romance. Christian L. *crŭcifīxus, crŭcifīgĕre, -fīcāre*, by its widespread occurrence, made possible other formations with nominal first constituent, e.g., Med.L. *panificare* 'to make bread', OFr. *pannechier*.

the time *manūtenēre* appears in Charlemagne's 4th Capitulary, chap. 9 (ca. A.D. 800), it has come to mean 'defend, protect, support, aid', its nominal element, like the *manū* of *manūmittĕre*, representing 'by the hand = power' (of the slave owner or feudal lord). Its compound status at the Classical stage can be inferred, if not absolutely demonstrated. As mentioned above, graphic coalescence cannot suffice as proof of Latin compounding; more telling by far are its early, clear collocation, conducive to coalescence; its semantic isolation, as a term which found its way into everyday usage; and its pan-Romance status, [19] from the earliest vernacular monuments, which argues its presence at the stage of spoken Latin.

The claim made here for compound status of *manūtenēre* in spoken Latin finds support in Bloch–Wartburg (s.v. "main"); why, then, should the first element of Fr. *main-* have a form suggesting independent tonic stress? The answer must be: through remodeling of an earlier northern Gallo-Romance **mantenir*, i.e., through a conscious search for transparency. [20] Such remodeling stands out against the shape of atonic *man-* in *manuvrer* ([11th c.] 'to put with the hand', [12th c.] 'to work'), particularly in light of the early dating, ca. A.D. 800, of both *manūtenēre* and *manūŏpera* in Med. Latin. The morphological transparency of nominal *main-* also argues for a certain degree of productivity in N + V compound verb formation, since the pattern must have been in use for such a remodeling to have taken place. By A.D. 800, *manūtenēre* is clearly compounded: witness its occurrence beside an exact synonym in a 9th-c. Carolingian text: "et per se, aut ad nos, aut filium nostrum caput teneant ['protect'], id est, seipsos per se, aut per nos, etc. manuteneant" (DuC, s.v. "captenere"). This pair, owing its existence to "enchaînement associatif" (*caput* for *manus*, with no change in meaning), figures prominently with other examples of analogical influence, both assimilative and creative, in our examination of the multiple sources of N + V compounding in Latin and Romance.

A number of early N + V compounds, e.g., Cl.L. *mĕnte habēre* 'to remember', *manūmittĕre* 'to free a slave', and so on, clearly show semantic isolation, just as they are sufficiently transparent to have given rise to analogical imitation. *Manūmittĕre* 'to emancipate', "leader" word at the Cl. Latin stage of N + V, must have been widely known, given the importance of freed slaves in Roman society; the verb remains alive to this day in the legal terminology of Romance (*manumetre*, *mainmise*, and so on). Classical examples, however, were destined to survive only marginally in spoken Romance, e.g., *mentaure*, *mentaver* in a number of Occitan dialects. It is *manūtenēre*,

---

[19]See Chapter 1, note 6.

[20]Edouard Bourciez posited just such a primitive, in his *Précis de phonétique française*, 9th ed. (Paris: Klincksieck, 1958), §88 II; Gallo-Romance reflexes in *-ir* resulted from a change of conjugation class (TENĒRE → *tenir* through pressure of *venir*).

generalized from a technical term into everyday speech, that furnishes the clearest example of N + V compounding in Med. Latin and early Romance. Today the reflexes of this leader word are opaque, no longer felt as compounds; but throughout the medieval period, as long as Latin and Romance could continue to borrow from each other, it provided a morphological model for legal coinings, just as, e.g., "Lent" came to be represented by a rich series of words combining 'meat, flesh' + 'remove/ prohibit'. Because of the continued transparency and concreteness of *manūtenēre, maintenir, mantener,* etc., creation of semantic doublets was also possible in the medieval period: cf. 'hand' + 'hold' (OPr. *mantenen,* MFr. *maintien*) as names for balustrades and handles. Much of the interest of *manūtenēre, maintenir,* etc., today resides in the contrast between its present status as a morphologically distinguishable compound (Darmesteter invokes "la composition proprement dite") and its origins in unmarked syntax, as a so-called syntactic or juxtaposed compound. A pattern based on *manūtenēre* could develop only after the shift to composition with inflected, and eventually transparent, compositional elements was clearly under way, as a concomitant of the rise to prominence of compounding with independent lexemes.

3

MEDIEVAL AND RENAISSANCE EVIDENCE OF MANŪTENĒRE

1. LEARNED N + V BORROWINGS IN WESTERN ROMANCE

The following corpus of learnèd N + V compounds, lacking significant adjustment to Gallo- or Hispano-Romance phonology and morphology, complements the discussion in Chapter 2 of Classical Latin and Late Latin juxtaposed compounds, e.g., *animadvertĕre, manūmittĕre*, since many of those were taken bodily into the vocabulary of learnèd spheres of medieval and Renaissance Romance. N + V borrowings from all stages of Latin are centered in a small number of Western Romance lexical domains: religion; administration; and, marginally, medicine. The oldest learnèd N + V compounds in French, for example, *crucifixion, manifester*, are taken from the Vulgate and other Christian texts; words and even whole phrases were frequently borrowed into literalistic vernacular translations (psalters, hagiography, lapidaries). After A.D. 200, new derivations and borrowings from Greek continued to swell the stock of written Latin vocabulary. It was not until the start of the 14th century that significant numbers of direct borrowings from Cl. Latin began to appear in Romance. Through the 16th century, simultaneous use of both Latin and the vernaculars in various official capacities facilitated bidirectional borrowing.

The majority of OV-ordered borrowings presented here in section 1 are nominal-adjectival forms. Of these, few have served as derivation bases for N + V infinitives, e.g., Med.L. *manūscrīptus* 'manuscript' (lit. 'handwritten') > Sp. *manuscribir; terraplēnum* 'embankment' > Cat./Sp. *terraplenar*, through It. *terrapieno*. Borrowed verbs in learnèd garb are frequently flanked by vernacular by-forms (Fr. *cloufir, cloufermer*, OCat. *crozficar, creuposar*, Arag./Ast. *croc[h]eficar* 'to crucify'). Judging from the evidence of this slender corpus, the late-medieval influx of nominal-adjectival Latin vocabulary played but a minor role in the appearance of vernacular denominal verbs with N + V structure.

Latinisms of the post-medieval period, such as Fr. *fructifère, manu-/mani-cure, pédicure*, have been grouped into a note to this section; since many represent very recent intraRomance borrowings, they hold only peripheral interest for the study of *manūtenēre*. [1] Neoclassical synthetics, e.g., Fr. *thermomètre, manucure, fructifère*, are paralleled by other thematic compounds, e.g., Fr. *gréco-latin*, all representative of those late-medieval Latinizing tendencies still operative at present. Vernacular forms (enclosed in double square brackets), repeated below in section 2, are also found with full glosses, analyses, and indexes in Appendices A–E.

Corpus of Learnèd N + V Borrowings in Western Romance

Cat. *capitiluvi* 'head bath' (cf. Med.L. *capitilavium* 'lotion for anointing the head'; the interplay of *-lav-* and *-luv-* is already Classical)

Church L. *crūcifīgĕre*: Fr. *crucifier* (adopted from *-ficar* to verbs in *-ifier*); OPr. *crucificar*; [[OCat. *crozficar*]]; Cat., Sp. (13th c.) *crucificar*; Fr. (1175) *crucifiement*

Church L. (8th c.) *crūcifīxus* 'Christ crucified': Fr. (12th c.) *crucifix* 'cross with image of crucified Christ'; OPr. *crucific*; Occ. *crucifis, crucefi*; Cat. *crucifix*; Sp. (1220–1250) *crucifixo*; MFr. (ca. 1500) *crucifixion*; Sp. (18th c.) *crucifixión*

Late L. *fidĕ(i) committĕre*: Cat. *fideicomitent* 'testator who wills a legacy. . .' (see next entry)

Late L. *fidĕicommissārius* 'fideicommissary' ('the recipient of a fideicommissarium'; 'of, or pertaining to, a fideicommissum'): Fr. (13th c.) *fidéicommissaire* 'fideicommissary, receiver of a *fidéicommis*'; Occ. *fideicoumessàri*; Cat. *fideicomissari*; Sp. *fideicomisario*

---

[1]A representative sampling of learnèd compound elements: each item within double brackets is analyzed in its corresponding vernacular corpus (Appendices A–D).
-COLA Fr. *terricole*, Sp. *terrícola* 'earth-dweller'
-FER Christian L. *crucifer*; Fr. *crucifère* (1701) 'cross-bearing'; (1762, bot.) 'having petals arranged in a cross'; Occ. *crucifèr*, Cat., Sp. *crucifero* (1611)
-FRĂGUS; *ossifrage* (literally calqued, but in V + N order, by Sp. *quebranta-huesos*) 'vulture'; Fr. *saxifrage*
-FUGUS Med.L. *tergafuga* 'fleeing' (?); Fr. *-fuge* (*vermifuge*, 1738), Cat. *-fuc*, Sp. *-fugo*
-GĔNUS Fr. *-gène* (*indigène* 'indigenous'); Cl.L. *terrigena* 'born of the earth' (a poetic compound), and its calque, [[Mid./Mod.Fr. *terre-né*]]
-TERGUS Fr. *manuterge* 'towel used during the Holy Office'; [[OPr. *mantersa*]]
-VORUS Fr. *-vore* (Fr. *carnivore*, Sp. *carnívoro* 'carnivorous')

Late L. *fidĕicommissum* ("entrusted to good faith") 'feoffment in trust, testator's request that his heir convey a specified part of the estate to another person or permit another person to enjoy such a part': OFr. (13th c.) *fidéicommis* (found in a translation of the 6th-c. *Digesta* of Justinian); Occ. *fideicoumés*; Cat. *fideicomís*, Sp. (17th c.) *fide(i)comiso*

Late L. *fidĕ(i)iussiō* 'bail': Fr. (15th–16th c.) *fidéjussion* 'guaranty for another party, debt', [[OBéar. *fedessos*]]

Late L. *fidĕijussor* (for *fidĕiussor*): OFr. (1308) *fidéijusseur* 'one who guarantees the debt of another'; [[OBéar. *fedexor*; OIt. *fedesor*]]

Late L. *genuflectĕre* 'to genuflect'

Late L. *genuflectiō* (deverbal) 'genuflection': Fr. *génuflexion*, etc.

Cl.L. *iūreperītus* (Aulus Gellus) 'one versed in the science or philosophy of law': Cat. *jurisperit*

Cl.L. *iūriscōnsultus* (Roman and civil law) ("learned in law") 'one authorized to give legal advice, a master of the civil law': Fr. (1393) *jurisconsulte* 'legal expert'; Occ. *juriscounsulte*; Cat. *jurisconsult*; Sp. (ca. 1450) *jurisconsulto*

Cl.L. *iūris dictiō* ("action of saying justice") 'administration of the law, authority': Fr. (13th c.) *juridiction* (replacing *jurisdiction*, on model of *iūridicus*); Cat. *jurisdicció*, Sp. (ca. 1440) *jurisdicción*; OFr. *jurisdictionable, jurisdiciable* 'which can be assigned to a jurisdiction'; *jurisdictionnel* 'who has jurisdiction'

OFr. *litiscontester* 'to introduce a trial'; *litiscontestacion* 'first act of procedure, opening a judicial contestation'

Med.L. *locum tenēns* 'representative, substitute': [[OFr. (1287) *luetenens* ('second in command'), Fr. (1669) (milit.) *lieutenant*]]; [[OPr. *loctenen*]]; [[Cat. *lloctinent*]]; [[Sp. (ca. 1590) *lugarteniente*]]; [[It. *luogotenente*]]

Cl.L. *mancipāre* 'to sell property': Sp. *mancipar* 'to enslave' (*emancipar* 'to emancipate')

Cl.L. *manifestus, manufestus* ("which can be seized with the hand") 'palpable, evident': OFr. (1190) *manifeste*; Cat. *manifest*; OSp. (1220–1250) *manifiesto*

Imperial L. *manifestāre*: OFr. (1120) *manifester*; Occ. *manifesta*; Cat. *manifestar*; [[OSp. *manfestar, malfestar*]], Sp. (1220–50) *manifestāre*;, OPtg. *mēefestar*

Church L. *manifestātiō* 'act of becoming evident; revelation': Fr. (1200) *manifestation*, Sp. (1495) *manifestación*; Fr. (1849) *manifestant*

Med.L. *maniluvium* (from Cl.L. *malluviae* 'basin for washing the hands'): Sp. (medic.) *maniluvio* 'hand-bath'

Fr. (1877) *manucure* 'hand-care', *manucurer*; Occ. *manicur*; Cat. *manicur,-ra*; Sp. (1914) *manicuro*

Med.L. (10th c.) *manū factus* 'made by hand': [[OPr. *mafa(i)t*]]

Med.L. *manūfactūra* "action of making by hand": Fr. *manu-, manifacture* (1500–1550 through mid-18th c.) 'manual production', (Mod.) 'factory'; OPr. (1450) *manufatura*; Cat. *manifactura, manufactura*; Sp. (1633) *manifatura, manufactura* Fr. (1644) *manufacturier* 'manufacturer'; Sp. (1843) *manufacturero*

Low L. *manūfacturāre* (denom.) 'to manufacture': Fr. (1605) *manufacturer, manifacturer* 'to manufacture'; Cat., Sp. *manufacturar*; Fr. (1877) *manifacturable*

Cl.L. *manū missiō* 'act of manumitting, state of being manumitted': OFr. [[(12th c.) *marmissio*]], (1324) *manumission* 'liberation of a slave'; [[OPr. *marmessió*]]; Sp. (17th c.) *manumisión*

Med.L. *manūmissor* 'manumitter, liberator': [[OBéar. (1307) *mamessor* 'servant']], [[Cat. (13th c.) *man-, marmessor*]], (1503) *manumissor* 'testamentary executor'; [[Sp. (1323) *marmessor, mansessor*]], *manumisor*

Late L. *manūmittĕre* 'to release from slavery': OFr. [[*manumetre*]], [[*manumitter*]]; OPr. *manumitar*, [[*marmetre*]]; Sp. *manumitir* 'to free a slave'; [[MFr.–Mod.Fr. (1342) *main-mise* 'confiscation, seizure', with later semantic extension to 'domination']]; Sp. *manumiso* 'freed'

Med.L. *manūŏpera*: Fr. *main-d'œuvre* (1706)

Med.L. *manūscriptus* (used adjectivally to qualify *liber* or *codex*): Fr. (1594) *manuscrit*; Occ. *manuscri(t), manuscrich*; Cat. *manuscrit*; Sp. (1650) *manuscrito*; Sp. *manuscribir* 'to write by hand'

Med.L. *manūtenēre* 'to defend, protect, maintain': Sp. *manutener* 'to support, maintain'

Med.L. *manūtentiō* (deverbal): Mid.Fr. *manutenance*; Fr. *manutention* (1478) 'maintenance' [[syn. *maintien*]], (16th c.) 'management', (Mod.) 'handling of merchandise'; Occ. *manutencioun*; Cat. *manutenció*; Sp. *man(u)tención*; Fr. (1820) *manutentionner*; (1907) *manutentionnaire*

Low L. *manūtergium* ("wiping [with the hand]") 'towel': [[OPr. *mantersa* 'towel']], Fr. (1809) *manuterge* 'towel used in the Lavabo of the Holy Office'

Low L. (5th c.) *manutigium* 'a touching or feeling with the hand' (related to *tangō*, *tetigī* 'to touch'): Sp. *manutigio*

Fr. (1781) *pédicure* 'foot care, chiropodist'; Cat. *pedicur*; Sp. *pedicuro*

Med.L. *pediluvium* (from Cl.L. *pelluviae* 'basin for washing the feet'): Fr. *pédiluve* 'foot-bath' (1738), Sp. *pediluvio*

Med.L. *tergiversātiō* 'evasion, subterfuge': Fr. (1300) *tergiversation*; OSp. (1438) *tergiversación* 'turning the back'

Late L. *tergiversārī* ("to turn the back"): Fr. (1532) *tergiverser*; Occ. *tergiversar*; Cat., Sp. (1607) *tergiversar*

Cl. L. *terrae mōtus*: [[Cat. *terratrèmol,* infinitival *terratrèmer*]]

Med.L. *terraplēnum*: It. *terrapieno*; *terrapienare*; Sp. *terraplén*; Cat./Sp. *terraplenar* 'to fill with earth'

Med.L. *ventriloquus* ("who speaks from the belly"): Fr. (1552, Rabelais) *ventriloque* 'ventriloquist'; Occ. *ventriloque*; Cat. *ventríloc*, Sp. *ventrílocuo*; cf. coll. Amer. Eng. *belly-talker*, Gm. *Bauchredner*

2. MEDIEVAL AND RENAISSANCE N + V COMPOUNDS

Medieval and Renaissance N + V compounds are presented onomasiologically in French, Occitan, Catalan, Spanish, and Med. Latin. Evidence from the five corpuses (alphabetized, glossed, and analyzed in Appendices A–E) is distributed among twenty informal lexical fields: nature (A–E), feudal practice and warfare (F–G), administration and law (H–I), food (J), trades (technical, nautical) (K), religion (L), medicine (M–N), the world of physico-mental sensation (O–V), sports and pastimes (W), and everyday life (X), with a miscellany of items difficult to classify (Y).[2] Category labels are representative rather than exhaustive, e.g., category B, Animals, encompasses animals, birds, fishes, etc.

A	Plants
B	Animals
C	Farm Labor/Animal Husbandry
D/E	Terrain/Elements
F/G	Feudalism/Warfare/Politics
H/I	Administration/Law
J	Food
K	Trades (Technical/Nautical)
L	Religion
M/N	Medicine, including Veterinary
O	Mental and Emotional Processes
P	Sad/Embarrassed
Q	Angry/Hurt
R	Curious/Worried
S	Physical Description
T	Tumble/Turn Over/Die
U	Personal Violence

---

[2]Certain sections, particularly those devoted to the physical universe, resemble the onomasiological divisions found in Hallig & Wartburg's *Begriffssystem*, originally developed for the *FEW* (cf. Rudolf Hallig & W. von Wartburg, *Begriffssystem als Grundlage für die Lexikographie*, rev. 2d ed. [Berlin: Akademie-Verlag, 1963]). On the whole, however, the organization of man's physical and intellectual attributes has been considerably simplified; category Y highlights the semantic and geographic discontinuity of vernacular N + V compounding.

V   Physical Movement
W   Sports and Pastimes
X   Everyday Life
Y   Miscellaneous

Only a handful of early lexical items occur in categories A–E, as against a significant number of modern N + V compounds pertaining to nature.

[B.1] 'to molt': In the four target vernaculars, the sense of L. *mūtāre* 'to change' was specialized to 'to molt' (skin or feathers) (Bambeck 1959, *FEW* "mutare"), making redundant the phrase *pĕllem/pĭlum mūtāre* 'to molt', lit. 'to change skin/hair'. To these correspond Arag. *pelmudar* (Occ. *pelmudar*), Sp. *pelechar*. [C.1] OBéar. *capbirà* 'to train oxen to pull either to right or left' is the earliest N + V Infin compound concerning farm labor and animal husbandry bereft of any parallel in Med. Latin. Also in this category are: [C.2] Arag. (arch.) *camajuste* 'ladder for picking olives'; [C.3] OFr. *chanfrein* 'bridle'; [C.4] OFr-Pr. *chateni* 'to stop a bull by the horns'; [C.5] MFr. (15th c.) *maintien* 'handle of the flail' (see category K as well); [C.6] Cat. (14th c.) *palafanga* 'three-pronged spade', with denominal verb in the modern period. [C.7] OFr. *mainplant* 'plantation (by the hand of man)' structurally echoes *manū factu(m)* and vernacular OPr. *mafa(i)t*.

[D.1] Med.L. *aquisfluis* 'currents' lacks Romance parallels; [D.2] Med.L. *aqua(e)-, aquis-versus* 'slope', and *aquivergium* 'declivity into which water flows' parallel OPr. *aigaversar* 'to divide waters', Cat. *aiguavé(r)s* and *aiguavessant*; although Catalan at no time developed an infinitive from this noun, Mod. *aiguabarreig* 'confluence of two rivers' is flanked by *aiguabarrejar*. [E. Elements] contains only [E.1] OFr. *signeportant* 'zodiac'.

Medieval feudal vocabulary [F] is richly attested, its vocabulary offering proof of several essential semantic notions, of which [F.1] 'to defend' is assuredly among the earliest, and also the one central to the overall success of the N + V pattern.

[F.1.a] 'to defend, govern, conduct', compounded of *manū* + *tenēre*
> Med.L. *manūtenēre* 'to defend, support, conduct, govern'; *manūtenēns* 'protector'
> OFr.–Mod.Fr. *maintenir*, OFr. *maintenoir, mantoivre*
> OPr. *mantener, mantenir*; deriv. *manteneire, mantenedor, mantenent*; Mod.Occ. vars. *manténer, mantenir, mantenei*
> Cat. *mantenir*
> Sp. *mantener*; (law) *manutener*
> Arag. *mantení, mantenere, mantinre*; ONav.-Arag. *manten-iença*, OCast. *-encia* 'financial management'
> Other Romance: Ptg. *mantêr*; *mantedor* '(legal) guardian'; It. *mantenere*; Engad. *mantnair*

[F.1.b] 'to defend', compounded of *cap[ut]* + *tenēre*
    Med.L. *cap[ut] tenēre, captenēre*
    Med.L. *capitennium* 'support'
    OFr. *chatien* 'support'
    OPr. *captenium, captein* 'support', OGasc. *captenh*
    OSp. *captener* 'to protect'
    OArag. *captener* 'to protect, maintain, represent'
    Astur. *caltener*, Occ. *captener* 'to stand firm'

[F.1.c] OHG *mundeboro* 'defender, protector, (legal) guardian' (from Gmc. N *mund* 'hand' + V *beran* 'to protect')
    Med.L. *mundiburdus, mundeboro, mandeburda, mamburnus*
    Med.L. *maniburnia* (from OFr. *mainbournie*)
    Med.L. *munburn-āre, -īre, mamburnīre* (from OFr.)
    OFr. *mainbour*, deriv. *mainbournie, manbournir*
    OPr. *manbor* 'guardian' (Diez 1887)
    OSp. *manbor* 'protector, guardian'

[F.1.d] **manū adiūtāre* 'to support' (*REW* §5339)
    OFr. *manaie* 'support', deriv. *manai(d)ier*
    OPr. *manaya* 'support'

[F.1.e] **manū pāstus* 'supported, fed [by the hand = power]' (*REW* §5338)
    Med.L. *manū-, manipāstus*, Brit.L. *mainpastus*
    OFr. *mainpast* 'household (protégés of a lord), servant'
    A.-Norm. *manupast* 'servant, farmhand' (hap.) OSp. *mampastor* 'household dependent'
    Other Romance attestations: OPavia *manipasto* 'servant', Val. *mēpá* 'master herdsman's third helper', Suisse Rom. *māpa* idem, *paschamaint* 'sustenance for Alpen herdsmen', *mampat* 'suspicious-looking fellow'; Eng. (arch.) *mainpast* 'household' (Webster's [2d ed.])

[F.1.f] **manūparāre* 'to support' (*REW* §5337); currently, derivation from *ante* + *parāre* (*DCE[LC]*) is accepted)
    OSp. [OPtg.] *mamparar* 'to protect, defend, support'
    Cat. *mampara* 'inner door, folding screen'
    Sp. *mampara* 'screen, small door'

[F.1.g] *manū* + **posĭta*
    OSp. (12th c.) *mampuesta, manu posta* 'protection', *mampostero* 'protector'

The next notion from feudal practice, [F.2] 'to abandon', is no more than a negative derivation from several compounds meaning [F.1] 'to defend, protect'.

[F.2.a] *dis-* + *manūtenēre* 'to abandon'
    OPr. *desmantener* (Girart de Bornelh)
    OCat. *desmantenir* (11th c., from Med.L. *dēmanūtenēre*)
[F.2.b] OPr. *descaptener* (Bernard de Ventadorn)

[F.2.c] OSp. *des(m)amparar* 'to abandon', Mod. *desamparar*

Gestures of the hand figured widely among feudal rituals: [F.3] Med.L. *manum dare* 'to swear allegiance'; *manum levāre* 'to raise the hand to swear an oath' (cf. synon. *fidem levāre, fidem iūrāre*). The loyal warrior ([F.4] OFr. *foitenant*) kept faith with his lord, who signaled his knighthood with a blow of the hand, [F.5] OSp. *manferir* 'to designate for military service by a touch of the hand on the shoulder'. [F.6] *mainfait* 'loss of rights of lineage'. 'Treachery' was Med.L. *fidementūta, fidēs mentūta, fidefragium* (lit. 'broken faith'); the traitor [F.7] was characterized as

[F.7.a] Med.L. *fidementūtus, fidementirōsus* 'traitor'
  OFr. *foimenti, -mentif, -mentu*
  OPr. *fementit, femendit*, OBéar. *fee-mentit* 'renegade'
  OCat. *fementit*
  OSp. *fementido*

[F.7.b] Med.L. *fidefragus* 'traitor'

[F.7.c] OFr. *dieumenti, deumentiz* (synon. *dieuparjur*) idem

[F.7.d] Cat. (16th c.) *caragirat* 'turncoat, traitor'

In feudal times, warfaring men (as against smooth-shaven clerics) sported beards: [F.8] Sp. (16th c.) *barbiponiente* (from *pŭngĕre*, later reassigned to *poner* < PONĔRE); cf. Med.L. *barbam tangĕre* 'to grow one's first beard'. 'Warriors' were armed with iron weapons: [F.9] OFr. *fervesti, fervestu* 'armored, iron-clad', OFr. *fervestir* (also *ferarmer*); OPr. *fervestit*; and with crossbows: [F.10] OPr. *coa-leva* 'lever or pulley of a crossbow'. In doing battle ([F.11] OSp. *manentrar* 'to attack, assault'), they occasionally fell on the field of honor: [F.12] adj. OFr. *champcheü*.

Military functions [G] were specified in the later Middle Ages by a number of compounds calqued from Med. Latin:

[G.1.a] MFr. *terratenant* 'foot-soldier'
[G.1.b] Cat. *camptinent* 'corporal'

[G.2] MFr. *terraguarde* 'police'
  OPr. *terragardar* 'to police, act as game warden; make an inspection'

[G.3.a] Med.L. *terraplēnum* 'embankment'; Mod. vars. Fr. (16th c.) *terre-plein*, Sp. *terraplenar* (from It. *terrapieno*)
[G.3.b] OPr. *terragiet* 'earth dug out of a moat and thrown up along the sides'; Fr. *terrejeter* 'to plant in rows', 'labourer par la culture en planches'

In the joint administrative-legal domains [H/I], a key notion appeared decidedly early, ca. A.D. 800, to be quickly paralleled within the context of feudal financial practice: widespread [H./I.1] *manūŏpera* 'manual service' was flanked by lesser-known [H./I.2] *car(r)ŏpera* 'cart-service':

[H./I.1] *manū + ŏpera* 'manual work-service', 'corvée manuelle'
   Med.L. *manūŏpera*, vars. *manopera, maneopera, manuumopera, mannopera, mannwerch*
   Med.L. *manū ŏperāre, manūŏperor*, Brit.L. *manūŏperāre*

[H./I.2] Med.L. *car(r)ŏpera* 'cart-service', var. *carriopera*
   Med.L. *carŏperāre*

Yet another key notion made its appearance by the 12th century: [H./I.3] 'to swear on raised hand so as to free a person or an object that has been seized', with the additional sense of relinquishing property, which subsists today in Mod.Fr. (law) *mainlevée* 'withdrawal, release of mortgage, restoration of goods'.

[H./I.3.a] *manū + levāre* 'to give a pledge, guarantee, post bail'
   Med.L. *manūlevātiō, manūlevātum* 'bail'
   MFr.-Mod.Fr. *mainlevée* 'withdrawal, release of mortgage, restoration of goods'
   OPr. (12th c.) *manlevar* 'to post bond or bail'
   OCat. *manleuta* 'bail', Cat. *manlleutar* 'to post bail'
   OSp. *manlieva* '[act of posting] bail'
   OArag. *manuleuta* 'relinquishing of a piece of property'
   OArag. *maleuar* 'to leave [an object as] a pledge against a sum of money, guarantee a debt'

[H./I.3.b] *cap[ut] levāre* 'to give a guarantee, to post bail'
   OCat. (1346) *capleuta* 'legal evidence'
   OCat. (1460) *capleuta* 'bail, [object left as] pledge', Cat. *capllevar* 'to post bail'
   OSp. (13th c.) *cablieva* 'bail, pledge, guarantee'; *caplevar*
   OArag. *caple(u)ta* 'bail, pledge'; *caplevador* 'guarantor'; Mod.Arag. *capletar* 'to jail for debt'
   (also OSp. *sobrelevar* 'to guarantee', *sobrelevadura* 'bail', and hybrid OArag. *superlevador* 'guarantor')

[H./I.3.c] *manū + prendĕre* 'to guarantee, accept a pledge'
   Brit.L. *manuprisa, meinprisa* 'mainprise, bail'
   A.-Norm. (ca. 1300) *meynprendre*, (14th c.) *meynpernor, -preneör* 'guarantor', (14th c.) *mainprenable* 'capable of guaranteeing another'; Eng. (arch.) *mainpernor* 'pledge, bail, surety'
   OFr. (1304) *meynprise* 'guarantee, bail'

[H./I.3.d] *fide(m) + iubēre* 'to post bail, guarantee'
   Med.L. *fidejussiō* 'bail', Brit.L. *fedejusseō*

OBéar. *fedessos* 'bail, relinquishing of a piece of property'
Late L. *fideiussor, fideiutrix*

[H./I.3.e] Late L. *fidedictor* 'bail'; *fidedīcĕre* 'to guarantee'

[H./I.3.f] Med.L. *fideprōmittĕre* 'to go bail for'

[H./I.3.g] Med.l. *manūcaptiō* 'bail', *manūcapĕre* 'to go bail for', *manūcaptor* 'guarantor'

[H./I.3.h] OPr. *marmes, marmetre* 'to abandon', *marmessió* 'action of abandoning'

Old Spanish borrowed both *caplieva* and *manlieva* from OCat., through OArag. *cablevar, capleuta, maleuar*; the original meaning of OSp. *manlieva* ('act of posting bail or giving a pledge') was rapidly lost, and it came to mean 'loan', 'amount borrowed', 'renta, tributo'.

[H./I.4.a] *manū + levāre* 'to borrow' (from the 12th century)
    Med.L. *manūlevāre* 'to borrow'
    OPr. *ma(n)levar; manleu, manleuta* 'loan'
    Occ. *manlevar* 'to borrow, be guilty of extortion'
    Cat. *man(l)levar*
    Cat. *manlleu(ta)* 'loan'
    OSp. *manlieva* 'loan', Sp. *manlevar* 'to contract debts'
    Arag. (from Occ.–Cat.) *manlebar* 'to borrow'
    Other Romance reflexes: OPtg. *malevar*; OIt. *mallevare*

[H./I.4.b] OPr. *prestlevar* 'to lend, borrow'

[H./I.5] 'to emancipate'
    [H./I.5.a] Late L. *manū mittĕre* 'to emancipate, free (a slave) from the power
        of his/her master', Cl.L. *manūmissiō* 'emancipation'
    Med.L. *manmessiō, marmissiō* 'freed slave'
    OFr. *mainmetre* 'to free', OFr.–MF. *mainmission* 'emancipation'
    MFr. *manumetre, manumetter* (DuC)
    OGasc. *mamessor* 'servant'
    OSp.–Mod.Sp. *manumitir* 'enviar los esclavos lejos del poder del dueño',
        manumisor 'el que manumite'

[H./I.5.b] Arag. (arch.) *manifestar* 'to liberate'; *sacar manifestada* 'to free a young
    woman of legal age from her home and father's power so that she may
    contract marriage'

[H./I.6] Med.L. *manūmissor* '(testamentary) executor', agentive from *manūmittĕre* 'to
    leave a bequest to a third party'
    OCat. *manumissor*

Cat. *marmessor*
OSp. *mansessor*, (14th c.) *marmessor, manumisor*

[H./I.7.a] *manū + mittĕre* 'to put s.o. in possession of, give over to, seize'
    Fr. *mainmise* 'confiscation, seizure'
    OPr. *man-mesa, -misa* 'confiscation'
    OBéar. *manumitar*, Béar. *mâ-méte* 'to seize'

[H./I.7.b] OBéar. *mansaizir* 'to seize'

[H./I.7.c] Med.L. *manleita* 'requisition'

[H./I.8] 'to change hands' (of a property)
[H./I.8.a] Med.L. *manūprisum* 'handing over, transfer of a slave to a buyer'
[H./I.8.b] Med.L. *manūtrādĕre* 'to deliver, transfer'
[H./I.8.c] OFr. *mainmuable* 'who can change hands'
[H./I.8.d] OBéar. *maamudar; maamude* 'transfer of property'

[H./I.9] OSp. *man(i)festar* 'to make public admission of a debt or crime'

[H./I.10.a] Béar. *caplheba* 'to levy a tax'
[H./I.10.b] Med.L. *manūpos(ī)ta, mampostarium* 'type of tax'
    OSp. *manpuesta* 'tax', *mampostero* 'tax collector'

[H./I.11] 'representative, administrator, government agent'
[H./I.11.a] Med.L. *locum tenēre* 'to replace'
    Med.L. *locumtenēns, locatenentēs* 'lieutenants', *locumtenentēs generālēs*
        'provincial governors'
    OFr. *luetenant* 'administrator, deputy'
    OPr. *loctenent*, OBéar. *leotenent, locstenentz*
    OGasc. *logtient* 'lieutenant'
    OArag. *lugartinient* 'representative of the Justicia Mayor de Aragón'
[H./I.11.b] Med.L. *locōposĭtus, locumservāns, lociservātor*
[H./I.11.c] OBéar. *fedexor* 'agent communal, local government agent'

[H./I.12] 'owner, tenant, heir'
[H./I.12.a] OGasc. *terratenen* 'tenant'
    OCat. (13th c.) *terrestinent* 'land-owner'
    OArag. *terrastenentes* 'tenants'
[H./I.12.b] OPr. *cazatenen* 'house-owner'
[H./I.12.c] OFr. *jointenant* 'joint tenant'
[H./I.12.d] OPr. *benstenen* 'heir'

[H./I.13] 'to do a wrong'
[H./I.13.a] OFr. *torfaire* 'to do a wrong'; *torfait* 'wrong'; *torfesor* 'wrongdoer, enemy'
[H./I.13.b] OGasc. *fort[s]-fasedor* 'wrongdoer'
[H./I.13.c] OFr. *poifait* 'negligence'; *poifaisant* 'negligent'

[H./I.14] 'emprisonment'
[H./I.14.a] OGasc. *cu-bagnadei* 'punishment for shrews'
[H./I.14.b] OGasc. *cu-labadei* idem
[H./I.14.c] Cat. (arch.) *claupresó* 'imprisonment'
[H./I.15] OGasc. (14th c.) *deit-dizador* 'referee'
[H./I.16] MFr. (15th c.) *blanc-signé* 'signature to a blank document'

[H./I.17] Pr. (16th c.) *manbestir* 'to invest'

[H./I.18] OBéar. *conde-finar* 'to close out an account'

In the category of expressions pertaining to food, J, with the exception of [J.1] OFr. *escalbotter* 'to shell peas', the few compounds encountered have *sal* 'salt' as their first element.

[J.2] OFr. *saupiquet* 'spicy sauce or stew' (no verb is attested); MFr. *saupiqueter* 'to give a spicy taste'

[J.3] OFr. *saupoudrer* 'to sprinkle (with salt)'

[J.4] OPr. *salpicar* 'to spread with ashes'
       OCat. *salpicar* 'to sprinkle, splash'
       Sp. (16th c.) *salpicar* idem

[J.5] 'food preserved with salt'
       Med.L. *salpresa*
       OPr. *salprés* 'salt pork'
       OCat. *salp(r)endre* 'to preserve with salt', *salpres*
       OCat. *salpebrar* 'to preserve meat with *salpebre* (salt and pepper mixture)'
       OSp. *salpreso* 'preserved with salt'; deriv. (17th c.) *salpresar*

Category K includes terms from the trades and crafts other than farm labor, as well as technical terms, the earliest among them being the *corvée manuelle*, or quota of manual labor owed to a feudal lord.

[K.1] '(manual) labor'
[K.1.a] Med.L. (ca. A.D. 800) *manŭŏpera*, *manŭŏperāre* (according to *REW* §5336, French is the source for all other Romance reflexes)
       OFr. *manuevre* 'manual labor'; *manuvrer, manovr(i)er* 'to work or put with the hand', Mod. *manœuvrer* 'to maneuver'
       OPr. *man(a)obra* 'manual labor'; OGasc. *manobrar* 'servant'; *man(a)obrar* 'to work or put with the hands'
       Cat. *manobre* 'workman, peasant'
       Sp. (18th c.) *maniobrar* 'to maneuver'; *manobra* 'worker', *manobre* 'hod-carrier'
       It. *manovra, manovrare*
[K.1.b] OGasc. *mantreyt* '(hand)work'

[K.2] OPr. *mafa(i)t* 'handmade'

[K.3] OFr. *orbateör, -batteur* 'goldsmith'; *orbatre* 'to work gold'
[K.4.a] OFr. *orfergié* 'embroidered with gold'
[K.4.b] OFr. *orpoignant* 'gold embroidery'

[K.5] OFr. (14th c.) *chanfraindre* 'to bevel'; *chan-fraint, -freint* 'bevelled'

[K.6] OFr-Pr. *carbon-fadere* 'charcoal-maker, -merchant'

[K.7] MFr. (15th c.) *colport-euse, -eresse* 'female vendor'; *colporter* 'to carry on the neck, peddle'

[K.8] OFr. *cuirpaner* 'to cover with leather'

[K.9] OFr. *pele-fouans* lit. 'digging with a shovel'

[K.10] OFr. *estanfique* 'slender column dividing the masonry of a bay window'

[K.11] OPr. *mantenen* 'balustrade'

[K.12] Fr. (15th c.) *maintien* 'handle of the flail'

[K.13] OPr. *pèe-lhèbe* 'trap'

One particularly fruitful field of inquiry for N + V compounds is religious vocabulary [L]. Within the semantic notion of [L.1] 'to crucify' (Med.L. *crŭcifĭxus, clāvifĭxus* '[crucified] Christ') are:

[L.1.a] OFr. *cloufire, claufir*
[L.1.b] OFr. *cloufich-ier, -ir*
[L.1.c] OFr. *claufiiés*, OPr.–OCat. *clauficar*, OCat. *clavificat*
[L.1.d] OFr. *clo(u)fermer* 'to attach (with nails)'
[L.1.e] OPr. *clauponh* 'crucifixion'
[L.1.f] A.-Norm. *croizficher*
[L.1.g] OCat. *creuclavat*
[L.1.h] OCat. *creuposar*
[L.1.i] Med.L. *crucem figere* 'to crucify'
[L.1.j] OCat. *crozficar*, Arag. *croceficar*, Astur. *crocheficar*

A host of compounds representing [L.2] 'Lent' straddle learnèd and vernacular vocabularies. The Rumanian noun *cîrne-le(a)gă* has an exact converse in *câşle(a)gă* (Mod. *cîş-*) 'period of the year exempting one from fast' (cf. OFr. *charnage* idem).

[L.2.a] Med.L. *carnemlaxāre*, OIt. *carlasciare*
[L.2.b] *carne + levāre*

Med.L. *carnelevamine*
It. *carnelevale, carnavale* (borrowed into Fr., Occ., Cat., and Sp. in the 16th century; cf. also OFr. [13th c.] *quarnivalle*)
[L.2.c] *carne* + *liga* (*ligāre*)
Rum. *cârnele(a)gă* (*REW* §1706 "carō"), Mod. orthography *cîrnele(a)gă*
[L.2.d] Med.L. *carniprivium, carnisprivium*
[L.2.e] *carne* + *siccāre* (lit. 'to dry')
Logud. *carrasecare*
[L.2.f] *carne* + *tollĕre* (lit. 'to remove')
Med.L. *carnestoltas* 'abstinence from meat'
OCat. *fer carnestoltas* 'to abstain from meat'
OCat. *carnes-, carnistoltes* 'Lent'
OSp. *carnes-, carnistolendas*
[L.2.g] *carne* + *vetāre* (lit. 'to forbid')
OBéar. *carn-bedar*

In Gallo-Romance, 'Lent' was originally signified by compounds based on L. *quadragesima* 'period of 40 days', whose syntactic relationship is still found today in Occ. *l'annado entrant* 'at the start of the new year'.

[L.2.h] Med.L. *carementrannus* 'Mardi Gras; first Sunday of Lent'
OFr. *quarem pernant* (northern Gaul from Berry to Bourgogne, except Walloon and Picard)
OPr. *carema prenens*
OFr. *caresmentré, quaresmentrant*, OPr. *caramantrant*, Fr-Pr. *carimentrant* (through 16th century in remainder of Gaul)

[L.3] 'pilgrim (= traveler)'
OPr., OCat., OPtg. (13th c.) *vian(d)an(t)* 'pilgrim', Béar. *biandant*
OSp. *viandante*

[L.4] Med.L. *crucis(s)ignatio* 'sign of the cross'
Med.L. *crucesignati* 'Crusaders'

[L.5] OFr. *painquerant* 'mendicant [friar]' (lit. 'seeking [gifts of] bread')

[L.6] '(Catholic) priest' = 'one who recites Mass'
[L.6.a] (cf. Med.L. *canĕre missam, cantāre missam* 'to say Mass')
OBéar. *missecantaa*, OBéar. *missecandera* 'priest's housekeeper'; (Mod.) Gasc. *misso-canta* 'to be a priest'
OSp. *misacantano*
Cat. *missacantant*
Med.L. *missacantania* 'ecclesiastical gift offered for celebration of Mass'

[L.6.b] (cf. Med.L. *dīcĕre missam*)
Cat. *missadient* 'priest'

[L.7] Med.L. (10th c.) *deōdicāta (femina)* 'nun'

[L.8] OFr. *dieulever* 'raising, elevation of the Host'

[L.9] OPr. *mantersa* 'towel'

[L.10] Occ. *Dieu-Trouva* (name of a folktale hero from Provence)

Within the realm of veterinary medicine, M, a single verb (L. *fŭndĕre* 'to melt') occurs with a variety of nominal elements:

[M./N.1] OFr. *morfondre* 'to catch cold' (of horses)
OPr. *morfondre, marfondre* (cf. Cat. *marfondre* 'to die of consumption, lose one's strength')

[M./N.2] MFr. *nerf-féru* '(equine) inflammation of the tendon'

[M./N.3] MFr. *graisse-fondre* 'to stifle with heat'; *gras-fondure* '(equine) loss of weight consequent on a disease'

[M./N.4] 'to flush, become suffused with blood'
A.-Norm. *sancfuison* 'bloodshed, loss of blood'
OPr. *sancfoizó*, OLang. (12th c.), Albi (13th c.) *sancfois* idem
OCat. *sangfondre* 'to flush, overeat', and action nouns *sangfús, sangfoniment*

[M./N.5] OFr. *sangmuer* 'to catch cold'

[M./N.6] Cat. (15th c.) *aiguatoldre* 'to defecate'

Medieval vernaculars contained as yet few attested relevant expressions of mental or emotional processes.

[O.1] *mĕnte(m)* + *habēre* 'to remember, mention'
OFr. *mentevoir, mentoivre*
OPr. *mentaure, mentaver, mentaire (Jaufre)*
OGasc. *menthaber*, OBéar. *mentabe* 'to mention'

[O.2] OSp. (13th c.) *caboprender* 'to understand'

[O.3] OSp. *mientesmetudo (Alixandre)* 'prudent, sane'
[O.4] Sp. (16th c.) *mentecapto* 'weak in the head'

L. *mĕnte(m)* succumbed in French; Occ. *ment* 'mind', however, was still listed by Mistral, who qualified opaque *mentaure* as archaic and recorded no extant verbs; only in Gascon is *mentábe(r)* (with Mod. *habe*) 'to mention' still current, according to Lespy.

In the modern Catalan and particularly Occitan corpuses (Chapter 4), categories P Q R show major extension vis-à-vis the slender evidence of, e.g., [Q.1] OFr. *sancmesler* 'to become angry', and [Q.2] MFr. *se boffumer* 'to be angered'. [R.1] OSp. *fazferir* 'to wrong, offend' (lit. 'to slap s.o. in the face'), surviving today as *zaherir* 'to reproach, criticize', is doubly interesting in that so few innovative N + V compounds developed in Old Spanish.

[R.2] OBéar. *coo-transi* 'to pierce the heart'

[R.3] OPr. *(se) carabirà* 'to feel strong emotion'

[R.4] OCat. *capgirar* 'to bother, (be) upset, change one's mind'; cf. Cat. (16th c.) *caragirat* '(political) turn-coat', and OPr. *caravirar* 'to change political party'

[R.5] Cat. (15th c.) *capfic* 'worried'

[R.6.a] OFr. *chafresner* 'to repress strong emotion'
[R.6.b] OPr. *c(h)apfrenar* idem

[R.7] OFr. *sancmesler* 'to become upset or angry'

[R.8] OFr. *avoir le sang mué* 'to be troubled'; *sangmueçon* 'agitation'

Medieval evidence of physical description, S, allows only a hint of later creations in this category.

[S.1.a] OFr. *boranfler* 'to swell'
        OPr. *botenflat* 'swollen'
[S.1.b] OFr. *borsoflé* 'swollen'
[S.1.c] OFr. *charboter* 'to swell'

[S.2] A.-Norm. *sangterné* 'mixed with blood'

[S.3] OFr. *koñibote* 'to walk swinging the head to and fro'

[S.4] OCat. *solabatut* 'tired, worn out'

[S.5] OCat. (14th c.) *carafaxada* 'split'

[S.6] MFr. (14th c.) *être grosse d'enfant sentant* 'to feel one's unborn child moving'

[S.7.a] OPr. *cap-tenh, -tein, -tenemen* 'conduct, countenance'
[S.7.b] Cat. *capteny* 'appearance'
[S.7.c] OSp. *captenencia* idem

[S.8] OFr. (13th c.) *vermoulu* 'worm-eaten'

There remains in this category a series of French literary adjectives, calqued on Greek models (MFr. *jour-apporte* 'bringing light', Gr. *phōsphóros*, L. *lūcifer*) by Ronsard and the 16th-c. poets of the Pléiade: *aile-porte* 'wing-bearing', *cœur-rongeant* 'which gnaws at the heart', *cuisse-né* 'born from the thigh', *feu-soufflant* 'firebreathing', *feu-vomissant* 'fire-spewing', *jour-apporte* 'bringing light', *lierre-porte* 'ivy-bearing', *montagne-porte* 'mountain-bearing', *nuit-volant* 'flying by night', *Ourse-gardant* 'watching the heavens' [lit. the constellation Ursa].

In category T, Tumble/Die, modern compounds with *girar/virer* are frequent; lacking reflexes of *virāre*, Italian has pressed into service *volgere* and *voltare* instead. Reflexes of **tumbāre* 'to tumble' (from Gmc. **tûmôn* 'to turn around'?) are found in Catalan (*capitombar* 'to fall headlong'), Italian (*capitombolare* idem), and French. By the 16th century, Fr. *tomber* (12th-c. *tumber*, *tumer*) 'to take a spill, fall head over heels' had displaced *ch(e)oir* (L. CADĔRE 'to fall', via VL. **cadēre*); the borrowing of Fr. *chavirer* 'to capsize' from Occ. *capvirar* postdates 1600. In the medieval corpus, the development of these related notions is already visible:

[T.1.a] OPr. *capgirar* 'to twist one's neck'
      OCat. *capgirar* lit. 'to turn upside down', (15th c.) *capgirant*
[T.1.b] Fr. (16th c.) *bouleverser* 'to upset, turn over'

[U] Personal violence
[U.1] OFr. (13th c.) *go(u)rfouler* 'to beat, trample, damage'
[U.2] Gasc. (16th c.) *pernabatre* 'to fight with the feet'
[U.3] Cat. (15th c.) *peucalcigar* 'to trample under foot, press'

[X] Everyday life
[X.1] Cat. *cama-lliga*, *-lligues* 'garter'
[X.2] OPr. (13th c.) *pelpartidura* 'part (in the hair)'

In the miscellaneous residue of medieval and Renaissance fall a number of compounds similar to the literary calques in S: [Y.1] OFr. *nientdisant* 'insignificant', [Y.2] OFr. *nongresachant* 'unthankful'. The majority, however, share no similar structure:
[Y.3] Fr. (16th c.) *lettre-féru* 'fond of letters, well-lettered'
      Gasc. (16th c.) *letre-herit*
      Cat. (arch.) *lletreferit*

[Y.4] OCat. (14th c.) *mampendre* 'to begin'

[Y.5] Cat. (15th c.) *ullprendre* 'to bewitch, fascinate [with one's eyes]'

3. ANALYSIS OF THE MEDIEVAL LATIN EVIDENCE

Analysis of the substantial corpus of medieval and Renaissance N + V compounds presented in section 2, as well as in Appendix E, illustrates the continued inter-dependence of Med. Latin—still in use as a chancery language and in the sciences—and the vernaculars throughout the medieval period. After the 16th century, when it was shorn of any last vestiges of direct support from Med. Latin, N + V compounding would either stand or fall on the basis of language-internal criteria in each Romance vernacular.

Within the contexts of feudalism and Christianity (categories F–L), Med. Latin compounds closely resemble their Romance counterparts, despite occasional differences. Med. Latin elements allowed readily of replacement, both nominal (Med.L. *cap[ut]-, manū-tenēre* 'to defend, protect'; *clāvi-, crŭci-fīxus* 'crucified'; *fīdem-, manū-levāre* 'to swear an oath') and verbal (*fide-fragus, -mentūtus* 'traitor'; *fide-dīcěre, -prōmittěre* 'to go bail for'; *locum-servāns, -tenēns* 'substitute'; *missa caněre, cantāre, dīcěre* 'to say Mass'). Noun constituents served at times to reinforce the following verb (Med.L. *fidejūrāre* 'to swear [= *jūrāre*]; *manūtrāděre* 'to transfer' [= *trāděre*]), possibly retaining minimal semantic substance. Equally noteworthy is the partial/complete reinterpretation and replacement of Romance constituents in *manūŏpera* by near-homonymous Gmc. *Mann* or by 'work': *mannopera* and *mannwerch* 'opus hominis'. [3]

Among the most salient characteristics of Med. Latin N + V compounding is the morphological transparency of both nominal and verbal elements, or their renewed transparency ("re-etymologizing", "recomposition") in such cases as Cl.L. *malluviae* → Med.L. *maniluvium, manulavium*, no matter what their regional pronunciation. Not all of them were syntactic or juxtaposed compounds, but within the context of disappearing nominal declensions, the vacillation between, e.g., *man-* and *manū-* (Med.L. *mandŭctō* and *manūductō*, post-Carolingian *maniteneo* and *manuteneo*) represents little more than graphic variation—spelling variants of a single lexeme rather than accurate phonetic representations.

These Med. Latin compounds were built up of recognizable whole words, being, like their earliest Romance counterparts, of a type made syntactically possible by nominal declension: L. *manūtenēre* 'to defend (by the hand = power)', *terraplēnum*

---

[3]This last term is still listed in glossaries of OHG and MHG, meaning 'amount of work which one man and two oxen can do in a day'; since it is absent from Mod. German, where OV-structured compounds like *Handwerk* continue to flourish, one may conclude that Med. Latin was the original source for Germanic (compare near-homonymous *manu* and *Mann*, in *mannopera, mannwerch* 'opus hominis') rather than vice versa.

'embankment' (lit. 'full of earth') and later OFr. *fervestit* (lit. 'clothed in iron'). The grammatical relationship (neither nominative nor accusative) between N and V in *manūtenēns* 'powerful personage' and *locōposĭtus* 'deputy, substitute' contrasts with that of *locumservāns* (lit. 'place-reserving') and long-lived *locumtenēns* (lit. 'place-holding'), both of which display N Dir Obj + V structure. [4] No compound, however, depends on the presence of explicit case-endings to convey its meaning. Med.L. *aqua(e)-, aquis-versus* clearly show hesitation in marking the case of the nominal element; the syntactic relationship must have been hazy, not to say inessential—and its very marking in this example has an after-the-fact flavor. *manūŏpera* shows a different range of variants, alternately lacking any composition vowel (*manopera*), or showing a change either of declension class (*maneopera*) or else of case and number (*manuumopera*).

The Med. Latin corpus contains a number of innovations, alien to Romance, which nevertheless usefully illuminate the vernacular corpus. *Manūŏpera*, in its most neutral form, contains either a genitive or ablative relationship between its two nouns; this financial term was flanked in Med. Latin by a similarly structured N + N compound, *car(r)ŏpera* 'cart-service'. The lack of *carŏperāre* 'to cart, supply cart-service' in Brit. Latin, where *car(r)ŏpera* occurs regularly, reinforces the derivational primacy of nominal *manūŏpera*. Also absent from Romance is (5th c.) *fidēdictor*, coined by St. Augustine. Med. Latin N + V derivations and innovations were mostly juxtaposed forms (*fĭdem levāre*, synonym of *manūlevāre*). But there did exist a handful of synthetic N + V compounds coined in Med. Latin on classical models, both Greek and Latin:

> *aquitanigenus* (A.D. 962, "pro aquitanus")
> *architenens* (8th c.) 'one who holds chief place', its opening ingredient from
>   Gr. *arkhi-*
> *francigenus* ("pro francicus")
> *missiocaptus* (*NGML* "hybride pour *musiocattus* 'ingenious'")
> *odorisequus* 'following a scent, having a good nose; hunting dog'
> *tergafuga* (11th c.) (Du Cange "dicitur, inquit Papias, quoties milites fugientes
>   a tergo caeduntur")

In Chapter 2 no objection was voiced to the argument that the earliest N + V compounds demonstrate an "oblique" (neither nominative nor accusative, as per Benveniste [1966] and Kuryłowicz [1976]) relationship between N and V, with the accusative appearing only in later examples. Constituent function within a compound, however labeled, is frequently debatable: *manūŏpera* has been glossed as both 'work

---

[4]In colloquial Mod. Brit. English, *locum[tenens]* still retains its value of '(professional) replacement, stand-in'.

with the hand' and 'work of the hand'. [5] *Manum levāre*, to select a more telling example, appears to blur any neat distinction between accusative and other so-called oblique cases in the first constituent: OPr.–OCat. (12th c.) *manlevar* 'to borrow' can be understood as 'to raise the hand = swear an oath', or '*ā manū levāre*' = 'to remove from s.o.'s power' (*DECC*, s.v. "mà"). L. *manus* boasted a number of differing values, ranging far beyond the physical, and this very polysemy allowed it to figure in compounds with differing case roles.

Caput, the second most frequent nominal element in the listings of medieval and Renaissance vernacular N + V compounds, occurred very rarely in Med. Latin. In *capitilavium* 'lotion for anointing the head' it represents, quite literally, 'head', but its exact sense is difficult to paraphrase in *cap[ut] tenēre* (synonymous gloss of *manūtenēre* 'to defend, protect, etc.' in Charlemagne's capitularies). The possibility of substantial nominal value accruing to *cap* in *caplevar* 'to deliver a pledge' (lit. 'to raise the head = be present') has recently been made explicit in *DECC*, s.v. "cap": "entre altres coses es pot suggerir que hi hagi la idea d'alçar el cap fent act de presència, acord o solidaritat". Reflexes of *caplevāre* are lacking in Med. Latin and anywhere in medieval Romance except to the south of the Pyrenees; witness OCat.–OArag. *capleuta*, *caplevador*, transplanted onto Old Spanish. Such a distribution can be construed as support for vernacular impetus for any and all Med. Latin compounds showing *caput*, particularly in the absence of corroborating evidence from Brit. Latin.

Manu(m) far outnumbers other first constituents in Med. Latin N + V compounds; in Appendix E are listed fifteen forms with *manu(m)*, plus *mundeboro*, blended with *manu(m)*. Of these, only *manūmittĕre* 'to emancipate' directly continues Cl. Latin. In addition there are nine examples with *fidēs*, four with *carō*, three with *locus* and *mĭssa*, two each with *aqua* and *caput*, and single examples of *carrus*, *clāvus*, *crŭce(m)*, *dĕus*, *sāl*, and *terra*. Among verbal second constituents figure four examples with *tenēre*, three with *levāre*, two each with *dicĕre*, *factus*, *lavāre*, *posĭtus*, and *praehendĕre/prē(n)sus*. Twenty-six verbs occur singly.

From these numerical tallies, and from the statistical charts of French, Occitan, Catalan, and Spanish provided in Appendices A–D, it follows that reflexes of *manus* and *caput* are the two most common nominal constituents in the N + V compounds under investigation here. These two parts of the body are perhaps the most characteristic of humans; hence their widespread metaphoric applicability. *Manus*, which also figured prominently in the discussion of Cl. Latin compounds above

---

[5]Its second nominal element falls short of continuing the exact sense of Cl.L. *ŏpera* (i) 'work(s) which suppose free will and a desire to serve' (Lewis & Short, s.v. "opus"); (ii) (applied to material objects) 'handiwork' (Glare, s.v. "opus").

(Chapter 2), was the most widely used nominal element at the early stage of all four languages; it was continued into each one, whereas the general fate of *caput* in Western Romance was uneven: it was replaced in French by (originally slangy) *tête* and in Spanish by *cabeza* (cf. Ptg. *cabeça*). The hand is associated with power, in its capacity to grasp and wield weapons, and with work; it is intimately connected with battle (L. *venīre ad manūs*, Fr. *en venir aux mains*, G. *handgemein werden* 'to come to blows, grapple'), as well as with the making of ritual gestures, both religious (*the laying on of hands*) and feudal (Med.L. *manum dare* 'to swear allegiance').

Med.L. *manus* represented 'hand', 'power', 'possession', 'feudal service', 'signature', and 'faith'. [6] Med.L. *manūtenēre* only indirectly continues Cl.L. *manū tenēre* 'to have tangible evidence of, know to be evident'; but many legal terms, particularly *manūmittĕre*, as well as Med.L. *manum levāre*, Med.L. *manūprisum/* A.-Norm. *main-, meyn-prendre*, etc., represent the continued practice of Roman law and the later institutions of feudal life. [7]

Caput could mean 'head', 'end', 'chapter, paragraph', or 'legal head of family'. *Caput* was also semantically blurred to the point of becoming a simple prefix, both positive ('head', 'chief') and negative, the latter particularly well represented in Occitan and Catalan (see Schwegler [1986]). In 13th-c. OSp. *caboprender* 'to understand', indexed below in Appendix D under N *cabo* 'head' + V *(em)prender* 'to (under)take', *cabo-* was analyzed unhesitatingly by Ayala (see Gili y Gaya [1947], s.v. "caboprender") as a reinterpretation of *com-*, a role commensurate with prefixal status. OPr. *capgirar* 'to twist one's neck' (cf. late medieval Cat. [1490] *capgirant* 'turn(ing) upside down') and Pr. *capvirar*, borrowed into late 17th-c. French as *chavirer* 'to capsize', argue instead for continued transparency, hence retention of full semantic value, as in Béar. *cap-préne* 'to get a head-ache'. The range of nominal elements in the medieval corpus was by no means limited to body parts. The modern vernaculars show an even higher concentration of body parts in first position, and this for the following reason: after the disappearance of Med. Latin, the N + V pattern seems to have been most strongly supported by factors inherent in the development of the vernaculars themselves, in particular the exploitation of vernacular N + Adj

---

[6]Bloch–Wartburg (s.v. "mainmorte") note that OFr. *mainmorte* 'mortmain, inalienable ownership' probably calques Med.L. *manus mortua*, rather than the reverse, since in legal phraseology L. *manus* already meant 'possession, authority'.

[7]OGasc. (1440) *manumitar* is still represented by Béar. *mâ-méte* 'confiscation, opération de mainmise'. Older Fr. *mainmetre*, however, was replaced by MFr. *manumettre*, which survived longer (1338–1665) than *manumiter* (1354–1474)—an instance of partial re-Latinization akin to the remodeling Sp. *mantener*/(law) *manutener*.

compound patterns, from which N + V compounds have been liberally back-formed since the 19th century.

Throughout the medieval periods of French, Occitan, Catalan, and Spanish, morphologically transparent Latinate forms (whether originally Latin or Romance, and whatever their pronunciation) were to continue to provide a powerful source for both borrowing and analogical derivations, just as Latin OV word order continued to provide a syntactic mold. Support from Med. Latin religious, legal, and scientific vocabulary, and from syntax itself, disappeared definitively by the 16th century. It matters little whether, after the time of Charlemagne's reforms, Med. Latin syntax was VO or OV, since there remained numerous OV syntactic constructions throughout the period of medieval Romance. Before vanishing, the Latin of the Middle Ages had put its own stamp on a pattern that had developed from unmarked OV syntax to become one of the earliest types of juxtaposed compounds in Romance.

4. VERNACULAR NOMINAL AND VERBAL ELEMENTS IN THE MEDIEVAL AND RENAISSANCE CORPUS

Noun elements in the Romance compounds have been tallied in the chart below. There are, for example, fifteen different Old Occitan compound lexemes that display *man-* as first element: *manaya, manbestir, manbor, mafa(i)t, manlevar, manleu(ta), mamessor, marmetre/marmessia, maamudar, manobrar, mansaysir, mantenen, mantener, mantersa, mantreyt*. Artistic innovations, insofar as they have found their way into dictionaries, are included in the chart below, but their first constituents, generally one-of-a-kind, do not obscure the over-all frequencies that emerge from comparison of the four target vernaculars.

N + V compounds alone figure in the analysis here. From the sections in Appendices A–D devoted to structures approximating N + V, the following have been eliminated from further consideration: OFr. *caillebotter,* (16th c.) *culbuter* (also *jouer au cul levé*), MFr. *escalventrer,* OFr. *ferlier, fernoer,* MFr. *gras-fondure,* OFr. *g(u)aimenter, houcepignier* (Mod. *houspiller*), OFr. *jambaterrer,* OFr. *jointenant,* MFr. *peslemesler,* A.-Norm. *sancfuison, sancterné,* (16th c.) *saugrenu,* (15th c.) *tient-main,* OFr. *tourneboeler,* MFr. *tournevirer;* OPr. *calpizar, cambaterrar, palferre;* Cat. (16th c.) *aigua-baixant,* OCat. *cap-brevar, -lletrar, -salmar,* OCat. *solabatut;* Sp. (16th c.) *terraplenar* (cf. Mod. Cat. *terraplenar*). Among formations qualified as "dubious" in Appendices A–D, the following have been omitted: OFr. *chapignier,* (15th c.) *courbatu,* (13th c.) *vermoulu;* OPr. *mantuzar;* Cat. (15th c.) *capvivar;* Sp. (16th c.) *carcomer, escamondar.*

Comparative Frequency Chart of Nominal First Elements:
Constituents Shared by Three or Four Languages

	Fr	Occ	Cat	Sp
manu(m)	11	15	4	1 0
caput	3	5	4	4
sāl/săle	2	2	2	2
fĭde(m)	2	3	1	1
carne(m)	1	1	1	1
lŏcum	1	1	1	1
terra(m)	3	1	1	1
clāve(m) 'nail'	2	2	2	0
mente(m)	1	1	0	2
mĭssa(m)	0	1	2	1
sangue(m)	2	1	1	0
lĭtterā(s)	1	1	1	0
murr-	1	1	1	0
vĭa(m)	0	1	1	1

The 4- and 3-way tallies above suggest, foremost, that many shared items were inherited from Proto-Romance, or borrowed early from ecclesiastical Latin (*clou*, *clau* 'nail' in compounds with *fīgĕre*, **fīgĭcāre* and other vernacular elements). No nominal constituent is able to compete with the overwhelming frequency of *manu(m)*, whether arrived at by diffusion among the vernaculars or through independent innovation; nevertheless, in OSp. *malfestar* (MANIFESTĀRE), there has occurred a—semantically motivated—blend with L. *mal(e)*. In the earlier examples of a feudal or administrative nature, *caput* runs *manu(m)* a clear second, but becomes increasingly more visible in the ensuing rise of N + V compounds in semantic fields minimally influenced by Latin, i.e., other than feudal/administrative/religious/ scientific: OBéar. *capbira* 'to train oxen to pull either to right or to left', OPr. *capgirar* 'to twist the neck', MFr-Pr. *chateni* 'to restrain a bull by the horns' (cf. [13th c.] *chafresner* 'to restrain, tame'). As regards borrowings between Med. Romance and Med. Latin, great caution must be exercised in attributing original provenance to either: identically structured OFr. *foimenti*, OPr./OCat. *fementit*, Sp. (13th c.) *fementido* 'traitor' cannot conclusively be labeled borrowings, although they are flanked by Med.L. *fidementūtus*, attested as early as A.D. 794. In all likelihood, the Med. Latin form is calqued on Romance.

Like the compounds with 'fidem' + 'mentīrī', adj. Fr. (16th c.) *lettre-féru*, Gasc. (16th c.) *letre-herit*, Cat. *lletraferit* 'fond of letters (= humanities), well-lettered' represent but a single combination of 'letter' + 'stricken', the French example having been calqued on southwestern Occitan by Montaigne himself. A given constituent may appear once in each medieval vernacular but in more than a single lexeme: in OFr. *charboter* 'to swell'/*encharboter* 'to embarrass', the reflex of *carne(m)* lacks semantic affinity with OBéar. *carn-bedar* (lit. 'flesh' + 'to prohibit'), OCat. *carnestoltes*, OSp. *carnes tolendas* 'Lent' (lit. '[pieces of] flesh' + 'removed'), but seems, rather, to align itself with the notion of 'swelling' found also in OPr. *botenflat*, etc. Many pairings operate on regional grounds, setting off Gallo-Romance from Hispano-Romance, etc., or otherwise pitting two or three languages against the remainder.

French, Occitan, and Catalan join in so using *sang* + *fŭndĕre*, but the N + V status of the Catalan compounds has been questioned: Corominas rejected any notion of **sanguifŭndĕre* for 14th-c. *sangfondre*, favoring instead a reinterpretation of prefixal SUB- (*DECC*, s.v. "fondre"). Gallo-Romance (French + Occitan) is alone in favoring *carême* (*quaresme entrant*/*caramantrant*, *quaresme prenant*/*carema prenens* 'Lent'); *ferru(m)* + *vestūre*; *mĕnte* + *habēre*. In the modern period, *carementrant* has yielded a N + V Inf compound, Occ. *carementrar* 'to enter into Lent'; cf. also Occ. *l'annado* (*la semano, lou meis*) *entrant* 'the coming year (week, month)'. Given later Gasc. *goudeslat* 'swollen' and Hispano-Romance *bodinflao, -inflón*, there are precedents for identifying the root *bod-* 'round shape' (= 'stomach', 'sausage', e.g., Fr. *boudin* 'blood sausage') in OFr. *boranflé* 'swollen'. OPr. *botenflat* is listed only in *DECC*, s.v. "botir-se"; however, on chronological grounds the *FEW* rejects *bod-* in OFr. *borsoflé* 'puffed up' and MFr.–Mod.Fr. *boursouf(f)ler*, preferring *bŭrra* 'hair, stuffing' as etymon, all of which makes early Gallo-Romance evidence inconclusive as to the presence of *bod-*.

French and Catalan have in common *pāla* 'shovel', compounded with a verb of digging; and *campu(m)*. Occitano-Romance (Occitan + Catalan) share *aigua* (cf. Med.L. *aquaeversus*); *cam(b)a*; *cara*; and *pè*/*peu* 'foot'; the presence of *cam(b)a*, *gam(b)a* 'leg' in Spanish, e.g., Cast. *ligagamba*, carries a hint of nonCastilian sources. Occitan and Spanish have compounds with L. *pĭlu(m)* 'hair'. OPr. *pelpartidura* is a hapax, clearly involving artistic coinage; *pelechar* 'to shed, molt, get new hair' points to *pĭlu(m)*, although *pĕlle(m)* and *pĭlu(m)* are listed as equally possible etyma in the index to medieval and Renaissance Spanish compounds (Appendix D); and OArag. *pelmudar* 'to molt' (similarly attributed to either *pĕlle[m]* or *pĭlu[m]*) ranks as only the earliest attestation of a widespread reinforcement of semantically specialized L. MŪTĀRE 'to change [hair or feather]' (> Fr. *muer* 'to molt'). OPr. *cazatinent* 'house-owner, -holder' is continued by Cat. (18th c.) *casatinent* idem. Hispano-Romance (Catalan + Spanish) shares reflexes of CRŬCE(M) (OCat. *creuclavat*, *creuposar, crozficar*; OArag. *croceficar*/Ast. *crocheficar*) with OFr. *croizficher*. The feudal tradition of Catalonia also provided medieval Aragonese (hence Castilian) with borrowings, e.g., *caplevar, capleuta,* as did early French, e.g., OSp. *manbor, mampastor.*

Certain formations in each corpus contain nominal elements uniquely represented. French is alone in having: *or* (three unassailable examples), *bourre* (of three possible examples of *bourre,* only OFr. *borsoflé,* (Mod.) *boursouf(f)ler* is unproblematic, unlike *boranflé;* in addition, although OFr-Pr. *burdemeclia* is listed under *bŭrra* (*FEW* I, 644a), *bourre* is phonetically outranked by **borda* 'fraud, cheat, dizziness', alien to any other medieval vernacular); *dieu, feu* (two examples); and one example each of *aile, bille, blanc, boule, chant* 'edge', *charbon, col, corne, cuir, cuisse, *estan, go(u)r(t), goutte, graisse, gré, jour, lierre, montagne, nient, nuit, Ourse, pain, part, poi* (Mod. *peu*), *signe, *skala, tort.* Occitan is alone in displaying: *cul* (two examples); *ben* 'goods', *casa, coa, conde, deit* (Mod. *dit*), *fort[s], pel, perna, prest* (one example each). Catalan alone displays: *ull* (one example). Spanish alone claims: *barba, bota, cam(in)al, faz* (one example of each).

MFr. *boffumer* 'to become angry' is isolated in featuring an onomatopoeic first element (*buff-, puff-*), although the *FEW,* paradoxically, attributes Mod. *embaufumer, -fumé* to both *buff-* (1, 596b) and to *balsamu(m)* (1, 226a). There are no conspicuous numbers of Germanic elements, directly absorbed without passing first through Proto-Romance, in any corpus above save in three Old or Middle French words: (i) *mainbor,* whose initial element (Gmc. *mun[d]-,* cognate with L. *manu(m)* 'protection') has been blended with, or reinterpreted as, *main-;* (ii) *estanfique* 'small column in the masonry of a bay window' (cf. also Pic. *estafiker* 'to settle into one spot'), in which Gamillscheg identified Gmc. **estan* 'supporting beam' + *fichier; FEW* XII, s.v. "stare" (238a*n*7), also suggests a V + V construction, *stare* + *-fiche,* from *fichier;* and (iii) *escalbotter* 'to shell peas, beans', with Gmc. **skala,* cognate to Eng. *scale* (cf. Pic. *décafiker* 'to husk [nuts or fruit]'). In the modern (Northern) French corpus, Germanic elements appear far more frequently—but this fact may, in part, reflect superior documentation rather than actual numbers of vernacular medieval compounds.

Germanic elements are found in Fr. *bouter* (Frk. *bôtan* 'to strike'), *garder* (**wardôn* 'to guard'), and Gmc. *beran* 'to defend' (verbal constituent of MUNDEBORO → OFr. *mainbour,* OPr. *manbor,* etc.). *Tenēre,* in its various Romance forms, is undoubtedly the most frequent verbal constituent of N + V compounds, with *lever, -ar* clearly in second place. *Levĭta* (OCat. *caplleuta,* OArag. *caple[u]ta,* OPr. *manleu[ta],* etc.) is patterned on *dēbŭta,* and cf. OSp. *debda.* All four languages have absorbed partially or wholly vernacular reflexes of MANŪ-MITTĔRE, -MISSOR; in addition, Old Spanish shows a single innovative form with *meter,* namely *mientes-metudo.*

Comparative Frequency Chart of Verbal Second Elements:
Constituents Shared by Three or Four Languages

	Fr	Occ	Cat	Sp
tenēre	5	7	4	4
levāre	2	5	2	2
prae-, prē(he)ndĕre	4	1	4	2
*figicāre	3	1	2	1
mentīrī	2	1	1	1
mūtāre	2	1	1	1
mittĕre	1	1	1	2
pikk-	1	1	1	1
fŭndĕre	2	2	2	0
versus (versar)	1	2	2	0
levĭta	0	1	2	2
batt(u)ĕre	1	1	1	0
*am(bu)lāre	0	1	1	2
cantāre	0	1	1	1
prē(n)su(m)	0	1	1	1
dicĕre	1	1	1	0
intrāre	1	1	0	1
pŭngēns, pŭnctu(m)	1	1	0	1

Not unexpectedly, cognates of *an(d)ar* are absent in northern Gallo-Romance, again as a result of lexical differentiation. The verbal element of OPr. *sanc-fois, -foizó* 'bloodshed' shows contamination of *fūsiō, -iōne(m)* by the ŭ of *fŭndĕre*, as against OCat. *sangfús* 'flushed', A.-Norm. *sancfuison* 'bloodshed'. Traces of L. *pŭngente(m)*, *pŭnctu(m)* occur in OFr. *orpoignant*, OPr. *clauponh*, and OSp. *barbiponiente*; in the latter, *pŭngente(m)* (a remnant of now-defunct Hispano-Romance *pŭngĕre*) has been replaced by the nearly homonymous *pōnente(m)* through internal contamination of vowel length.

Again, two languages may be set off from the remainder: French and Occitan share reflexes of ADIŪTĀRE, *FA(CĔ)RE, *FRĒNĀRE (*frener, -ar* 'to restrain, bridle'), HABĒRE, INFLĀRE, LIGĀRE, MŪTĀRE, ŎPERĀRE (*œuvrer/obrar* 'to work'), and VESTĪRE, as well as Gmc. *wardôn*. Occitan and Catalan agree on *capgirar*, with Catalan choosing *capgirar, caragirar* where Occitan has *capgirar/capvirar, caravirar*; Spanish and Catalan are in agreement on *TOLLĬTA (Cl.L. *sublātus*)/TOLLENDA, although only Catalan has a fully vernacular compound, *aigua-toldre*. OSp. *mampastor* is taken here as a reflex of PĀSTU(M) 'nourished' (J. Barthe [1979]), and cf. OFr. *mainpast*; French and Spanish also share FERĪRE (in part, as heir to FERRE).

French alone has: *porter* (five examples); *bouter* (three examples); *mêler, naître, souffler* (two examples each); and one example apiece of *apporter, armer, barrer, choir, fergier, fermer, fouir, fouler, fraindre, fumer, paner, planter, poudrer, querre, ronger, (non) savoir, signer, voler,* and *vomir.* Occitan alone deserves credit for *virar* (two examples); and *banhar, finar, getar, investir, lavar, partir, saisir,* OPr. *trachar, transir, vetar* (one example each). Catalan monopolizes *calcigar, faixar (feixar), fangar, lligar,* and *posar* (one example each). Spanish exclusively has one example each of *ajustar, alzar, amparar, catar,* and *echar.*

Despite instances of common inheritance from Proto-Romance (OFr. *mentevoir,* OPr. *mentaure*), of borrowing from Latin (OCat. *crozficar,* etc.), or of loan translation (OFr. *luetenant,* OPr. *loctenent,* etc.), the accumulations of isolated verbs suggest that innovations in the medieval vernaculars centered around the verb; OFr. *ferarmer, -vestir* are good cases in point, flanked as they are by two additional examples relegated, in Appendix A, to "Other Compound Structures Approximating N + V": *ferlier, -nouer,* with initial *firmus* (cf. OWall. *ferm lier* 'to bind tightly', *FEW* III, s.v. "firmus"). While there may be some justification for regarding nominal elements, particularly frequent ones such as *manu(m)* or *caput,* as prefixes, the verbs in N + V compounds never seem to lose their individual identity, allowing easy replacement within a number of identifiable ranges of semantic notions.

5. SUPPORT FOR THE VERNACULAR PATTERN

In addition to two-way borrowing from Med. Latin, innovative N + V compounds appeared freely in the medieval vernaculars by a number of processes. One can usefully distinguish, as major sources of support for ongoing N + V compounding, syntax, lexicon, and semantic notions. The importance of semantic notions in the spread of Med. Latin N + V compounds, including their ultimate dependence on Romance, was examined in section 3 of this chapter. Lexicon and semantics provide a powerful key to understanding the actual proliferation of N + V compounding in the target vernaculars as well, with the noun and verb tallies (section 4) aiding in the determination of shared innovations or borrowings. This section is devoted to an examination of synchronic supports for the vernacular pattern, particularly the processes by which existing lexical items were reinforced, and their constituents reinterpreted or replaced.

The pattern of *manūtenēre* was clearly attested in both Med. Latin and the medieval vernaculars before unmarked OV syntax had entirely disappeared. "O" here refers to any noun standing in an oblique relationship to V, including that of direct object; in the context of this study of *manūtenēre,* no mention will be made of adverbs (of time, manner, place, or quantity) or complements other than nominal. Since French happens to be the best documented of the four chosen target languages, it has been most widely used in illustrating various OV-ordered syntactic structures and phrases, where neither emphasis nor expressivity matters in connection with pre-verbal position. All four languages show considerable incidence of object + V ordering, a situation which continues to hold true in modern complement pronoun position (Fr. *je la vois, je l'ai vue*). A number of examples still extant in the modern languages are included as well, e.g., Fr. *sans coup férir* 'without striking a blow'.

Medieval Romance retained a good measure of the freedom in word order that had characterized Cl. Latin, although that freedom was constrained by the need to ensure comprehensibility. In the oldest vernacular texts, OV order continued verb-final Latin syntax; there was also a dosage of artistic experimentation with Latinate syntax during the 15th and 16th centuries, e.g., in Spanish, but by then SVO had become generalized throughout Romance. In Old French and Old Provençal, a nominal two-case system was available to clarify syntactic relationships; this system was never the sole means of marking logical relationships between nouns, since even in early texts several set patterns of word order are recognizable. The position of the OFr. object noun was still rather arbitrary. It could easily open the clause, particularly where its function was clearly marked by a case form: *Humes devure, grant mal fait* 'he eats men, [and] does great damage' (Marie de France, *Bisclavret*, verse 11); traces of this order are still found at present in fossilized proverbs and sayings, e.g., *qui terre a guerre a* 'he who has land has war', *qui dort bien puces ne sent* 'he who sleeps well feels no fleas', *grand bien lui fasse* 'much good may it do him/her'. Indirect-object function could also be marked by word order: OPr. *pos Dieu platz* 'if it [so] please God'.

Lucien Foulet's *Petite Syntaxe de l'ancien français*, rev. 3d ed. (Paris: Champion, repr. 1965:§§447ff.) lists six different combinations of S, V, and O; among these, three patterns display O preposed to V: OSV, OVS, SOV. The first survives today as normal order after a relative pronoun: Fr. *[l'homme] que je vois* '(the man) whom I see'. The second, OV(S), abounded in poetry, being less common in prose; subject inversion was, and still is, frequently motivated by stylistic considerations, although it need not be so, e.g., OCat. *aquestes paraules entengueren los mesatgers* 'the messengers heard these words'. SOV, finally, decidedly poetic in main clauses (§480), was abundant in subordinate clauses after certain conjunctions (*quant, se, si . . . que, que*), e.g., *se vos ceste desloiauté soufrez* 'if you suffer this disloyalty' (*La Mort le roi Artu*); and in relative clauses (§462).

The substantival object of an infinitive normally preceded the latter: OFr. *Galahad chevauche mainte jornee sans aventure trover* 'G. rides many days without encountering adventure' (*Mort Artu*), *ils s'en partent pour leur leu tenir* 'they go off to defend their position', OPr. *per pels partir* 'to part the hair'. The construction was frequent, enclisis occurring between the preposition and a following definite article with which it lacked close syntactic connection: *essamples . . . del miracle représenter.*

Dictionary research also yields a number of N + V–ordered expressions, both medieval and modern: OFr. *pié estant* 'immediately' (cf. Wall. *pî-stant, stant-pî* 'standing'), OFr. *une lance tenant* 'a lance-throw away' (*Chanson d'Aspremont*), OPr. *a un tenen de* 'contiguous', Fr. *être grosse d'enfant sentant* 'to feel one's unborn child stirring', Fr. (Norm.) *à chiffe-tirer* 'in disagreement', Occ. *en terre-estant* 'during one's lifetime', *à palavira* 'in profusion'. These are complemented by idioms combining Obj + Inf: OFr. *corda toccar* [*sic*] 'to touch the strings of a lyre', 18th-c. Fr. *eau donner* 'to soak before adding indigo' (step in the dying process) and Mod. Occ. (H.-Alpes) *pate tetiar* 'to caress', which echo in reversed format the mass of Inf + Obj idioms of the vernaculars, e.g., OFr. *porter a col* 'to carry on one's back', Fr. *perdre pied* 'to lose one's footing', Occ. *cantar messa* 'to celebrate Mass', *metre man* 'to put one's hand to', *prendre sal* 'to absorb salt', *téner pé, cap* 'to keep one's footing, one's head', *perdre temps* 'to waste time', OSp. *meter mientes* 'to be prudent', which share several of the attributes of compounds (idiomaticity, uninterruptibility).

OFr-Pr. *janbe terrat* '(having) dismounted' (*Girart de Roussillon*) illustrates the coalescence of a multipartite phrase, **metre jambe a terre*, into a juxtaposed compound—the process ultimately responsible for all composition. From *janbe terrat* or its congeners, infinitival OFr. *jambaterrer* 'to dismount' and OPr. *cambaterrar* (*Jaufre*) appear by back-formation, one of the major sources of N + V at any stage in the progression from Latin to Romance. The range of early vernacular lexical items coalesced from verb-final syntax is limited to a few examples inherited from spoken Latin, e.g., reflexes of Cl.L. *mĕnte habēre* (OFr. *mentevoir*, OPr. *mentaure*). Med.L. *manūtenēre*, also considered to be a juxtaposed form, represents a Romance compound with N obl. first constituent, on a Latinate N + V pattern (cf. Cl.L. *manūmittĕre* ← *manū missus*). Similarly, OFr. *foimenti*, OPr.–OCat. *fementit*, OSp. *fementido* are Romance creations on an N + V Past Ptc pattern, ultimately of Indo-European origin. *Foimenti*, etc., demonstrate, not syntactic, but lexical motivation, as does *manūtenēre/cap(ut) tenēre*; in either case, new compounds appear analogically on the basis of an established pattern.

Within a fixed N + V pattern were operative a number of processes by which (i) associated compounds could gain in resemblance (associative analogy); (ii) new compounds could appear through the agency of paradigmatic replacement (creative analogy, or "enchaînement associatif"); (iii) simplex verbs could undergo reinforcement by a nominal element. Back-formation (iv) from agentives, action nouns, and other nominal/adjectival formations also accounts for a significant proportion of the medieval and Renaissance corpus, e.g., OFr. *orbattre* (← *orbateör* 'goldsmith'), OFr./ OPr. *manuvrer/manaobrar* 'to work or put with the hands' (*manuevre/manobra*).

The majority of compounds in the medieval corpus are not isolates: 16th-c. Cat. *caravirat* is flanked by contemporary *caragirat*; OFr. *foitenant* is strongly evocative of *foimenti, -eör*, despite the discrepant shapes of the verbal element involved. Beyond such instances of paradigmatic replacement, isolates could also occur, e.g., OFr. *charboter, cuirpaner,* MFr-Pr. *chateni* (cf. OFr. *chafresner* 'head' + 'hold'), OBéar. *coo-transi, prestlevar,* OCat. *ullprendre,* Arag. *camajuste.* Some degree of lexical support can generally be adduced, however, on the basis of strong formal or semantic parallels between sets of compounds (e.g., the 'Lent' series) or between isolates and their assumed prototypes: e.g., Fr. (14th c.) *saupiquet* (*saupiquer; cf. MFr. *saupiqueter,* OPr.–OCat. *salpicar*).

Prefixal reinterpretation accounts for MFr. *colporteuse, -eresse,* (16th c.) *colporter*—the infinitive remodeled from *comporter* under influence of *porter a col* (*REW* §2104 "comportāre," etc.); OSp. (13th c.) *caboprender* is suggestive of *comprender* 'to understand'. Levy (1973) lists OPr. *cap-, con-tener* 'to govern, support, protect'; (refl.) 'to behave'; *cap-, contenemen, cap-, contenensa* 'behavior'. Similarly, OSp. *captenencia* 'conduct, appearance' was flanked by vars. *cac-, cau-,* and *contenencia* (Alvar 1976:235). OSp. *caplevar, -lebador* are doubled by *sobrellevar, superlevador.* In 16th-c. Occ. *manbestir* 'to invest', there has clearly occurred remodeling of prefixal *investir* idem, but no clear semantic value here accrues to *man-* itself from this process (cf. dial. Fr. *manpatient* 'impatient' and *mainfait* 'mal fait'). However, *man-* is identifiable in OSp. *mamparar* 'to protect, defend', where it occurs through blending with prefixal *ante-*, in this instance retaining something of the value of 'power, authority' (*REW* §500a "anteparāre," §5337 "manū parāre"). OCat. *comprès* yielded to *corprès* '(emotionally) moved' under pressure from a series of semantically similar adjectives: *corfós* 'confused, faint', *cor-ferit* 'afflicted, heart-stricken', etc. (*DECC,* s.v. "cor").

Verbal elements less frequently succumb to this type of reinterpretation, unless they are remodeled in tandem with their initial constituents: through the agency of so-called folk etymology, Mod. Sp. *escarapela* 'quarrel ending in hair-pulling' (from EXCARPĒRE, through Ptg. *escar[a]pelar-se, BDE[LC],* s.v. "escarapela") has been popularly analyzed as *cara + pelar;* *ēscam mundāre has been suggested for Sp. *escamondar* 'to prune trees', since superseded by *escamoch(e)ar × mondar (BDE[LC],* s.v. "escamocho"); Diez (1887) suggested CARNEM COMĚDĚRE as the etymon of *carcomer,* today accepted as a denominal from *carcoma* 'wood-borer, species of worm' (*DCE[LC],* s.v. "carcoma").

Throughout each corpus, there is considerable evidence from attested pairs that both noun and verb elements within compounds were replaceable by synonyms: OFr. *clo(u)fermer, cloufire, cloufichier, croizficher* 'to crucify'; *fervestir, ferarmer* 'to cover in armor'; Sp. (late 15th c.) *pelechar,* Mod. Arag. *pelmudar* 'to molt'. OCat. *camptinent* 'corporal' parallels *lloctinent*; OCat. *missacantant* 'priest' is paralleled by a synonym, *missadient* (cf. Med.L. *missam canĕre/cantāre/dīcĕre*). Combining evidence from Med. Latin and Romance as a whole, the 'Lent' series, L.2 above, offers an outstanding illustration of paradigmatic replacement, i.e., of lexical support for N + V: *carne[m] + laxāre, levāre, ligāre, privārī, sĭccāre, tollĕre,* and *vetāre*.

Also through the process of replacement, new N + V derivations could be modeled on Adv + V or Adj + N compounds, e.g., OFr. (11th c.) *forfait* 'forfait', *forfaire* (Adv + V)/*torfait* 'wrong-doing', *torfaire*, and later (in Brittany) *poifait* 'negligence', *poifaisant*. *Jointenant* 'joint-tenant' parallels *foitenant* 'faithful', *terretenant* 'landholder, tenant', *benstenen* 'heir', *cazatenen* 'house-owner'. It is also possible to analyze *torfait* as N + Adj (lit. 'wrong done'), an ancient Indo-European pattern clearly underlying in OFr. *orfergié, orpoignant*. N + Adj (= V Past Ptc) must figure here in its unquestionable capacity to motivate new N + V compounds by back-formation, but cannot approximate the verbal force of N + V as closely as does N + V Pres Ptc (even in calques). Other N + V Past Ptc compounds (their corresponding infinitives, if any, enclosed within parentheses) encompass: OFr. *blanc-signé* 'signature to a blank document', later remodeled to *blanc-seing*; *borsoflé* (*-er*) 'swollen'; *chanfraint* (*-fraindre*) 'bevelled'; *dieu-menti* (mid–13th-c. *mentir Dieu* [hap.]) 'one who betrays his solemn oath'; *fervesti, -vestu* 'armored, iron-clad (warrior)' (*-ir*); *sangmeslé* 'troubled by a strong emotion' (*-er*); OCat. *aiguavés, -vessant* 'slope (of terrain)', *peucalcigat* 'trampled' (*-ar*), *sangfús* 'flushed' (*sangfondre*), *solabatut* 'weary, footsore'; OSp. *mientesmetudo* 'prudent', (16th c.) *menteca(p)to* 'weak in the head', *maniatado* 'manacled' (*-ar*).

Occasionally, verbs were reinforced by adjunction of semantically redundant nouns: Hispano- and Gallo-Romance reflexes of MŪTĀRE signified 'to molt [skin, hair, or feather]', making OArag. (and Mod.) *pelmudar*, and innovative Sp. (15th c.) *pelechar*, redundant. Verbs could be otherwise remodeled: OFr. *vermoulu* 'worm-eaten' was convincingly analyzed as a reinterpretation of *vermelé* 'wormy' by Orr (1951). *REW* §9296 lists OPr. *viandant*, OCat. *vian(d)ant*, OSp. *viandante* as reflexes of *viāns, -ntis*, but there has been remodeling of *viāre* on *an(d)ar* (Battisti–Alessio, s.v. "viandante"; *DCE[LC]*, s.v. "via"). Given OPr. *anar via* and It. *andare via*, this item qualifies for inclusion among true N + V compounds.

Lexical items distributed among the twenty informal semantic categories of section 2 above highlight the overwhelming importance of lexical and semantic support in the survival and propagation of a compound pattern. Syntactic phrases can provide raw materials for new compounds, but the majority of compounds examined here resist syntactic analysis. Rather, reinterpretation of existing compound constituents, replacements of noun or verb within a given semantic notion or field, even reinforcement of verb by noun—these major analogical processes, taken in conjunction with back-formation, are primarily responsible for the corpus of medieval and Renaissance N + V compounds.

6. CONCLUSIONS

The pattern of *manūtenēre* was kept alive in medieval and Renaissance Western Romance by a concatenated series of circumstances: a single N + V–ordered leader compound, adopted very early from the legal sphere into general vocabulary ('maintain'), was supported, internally, by (i) still-viable OV vernacular syntactic structures and (ii) ongoing lexical support from other compound patterns; plus, externally, by (iii) the contexts of feudalism and Christianity, at least in the earlier Middle Ages; and (iv) the morphological transparency of Med. Latin.

In the genesis of an N + V pattern, Med. Latin and the vernaculars provided each other with raw materials for innovations and substitutions. A curious correlation emerges from a close second look at each medieval corpus in connection with the seemingly interchangeable compounding of *manu(m)* and *caput* + *tenēre* and *levāre*: *manūtenēre* = *captenēre* 'to protect'; *manūlevāre* = *caplevāre* 'to swear (with raised hand), post bail'. Precisely where the analogical equation drawn from *manus, caput, tenēre*, and *levāre* is not fully or to a reasonable extent fleshed out, N + V compounds have enjoyed scant success beyond the medieval period. [8] It thus appears that a tendency toward greater or lesser N + V compounding activity is already identifiable in the medieval vernaculars. French shows no more than fragmentary traces of *captenēre* (*chatien*), *manūlevāre* (*mainlevée*); many of the early Spanish examples are in all likelihood borrowed from Catalan or else represent Gonzalo de Berceo's Riojan dialect, essentially Navarro-Aragonese (hence more representative of Pyrenean Romance than of Castilian Spanish). This correlation allows us to argue for a major degree of osmotic, bidirectional borrowing between the vernaculars and Med. Latin, as well as among the Western vernaculars, even in the domains of law and ecclesiastical terminology.

Paradoxically, the polysemy (taken here to stand for loss of semantic individuality) of *manus* and, to a lesser extent, *caput* was unaccompanied by any considerable degree of phonic or morphological blurring. In general terms, analogy cannot function

---

[8]It is less persuasive to pinpoint semantic patterns in a compound than in a suffixal formation, particularly in a relatively noncompounding language such as any of the RLs or Latin. No single element will suffice in a given slot, or else we have affixation (c.f., CAP[UT]-, -*(I)FĬCĀRE), rather than genuine compounding. But there is no reason why even two elements alternating within a given position and a single semantic pattern cannot set the stage for analogical extensions.

with opaque elements on either side of an equation. Transparency was needed if the sense of compoundedness was to be maintained, which, in consequence of the loss of *měnte(m)*, clearly was not the case with Cl.L. *měnte habēre* > OFr. *ment-evoir, -oivre*.

The two elements in Fr. *maintenir*, OPr. *mantener*, etc., could not have remained phonetically distinct under normal elocutionary conditions, yet the wide range of synonyms flanking that leader word was surely supported by its continued (or renewed, in the case of *maintenir ← *mantenir*) morphological transparency as much as by its distinct semantic and cultural importance. Once a morphological mold (including word order and compoundedness) had become identifiable with a number of key semantic notions favoring easy replacements, an actual N + V Inf pattern became available for further exploitation.

Section 5 above examined several processes that motivated much of the medieval corpus: coalescence from OV syntactic structures; reinterpretation; paradigmatic replacement within a given semantic notion; reinforcement; and back-formation. To these must be added calquing, or loan translation, as well as straightforward borrowing or diffusion. In reinterpretation and replacement one recognizes the workings of analogy, the only factor apt to explain the continued exploitation of verb-final and other OV patterns (as well as reversibility in compounds) in the face of the progressive triumph of VO syntax throughout Romance.

In the N + V corpus under scrutiny here, no single resultant part of speech qualifies as primary, although compound verbs abound in many semantic notions thus far examined from the Med. Latin corpus. Against the originally verbal shape of *manūtenēre*, flanked by deverbal OFr. *maintien*, other nominal forms serve as counterevidence: OFr. *mainbour*, OFr. *mainpast*, OCat.–OSp. *cap(l)leuta*, even Rum. *cîrnele(a)gă, cîş-le(a)gă*. In their functions, medieval and Renaissance N + V nominal compounds fall into three broad categories: technical, poetic, and insulting/vulgar; in this respect, they faithfully continue major Indo-European nominal compound types.

A Latin N + V compound pattern was already available by the beginning of the Christian era. In pre-literary Romance, as in post-Classical Latin, a recognizable N + V pattern was productive, although less than prolific. The continued or renewed morphological transparency of vernacular N + V compounds, which attests to their productivity, also made possible the assignment of new semantic values to certain N + V combinations, e.g., 'hand' + 'hold' = OPr. *mantenen* 'balustrade' as well as *manūtenēre, maintenir*, etc. Northern Hispano-Romance *caplevar* was originally limited to the northern section of the peninsula: Cat. (13th c.) *capllevar*, OArag. *cap-, cablevar* 'to deliver a pledge, post bond', synonymous with Med.L. *manūlevāre* 'to post bail'. However, this older value contrasts sharply with OPr. *cap-lève* 'seesaw', Occ./ Cat. *caplevar* 'to raise the end/head', [9] and pre–17th-c. Sp. *caulevar.* [10]

No new derivational pattern has appeared with the advent of *mantenen, cap-lève*; rather, transparent *caplevar* ('head' + 'raise') continues OPr. *cap-lève* and other concrete N + V compounds of the early period, e.g., *pelpartidura*, OBéar. *cap-bira*, OPr. *pèe-lhèbe* 'trap', all morphologically clear-cut and all deriving strong analogical support from N + Adj compounds in which a body part is followed by an adjective (OCat. *solabatut* 'tired', Gasc. *capbourrut* 'headstrong'). [11] Body parts, to be sure, are not intrinsically synonymous, yet onomasiological variants in the prolific modern 'tumble' series (Chapter 4, section 1, category T) range among nom. constituents *cap*, *camba, cara, coa, cul, pata, pè, pèl*, and *perna*, compounded with *virar, girar*, etc.

Is literary innovation in the medieval vernaculars to be inseparably linked with Med. Latin N + V compounding, or do individual artistic creations stand against both the spoken vernacular and feudal/legal Latinate examples or calques? [12] While there is scant evidence of spontaneous N + V compounding in any medieval corpus, modern examples in Chapter 4 give firm assurance of ongoing derivation in many semantic fields least affected by literature—farm labor (Arag. *mancuspir* 'to spit into one's hands and rub them together before taking hold of a tool'), animal husbandry, and everyday life (Gasc. *causse-ha* 'to knit socks').

By no means were N + Adj compounds limited to literary uses, although they underwent remodeling due to the influence of humanistic Latin. In 16th- and 17th-c.

---

[9]There has even been a crossover from *manlevar* to Mod. *caplevar*: in one dialect of Occitan, *manlevar* has been attracted into the semantic orbit of Occ. *caplevar* 'to seesaw', although the former still retains the value 'to borrow' in Gascon, Languedocien, and Limousin, as well as Catalan.

[10]Gili y Gaya (1947), s.v. "caulevar, caulevado," cites Palet's [1604] gloss 'soubslever', a bit of information from which one may infer that the word was available already in the medieval-Renaissance period.

[11]Darmesteter (1894:50ff.) goes to great lengths to differentiate true *bahuvrihi*, or possessive compounds (e.g., Lat. *longimanus*, Sp. *boquiabierto, perniquebrado*, Pr. *bocatortz*), from juxtaposed expressions characterized by synecdoche (e.g., Pr. *golabadata*, Fr. *rouge-gorge, blanche-queue*). He bases his argument on presence or absence of internal agreement; the very lack of concord is his main criterion for "ellipsis." His argument remains useful primarily in a morphologically oriented analysis aiming to establish watertight categories or taxonomies of compound formations.

[12]Gonzalo de Berceo offers a neat example of the cleric steeped in Latin who was capable of carrying over Latin compounds and constructions into his literary activities: *captener*, used in his poetry, and "eres misa cantan," perhaps on model of *locumtenent, terretenant*. Berceo also had access to words imported from France by pilgrims. His dialect, entering into Old Navarro-Aragonese, was not immune from Catalan influences.

Spanish the Latin theme vowel *-i-* (*boquiabierto*) was pressed into widespread service, appearing in borrowings: *maniobrar* (from Fr. *manœuvrer*) and novel formations: *perniquebrado, -ar*; (1607) *maniatado, -ar*.

Mid. French seems to have had no such learnèd favorite, although the 16th century marked a significant increase in V + N structures. Rabelais was responsible for coining *nasitort* 'stinking'. His rich harvest of newly devised compounds was based on both Classical and vernacular patterns. His innovations with vernacular elements include V + N (*pissechiens, grippeminaud*); V + Adv (*pissefort*); V + V (*torchelorgne*); and three-part formations (*chienlit* ← *chie en lit, soufflemboyau* ← *souffle en boyau*). In his study of Rabelais's (and Gué de Balzac's) word formation, Spitzer (1910) makes no specific mention of N + V examples, with the possible exception of *fretinfretailler*, one of fifty-five synonyms for 'to make love'. Ronsard directly calqued Greek OV-structured adjectives with French elements, e.g., *jour-apporte* (cf. Gk. *phōsphóros*, Lat. *lūcifer*); his *aile-porte*, as used in the first edition of one poem, was later replaced with the less exotic phrase "qui le sup(p)orte." Ronsard's experimentation went beyond N + V to include Adj + Adj (*blanc-vermeil, aigre-doux*); Adj + Pres Ptc (*aigu-tournoyant, triste-riant, clair-voyant*); and, most frequently, V + N (*forge-foudre, rase-terre*). The Pléiade's penchant for adjectival use of V + N compounds scarcely outlasted the 16th century. [13] During the next, most of the product of earlier lexical experimentation was eliminated during the explicit codification of literary French and the birth of the Académie Française.

Sp. *cultilatiniparla* (a derisive tag, coined by Quevedo and echoed today in, e.g., Cat. *llatinoparlant* 'speaker of Latin') illustrates the same vein of relatively untrammeled individual artistic creation. It is perhaps to be expected that much of the 16th-c. experimentation would be doomed to failure, at least partially in reaction to excess. Occitan, and particularly Gascon, 16th-c. production can be roughly approximated through examination of a few excerpts in verse and prose from Lafont's *Anthologie des baroques occitans*, where casual inspection finds, not N + V compounding per se, but (i) proliferation of N + A compounding: *barbagelat* 'white-bearded' (Lafont: "un trait de langage populaire"), *córherit* 'heart-stricken', *córnatrèits* (lit.) 'with pulled horn', *gautacousut* ('tight-mouthed'), *maucròcs* ('tightfisted, tightwad' [?], 'main crochue'), *[unglas] pauhicadas* (lit. 'with pierced nails'); (ii) an occasional Adv + V formation (Gasc. *hòranisar, mauhasèc*); and (iii) V + N sequences, often endowed with adjectival function (*peta-òsses* 'bone-breaker', 'brise-os'; *curamaisons* 'thief' [?], lit. 'house-cleaner').

---

[13] A brief summary of artistic Mid. French N + V compounds: *aile-porte, cœur-rongeant, cuisse-né, feu-soufflant, feu-vomissant, jour-apporte, lierre-porte, montagne-porte, nuit-volant, Ourse-gardant, signeportant* (*signiferant*), and *terre-né*.

N + V compounding continued to occur in pre–17th-c. Western Romance, however infrequently, as long as it was supported by vestiges of OV syntax in Med. Latin and the vernaculars, through use of Med. Latin as a chancery language, and through the resultant possibility of interlanguage borrowings and calques. Overlooked amid the renewal of Classical compound types that began in the 14th century—since it was at no time identified with Cl. Latin—ongoing N + V compounding found substantial analogical support from other compound patterns with nouns as their first constituents. It was available then, even as it occurs sporadically today throughout the French dialects: the *FEW* offers eloquent testimony, visible in the modern corpus of Chapter 4.

Old French seems to have exploited the pattern in more ways than Old Provençal (or is the scheme simply better attested?). In Occitan, where the pattern proliferated, no more significant percentage of early examples can be found than in any of the other medieval and Renaissance vernaculars. When we consider regularity of derivation, even the substantial Old French corpus begins to look less impressive, however, despite a higher number of isolated noun and verb elements than in Old Provençal, Old Catalan, or Old Spanish. The medieval Spanish corpus, e.g., shows variation mostly in the nominal element. This is not exploitation in which one or both elements of a compound can be replaced. But such exploitation, taken in connection with Séguy's "enchaînement associatif", allows us to capture the essence of analogy. Sixteenth-century artistic innovation (essentially a newer wave of borrowing from Latin and Greek) may help to explain later literary creations but remains powerless to account for continued survival in spoken Occitan and Catalan, in northern Spanish dialects, and in nonstandard dialects of Northern French. To paraphrase an old saying, borrowings and lexico-stylistic innovations may propose, but the language itself will eventually dispose, on the basis of its own internal design and predisposition.

4

MODERN EVIDENCE OF MANŪTENĒRE

1. KEY NOTIONS IN THE MODERN CORPUS

Modern N + V compounds from the four target Romance languages, as presented here, are spread among twenty informal lexical fields. Within each onomasiological category, evidence from French, Occitan, Catalan, and Spanish is grouped separately so as to facilitate cross-reference with Appendices A–D; lexical items within each category are listed alphabetically rather than being numbered as they were in Chapter 3, section 2.

    A   Plants
    B   Animals
    C   Farm Labor/Animal Husbandry
    D/E Terrain/Elements
    F/G Feudalism/Warfare/Politics
    H/I Administration/Law
    J   Food
    K   Trades (Technical/Nautical)
    L   Religion
    M/N Medicine, including Veterinary
    O   Mental and Emotional Processes
    P   Sad/Embarrassed
    Q   Angry/Hurt
    R   Curious/Worried
    S   Physical Description
    T   Tumble/Turn Over/Die
    U   Personal Violence
    V   Physical Movement
    W   Sports and Pastimes
    X   Everyday Life
    Y   Miscellaneous

A. Plants

A. FRENCH (Plants)
    champbrûler, champler 'to frost' (of vines)

A. OCCITAN (Plants)
    came-tòrse 'to break a leg, a plant stem'
    cap-seca-s 'to dry' (from the top inward)
    chanlevâ 'to crack open a walnut husk'
    colormudar, coulou-muda 'to change color' (of ripening wheat)
    còrmanar 'to spoil, rot' (of wood)
    còrsecar, co(r)-seca 'to dry thoroughly' (of chestnuts)
    florcurar, flourcura 'to wither'
    Gasc. *eslou-passà* 'to lose its flowers, wither' (of a plant)
    Gasc. *terre-pouyrì* 'to rot in the ground'
    Also: *mourado* 'layered vine', 'provin'

A. CATALAN (Plants)
    colltorçar, -tòrcer 'to wither, spoil; bend under its own weight' (of wheat)
    collvinclar-se 'to bend over onto the stem' (of a flower)
    corgelar 'to freeze, harden from the cold' (of plants); 'freeze, even the innermost
        part'
    corsecar 'to dry out from the cold' (of fruit)
    pellobrir-se 'to crack, burst open' (of fruit)
    pellpartir-se idem
    pelltrencar-se 'to excoriate, crack'
    salpassar (bot.) 'hyssop'

B. Animals

B. FRENCH (Animals)
    chanfrein 'bit' (of a bridle)
    chateni 'to stop a bull by the horns'
    corni-, cornu-fiker 'to butt with a horn'
    encoubaissé 'to tie up an animal with the end of the halter'
    (ils) s'épatvoulant '(they) squawk and flap their wings' (of chickens in a henhouse)
    gourmacher 'to ruminate'
    konbrüšé 'to scratch with a horn'
    patevôler 'to flutter around in circles' (of chickens)
    pativoler 'to flutter the wings and push with the feet' (of chickens)
    peaumuer 'to molt'
    Also: *nerf-férure* 'equine inflammation of the tendon'
        nerfrē 'limping; incapable of walking' (of an animal)
        vermoulu 'worm-eaten'

B. OCCITAN (Animals)
    Prov. *chanfrin* 'part of horse's nose from forehead to nostrils'

Gasc. *corne-bachà* 'to lower the horns, pull on the yoke with lowered head' (of an ox)
Gasc. *corne-quilhà* 'to raise the horns'
culhebét 'horse's kick', *culhebeta* 'to jump'
lanaperdent lit. 'wool-losing'
mournifla 'to sneak, snoop around'
mourre-finta 'to sniff hesitantly'
mourre-senti 'to sniff' (cf. *cu-senti*)
Gasc. *pè-jùgne, -juntà* 'to join the feet, gallop'
pelbufar 'to have a dull coat' (of cattle)
pèlmudar, pèu-, pèt-mudà, péumia 'to molt'
pernabatre 'to fall with the hoofs in the air', 'tomber les quatre fers en l'air'
Gasc. *péu-passà* 'to molt'
plu(mo)muda, plooumiar 'to molt'
recapvirar 'to rear' (of horses)
Gasc. *sère-birà-s* 'to fall from horseback'
sole-batut 'footsore' (of cattle)
Also: *foul-fina, -sina*; *mourfina, moufida*; *soulfina, -una* 'to sniff hesitantly'

B. CATALAN (Animals)
   camatrencar 'to break a(n animal's) leg(s)'
   colltrencar-se 'to die a violent death from a fall, etc.' (Pyrenees, said of animals)
   pèl-mudar 'to molt' (hair, skin, or feathers)
   Also: *colltort* (ornith.) 'wryneck'
         pernagirat 'having the front legs toward the flanks'
         potaferit 'wounded in one leg'

B. SPANISH (Animals)
   alicortar 'to cut off the wings'
   cachipegar 'to copulate' (of dogs)
   pelechar 'to molt'
   pelmudar 'to molt' (of animals); *per-, premudar* 'to molt' (of mammals and birds)

C. Farm Labor/Animal Husbandry

C. FRENCH (Farm Labor/Animal Husbandry)
   bafumer 'to fumigate'
   bastorner 'to beat (nut or fruit) trees'
   chaufumer 'to douse a crop with lime'
   cubassieu 'to distort, mix'
   embaufumer 'to stink (out)'
   encauchumer 'to spread lime'
   maintint, mantagne 'handle of a flail'
   mēpa, māpá 'master herdsman's third helper'; 'sustenance for Alpen herdsmen'
   pallemener 'to scrape soil around vines with a shovel'
   paufichonner 'to tear to shreds'; *pauficher* 'to work clumsily'
   pelleverser 'to shovel'

tarabuta 'to uncover the base of a wall or tree'
terrebécher 'to hoe'
terrejeter 'to plant in rows', 'labourer par la culture en planches'

C. OCCITAN (Farm Labor/Animal Husbandry)

Béar. *amaligá* 'to assemble s.th. into a handful'
cambira 'to dig up a field'
cap-, cha-, tso-batre 'to shell (wheat, corn) with a stick'
cap-bordelar, -bourdilha 'to roll a cask, pushing either end alternately'
capescodre 'to shell (wheat, corn) with a flail, beat (nut trees)'
Gasc. *cap-hen(d)e* 'to split the head (of a stalk)'
cap-herrà 'to shoe one end of a stick'
cap-pouda 'to knock off the head'
Gasc. *care-birà* 'to open new cuts on a pine tree'
Gasc. *cot-juntà* 'to join two objects'
Gasc. *cot-ligà* 'to bind the neck'
Gasc. *cot-panà* 'to twist a beast's head toward the shoulder, so as to tame it'
coubeissà 'to lower the head, deliver a blow in the neck to make the head drop'
Béar. *coude-poudà* 'to crop the tail'
Gasc. *cour-bagna* (hort.) 'to layer, fix a vine shoot in the ground so as to create a new vinestock'
courcreva 'to press a person or animal against a wall so as to flatten or stifle him/it'
Gasc. *croustemaligà* 'to crisscross'
Gasc. *cu-bouchà* 'to rub, clean the insides of a container'
Gasc. *cu-pédasá* 'to protect a ewe from the ram'
Gasc. *cu-toune* 'to shear a sheep around the anus'
Béar. *entermaligá* 'to bind several sheaves'
Périg. *fiau-tirâ* 'to string barbed wire'
florcurar, flourcura (hort.) 'to set'
Gasc. *mâ-ligà, manouliâ* 'to bind the hands, gather into a handful'
marfoundre la terro 'to plow out of season'
manobrar 'to maneuver, handle carelessly'
mourfica (hort.) 'to layer, fix a vine shoot in the ground so as to create a new vinestock'
Gasc. *obre-léche* 'ringing of church bells, signaling an end to work in the fields'
Gasc. *palabentà* 'to winnow with a shovel'
palaficar, paufica 'to plant in the earth, push with a pole'
pala-versar 'to dig with a shovel'
palavirar, pale-bira 'to shovel, turn over with a shovel'
panminjant '(long-term) day-laborer'
pèiraficar 'to pave'
pèu-bouli, pèt-bouri 'to scald'
pot-ligà 'to bridle (a horse)'
Gasc. *sou-coélhe* 'to harvest with the sun'
Gasc. *sòulhebà* 'to remove surface dirt', 'lever un sol'
Also: *caus-fourna, chaus-fournâ* 'to make lime'
     palabessar 'to dig with a shovel' (*pala-bes*)
     pala-grilha idem (*palagrilh* 'double-pointed shovel')

pala-herrà idem (*palahèr* 'iron shovel')
Gasc. *pèyrecayrà* 'to place dressed stones in the corner of a piece of masonry work'

C. CATALAN (Farm Labor/Animal Husbandry)

capalçar 'to raise the head, raise one end of an object'; (dial.) 'to plough sideways'
capficar (hort.) 'to layer, fix a vine shoot in the ground so as to create a new vinestock'
capllevar 'to pull up plants'
capterrar 'to cover a haystack's thatch with dirt, place stones atop a dry-wall for reinforcement'
mamposteria 'dry-wall, stonework'
maniobrar 'to manipulate, work with the hands'; *manobre* 'laborer, day-worker'
mantega 'handle of the scourge'
mantornar 'to plough again'; (dial.) 'to patch clothing'
palafangar 'to dig with a *palafanga*'
Also: *aygua-baxant* (n.g.)
    capllaçar 'to tie a bull by the horns with a rope'
    capmallolar 'to prune the first offshoots of a vine'
    capmartellar 'to wield a hammer'
    manobrejar 'to toil as a day-worker'
    terraguixar 'to repair walls with *terraguix*'
    terraplenar 'to embank, fill in, terrace'

C. SPANISH (Farm Labor/Animal Husbandry)

cachipodar 'to prune'
camajuste 'ladder for picking olives'
mampostear 'to build a dry-wall of rubble or stones'; *mampuesto* 'rubble, rough stone'; *mamposteria* 'rubblework'
mancuspir 'to spit into one's hands and rub them together before taking hold of a tool'
maniobra 'bricklayer's materials'
maniobrar 'to work with the hands'
manobre 'hod-carrier'; *manobra* 'worker, peasant'; *manobrero* 'keeper of irrigation ditches'
mantorn(i)ar 'to plow a second time'
Also: *mampresar* 'to capture horses'
    mancordiar 'to tie à cow to a pole, with one end of the rope in one's hand'
    mancornar 'to join or yoke two things together'
    mancorniar 'to wrangle a bull'; *mancurniar* 'to tie a cow's leg before milking it'
    terraplenar 'to embank, fill in, terrace'

D./E. Terrain/Elements

D./E. FRENCH (Terrain/Elements)

bècbassieu [*sic*] 'to meander'
chantourner idem

(geler) à pierre fendre 'to freeze'
tarmené 'to rumble'

D./E. OCCITAN (Terrain/Elements)
  Gasc. *aiga-pich* 'small waterfall'
  aigo-pendent 'slope of a hill'
  aigo-vers 'water divide'
  pèirabatre, peirobate 'to hail'
  Gasc. *(tourrà) a pèira-héner* 'to freeze', '(geler) à pierre fendre'
  Also: *l'aigo pren la cap-baissado* 'the water level is falling'
       jon-gibrá 'to freeze'

D./E. CATALAN (Terrain/Elements)
  aiguabarrejar-se 'to converge' (of two rivers)
  aiguabatent 'surface or slope exposed to rain'; *-batut* 'rain-soaked field'
  aiguabatre 'to run, beat down' (of water), 'to rain'
  aiguadeix 'alluvium, alluvial deposit'
  aigualleix idem
  aiguaneix 'source of a spring'
  aiguavés, -vers, -vertent 'slope' (of terrain or roof)
  aygua-regant 'irrigable [land]'
  terra-lleva 'land for growing fruit'
  Also: *aigues-juntes* 'confluence of two rivers'
       terratrémer 'to shake' (of the earth)

D./E. SPANISH (Terrain/Elements)
  aguallevado 'dredging (of a riverbed)', 'mountain gorge'
  Also: *aguas vertientes* 'watershed, water running downhill'

F./G. Feudalism/Warfare/Politics

F./G. FRENCH (Feudalism/Warfare/Politics)
  lieutenant 'lieutenant'
  tranche-maçonné (heraldry) 'se dit d'un écu dont une division est en maçonnerie'

F./G. OCCITAN (Feudalism/Warfare/Politics)
  loc-tenent 'lieutenant'

F./G. CATALAN (Feudalism/Warfare/Politics)
  caragirat, caravirat 'turn-coat'
  fementit 'traitor'
  lloctinent 'lieutenant'
  mantenents (heraldry) 'two lions or other animals that support s.th.'

F./G. SPANISH (Feudalism/Warfare/Politics)
  lugarteniente 'lieutenant'
  mampara 'protection'
  maherir 'to designate for military service'

Also: *terraplenar* 'to embank, fill in'

H./I. Administration/Law

H./I. FRENCH (Administration/Law)
banjointant 'contiguous, abutting on' (of territories or communes)
mainlevée 'withdrawal of a legal seizure'
mainmise 'legal confiscation'
mamborner 'to direct a legal ward; govern'
part-prenant 'legatee, one who has a share in an inheritance'

H./I. OCCITAN (Administration/Law)
bèn-tenent 'landowner'
Gasc. *coùmpte-dà* 'debt'
Gasc. *coumpte-fina* 'to finish paying a debt, close an account'
cu-bagnadei 'ordinance fixing punishment (at Bayonne, 1317–1789) similar to the
    dunking stool'
cu-labadé idem (currently, 'public baths at Bayonne')
Gasc. *débe-dà* 'debt'
Gasc. *ha déute-pague* 'to pay cash'
Gasc. *mâ-méte* 'to confiscate'
manlevar, malheba 'to borrow, be guilty of extortion'
Gasc. *sosmalhebar* 'donner, obtenir mainlevée'; *sosmalheute* 'mainlevée'
tèrratenent 'landowner'; Périg. (adj.) 'adjoining another property'
Gasc. *terre-passà* 'to overstep a boundary, go beyond one's rights'
tèrre-tièn 'adjoining land'

H./I. CATALAN (Administration/Law)
caplleuta 'bail'; *capllevar* (13th c.) 'to post bail, free'
casatinent 'householder'
claupresó 'emprisonment'
fefa(ci)ent 'authentic'
manllevar 'to borrow'; *manlleuta* 'bail; loan'
manlleutar 'to guarantee, to post bond, bail'
marmessor (13th-c.) 'testamentary executor'
terratinent 'landowner'
Also: *capbrevar* 'to make an inventory or contract; measure lands'

H./I. SPANISH (Administration/Law)
capleta 'bail'; *capletar* 'to jail for debt'
fehaciente 'authentic'
manlebar 'to borrow, guarantee a debt'
mansesor, marmesor 'executor'
poderdante 'constituent'
poderhabiente 'attorney, proxy'
reivindicar 'to claim one's rights, lay hold of'
terrateniente 'landowner'

J. Food

J. FRENCH (Food)
>   *croulever* 'to rise and separate from the crumb' (of the breadcrust); (*pain*) *croulevé*
>   'bread with separated crust'
>   *dékafiker* 'to husk, hull (nuts or fruit)'
>   *escalbotter* 'to shell peas'
>   *saupiquet* 'spicy sauce or stew', *saupiqueter* 'to give a spicy taste'
>   *saupoudrer* 'to sprinkle (with salt, etc.)'
>   *taramatsié* 'to chew'

J. OCCITAN (Food)
>   *aigo-pico* 'mineral water, sparkling water'
>   *barbo-leca, -lequa* 'to lick one's chin, eat voraciously'
>   *esse corfalit* 'to be hungry'
>   *se crousto-leva, crouste-lheba* 'to detach from the crumb' (of the breadcrust)
>   *fial-frexa, fiel-freja* 'to ravel, be stringy' (of cloth or foods); Périg. *fialfros* 'stringy'
>   *gorjo-vira, gorje-bira* 'to eat gluttonously'
>   *pahourra* 'to gorge on bread'
>   *salicar (se)* 'to savor one's food'
>   *salpicar, saupicá* 'to sprinkle with salt'
>   *salposcar* idem
>   *salprene, saupren(dr)e* 'to absorb salt' (of meat)
>   Gasc. *saugrenade* 'ragoût', 'saugrenée' (condiment of peas, beans, etc.)
>   Gasc. *saupoudra* idem
>   Also: *cambavirotat* 'poisonous mushroom'

J. CATALAN (Food)
>   *colltrencat* 'sour wine'
>   *salp(r)endre (salprémer)* 'to cover with salt, conserve'
>   *salpi(s)car* 'to sprinkle with salt, spatter'
>   Also: *caragirats* 'black-eyed beans'
>   *salpebrar* 'to conserve with salt and pepper'

J. SPANISH (Food)
>   *salpicar* 'to splash, sprinkle'
>   Also: *aguamelar* 'to sweeten (water)'
>   *salcochar* 'to boil or cook in salted water'
>   *salpimentar* 'to season with salt and pepper'
>   *salpresar* 'to preserve with salt'

K. Trades (Technical/Nautical)

K. FRENCH (Trades [Technical/Nautical])
>   *champlever* (engraving term) 'to remove material around a pattern, leaving it
>   raised'
>   *chanfreiner, chanfrer* 'to bevel'
>   *chavirer* 'to capsize'

colporter 'to peddle'
eau donner 'to soak before adding indigo' (step in dying process)
étanfiche 'slender column in the masonry of a bay window'
manœuvrer 'to maneuver'
pattefiche (woodworking) 'triangular nail'
Also: *tientmain* 'handhold'

K. OCCITAN (Trades [Technical/Nautical])
Gasc. *(à) barre-lùua* '(to) raise with a lever'
blaugetar, blauguela 'to incrust a fine strip of gold, silver, or copper in a metallic surface', 'damasquiner'
cant-birà 'to set edgewise'
cap-aussà (woodworking) 'to raise'
capbilhar, cap-bilha, capilia 'to join two pieces of wood with dowels'
cap-hautà 'to raise'
Gasc. *cap-lissà* 'to join, link (ends), sharpen'
cap-pountà (woodworking) 'to raise a scaffolding'
Prov. *chamfrenat* 'chamfer'
chanfrena, chamfrenar 'to bevel', 'chanfreiner'
chanlevâ 'to remove material around a pattern, leaving it raised, before applying enamel', 'champlever'
chantournâ, tsan-, cantourná 'to cut out along a given pattern', 'chantourner'
chavirâ 'to capsize'
còlportar 'to peddle, carry on one's shoulders'
Gasc. *cu-boussà* 'to stanch a leak, close up the bottom of a container'
cu-ligà 'to bind up the bottom of a sack'
matrifusar, motrifusá 'to mix good stuffs with poorer merchandise'
tal(h)-, tai-vira 'to ruin the edge (of a knifeblade)'
Périg. *trancho-daurâ* 'to gild the edges of books', 'dorer sur tranches'

K. CATALAN (Trades [Technical/Nautical])
capalçar 'to raise one end of an object'
cap(i)alçat 'top of a door frame'
capfermar 'to attach a cord to a fixed point'
caplliga 'oarlock'
collportar 'to carry on one's shoulders'
mampara 'inner door, folding screen'; *mamparo* 'bulkhead'
mantega 'handle of the scourge'
Also: *capserrat* 'angle of two walls; protractor'

K. SPANISH (Trades [Technical/Nautical])
botalima 'inefficient bootblack'
capialzar 'to bend the face of an arch or lintel into an outward slope'; *capialzado* 'curve or bend of an arch'
caulevar 'to lift, support'; *-levador* 'supporting'
mampara 'screen, small door'; *mamparo* 'bulkhead'
manobrar 'to work with the hands'

L. Religion

L. OCCITAN (Religion)
   camalhegue 'new mother's prayer of thanks'
   careimentrâ 'to enter the period of Lent'
   Dieu-Trouva (proper name of a folktale hero from Provence)
   Gasc. *diu-bedë* 'raising, elevation of the Host'
   manstraire (se faire) 'to be blessed at church' (of mothers after childbirth)
   Gasc. *misso-canta* 'to be a priest'

L. CATALAN (Religion)
   carnestoltes 'the last (3) day(s) to eat meat before Lent'
   clauficat 'nailed'
   creuclavat 'nailed to the cross'
   salpassar 'container for holy water'

L. SPANISH (Religion)
   carnestolendas, garrastolendas 'Carnival'
   misacantano 'priest'
   Also: Andal., Mex. *cantamisano* 'priest'

M./N. Medicine, including Veterinary

M./N. FRENCH (Medicine, including Veterinary)
   embaufumé 'ill, swollen'
   nerf-férure 'equine inflammation of the tendon'
   pore-levet 'male midwife'
   se san(g)-glacer 'to catch pleurisy, be hot and cold'; *sangglacé* 'chill'
   sang mêlai 'illness said to be caused by a panic';
   sang-meslé 'blood-curdling' (of a fright)
   se sanzevra 'to catch cold'; *avé un sanggivre* 'to be in a cold sweat'; *sanzáivre* 'fever
      with chills'
   Also: *gras-fondu* 'emaciated'
      nerf failli 'tendon du cheval qui diminue vers le pli du genou'
      nerf-foulure 'equine sprain of the tendon'
      solbatu 'footsore'; *sole battue* 'wound on sole of horse's hoof'

M./N. OCCITAN (Medicine, including Veterinary)
   aboudenfli 'to bruise'
   aiga-prene 'to catch cold from humidity or sweat'
   Béar. *ale-bate* 'to feel unwell'
   Béar. *bente-boueita, bénte-boeytà* 'to disembowel, gore, purge'
   came-pouda-s 'to break one's leg'
   came-tòrse 'to break a leg or plant stem'
   cap-préne-s 'to develop a headache'
   Lim. *carfouladis* 'sprain'
   carn-matar 'to wound, bruise'
   char-mountâ 'to heal' (of a wound)

Gasc. *coechipoudá-se* 'to break one's thigh (bone)'
còlcrebar 'to break the neck, die'
còltòrcer, cot-torse 'to twist the neck'
co-bouri 'to be troubled by a physical ailment'
co-clabà 'to break the heart'
co-mourì 'to faint, feel unwell'
còrcachar 'to squeeze, press the heart'
còrcrebar, cor-, co-crebà 'to break the heart; become exhausted, die'
cot-birà 'to twist the neck'
cot-crouchì idem
co-transì idem, 'pierce the heart'
Gasc. *cu-bagna* 'to bathe'
Gasc. *cu-labà* idem
enchifrenà 'to have a stuffy nose'
Gasc. *frèbe-passà* 'to shake with fever'
(es)gorrobàte 'to be delirious' (of a sick person)
Gasc. *goute-préne* 'to contract gout'
Gasc. *gouto-herì-s* 'to be numb with cold, chilled to the bone'
graisfondre (se) 'to become overheated, sweat profusely'
marfondre, -fondir, etc. 'to catch cold, lose weight'
Gasc. *nas-tapà* 'to catch cold'
Gasc. *oélh-birà* 'to squint; die'
Gasc. *oélh-perì* 'to blind'
Gasc. *oélh-tirà* idem
pelferit 'numbed'
sang-bégut 'numbed with cold'
Gasc. *sang-bourri, sang-bourrit* 'to overheat' (of the blood)
sanglaçar, songloçá, sanglaceja, etc. 'to cause a sudden, dangerous drop in temperature'; *sanglaçat* 'pleurisy'
Also: *chaupica* 'to sprain one's ankle'
    Viv. *ner-ferodure* '(equine) inflammation of the tendon', 'nerf-férure'
    Viv. *ner-fouladuro* '(equine) sprain of the tendon', 'nerf-foulure'

M./N. CATALAN (Medicine, including Veterinary)
ayreferir-se 'to suffer an attack of apoplexy, be incapacitated'; *aireferit* 'incapacitated, lamed, suffering from apoplexy'
claupassat 'stricken by illness; pierced by a nail'
collgirada 'sprain, dislocation of the neck'
cuixatrencar 'to break one's leg', *cuixatrencat* 'having a broken leg'
greixfondre 'to lose weight'
morfondre, marfondre, marfondir 'to waste away, lose one's strength'; *morfonada* 'dead of consumption'
(arch.) *sangfondre* 'to flush, overeat'
sangtrair 'to bruise, get bruised'
Also: *carn-esquixat* 'torn muscle'
carnfu(g)it 'bruised flesh'
sangprés 'coagulation'
sangtrait 'bruise'

M./N. SPANISH (Medicine, including Veterinary)
   perniquebrar 'to break the leg(s)'
   Also: *mamporro* 'bump, contusion'

O. Mental and Emotional Processes

O. OCCITAN (Mental and Emotional Processes)
   acabourrá , encabourrí 'to be stubborn'
   Gasc. *bouque-barrà* 'to remain silent'; *bouque-barrat* 'discreet'
   Gasc. *capbiroulète* 'scatterbrained'
   Gasc. *cap(i)lheban* 'uppity'
   Lang. *carnabal* 'harebrained', 'joker'
   còr-dòldre 'to faint, be overcome with emotion'
   Gasc. *cu-bouhà* 'to brag, incite against s.o.'
   Gasc. *gay-hasén* 'pleasing'
   Auv. *incorovira(t)* 'obstinate'
   Béar. *(re)mentábe(r)* 'to mention, cite, remember, call'
   morlevar 'to show off, be vain, brag'
   mourlecá 'to show off'; Nice *mourre-lec* 'gourmand, dilettante'
   Gasc. *nas-lhebà* 'to be arrogant, raise one's nose'; *nas-levat* 'insolent woman'
   pellecar 'to spoil' (a child or pet)
   Gasc. *pèt-eslà-s* 'to swell with pride'
   sangbeure, sangveure 'to desire ardently'
   sangpausa 'to calm'
   Gasc. *sère-birat, -biroû* 'deranged'
   Also: *pè-herrà, perrà* 'to plant one's feet in the ground, stand fast'

O. CATALAN (Mental and Emotional Processes)
   capfilar 'to ponder over'
   capguardarse 'to foresee or prevent a mishap, notice'
   caragirar 'to change one's mind'
   cor-doldre 'to be overcome with emotion'
   corprendre 'to stir one's heart, be moved'
   culbufar 'to give bad advice'
   feina-fuig 'lazy'
   fer corcruix 'to be compassionate'

P. Sad/Embarrassed

P. OCCITAN (Sad/Embarrassed)
   Béar. *ale-bacha* 'to be humiliated'
   boudenflar, -ifla, bauduf(l)a 'to be sad, cry'
   cap-bacha, -baissa 'to lower one's head, be ashamed'
   Gasc. *cu-, cuou-bacha* 'to crouch, humiliate oneself'
   Gasc. *cu-barrà* 'to keep silent'
   lengue-plegà 'to keep silent'

P. CATALAN (Sad/Embarrassed)
  capbaixarse 'to cower, abase oneself'

Q. Angry/Hurt

Q. OCCITAN (Angry/Hurt)
  chaplavar 'to raise one's voice' (Béar. *labe-cap* 'reprimand')
  pellevar (se), *peu-leba* 'to get riled, angry'

Q. CATALAN (Angry/Hurt)
  corferir 'to afflict, cause pain'
  cortrencar 'to suffer, cause pain'
  ullprès 'disliked, inconsiderate'
  Also: *cornafrat* 'wounded in the heart'

R. Curious/Worried

R. FRENCH (Curious/Worried)
  ensangmêler 'to be troubled'
  morfondre 'to mope, fret'
  sangtourner 'to be bothered, afraid'
  tenduement 'ennui, melancholy'
  Also: *corfoundut* '(emotionally) moved'
       sanmu idem

R. OCCITAN (Curious/Worried)
  aigatrebolar 'to be agitated'
  cap-mounta 'to get worried'
  caravirar 'to become upset'
  clauhicàn 'indiscreet'
  Gasc. *co-passà* 'to be surprised, dismayed'
  còrfalir, cor-fa(i)lhi 'to faint, quiver with emotion'
  còrfendre, co-héne 'to break the heart'
  còrferir, co-heri 'to trouble, move'
  còrfondre 'to melt (the heart)'
  còrvirar, co-bira 'to upset one's stomach'
  Gasc. *co-sarrà* idem
  Gasc. *co(r)s-passa(r)* 'to oppress'
  cuolfregar, cuou-, quieu-, cu-regà 'to quiver, tremble, become agitated'
  Gasc. *cu-senti* 'to be indiscreet, spy on'
  Landes *desmoumbirà* 'to trouble'
  pè(d)batre 'to shiver, become agitated'
  Gasc. *pè-hican* 'indiscreet'
  Gasc. *pè-picà* 'to be impatient'
  Gasc. *póu-herit* 'fear-stricken'
  Gasc. *sang-birà* 'to upset, be troubled'
  Gasc. *sang-bouri, sang-boure* 'to be impatient'

sang-dévorant 'restless'
Gasc. *sangtradi* 'to surprise, render speechless'
Gasc. *sang-transi* idem
Also: *aqueferar* 'to be worried'

R. CATALAN (Curious/Worried)
capficar-se 'to worry too much about something'; *capficat* 'preoccupied, worried'
capgirar 'to bother, upset'
corcaure 'to lose one's nerve, lose heart'
corcorcar-se 'to be consumed with worry'
corfondre 'to become confused'
corglaçar-se 'to be frightened'
corlligar 'to fail (in one's nerve)'
cornuar-se idem, 'have a fainting spell'
corsecar 'to worry, fade away'
culmenejar 'to snoop around'
greixfondre 'to worry excessively'
sangcremar-se 'to become impatient'
sang-girar 'to irritate, become irritated'
sangglaçar-se 'to take fright'; *sang-glaçat* 'indecisive'
terramanejar 'to meddle, interfere'
Also: *capmassar-se* 'to worry'
    corfallit 'having lost one's nerve, lacking in courage'
    cormigrat 'very worried'

R. SPANISH (Curious/Worried)
Arag. *culmené* 'snoopy, meddling'

S. Physical Description

S. FRENCH (Physical Description)
billebarrer (intr.) 'to be striped or variegated'
bourenfler 'to swell'
boursouffler idem
chère en caillmachâ 'to fall to pieces'
embaufumé 'ill, swollen'
goulimacher 'to chew slowly'
gourmelai 'to speak between clenched teeth'
gournâcher 'to nibble, peck at' (without appetite)
pî-stant, stant-pî 'standing'
terre-né 'earthborn'
Also: *vermoulu* 'worm-eaten'

S. OCCITAN (Physical Description)
boudenflar, -ifla, bauduf(l)a 'to swell'
cap-enfla-s, -inla-s 'to swell' (of the head)
Gasc. *cap-eschaureya-se* 'to get disheveled (in the wind)'
cariboussa 'to be deformed, deform'

char-uflâ 'to swell'
Gasc. *cu-agusà* 'to dwindle to a point; swing one's butt in walking'
Gasc. *cu-dà* 'to turn one's back'
èl-traire 'to tear one's eyes away'
Prov. *s'empalaficar* 'to be petrified, remain immobile'; *empalaficat* 'immobile; pale
     with cold'
esgautirà 'to yawn'
espelferi 'to make the hair stand on end'
Rouerg. *espelofrit* 'hairy; weak'
Gasc. *gorgibirad* 'with a twisted mouth'
gorjo-bada 'to open one's mouth'
Gasc. *gorrebat* 'noisy'
goudenfla (*boudenflà* q.v.) 'to swell'; *-eslat* 'swollen'
Landes *goudeslà* idem
lenga-bira-s 'to trip over one's tongue, stutter'
lengue-bourrà-s idem
Gasc. *pèu-lia, se peulha* 'to tie one's hair'
Gasc. *péulissà* 'to comb, smoothe the hair'
Gasc. *pot-birà* 'to turn up one's lip, grimace'
Gasc. *prouhasent* 'comely'
sucapelar, suco-pela, -pola, supela 'to become bald'
en terre-estant 'during one's lifetime'

S. CATALAN (Physical Description)
barbapunyent, barbapunta 'starting to have a beard'
botinflar-se 'to swell', *boti(n)flat* 'swollen'
cappelar 'to lose one's hair'; *cappela* 'bald head', *capelat* 'bald'
corbategar 'to beat, palpitate' (of the heart)
llampferit 'struck by lightning'
manllevat 'false, out of place'
palplantar 'to stand tall and immobile'
pernabatent '(one) who hurries; death jerks'
solprès 'sunburned'
testavirar 'to turn s.o.'s head, make his head spin, make dizzy'
Also: *carnxancar-se* 'to feel bruised' (after a horseride)
     colltort 'wry-necked, with twisted neck'
     galta-inflat 'very fat'
     gordinfleta 'corpulent'
     morroaterrat 'with nose to the ground'
     solabatut 'tired, worn out'

S. SPANISH (Physical Description)
barbiponiente 'starting to grow a beard'
botinchau, botinflau 'swollen'
botinflón idem
carnistoltas 'one who is odd'
maherido 'trained, guided, skillful, well-disposed'

T. Tumble/Turn Over/Die

T. FRENCH (Tumble/Turn Over/Die)
bouleverser 'to tip, turn over'
canverser idem
caraviri idem
chambarder idem
chambouler 'to turn upside down, stumble'
champbouter 'to replace an object upside down'
cuboulé idem
culbonder idem
culbuter idem
culvéchi 'to tip, turn over'
cusoter 'to bounce an object around, bob it in the air'
cutemelé 'to tip, turn over'
es cutoûrner 'to move, agitate'
külpeta idem
sanveri 'to tip, turn over'
Also: *culberger* 'to tumble backwards'
    s'écalpatrer 'to fall face down, prone'

T. OCCITAN (Tumble/Turn Over/Die)
banc-leva 'to seesaw, topple, fall over'
borramesclar 'to upset, turn over'
boulouversa idem, 'bouleverser'
camba-buou 'to kick up one's heels while lying on the ground'
cambavirar, combobira, came-bira(-s) 'to trip, take a tumble, twist one's leg, faint'
cambira 'to upset, turn over', 'bouleverser'
can-lheba, canleuà, calleva 'to topple by one end or side'
capbilhar, cap-bilha, capilia 'to tumble headlong'
cap-bourdilha 'to tumble'
capgira(r), cagirà 'to turn around, twist one's neck, upset'
cap-leva, caplheba 'to tumble, seesaw, raise the end or head'
capvirar, chavira 'to turn the head, upset, turn upside down'
capvirolar, ca(m)biroula 'to tumble, roll, fall head first'
caravirar, coro-bira idem
coalevar, collebà, coude-lhebà idem
Gasc. *coullebá , cot-lhebà* 'to raise the head, cause to topple'
Gasc. *cu-bachà* 'to tumble, trip'
Gasc. *cu-lhebà* idem
cupela 'to raise the head, cause to topple'
Gasc. *empataligà-s* 'to trip, get tangled in s.th.'
Gasc. *estrem-birá* 'to overturn'
manlevar 'to tip over, seesaw'
Gasc. *moun(de)-birà, moumbirà* 'to upset, lose one's balance'
palavirar, pale-bira idem
pan-, pallevar, pelleba 'to raise a heavy object, tip over'
Gasc. *part-birà* 'to upset, turn over, move'
Gasc. *part-mudà* idem

patavira, pato-vira 'to die'
pè-lhebà 'to raise the foot, raise with a lever'
Gasc. *pèrnabatre, espernobate* 'to agitate the feet, fall with one's feet in the air, wriggle about, die'
Gasc. *perne-bira* 'to tumble, turn over'
pèu-vira, pétbira, petchibira idem
sengirar 'to turn upside down, upset'
sens-birà 'to change direction, turn upside down'
Also: *cabiroulá* 'to roll down'
       capbordonar 'to trip, tumble'
       caprodelar idem
       chalibourdounâ idem
       cu-plata-s 'to fall on one's butt'
       Gasc. *peyraherrà, peyrahemà* 'to set up a lever', 'prendre un point d'appui'
       viropatá 'to turn over, tumble, die'

T. CATALAN (Tumble/Turn Over/Die)
capficar 'to dive, sink, make s.o. fall headlong to the ground'
capgirar 'to turn upside down'
capitombar 'to fall headlong, tumble; make s.o. fall'
colltorçar, -tòrcer 'to die'
Also: *capgirellar* 'to turn somersaults'

U. Personal Violence

U. FRENCH (Personal Violence)
abastorner 'to beat someone with a stick'
bornifiker 'to slap in the face'
Pic. *bornifle* 'slap'
(é)c(h)ampoussi 'to chase out'
chatourne 'slap'
chéuplâ 'to step on'
chifrenel 'slap'
corbattre 'to fight'
gormenó 'to bother, worry, pester'
gour-, garfoler 'to press, bruise, damage, crush, sprain'
harlifiker 'to beat with a strap (*hart*)'
se keurpiller 'to take by the hair'
mornifler 'to slap, swat the nose'
puoutirar 'to pull by the hair'
Also: *champihtar* 'to tread on s.o.'s feet'

U. OCCITAN (Personal Violence)
cambalevar, comboleba 'to trip s.o.'
Lang. *càmo-coupà* 'to break s.o.'s leg'
Prov. *chi(f)farneou* 'blow to the head'
dza(m)bardzá 'to trample'
cambotira 'to trip s.o.'

camboviroula, combobiroula idem
cap-batre, chabatre, tsobatre 'to quarrel'
capmaçar, -massar(-se) 'to stun'
captorse 'to twist the neck'
charmenâ 'to fight'
corquichar, cour-, escol-quicha 'to put one's feet on the throat (of an opponent),
    oppress, squeeze, bruise'
cou-, cot-poudà 'to break one's neck'
courcreva 'to flatten or stifle'
còutrenca, cot-trenca, cottrinca 'to decapitate, cut the neck'
Gasc. *cu-laurà* 'to drag oneself on one's butt'
Lang. *gauto-bira* 'to slap'
gòrja-, gorjo-fendre 'to slit the throat'
gorjo-vira, guourjo-bira, gorye-bira 'to kill by twisting the neck'
Gasc. *gorrebàte, esgorrobàte* 'to rampage'
Gasc. *lengamanjar* 'to speak ill of, tear into s.o.'
Gasc. *lengue-passa* idem
Gasc. *mâ-ligà, manouliâ* 'to bind the hands, manacle'
mournifla 'to slap the face'
pellevar (se), pel-, peu-leba 'to pull the hair'
pel-, peu-, espel-tira idem, 'pull s.o. by his hair or clothes'
péu-tireja, póutireja 'to pull at from every side'
salpicar, saupicá 'to beat, give blows'
Gasc. *sang-barrejà* 'to spill blood, cut the throat'
sangoula, sangulha 'to pierce and let the blood flow out'
talafissâ, tolofissa 'to torment'
Also: *calpisar, caupisa, chaupica* 'to crush underfoot'

U. CATALAN (Personal Violence)
    captrencar 'to strike, hit (in the head)'
    capxafar, var. *capxifollar* 'to crack (the head)'
    copbatre 'to beat violently'
    corferir 'to knock down'
    espeltirar 'to pull by the hair'
    peulligar 'to bind the feet'
    ullcegar 'to make blind'

U. SPANISH (Personal Violence)
    carabirar 'to disfigure' (from Occitan)
    mamprender 'to subdue by hand'
    man(i)atar 'to manacle'
    manferir 'to injure badly'

V. Physical Movement

V. FRENCH (Physical Movement)
    se coderser 'to stand up, stand stiffly'
    es cutoûrner 'to move, agitate'

faire dzarvolá 'to spin a dancer, make her petticoats fly'
jambälou 'to waddle, roll from side to side'
quesauter 'to hop about'
santourner 'to turn an object over and over carelessly'
Also: *escalborder* 'to embark'

V. OCCITAN (Physical Movement)
acourbacha-s, s'acourbaissa 'to lower oneself'
Béar. *bie-passà* 'to exceed, go beyond'
came-boutà 'to place one's foot, straddle'
càmo-malhà 'to cross one's legs'
cap-(es)dressa 'to stand upright'
Gasc. *cap-houradà(-s)* 'to pierce the end'
cap-mounta 'to raise the end'
Gasc. *cap-plegà* 'to bend or lower one end'
Gasc. *cap-quilha(-s)* idem
corde-lhebà 'to excite'
corde-mià 'to lead'
coullebá, cot-lhebà 'to raise the head'
cuolfregar, cuou-, quieu-, cu-regà 'to wriggle'
Gasc. *cu-lhebà* 'to empty a bottle', 'lever le cul'
s'empalaficar 'to settle down in an armchair'
Gasc. *mantasta* 'to grope for', 'pêcher à tâtons avec la main'
panaussa 'to hike up one's skirt or petticoat'
panavelear 'to float'
pè(d)batre 'to flee'
pè-birà 'to turn one's ankle, walk with difficulty'
pè-branla 'to move'
Gasc. *ped-descaussa* 'to take off one's shoes'
Gasc. *pè-hica* 'to walk pigeon-toed, stand fast'
Gasc. *pè-hourè, -hourì, -hourà-s* 'to trample'
Gasc. *pè-mudà* 'to move one's foot'
pè-pica 'to run away'
Gasc. *pè-tirà-s* idem
Gasc. *pè-tòrse* 'to twist the foot'
Gasc. *pè-tourtejà* 'to limp'
Gasc. *pè-triscà* 'to cross the feet while walking', 'marcher en croisant les pieds'
Gasc. *pè-troulhà* 'to trample'
Gasc. *quilhe-courneja* 'to walk, cross at an angle'
Gasc. *sole-bàte* 'to beat one's feet on the road'
Gasc. *terre-pèrdre* 'to lose one's footing'; *terre-perdèn* 'losing one's footing'
Also: *mantusar, mantuza* 'to handle, continue'
      pè-hremar, -remà, -herrà 'to stand one's ground'
      (se) pelleba 'to remove, raise'

V. CATALAN (Physical Movement)
capalçar 'to raise one's head or one end of an object'
capbaixarse 'to lower one end of an object'
capllevar 'to raise one's head'

colltombar 'to fall (from the neck)'
copbatre 'to beat violently'
coresforçar-se 'to make an effort'
culremena 'one whose hips sway while walking'
pernabatre 'to agitate violently (one's legs)'
peucalcigar 'to trample'

V. SPANISH (Physical Movement)
    gullibaixar 'to keep one's glance lowered'

W. Sports and Pastimes

W. OCCITAN (Sports and Pastimes)
    Gasc. *cu-baysà* 'to kiss the bottom of a frying pan or kettle' (loser's penalty in
        certain rural games)
    Gasc. *mahà* 'to have the lead (in cards)'
    Gasc. *manteneire* 'croupier; one who bets'

W. SPANISH (Sports and Pastimes)
    Also: *sietedoblar* 'to double repeatedly'
        siete(l)levar 'to raise seven points' (in a card game); 'levar siete [puntos]'

X. Everyday Life

X. FRENCH (Everyday Life)
    blanc-poudrer 'to whiten with powder' (of face or hair)
    bourniger 'to work without accomplishing much'
    patte-mouille 'damp cloth for ironing'

X. OCCITAN (Everyday Life)
    aiga-, aigo-muda 'to change the water'
    biandant 'traveller'
    cambaligar, came-liga(-s), cambalia-s 'to wear garters'
    carabrina 'to roast badly, scorch'
    Gasc. *caso-heyt* 'homemade'
    Gasc. *causse-ha* 'to knit socks'
    clau-hicà 'to introduce a key'
    Gasc. *cuulavader* 'bidet'
    Gasc. *cubagnader* idem
    Gasc. *dit-poustà* 'to position'
    Gasc. *espeuligà* 'to wind thread/yarn on a spindle'
    fi(e)lbastar, fiéu-, fiu-basta, fiolbosta 'to baste'
    Gasc. *hioupassa* 'to darn socks'
    man-estrena 'to tip, make a New Year's gift'
    Gasc. *queha* 'affair, business'
    Also: *chafena* 'to put hay in one's hair'
        que-hà 'affair'

X. CATALAN (Everyday Life)
camalliga, -lligues 'garter'
claupassar 'to sew the edges of a shoe to hide the stitches'
filbastar 'to baste', *filbast(a)* 'basting'
vian(d)ant 'pedestrian, traveller'
Also: *lligacama, lligacames* 'garter'

X. SPANISH (Everyday Life)
camaliga 'garter'
viandante 'itinerant, stroller, tramp'
Also: *ligagamba* 'garter'

Y. Miscellaneous

Y. FRENCH (Miscellaneous)
à bout portant/touchant 'point-blank'
à chiffe-tirer 'in disagreement'
bulleménaou 'noisy'
estafiker 'to settle down into one spot'
maintenir 'to maintain'
microchanter 'to sing into a microphone'
taneuser 'to waste time'
Also: *saugrenu* 'preposterous'

Y. OCCITAN (Miscellaneous)
Lim. *balafincar* 'to send'
cap-tener, -tení, -tiene, chatení 'to support, defend, contain, stand firm'
captraire 'to complete, conduct, examine'
cla(u)fir, cli(a)fi 'to cover, fill'
còpténer 'to resist'
Gasc. *cos-préne* 'to solidify'
Gasc. *escù-goaytà* 'to watch from hiding'
Gasc. *hum-dà* 'to give off smoke, incense'
letroferit 'fond of letters, well-lettered'
ma(n)bour 'complicated situation'
sangoulhá 'to agitate s.th. in the water'
Also: *cu-herrà* 'to stabilize, affix firmly'

Y. CATALAN (Miscellaneous)
capbatre (n.g.) 'to beat' (?)
captenir(-se) 'to behave, work'
carafeixar 'to split, slice s.th. partially'; *cara-xafat, caraffexat* 'split'
corfondre 'to melt, even in the innermost parts'
cuixapenjant 'getting poor'
firandant 'merchant at fairs' (Cast. *feriante*)
lletraferit 'fond of letters, well-lettered'
mampendre 'to begin'
mantenir 'to maintain, support'; (refl.) 'to persevere'

pellforadar 'to pierce the skin'
tallgirar-se 'to dull, blunt'
terra-batut 'fallen on bad times (financially)'
ullferir 'to strike one's eye'
ullprendre 'to bewitch, fascinate, give the evil eye'

Y. SPANISH (Miscellaneous)
caltener 'to stand firm'
cornicantano 'cuckold'
cultilatiniparla 'euphuistic or macaronic speech, excessive use of Latin words and
    phrases'
mampesada 'nightmare' (cf. *pesadilla*)
mantener 'to maintain, provide with food, keep'
perniabrir (n.g.)
zaherir 'to reproach, criticize'
Also: *cultilatiniparla* 'euphistic or macaronic speech'
    cultiparlar 'to speak with affected elegance'

2. NOMINAL AND VERBAL ELEMENTS IN THE MODERN CORPUS

Absent from the noun and verb frequency charts below are those modern compounds
relegated to the section entitled "Other Compounds Approximating N + V Structure"
in Appendices A–D, e.g., Fr.-Pr. *sampilli* 'to tear into rags' (*cent* 'hundred' + *piller* 'to
plunder'), Sp. *sietedoblar* 'to double repeatedly' (*siete* [*veces*] 'seven [times]' + *doblar*
'to double'). Nominal elements of the forms listed under "Other" frequently coincide
with those of N + V compounds in the main lists, e.g., Fr. *blanc*, Occ. *cap*, *cul*, *pè*,
pèira. Reinforcing the already high incidence of *cap* evident in the Occitan noun tally
(Appendix B), there are five Occitan compounds with *cap* under "Other": *cabiroula*
'to roll down'; *capbordonar* 'to tumble', with a possible additional variant in
chalibourdounâ idem; *capfinar* 'to smoothe the hair'; and *caprodelar* 'to tumble'. Occ.
pala-grilha and *palaherrà*, designating activity with different types of shovels,
complement N + V–structured *pala-ficar* 'to plant in the earth', *-bentà* 'to winnow
(Occ. *ventar*) with a shovel', *-versar* 'to dig with a *palavèrs*', and *-virar* 'to turn over
with a shovel'. Under Catalan "Other" (Appendix C), forms with *cap* outnumber any
other nominal element, but *cap* varies in function, being nominal in *capllaçar* 'to tie
a bull by the horns with a rope' and in *capgirellar* 'to turn a somersault', but adjectival
in *capmartellar* 'to wield a hammer'. In the Spanish "Other" category (Appendix D),
man-cordiar 'to tie a cow to a pole', *mancorn(i)ar* 'to rope a bull', and *mampresar* 'to
catch horses' similarly augment the numerous instances of *mano* among Mod. Spanish
compounds.

Occasionally, nouns absent from the N + V corpus occur as elements of "Other" listings, e.g., French and Occitan reflexes of *calce(m)* 'heel' (through L. *calcāre*); or Cat. *pota* 'leg' (*potaferit* 'wounded in one leg'). French compounds with *gras-* or *nerf-* listed under "Other" appear to descend directly from the medieval and Renaissance examples analyzed in Chapter 3; other adjectives have been borrowed from neighboring Occitan dialects, e.g., Fr-Pr. *corfoundut* '(emotionally) moved'. From N + Adj compounds, which are abundant in the modern period, verbs are frequently derived by back-formation, e.g., Cat. *cappelar* 'to become bald' ← *cappellat* 'bald'. [1] Structurally, they remain of less immediate concern to N + V compounding than N + V Pres Ptc compounds such as Béar. *gay-hasén* 'pleasure-producing', although the latter are less likely to engender new infinitives. The individual elements of these N + Adj compounds have been excluded from separate nominal and verbal listings of French, Occitan, Catalan, and Spanish in the Appendices, and from tallies below. No attempt has been made to account systematically for all correspondences between N + V compounds and "Other" forms in the Appendices.

Problematic etymologies relegated to the "Other" category involve several opaque forms with possible N + V structure: Sp. *mamporro* 'bump' (containing *puerro* 'leek', according to *DCE[LC]*, s.v. "mano"), *mampurra* 'tip'. Under "Dubious" are classified several affixal formations to which N + V structure has been attributed, through folk etymology or transfer of a word from one family to another: Sp. *escarapelar* 'to quarrel' (said of women), from EXCARPĚRE with reinterpretation as *cara* 'face' + *pelar* 'to peel'. There too are found prefixes that have been crossed with nominal first elements, e.g., Occ. *pelleba* 'to remove, raise' or Gasc. *pellecar* 'to spoil (a child or pet)', in which (prepositional) *per* 'by, with, through, out of, from, for, etc.' has been identified with *pel* 'hair'.

Onomatopoeic elements, on the whole infrequent, appear concentrated in the northern Gallo-Romance corpus: Fr. *gorr-* 'noise of swine' (*gourmacher* 'to ruminate'), and *tar-* 'noise' (*tarmené* 'to rumble'), with competition from *bruit* 'noise' (dial. Fr. [West] *bulleménaou* 'noisy' = *bruit* + *mène* + *haut*, cf. *FEW* VI/2, s.v. "minare"). Underlying the four-and three-way tallies opposite are three processes already examined in Chapter 3: (i) common descent from Proto-Romance (although in many cases shared lexical items are unattested in the medieval period); (ii) independent parallel coinage; and (iii) borrowing (or diffusion). There is limited overlap between medieval and modern vocabularies, a situation flowing in all likelihood from the unavailability of attestations rather than from actual nonoccurrence in the earlier

---

[1]See Y. Malkiel, "A Lexicographic Mirage" [pseudo-participles unaccompanied by finite verbs]," *MLN* 56 (1941), 34–42; and "The *amulatado* Type in Spanish," *RR* 32 (1941), 278–95.

Comparative Frequency Chart of Nominal First Elements:
Constituents Shared by Three or Four Languages

	Fr	Occ	Cat	Sp
caput	4	33	18	3
manu(m)	9	14	7	12
cūlu(m)	9	19	3	1
camba(m)	2	12	2	1
terra(m)	4	6	4	1
pĭlu(m)	1	9	1	2(?)
pĕlle(m)	1	5	4	2(?)
săle(m)	2	5	3	1
cara(m)	1	3	2	1
bod-	1(?)	1	1	3
lŏcu(m)	1	1	1	1
cŏllu(m)	2	12	6	0
pĕde(m)	1	16	3	0
sangue(m)	5	10 (+1?)	5	0
aqua(m)	0	7	7	1
murr-	3	7	1	0
carne(m)	0	6	1	1
ŏcŭlu(m)	0	3	2	1
pāla(m) 'shovel'	2	3	1	0
perna(m)	0	3	1	2
cŏrnu	2	2	0	1
fĭde(m)	0	2	2	1
mĭssa(m)	0	1	2	1
pālu(m) 'stake'	1	1	2	0
vĭa(m)	0	2	1	1
barba(m)	0	1	1	1

period: OFr. *blanc-signé* 'signature to a blank document' is echoed, not in early Occitan, but in Mod. Périg. *blanc-signat* (Daniel 1914). In the "Other" category, Old Catalan alone shows *solabatut* 'weary', but Mod. French, Catalan, and Béarnais all have *solbatu* 'footsore' (of cattle), the last of these figuring among N + V thanks to the presence of Béar. *sole-bàte* 'to beat one's soles on the road'.

The single most frequently encountered post-medieval nominal element is *c(h)ap* 'head, end' rather than *main, man(o)*, but the modern distributions of these two nouns differ markedly from those of the earlier period. Occitan and Catalan now favor *cap-*, while in French and Spanish (where *tête* and *cabeza*, respectively, stand in for 'head') *main, man(o)* continues to prevail numerically. French and Spanish show less innovation with *main, man(o)* than do Occitan and Catalan with *cap*. [2]*C(h)ap* is nonetheless represented in four French compounds, one of them a genuine northern innovation: Norm. *chatourne* 'slap causing the head to turn'. Of the remainder, one (Fr. *chavirer* 'to capsize') is borrowed from Occitan, and two descend from the earlier period (Fr. *chanfrein* 'bit'/*enchifrené* '[suffering from a] stuffy nose'), and MFr-Pr. *chateni* 'to stop a bull by the horns', lit. 'by the head'). Even without the evidence of the Occitan and Catalan corpus, Fr. *chatourne* and Sp. *capialzar* suffice to suggest that N + V compounding has not disappeared from either standard Western Romance literary dialects or from the various spoken languages.

Earlier compounds shared with Med. Latin are continued across the four target languages in: Fr. *lieutenant, mainlevée, manœuvrer, maintenir,* Occ. *loctenent,* etc. Occitan, Catalan, and Spanish hold on to *terratenent* as well. Beyond reflexes of *lŏcu(m), săle(m),* and *tĕrra(m)*, nominal elements shared by all four languages refer to body parts (e.g., *camba[m], cara[m], cūlu[m],* and *pĭlu[m]*), except for *bod-*, underlying Fr. *bourenfler* (cf. Occ. *boud-enfla,* Cat. *botinflat,* Sp. *botinflón, -inflao*). [3]

Among three-way tallies, Occitan and Hispano-Romance share *camba + ligāre* (*cam[b]aliga*), *caput + levāre, + tenēre* (*caplevar, captener, -ir*), *mǐssa(m) + cantāre* (*mi[s]sacantan[t]*), *terra(m) + tenēre* (*terratenen[t]*), *vǐa(m) + am(bu)lāre* (*viandant*), as well as *aqua(m), barba(m), carne(m), fǐde(m), perna(m),* and *ŏcŭlu(m)* (Béar.

---

[2]Fr. *main* figures in two new compounds, as against six from the medieval corpus; Spanish has seven new formations, against five older. Catalan has three new and four old compounds in *man*; but Occitan has gone farther, with *man* figuring in eight new compounds, as well as in another five inherited from the earlier period. As regards *cap*, Occitan leads the way with twenty-eight new compounds, against five older; Catalan has thirteen new, vs. four older; Spanish has lost one compound from the medieval period, retaining four; and French aligns two old with two new ones. As if to underline the innovative tendencies of Catalan, TESTA in the modern period occurs only in Cat. *testavirar.*

[3]*FEW* IV, s.v. "inflare," also identifies BŬRRA 'coarse cloth with long nap' (Fr. *bourre* 'hair, stuffing') as a possible etymon of *bourenfler*.

oélh-peri or *-tirà* 'to blind', *oélh-birà* 'to squint, die', *él-traire* 'to tear one's eyes away', Cat. *ullcegar* 'to make blind', *ullferir* 'to strike one's eye', *ullprendre* 'to fascinate, give s.o. the evil eye', Arag. *gullibaixar* 'to keep one's glance lowered'). Catalan and Gallo-Romance have in common *sang* + *glaçar, glacer* 'to freeze one's blood', (refl.) 'be hot and cold'; *sang* + *girar, virar, -er, tourner* 'to irritate, upset', (refl.) 'be troubled', as well as reflexes of *cŏllu(m)*, *murr-*, *pāla(m)* 'shovel', *pālu(m)* 'stake, stick', *pĕde(m)*, and *pĕlle(m)*. Fr. *gourfouler* 'to press, bruise' presents an etymological puzzle, since the nominal element may reflect *gŭrge(m)*, **gorga* 'throat'; **gorto* (Med.L. *gordus*) 'fence, stick'; or *gŭrdu(m)* 'fat'. *Gourfouler* would belong in the "Other Compounds" category with Cat. *gordinfleta* 'corpulent' and Sp. *gord-i(n)flón*, Arag. *-inflas* 'chubby, pudgy' only if its initial constituent unequivocally continued *gŭrdu(m)* 'fat'. [4]

French and Occitan coincide only in *corne, cuerno* with Spanish; the informal origins of Fr. *konbrüšé* 'to scratch with a horn', and of Béar. *corne-bachà* 'to lower the horns', *-quilhà* 'to raise the horns', contrast with Quevedo's ironic *cornicantano* 'cuckold', calqued on *misacantano* 'priest'. Acting in concert against Catalan and Spanish, Gallo-Romance (French + Occitan) agree on several nominal elements (see overleaf).

Most modern compounds sharing only nominal elements appear to spring from independent coinage: Fr-Pr. *patevôler* 'to flutter around in circles' (of chickens), Occ. *patavira* 'to die'. [5] Occasionally, shared nominal elements appear in fully synonymous compounds, e.g., northern and southern reflexes of *balsamu(m)* + *fumāre* (dial. Fr. [Center] *bafumer*, Pr. *embòufuma* 'to stink') and *crŭsta(m)* + *levāre* (dial. Fr. [West] *croulever*, Occ. *se crousto-leva* 'to detach from the crumb', of the breadcrust) or dial. Fr. (Center) *santourner* and Occ. *sengirar* 'to turn over and over, upset'. Lexical and

---

[4]On semantic grounds, I hesitate to accept *FEW* IV's straightforward attribution of *gourfouler* to GŬRDUS, by which *gor(t)* would have functioned as an adverb modifying *fouler* 'to beat soundly'. I have identified three conceivable sources for OFr. *gor(t)*: (a) GŬRDU(M) 'fat', (b) GŬRGES, -ITE(M) 'whirlpool' (later **gorga* 'throat'), and (c) Celt. **gorto* 'fence, stick' (cognate with L. *hortus* 'vegetable garden'). Why not assume significant influence from reflexes of GŬRGES and **gorto*, Med.L. *gordus*, which reinforce the idea of 'excess' in GŬRDUS with elements of an orifice somehow connected with liquids, i.e., the throat; and with an instrument capable of inflicting damage, i.e., a stick. *Gourfouler* would thus lurk on the periphery of N + V compounds with a body part in nominal position; cf. Norm. *corbattre* 'to torment', Béar. *(es)gorrebate* 'to rampage, be delirious', Lang. *co[u]rquichar* 'to put one's feet on an opponent's throat, squeeze, oppress, bruise'. See Klingebiel (1987), "Fr. *gorfoler, gourfouler* 'to press, hit, bruise.''

[5]Occ. *patavira* surely carries a humorous connotation beyond its lexical meaning; it may also function as a substitute for a taboo word.

Comparative Frequency Chart of Nominal First Elements:
Constituents Shared by Two Languages

	Fr	Occ	Cat	Sp
canthu(m)	5	4	0	0
bŭrra(m)	3 (+1?)	2	0	0
campu(m)	4	1	0	0
gŭrge(m)	1 (?)	12	0	0
balsamu(m)	2	1	0	0
Gmc. blank	2	1	0	0
bulla(m)	2	1	0	0
cauda(m)	1	2	0	0
cŏrpŏre	1	2	0	0
parte(m)	1	2	0	0
patt-	2	1	0	0
sēnsu(m)	1	2	0	0
crŭsta(m)	1	1	0	0
*trīnīcāre	1	1	0	0

structural overlaps in such frequently represented notions as 'to turn over, upset' may be due to semantic coincidence. The alternatives to independent mintage, as outlined in the Introduction, are: common Gallo-Romance derivation; loan translation; back-formation; remodeling of existing compounds; conversions; and borrowing or diffusion. More than one of these factors could be responsible for dial. Fr. (West) *croulever* and Occ. *se crousto-leva*. Suisse Rom. *quesauter*, Wall. *cusoter* 'to bob an object in the air', and Occitan reflexes of *cauda(m)* compounded with *levāre* (*coalevar*, *coude-lhebà*, etc.) all fall within the sphere of 'to raise the tail, seesaw, cause to topple', with additional applications to V + N–structured ornithonyms, where northern and southern Gallo-Romance show a close match: MFr. (ornith.) *hausse-queue*, Pr. *lèvo-cuou*, Aveyr. *coueto-lébo* 'wagtail'.

Borrowing has been bidirectional. Fr. *bouleverser* 'to overturn, upset' appears as Occ. *boulouversá*; Fr. *champlever* (engraving term) 'to remove material around a pattern, leaving it raised'/*chantourner* (wood-working) 'to cut out along a given pattern' were borrowed as Occ. *chanlevâ*/Mars. *chantournar* (where [k] > [š] would otherwise be etymologically troublesome). Occ. *capvirar* 'to turn one's head, upset, etc.' has become Fr. *chavirer* 'to capsize'; on semantic grounds it appears that the latter was borrowed back as Périg. *chavirâ* idem, although French-language glosses for *capvirar* in Alibert 1977 do include 'to capsize').

Occitan and Catalan (Alibert's Occitano-Romance), on the other hand, abound in shared items alien to French or Spanish N + V compounds:

Comparative Frequency Chart of Nominal First Elements:
Constituents Shared by Two Languages

	Fr	Occ	Cat	Sp
cŏr, cŏrde(m)	0	20	15	0
clāve(m) 'nail'	0	1	3	0
fīlu(m)	0	4	1	0
cŏxa(m)	0	1	2	0
casa(m)	0	1	1	0
*cŏlpus 'blow'	0	1	1	0
crassia(m)	0	1	1	0
crŭce(m)	0	1	1	0
lĭtterā(s)	0	1	1	0
sōle(m)	0	1	1	0
*taliāre (talh)	0	1	1	0

The overwhelming predominance of nominal *còr* arises from a mixture of concurring factors: phonetic blurring (cò[r] = CŎR, CŎRPŎRE, CŎLLU[M], CŪLU[M], as well as CON-, to be examined below in Part 3); the heart's semantic centrality as the seat of human thought, feeling, emotion; and the ready possibility of substitutions within a given semantic notion, e.g., 'to feel faint, have a broken heart, be moved, suffer' (see section 1, categories M/N, O, and R) as represented by reflexes of COR + CLĀVĀRE, + *COACTIĀRE, + CREPĀRE, + DOLĒRE, + FALLĔRE, + FERĪRE, + FINDĔRE, + FŬNDĔRE, + MORĪ(RE), + NODĀRE, + PRĒ(HE)NDĔRE, + TRANSĪRE. *Greix* 'grease' (< CRASSIA[M]), *l(l)etra* 'letter', and *tal(l)/talh* 'cutting edge' (< *TALIĀRE) occur once each, in identical words which strongly suggest diffusion rather than independent coining, *l(l)etra* descending from the earlier period (Chapter 3). CRŬCE(M), conversely, appears in dissimilar Béar. *croustemaligà* 'to criss-cross' and Cat. *creuclavat* 'nailed to the cross'; *cop* 'blow' (< *CŎLPUS) brackets Occ. *còptener* 'to resist' and Cat. *copbatre* 'to beat violently'. Reflexes of CLĀVU(M) + *FĪGĬCĀRE, + PRĒ(HE)NDĔRE are inherited from the medieval languages, although Cat. *claupassar* 'to pierce with nails, sew a shoe's edge to hide stitches', belongs to the modern period. Occ.–Cat. *fi(e)lbastar* 'to baste' are flanked by innovating Occ. *fial-frexa* 'to ravel, be stringy' (of cloth or foods), *-tirâ* 'to stretch barbed wire'; Béar. *coechipoudá* 'to break one's thigh (bone)' contrasts in its makeup but not its meaning with Cat. *cuixatrencar*, as against isolated Cat. *cuixapenjant* 'getting poor'.

Excepting *barba* + *poner/pondre*, Catalan and Spanish together lack exclusive pairs against their northern neighbors; although Sp. *alicortar* 'to cut off the wings' is semantically independent, *alicaído* 'with drooping wings, crestfallen' echoes Occ. *ala* 'wing' in Occ. *ale-bacha* 'to lower the wing, humiliate oneself', *ale-bate* 'to beat one's wings, not feel well'. There are a small but significant number of Occitan and Catalan infiltrations into northern Spanish dialects, e.g., Arag. *carabirar* 'to disfigure, disguise' (from Occ. *caravirar* idem, according to Andolz [1977]); or Arag. *culmené* 'meddle-some' (cf. Cat. *culmenejar* 'to snoop around').

French stands alone in having: (3 examples) *gorr-*; (2 examples each) *bout*, CALCE(M), *chaux, tar-, temps*; (1 example each) *ban, bâton, bec, bille, bruit, chiffe, coq, cuir, *estan, gras, gueule, hart, jarret, micro, patte, père, *skala*. Of these, *bille* and *estan* continue from the older corpus (*étanfiche, billebarrer*), but *cuir* appears in a new coining.

Occitan alone has: (5 examples) *lenga*; (3 examples) *pan* 'flap', *peira*; (2 examples each) *borda, compte, corde* '(heart)string(s)', *débe/deute, dieu, flor, gauta, gota, nas, pan* 'bread', *pot* 'lip'; (1 example each): *banc, barre, bèn, bente* (VĔNTRE[M]), *blau, boca, cama* 'bed' (from Spanish), *carèma, causse, clau* 'key', *color, det, estrem, fèbre, gauta, gay, gòda, gorre, hum* (FŪMU[M]), *lana, matiera, ment, monde, òbra, páur, pluma, prou, quilha* 'leg', SANIĒS (?), *sèla, sol* 'sole', *solu(m)* 'soil', *suco, talon*. Of these, *compte* alone is continued from the older corpus in Béar. *coùmpte-finà* 'to settle an account', with additional Béar. *coùmpte-dà* 'debt'.

Catalan is alone in offering: (1 example each) *aire, feina, fira, llamp, testa*; the last-mentioned is found in no medieval compound except OSp. *tiestherido*.

Only Spanish offers: (2 examples) *cach[orr]o, poder*; (1 example each) *cam[in]al, faz, gallo*, RE(M) 'object', and Quevedo's *culto latino*. *Faz* is continued, in disguise, from Old Spanish in *zaherir* 'to reproach, criticize', lit. 'to slap' (*faz-ferir*).

One observes proportionately greater variation among verbal than among nominal elements in the modern period, as shown by the high numbers of verbs limited to one language. *Virar*, even without additional evidence from synonymous *girar* and *tornar/tourner*, has replaced L. *tenēre* as the most frequently encountered verb. *Levar, -er* remains in second position, followed by Mod. *tener, -ir*. Verbs shared four ways in both medieval/Renaissance and modern periods are few: *levāre, pikk- + -āre, tenēre*.

Among compounds relegated to the "Other" category, excluded from further discussion are: (i) forms whose second element is nonverbal, e.g., Fr. *saugrenu* 'preposterous'; (ii) compounds whose verbal element fails to appear alone as an infinitive, e.g., Fr. *écalventrer* 'to burst a stomach by kicking' (*skala + ventre + -er*, to the exclusion of *ventrer*), Occ. *cu-platà-s* 'to fall flat (*plat*) on one's butt (*cul*)', *palagrilha(r)* 'to dig with a shovel (*palagrilh*)', *pè-(h)réma* 'to stand one's ground', 'être de pied ferme'; (iii) denominals such as Cat. *salpebrar*, lit. 'to salt-and-pepper', Sp. *mampresar* 'to catch (horses)', Cat.–Sp. *terraplenar* 'to embank'. Dubious forms encompass Fr. *vertaper* 'to plug up', and suffixal formations such as Occ. *coudasquejar* 'to flutter the tail' (*coude*), [6] Cat. *salobrejar* 'to lead baby goats toward salt-covered stones'.

Occitan and Spanish share *putāre* 'to prune', with five compounds in the former as against one in Spanish. Against four examples of *dare* in Occitan, Spanish offers Latinate *poderdante* (law) 'constituent'. Each language has one example of *habēre*, but in compounds of widely differing origin: Pr. (arch.) *mentaure*/Béar. *menthábe(r)* 'to mention, remember' (cf. L. *mente habēre*) and Sp. *poderhabiente* (law) 'attorney, proxy', the latter clearly a learnèd coining like *poderdante*. Occitan compounds with *crebar* (*còl-, còr-crebar* 'to break one's neck, one's heart'), however, show structural and notional affinity with Sp. *perniquebrar* 'to break one's leg(s)'.

Against Gallo-Romance, Catalan and Spanish share *mampostería* 'dry-wall, rubble- or stonework', with *poner*, as well as several lexical items descending from the medieval period: Cat. *barbapunyent*/Sp. *barbiponiente* 'starting to have a beard' (*poner* × PŬNGENTE[M]); *amparar*, paralleling medieval *mamparar* 'to defend', as in *mampara* 'protection', Cat.–Sp. 'firescreen, small door', Sp. *mamparo* (naut.) 'bulk-head'; and Cat. *carnestoltes*/Sp. *carnestolendas* 'Carnival, activities preceding Lent'.

French alone claims: (4 examples) *mâcher*; (2 examples) *bouler, sauter, toucher, voler*; (1 example each): BALLĀRE, *barder, barrer, bêcher, bonder, brûler, brüšé(r), buter, durer*, OFr. *frener* 'to restrain', *givrer, lancer, maçonner, mouiller*, NĀSICĀRE, *nicher*, PĀSTU(M), *péter, piller, pougner* (cf. *empoigner*), *pousser, sauter, souffler, sumer* 'to sow', *user*.

Only Occitan gives: (4 examples each) *fendre, forrar, lecar*; (3 examples) *bolhir*; (2 examples each) *banhar, barrar, beure, borrar, crebar, falhir, lavar, lissar, manjar, montar, perdre, plegar, quilhar, sentir, transir, virolar*; (1 example each): *agusar, badar, baisar, bentar, bilhar, bordelar, bouchar, boueitar* (*voidar*), *branlar, bregar, cachar, coelhe, colar, coquelar, copar, cornejar, curar, daurar, descaussar, devorar, entrar, eschaurejar, escodre, estrenar, ferrar, finar, fintar, fissar, (f)regar, fusar, goaytà (gaitar), grusar (grudar), laurar, maçar, malhar, manar, matar, mentir, morir, pagar, panar, pausar, pedaçar, perir, pichar (pissar), pontar, porir, poscar, postar, quichar, rabinar, sarrar, signar, tapar, tastar, tirejar, tondre, tortejar, trair* 'to betray', *trebolar, trescar, trovar, trulhar, velejar, véser*.

Peculiar to Catalan are: (1 example each) *bategar, calcigar, caure, cegar, corcar, deixar, dir, esforçar, fangar, feixar, fermar* 'to attach', *filar, fugir, gelar, manejar, nuar, obrir, partir, plantar, regar*, SPARSUS 'sprinkled', *terrar, tridar/trigar, vinclar, xafar*.

Spanish exclusively has: (1 example each) *ajustar, atar, cortar, cuspir, echar, limar, pegar, quebrar, vindicar*.

---

[6]The affixal element *-asc*, admittedly problematic, is presumably associated with Ligurian substratum.

Comparative Frequency Chart of Verbal Second Elements:
Constituents Shared by Three to Four Languages

	Fr	Occ	Cat	Sp
virāre	3	25	2	1
levāre	4	19	3	3
tenēre	3	5	5	4
*figicāre	7	6	3	1
prē(he)ndĕre	1	5	6	1
mūtāre	2	7	1	1
inflāre	1	5	1	2
tornāre	5	2	1	1
*bassiāre	1	6	1	1
fa(cĕ)re	1	6	1	1
pikk- + -āre	1	4	1	1
cantāre	1	1	1	3
ŏperāre	1	1	1	1
batt(u)ĕre	1	7	5	0
*tirāre	2	6	1	0
fŭndĕre	1	3	4	0
minārī	4	2	2	0
versus, -āre	4	2	1	0
glaciāre	1	1	2	0
pilāre	1	2	1	0
portāre	2	1	1	0
ligāre	0	8	4	1
ferīre/ferre	0	5	5	2
*altiāre	0	3	1	1
am(bu)lāre	0	1	2	1

Comparative Frequency Chart of Verbal Second Elements:
Constituents Shared by Two Languages

	Fr	Occ	Cat	Sp
nāscĕre	1	0	1	0
*tûmon/*tumbāre	1	0	2	0
botan (bossuer)	2	2	0	0
botan (bouter)	3	1	0	0
fūmāre	3	1	0	0
iungĕre	1	2	0	0
misculāre	2	1	0	0
niff- + -āre	1	2	0	0
pulv(e)r, -āre	2	1	0	0
*dīrēctiāre	1	1	0	0
frangĕre	1	1	0	0
*fullāre	1	1	0	0
iactāre	1	1	0	0
mittĕre	1	1	0	0
stare/ess(ĕr)e	1	1	0	0
passāre	0	9	1	0
*trīnicāre	0	1	7	0
gyrāre	0	2	5	0
torquĕre	0	4	1	0
(Mod.) barrejar	0	2	1	0
buff- + -āre	0	2	1	0
sĭccāre	0	2	1	0
*tragĕr	0	2	1	0
*bastjan	0	1	1	0
clāvār	0	1	1	0
cremāre	0	1	1	0
*cruscīre	0	1	1	0
dolēre	0	1	1	0
fŏrātum + -āre	0	1	1	0
*laxāre	0	1	1	0
mentīrī	0	1	1	0
pendĕre	0	1	1	0
*wardôn	0	1	1	0

As in Chapter 3, these tallies are insufficient to pinpoint the specific areas of innovation of which all four Western Romance languages have shown themselves capable—areas which emerge clearly from the comparative onomasiological presentation in section 1 above. However, N + V formations continue to appear spontaneously, without notional support, in the written and spoken modern languages, just as they could do in the medieval vernaculars; wide-ranging medieval evidence of the notion [F.1] 'to defend' (in category F, Feudalism/Warfare/Politics, Chapter 3, section 2) contrasted with isolated OFr. *pele-fouans* 'digging with a shovel', just as Gasc. *causse-ha* 'to knit socks' stands alone against the mass of synonymous modern compounds in category T, Tumble/Turn Over/Die.

3. ANALYSIS OF THE MODERN CORPUS

N + V compounds in the modern languages generally conform to a basic structure of two or three syllables for nouns, three or four for verbs. This is true as well for prefixed verbs, e.g., Lang. *espeltira* 'to pull at from every side', Occ. *aboudenfli* 'to bruise', Gasc. *rementabe* 'to remember', as for parasynthetics with both prefixes and suffixes, e.g., Béar. *acabourrá-s*, *encabourrí-s* 'to be stubborn' (← *cap-bourrut* 'stubborn'). Compound infinitives of five syllables are infrequent, e.g., Occ. *cap-eschaureya-se* 'to get disheveled', *chalibourdounâ* 'to tumble', *espalaficar* 'to plant in the earth', and tendentially haplological Occ. *cam(bo)biroula* idem.

The multiple attested forms of Occ. *cambaligar(-se)* 'to don or wear garters', e.g., offer evidence of wide regional variation, including Mistral's (1979) head entry *cambo-liga* (*se*), Palay's (1980) *came-ligà-s*, and Alibert's (1966) normalized *cambaligar*. The full range of variants includes *cam(b)o-liga*, *camliga*; *cambo-*, *camba-*, *cambe-lia*; *cambala*; and *combellá*. Much of the disparity must be attributed to a lack of graphic conventions among the Occitan dialects. Only recently have all four major dialects (here Gascon is included with Languedocien, Provençal proper, and northern Limousin-Auvergnat) achieved among themselves a comparable level of graphic standardization, some fifty years after Alibert made the first linguistically sound attempts at Occitan normalization. [7]

---

[7]For spelling of Languedocien, Alibert's grammar (1976 [2d ed.]) is standard; for Provençal, Robert Lafont's *L'Ortografia occitana, lo provençau* (Montpellier: CEO, 1972); for Gascon, Robert Darrigrand's *Comment écrire le gascon* (Pau: Per Noste, 1974 [2d ed.]); for Auvergnat, Roger Teulat's *Comment lire et écrire l'auvergnat méridional* (Clermont-Ferrand: CRDP, 1971); for Limousin, P. Desrozier & J. Roux, *L'Ortografia occitana, lo lemosin* (Montpellier: CEO, 1974). For details on morphological normalization, see Klingebiel (1986b).

Since the reintroduction of etymological evidence into Occitan spelling, normalized graphies represent a tool, however imperfect, for accurate representation of phonetic processes. True, constituents of N + V compounds appear to retain separate stress: Palay's Gasc. *pè-tirà-s* and Alibert's *pèyrecayrà* are noted with two tonic vowels ("level stress"), as is Taupiac's V + N compound *pòrtafuèlha* 'wallet'. But the eventual fate of compound words lies in gradual loss of constituent identity, an effect better documented in glossaries and dictionaries with phonetic spellings (e.g., the Félibrige orthography of Occitan, closely adhering to spoken characteristics of the southeastern dialect of Provençal proper) than in modern normalized reference works.

N + V compounds undergo a number of expected phonetic reshaping processes. To judge from pre-normalized graphies of variants, final consonants of a compound's nominal element at times become mute, e.g., *cagira* 'to turn around, twist the neck, upset' (cf. normalized *capgirar*); *calleva* 'to topple by one end or side' (cf. Béar. *cantlhebà*); Béar. *co-dòle-s* 'to faint, be overcome with emotion' (cf. normalized *còr-dòldre*). Even more striking is the assimilation of *(ca)p* to dental *n* in Fr. *chanfrein*, in part, in assimilation of the word-final nasal. In Sp. *gordi(n)flón* (from "Other Compounds," Appendix D), one observes sporadic dissimilatory loss of the first *n* in anticipation of the following nasal consonant. Lexeme-final Gasc. *-n* and *-r* are consistently affected (Gasc. *pa[n]hourra* 'to gorge on bread'; Béar. *mâ-mete* 'to confiscate'; *maa-tien* 'handle'; *cos-prene* 'to solidify', from CŎRPŎRE. [8] Lexeme-final and lexeme-initial segments at the juncture are subject at times to joint blurring; cf. Gasc. *perrá* 'to plant one's feet in the ground', var. of *pè-herrà*. Consonants followed by a word-final vowel appear less susceptible to loss; in Spanish, however, apocope of *-o* is general (Sp. *pel[o]*, and *man[o]*, and subsequent loss of secondary *-n* is documented in Sp. *maherir*, with false restoration of *l* in *malherir* and *malfestar* ← MANIFESTĀRE). [9] Final *-a* generally remains; in *vian(d)ant*, medial *-a-* is bivalent: *via* + **an(d)ar*. Other phonetic processes affect final segments in one or more of the four modern languages: regressive assimilation (Gasc. *catteni*; Ast. *caltener*, from *cap-*, *cab-tener*; vocalization of secondary *-b-* (16th-c. Sp. *caulevar* from CAP-); and *r/l* alternation (Lang. *corquichar* vs. Narb. *escol-quicha* 'to squeeze, oppress'; Occ. *còrcrebar* vs. *còlcrebar* 'to break one's heart'). Neutralization of the *b/v* contrast

---

[8]The doubled vowel suggestive of lengthening due to loss of final consonant in OBéar. *maa-mudar* 'to change hands' (of a property); *misacantaa* 'priest', and *coo-transi* 'to pierce the heart' has either been simplified in modern graphies or replaced by a superscript, e.g., *mâ*.

[9]This phenomenon, e.g., INFĀNTE(M) > OSp. *yffante*, has been studied by Diego Catalán, "La pronunciación [ihante], por [iffante], en la Rioja del siglo XI," *RPh* 21 (1968), 410–35.

(Gasc. *bira/virar* 'to turn' [*FEW* XIV, s.v. "vibrare"], *boueitar/voidar* 'to empty', Arag. *manlebar*) is common to Gascon, Spanish, and Catalan; [10] in contrast to Gascon reflexes of L. *vibrāre* (*bira*), the *b/v* confusion is camouflaged in a variant listed by Azaïs (1877–78), *capira*.

At times, phonetic (pre-normalized) spelling has thwarted proper analysis: in Occ. *courcreva* 'to press a man or an animal against a wall so as to flatten or stifle him/ it' (listed by both Mistral and *FEW* II/2, s.v. "cor" 'heart'), Azaïs labeled *cour-* "un préfixe augmentatif." Underlying *rebourdelá*, Vayssier (1879, s.v. "capbiroulà") somehow identified REVOLVĔRE, paying insufficient attention to medial clusters. Mistral's *Tresor* is free neither of faulty etymologies (e.g., *cl[i]afi* is identified with Low L. *caffium* 'measure used in Marseille' rather than CLĀVŪ FĪGĔRE) nor of methodological weaknesses. [11]

Clarification of opaque constituents all too rarely emerges from examining by-forms or nominal-verbal tallies. *Roula(r)* has been ruled out as a component of Biterrois *cambiroula* 'to tumble, roll, fall head first', given the absence of any other Occitan N + V compounds involving *roular*; as analyzed here, *cambiroula* contains *virolar* as its second constituent. Its nominal element could be *cap* or *camba* (or perhaps both are present?), since transparent synonymous *cap-biroula* and *cambo-viroula* 'to trip, fall head over heels' are both attested in Mod. Occitan. Variant *cabiroulà* idem lends unequivocal support neither to *cap* (by assimilation of *cap* + *b* to *camb*) nor to the opposite end of the body, *camba* (by haplological reduction of *cam[bo]biroula*). In *callevá, -ua* 'to tumble, seesaw, raise the end or head', both *cap* and *cant* 'side' are phonetically possible, with the written evidence of Béar. *can(t)lheba* 'to topple by one end or side' possibly tipping the scale toward *cant*. Lespy–Raymond (1877) credited *can-lhebà* to *cant*; Palay selected *cant-* as his first entry, but Mistral classified the variant under *cap-*. Various graphic solutions to such problems result from the compiler's proficiency as etymologist (and intuitions as a native speaker), occasionally not without contradictions.

Beyond Occ. *cap/camba/cant*, phonetic overlap is possible in two other nominal series: between *coa* 'tail', *cor* 'heart', *cors* 'body', *còu* 'neck', *cu(l)* 'butt', and the opaque element *cour*, which Azaïs analyzed as prefixal; and between *pan* 'part, portion', *pè* 'foot', *pèl* 'skin', *pel* 'hair', plus prefixal *per-*. Per- doubtless can preserve augmentative value, e.g., Occ. *perboulir* 'to parboil' (vs. *pèu-bouli* 'to scald'), *perlecar* 'to lick thoroughly', with a possible var. in Gasc. *pelleca* 'to spoil'. *Pelleba (se)* 'to pull one's hair' has been listed as an N + V compound, on the understanding that it may

---

[10]See Johannes Hubschmid, "*Virāre*: romanisch oder vorromanisch?," *RPh* 15 (1962), 245–53.

[11]See Hans-Erich Keller, "La Valeur du *Tresor dóu Felibrige* pour les études lexicologiques occitanes," *RLiR* 23 (1959), 131–43.

have arisen from reinterpretation of *per* (cf. Fr. *colporter* 'to peddle', originally from COM-). [12] This three-way puzzle is further expanded in another N + V series: Mistral's recorded permutations of normalized Occ. *pelmudar* 'to molt' (from PĔLLE[M] 'skin' and PĬLU[M] 'hair') include: *péu-, p(i)el-, pial-, per-muda; péu-, póu-,* and *par-mia;* as well as *permuda* and even *plumya.*

In dial. French *chôvanté* 'to dry out prematurely from warm winds' (of cereals), a nominal element fills the slot otherwise occupied in its standard French near-synonym (*éventer* 'to air, [refl.] go stale') by a prefix; without echoing any potential nom. element, opaque *jan-/jon-* (Occ. *jangoutá* 'to drip', *jon-girà* 'to freeze', both under "Other") appear to represent phonetic variants of CON-. In addition to local confusion of prefixes with nominal elements, prefix change in Gascon can occur in conjunction with loss of syllable-initial *f-*, e.g., Béar. *pèt-esla-s* 'to swell' and *goud-eslat* 'swollen', from INFLĀRE ([f] > [h], with false restoration of [s]). [13] Also straddling the limits of affixation and composition are several combinations of noun + suffix, e.g., Cat. *capmallolar* 'to wield a hammer', relegated in the Appendices to "Other"; *cabiroula* (classified as an N + V compound) lends itself to alternative interpretation as *cabirole + -a(r)*; cf. Cat. *cabriolar, gambirolar,* Fr. *cabrioler* 'to turn a somersault'; cf. also *cambiroular,* with (*camba +*) *biroular* rather than *roular.* Yet false segmentation cannot be ruled out as a factor in analogical formation of new N + V compounds.

Identification and specification of verb elements offer fewer problems than those of nouns. Verb elements in N + V compounds are conjugated like their simplex forms: Mistral (s.v. "cor-creba") notes "*cor-creba* se conjugue comme *creba,*" and so on. As a concomitant of the local loss of *f-*, Gasc. *cu-rega* (cf. Occ. *cuolfregar* 'to quiver, tremble' ← CŪLU[M] + FRICĀRE) presents no difficulty; Gasc. *pè-remà* 'to stand firm' (cf. *de pè hrem* < FĬRMU[M]) may hold a clue to Gasc. *peyrahemà* 'to set

---

[12]Mistral glossed *pelleba (se)* (← *per + levar*) as: (i) 'to raise, remove', with cross-reference to *pa(n)leva* idem; (ii) 'to pull s.o.'s hair'; (iii) 'to swallow quickly', with reference to *peleja,* Sp. *pelear* 'to fight, quarrel'; and (iv) 'to become angered', with cross-reference to *pu-leva* idem. *FEW* V, s.v. "pilus," provides MFr. *perlever* 'to blow away' (of the wind), 'to become angered', which may support *per*'s candidacy, if a single etymon indeed underlies the four glosses. In the Spanish corpus (Appendix D), *pel-echar, -mudar* is attributed to *piel/pelo*; elsewhere, my analysis relies on graphic differentiation of Occ. *pèl* (PĔLLE[M]) and *pel* (PĬLU[M]), of Fr. *peau* and *poil,* and of Cat. *pell* and *pèl,* respectively. For possible motivation of *plumya,* see Jules Gilliéron & M. Roques, "Etudes de géographie linguistique: VII *plumer = peler.* Mirages phonétiques," *Revue de Philologie Française et de Littérature* 21, no. 2 (1907).

[13]Cf. similarly prefixed *cap-esdressa,* accompanying a profusion of other Gascon compounds in which the nominal element carries the (typically, optional) prefix *es-*: *(esch)alabatre, escolquicha (corquichar), (es)gorrobate, espelferi (pelfrit), (es)peltira, espernabate (pernabatre).*

up a lever' (PETRA[M] + FĬRMA[M]?, or FĬRMĀRE?). Other Gascon pairs show morphological variation in medial and final as well as initial segments, e.g., Gasc. *sang-transi/-tradi* 'to surprise'; *cap-haussa, -hautà* 'to stand upright'; *cap-barià, -barreya* 'to be confused' (cf. OPtg. *desvairado* 'crazy'); Béar. *pè-hourè, -hourì, -hourà* 'to stamp on the ground'. Change of conjugation class (insofar as the infinitive indicates that class) is not limited to Occitan, being found as well in Catalan, e.g., Occ. *man-téner, -teni, -tiene* (Gallo-Romance TENĒRE being influenced by VENĪRE); Cat. *mor-fondre, marfondir*. Occasionally no change of class results from remodeling, e.g., *forar/foradar* 'to pierce' (Béar. *cap-houradà*, Cat. *pellforadar*); Occ. *capvirar/capvirolar* 'to turn'; Ast. *mancorn(i)ar, mantorn(i)ar*. [14] From Gasc. *lheba* 'to raise' is derived *culhebet* 'horses's kick', which in turn has made possible *culhebetà* 'to kick' (of a horse).

Compounds, like other lexical units, are affected by phonetic erosion and morphological blurring, being particularly vulnerable at their points of juncture, where composition vowels (= "Fugenvokale") occur in Spanish, Catalan, and Occitan, particularly Gascon. From Latin, French has inherited a single final vowel, *-e* (shwa), whereas Occitan, Catalan, and Spanish alike have *-e, -o*, and *-a* (with *-a* in many Occitan dialects amounting to [*o*]); and French alone lacks phonemic word stress. Neither circumstance has hindered the accumulated French corpus from surpassing the Spanish in size and variety, while Catalan barely exceeds the French, and Occitan easily doubles both in bulk. Has Cat. *capitombar* been influenced by It. *capitombolare* (*i* → *o* by dissimilation; cf. It. *capovolgere* 'to tumble')? Spanish has a handful of instances, e.g., *alicortar* 'to cut the wings off, wound' (from Cat. *capalçar*); *capialzar* 'to raise the end'; Arag. *gullibaixar* 'to keep one's glance lowered'; *maniatar* 'to manacle, tie the hands', and Quevedo's *cornicantano* 'cuckold', *cultilatiniparla* 'excessive use of Latin words and phrases'; cf. also Sp. *maniobrar*, remodeled from Fr. *manœuvrer*. Linking *-i-* is unexpectedly frequent in Gascon adjectives and verbs, e.g., adj. *cambitort* 'limping', *capilheban* 'raising the head' (also *cap-lhebàn*), *couditort* 'with a crooked tail', *manitòrt* 'with crooked hands', *nasitòrt* 'with a crooked nose', [15] and verbal Béar. *camipoudà* 'to break one's leg' (also *camepoudà-s*), *camitorse* 'to twist one's leg' (also *cametorse*), *chaliboudounar* 'to tumble', *cariboussà* 'to deform',

---

[14]See Malkiel, "The Five Sources of Epenthetic /j/ in Western Hispano-Romance: A Study in Multiple Causation," *HR* 37 (1969), 239–75, for a fuller discussion of Ast. *-iar*.

[15]N + Adj compounds include, e.g., Béar. *camiflouch* 'with wobbly legs', *coechiprim* 'with thin legs', *croustilhebàt* 'bad-tempered', *cornihàut* 'with upturned horns' (also *corne-haut*); Cat. *morritort* 'with a twisted muzzle', *poutigròs* 'with thick lips', *testibouhàt* 'with a bare forehead', *testileujè* 'scatter-brained'. Adj + V, with adverbial function, include, e.g., *carivent* 'who charges steep prices'.

coudiquejà 'to flutter one's tail' (also *coudasqueja*), *manicouquear* 'to handle, manipulate', *paliherrà* 'to dig with a shovel' (also *palaherrà*), *matri-*, *motri-fusà* 'to mix good stuffs with poorer merchandise', and *petchibirà* 'to mistreat, turn upside down' (= *pèt-birà*). Thematic vowels in this most sharply characterized of Occitan dialects appear to occur most frequently as phonetic variants rather than as a result of remodeling or dissimilation (Sp. *boquiabierto, maniatado, perniquebrado,* It. *capitombolare,* etc.).

In the process of their reworking into more authentically Romance shape, borrowings and calques are subjected to different degrees of phonetic and morphological pressure attendant upon reanalysis, e.g, Gm. *Bürgermeister* → Fr. *bourgmeistre,* which offers no difficulty (cf. **man-* → *main-tenir*); *contredanse* (Eng. *country dance*), with its amusing companion piece, Fr. *danse de l'âne salé* (lit. 'dance of the salted ass'), from Eng. *dance of Aunt Sally.* Only one possible example of truncation in N + V compounds has come to light, Occ. *(pe)sigossar* 'to tickle' (apheresis of *pe-*; interpreted as 'foot'?), a process otherwise capable of producing new simplex forms, e.g., Fr. *pêche* 'peach' from L. *malum Persicam* 'Persian apple', Gr. *nephritis (nósos)* 'illness of the kidneys' > Fr. *néphrite.* These examples prefigure the tendency for (L. *nux muscāta* >) Fr. *noix de muscade* 'nutmeg' to undergo shortening to *muscade.*

In section 1 above, semantic notions in the modern corpus show a distribution discernedly different from the medieval (Chapter 3, section 2). There, the slots for categories A, Plants, B, Animals, C, Farm Labor/Animal Husbandry, and D/E, Terrain/Elements, turned out to be virtually empty; according to modern evidence, there has occurred significant, albeit unevenly distributed, innovation. Sp. *pelechar* doubles Arag. *pelmudar* 'to molt', both of them inherited from the medieval period; L. *pĭlu(m)/pĕlle(m) mūtāre* 'to lose one's hair/skin' reappears in Occ. *pelmudar* and Fr. *peaumuer,* suggesting early Western Romance distribution into which the rare Spanish N + V–structured synonym fits snugly. Occitano-Romance offers the most striking proof of ongoing spoken N + V compounding, particularly in the sheep-herding terminology of category C/D. The series of denominal Gallo-Romance verbs for 'digging' (Fr. *pelleverser, terrebêcher,* Occ. *palavirar,* etc.) lacks parallels in Hispano-Romance, save Cat. *palafangar.* The widespread attestation of PĀLU(M)/PĀLA(M) + **FĪGĬCĀRE* [16] supports Gamillscheg's (1966–68) analysis of OFr. *estanfique* 'slender column dividing a bay window' into Gmc. **estan* 'supporting beam' + *-fiche.* Compounds in G, Warfare, H/I, Administration/Law, J, Food, L, Religion, and M/N, Medicine, including Veterinary, are generally inherited from earlier Romance; It.

---

[16]It. *palafitta* '(prehistoric) pile, pole driven into the earth or lake', flanked by denominal *palafittare,* was borrowed into French as 19th-c. *palafitte* (→ Cat. *palafit*); cf. Béar. *pauhic* 'pile, etc.' (→ Béar. *pauhicá,* Pr. *palaficar*).

carnavale 'pre-Lenten period', now found in all four target languages, has replaced Gallo-Romance *caresmentrant*, *quaremprenant* 'Carnival', leaving reflexes of QUADRĀGĒSIMA to signify solely 'Lent' (Fr. *carême*, Occ. *carèma*). Sp. *lugarteniente* completes the four-way spread of modern 'lieutenant'. K, Technical, like category C above, includes innovations, e.g., Cat. *capfermar* 'to attach a cord to a fixed point', beside shared Occ. *talhvirar*/Cat. *tallgirar* 'to dull, ruin a knifeblade's edge'.

In the area of emotions, the Spanish corpus displays only one example, apparently borrowed from Catalan (Arag. *culmené* 'snoopy'); the meager French record involves figurative extrapolations from better-represented category M/N Medicine, including Veterinary. Catalan is generously provided with examples in categories M–R, but the number of Occitan examples by far surpasses Catalan.

Occitano-Romance compounds in these categories agree closely in their structure: nominal body part + verb of physical movement or, at least, swift change (hitting, falling, burning, turning, troubling, etc.). Within the confines of category M/N, compounds such as dial. Fr. *se sa(n)zevra* 'to catch cold', Cat. *sangfondre* 'to flush' evoke illness or disease through descriptive periphrases (cf. Eng. *heart attack*) rather than learnèd professional terms (*myocardial infarctus*). This imagerial quality is obviously suited to the description of emotional states as well. Compounds in categories S, Physical Description, T, Tumble/Turn Over/Die, and U, Personal Violence, overlap constantly, unlike one-of-a-kind French and Spanish examples in category V, Physical Movement, e.g., Arag. *gullibaixar* 'to keep one's glance lowered'. In addition to Occitan and Catalan isolates, e.g. Béar. *terre-pèrdre* 'to lose one's footing', however, category V displays occasional synonymous or nearly synonymous pairs (Gasc. *pè-troulhà*/Cat. *peucalcigar* 'to trample'), very much like the synonyms in categories S–U. The range of compounds found in Y, Miscellaneous, comprises few synonyms but significant evidence of sporadic innovation: Fr. *à chiffe-tirer* 'in disagreement'; Cat. *firandant* 'merchant at fairs' (on model of *vian[d]ant*); Béar. *causse-ha* 'to knit socks', lit. 'to sock-make', *hum-dà* 'to give off smoke'.

N + V compounds here, as above in Chapter 3, sections 4–5, are analyzed both on the basis of surface structure (see Appendices A–D), and also in terms of their origins: inheritance from spoken Latin; borrowing and diffusion; and a variety of analogical processes, primarily paradigmatic replacement and back-formation, with occasional reinforcement and reinterpretation.

Reinterpretation of a first constituent is particularly well exemplified by Occ. *plóu-*, *plumomuda*, *plumya* 'to molt' ('feather' + 'change'), from *pèl-*, *pel-mudar* idem ('skin'/'hair' + 'change'). Although few convincing instances of reinforcement are available in the modern corpus, dial. Fr. (Center) *peaumuer* 'skin' + 'molt' and Cat. *ullcegar* 'eye' + 'blind' both offer evidence of the process.

The ranks of modern N + V compound verbs have been greatly increased by de-adjectival derivation from N + V Past Ptc compounds associated with bodily description, e.g., Occ.–Cat. *cappelat* 'bald' (a very frequent adjective, which has spawned no compound verbs except Cat. *cappelar*). The structure of these adjectival bases parallels that of Gr. *gonuklinḗs* 'on bended knee', as *cappelar* parallels *gonuklineîn* 'to bend one's knee'. Denominal derivations occur less frequently, e.g., Cat. *aiguabarrejar*; Fr. *culbuter*.

The modern corpus is characterized by its large numbers of synonymous compound verbs, particularly in the areas of medical terminology, including veterinary (category M/N), of mental and emotional manifestations (categories O–R), and physical upsets (category T). Within the notions of 'twisting one's neck', 'breaking one's heart', 'swelling', and 'tumbling, tripping, see-sawing', there occur substitutions of N elements, frequently names of body parts, or synonymous V elements. To capture this process, the terms replacement, chaining, or "enchaînement associatif" (launched by Séguy [1953], in connection with Cental Occitan V + N–structured phytonyms, e.g., *grate-cu* [Rosa Canina], lit. 'butt-scratcher', *grate-pucie* [Euphorbia Lathyris], lit. 'flea-scratcher', etc.) can be put to use. The terms in Séguy's study, not uniformly synonymous, occur within a narrowly circumscribed field. Tags for body parts themselves, though not intrinsically synonymous, are nonetheless known to function in compounds where they are anatomically inappropriate, e.g., Eng. *heartburn*, affecting the esophagus rather than the heart. [17] Paradigmatic replacement operates in either compound constituent, e.g., (i) Cat. *corprès, salprès, sangprès, ullprès*; or the Gasc. *-tòrt* series (*cambi-, coudi-, mani-, nasi-*), above; (ii) Cat. *corprès* (from older *comprès*), *cor-fós, -ferit, -glaçat, -lligat, -migrat, -nuat, -secat* (*DECC*, s.v. "cor"), a series of words centering on emotional afflictions rightly or wrongly associated with the heart.

The most dramatic evidence of such replacement is furnished by the Occitan corpus. The multifariousness of noun shapes (e.g., *pèl, pièl, pial, pièul, péu* < PĬLU[M]) that pervades the Occitan dialects stimulates "enchaînement" and subsequent reinterpretation, resulting upon occasion in the rise of novel N + V compounds, e.g., *plumomuda* modeled on *péu/pel + mudar*. [18] However, residual or restored transparency, particularly in the noun, is essential to the process of replacement. The

---

[17]Cf. Sp. *corazón* 'heart' < COR *ĀRSIŌNE, discussed in the Introduction.
[18]Fr. *loup-garou*, from **lupus-garulfus*, with its transparent counterpart Ptg. *lobis-homem* 'werewolf', lit. 'wolf-man', presents a striking example of synonymous reinforcement in nominal compounds: 'wolf' (*loup*) + 'man-wolf' (*garou* < GAR-ULFUS = Gmc. *were* 'man' + *wulf* 'wolf'). For reinforcement in N + V compounds, cf. Med.L. *manūtrādĕre* 'to deliver, transfer'; *manuopera/mannwerch* 'manual labor'; dial. Fr. *peaumuer*.

recomposition (or reanalysis) of **mantenir → maintenir*, a key term in the strategic vagaries of feudal life, ensured its continued semantic translucency. During the Middle Ages, while the etymological transparency of *maintenir/mantener*, etc., received support from legal and administrative uses of Med. Latin, the temporal notion of 'supporting, defending' was subject to widespread substitutions in all four target vernaculars (Chapter 3, section 2 [F.1.a–g] *manu* + seven verbal elements). An identical number of verbal elements enter into the notion of 'Lent' (Chapter 3, section 2 [L.2. a–g]). Remnants of these medieval strings persist in various present-day vernaculars. But cumulative evidence suggests that the prolific 'swell'/ 'tumble' series (both N + V–structured compounds and similar compounds listed in the Appendices as "Other") has neither descended from early feudal and religious terms shared with Med. Latin (like *maintenir, carementran*), nor yet arisen from VO syntactic structures (like isolated Béar. *ha causses/causse-ha* 'to knit socks'). In French, this series must have been affected by the semantic shift of *tomber* from 'to (take a) tumble' to 'to fall' in the 16th and 17th centuries, occurring hand-in-hand with the loss of *ch(e)oir* 'to fall'. With impetus from verbal periphrases based on nominal compounds, e.g., Fr. *culbute* (*faire la culbute* 'to take a tumble', also *culbuter*), Béar. *(ha) capihoune/cabriole* idem (also *capbirolar*), Cat. *caure a capgirells* idem, It. *fare un capitombolo* idem, the 'swell'/'tumble' series derives principally from the adjectival sources termed "phrases nominales" by Ronjat, e.g., Occ. *cappelat* 'bald', *sang-begut* 'numbed with cold', demonstrably hospitable to paradigmatic replacement.

N + V compounding, bereft of direct support from Med. Latin, is far from extinct in any of the Western Romance languages here examined. Left to their own devices after the codification of standard French, the northern Gallo-Romance *patois*, not unlike their southern counterparts, continued to generate novel and synonymous N + V compounds, e.g., the series of 'tumble' synonyms in section 2, category T. On the whole, however, the scattershot quality of French dialect examples contrasts with the more patterned exploitation and substitutions found in Occitan and, although to a lesser degree, in Catalan. At the beginning of the modern era, the N + V pattern was still fully in bloom in French, Occitan, and Catalan. Spanish alone had become less than enthusiastic in its commitment, despite a number of innovative compounds unparalleled elsewhere (*mamparar, pelechar*). Of the Northern Hispano-Romance dialects, Aragonese and Asturian have borrowed from each other and from Catalan. The Catalan corpus presented above approaches the French in size (less than half that of Occitan), while the range of lexical constituents of Catalan N + V compounds closely resembles that of the Occitan corpus. Certain innovations suggest that N + V composition in Catalan remains viable: witness *feina-fuig*, lit. 'work-shirking', and *camatrencar, cuixatrencar* 'to break one's leg' (beside *pernatrencat*), corresponding element for element to Béar. *came-poudà, coechipoudà*, and Sp. *perniquebrar*.

Various examples in the Spanish corpus actually originated in northern Hispano-Romance dialects, particularly Aragonese, or were borrowed from Catalan (*camaliga, capialzar*). The accumulated Spanish N + V corpus proves to be not only the smallest in numbers but also the least productive in terms of any recognizable N + V pattern—that is, any systematic exploitation of the local lexical resources. The 16th and 17th centuries witnessed a renewal of individual artistic experimentation with this particular compound pattern, which included Spanish in a most limited way. Against, e.g., 16th-c. Fr. *jour-apporte* (Ronsard), stand only a handful of Spanish examples: (17th c.) *cultilatiniparla, cornicantano, perniabrir, terreplenar*, from the writings of Lope de Vega and Quevedo. Yet the possibility for continued innovation clearly emerges in Hispano-Romance dialectalisms of varied origin, i.e., other than back-formed compounds such as Arag. *mancuspir* 'to spit into one's hands and rub them together before taking hold of a tool'; or back-formations such as Arag. *gullibaixar* 'to keep one's glance lowered'.

This latter item, from the Bielsa Valley, may well be an artistic creation; appearing only once (in a recent dictionary of Aragonese, Andolz [1977]), it may even involve a lexicographer's extrapolation from adj. *gullibaixo* 'one who keeps his glance lowered', since both are listed. Yet the mere presence of the infinitive is relevant; it testifies to the continuity of Pyrenean word formation patterns, as it echoes other primary or secondary N + V formations sheltering reflexes of Lat. ŏCŬLU(M) in opening position: Cat. *ull-cegar, -ferir, -prendre*, Gasc. *olh-bira, -peri, -tira, èl-traire*. Comparison of nominal tallies of the four target languages underscores the innovative quality of Arag. *gullibaixar*, a compound of admittedly marginal type, but latently ever-present and worthy of eventual lexicographic adoption even under the relatively inhospitable circumstances of Spanish compound word formation.

Curiously, N + Adj–structured sources for back-formed verbs (e.g., adj. Cat. *gullibaixo*, or Occ.–Cat. *cappelat* 'bald'), have VO structure, while the resultant N + V infinitives, e.g., Cat. *cappelar* 'to lose one's hair' (no Occitan example is attested), are OV-ordered. N + V Pres Ptc compounds, say, Béar. *panminjant* 'day-laborer', *lanaperdent*, lit. 'wool-losing', have given rise to no new compound verbs, except possibly for Béar. *terre-perdén* 'losing one's footing' (cf. *terre-pèrdre*), which ranks here, however, as a deverbal.

Modern-day N + V compounding enjoys livelier productivity than is document-able through the 16th century. Examples from the earlier period have survived (Fr. *maintenir*, Lang. *letroferit*, etc.), disappeared (OSp. *mane[n]trar* 'to attack', OFr. *mentevoir*, etc.), or failed to gain currency, particularly many one-of-a-kind artistic creations (OFr. *orfergi* 'embroidered with gold') and legalistic terms (A.-Norm. *meynprendre*, which, oddly, has enjoyed longevity in British legal jargon). Among Gallo-Romance reflexes of L. *mente habēre* only Pr. *mentaure*/Béar. *menthábe(r)* lingers on. Other examples continue, with a shift in meaning: Mod.Fr. *morfondre* 'to mope, fret'; Occ. *caplevar* 'to seesaw' (vs. earlier 'to post bail; raise a tax'; and the like). On a synchronic level, *maintenir* is no longer a compound at all, with speakers unaware of its bipartite structure; even in the late Middle Ages it could well have been opaque, since no new synonyms post-date the 13th century (see category F.1, 'defend, protect, support', in Chapter 3, section 2). Ronsard's N + V–structured neo-Classical *feu-vomissant* was fated to suffer the same rapid demise that befell V + N adjectives in the 16th century, but for different reasons. V + N compounds were doomed as adjectives in formal poetry and prose because of ongoing semantic specialization with ironic and negative meanings, e.g., *pique-assiette* 'scrounger, sponger' (Bierbach 1982:75). N + V compounds have undergone no such pressure of semantic competition; nor has syntactic change eradicated them.

Béar. *causse-ha*, like Arag. *mancuspir*, demonstrates the existence of a truly vernacular Romance N + V pattern, owing no direct debt to verb-final syntax or to the analogical processes of reinterpretation or replacement examined above. These examples, rare as they are in modern Western Romance, complement the gratifyingly large corpus of N + V–structured back-formations gathered for this study. While (S)VO languages such as Romance and English prove relatively inhospitable to verbs like *causse-ha*, *mancuspir* (see Pennanen 1966:§§7.1–5 for discussion of similarly compounded Eng. *bulb-snatch* ← *to snatch bulbs*), no such penury characterizes the products of back-formation. The presence of N + V compounds versus their disappearance from post-medieval literary French and Spanish rests upon a complex set of interlocking factors including phonetic conditioning, morphosyntax, word-order change, semantic patterning, and analogy within the compositional process.

NOUN + VERB COMPOUNDING IN
WESTERN ROMANCE: CONCLUSIONS

With the gradual triumph of (S)VO syntax in Romance, *maintenir* and its N + V-structured analogs became morphologically distinguishable from unmarked syntactic structures. The pattern of *manūtenēre* has withstood phonetic blurring and syntactic evolution with surprising tenacity in the spoken vernaculars examined here, particularly dialectal French (the northern Gallo-Romance *patois*) and Pyrenean Romance (Occitan, Catalan, and the northern Hispanic dialects). When Med. Latin disappeared from common use after the 16th century, N + V compounding was shorn of any last vestiges of verb-final support. As evidenced by Fr. *chatourne* 'slap', Béar. *causse-ha* 'to knit socks', Cat. *ullcegar* 'to make blind', and Arag. *mancuspir* 'to spit into one's hands ... before taking hold of a tool', N + V compounding in Gallo- and Hispano-Romance did not perish with Med. Latin in the late Middle Ages; given dial. Argentine *culanchar-se* 'to be frightened', future investigation of New World Spanish may well confirm post-medieval N + V compounding. Within the Western Romance domain surveyed, Gascon remains particularly active in producing compounds of this type, but other dialects throughout the target areas present clear evidence of nonliterary, spoken compounding (e.g., Pic. *harlifiker* 'to bind with a *hart* [strap]', Wall. *gour-, mour-macher* 'to chew'), as well as of artistic or scientific coining (e.g., MFr. *lierre-porte* 'ivy-bearing', Sp. *cornicantano* 'cuckold').

There exists a wider base of shared origins than previous studies of N + V compounding have assumed, e.g., OFr. *gouteprenant* 'dignified', lit. 'gouty'/Béar. *goute-préne* 'to contract gout'; OPr. *cazatinent*/Cat. *casatinent* 'householder, houseowner', dial. Fr. *peaumuer*/Occ.–Cat. *pèlmudar* 'to molt'. Comparison of modern with modern, or medieval with modern, word lists brings to light other illustrations of borrowing or diffusion, e.g., trans-Pyrenean: OPr. *caravirar* 'to change political parties', Cat. *caravirat, -girat*, Arag. *carabirar* 'to disfigure, disguise'. The four-way corpus of vernacular N + V compounds assembled for this monograph testifies to the vitality—somewhat uneven, but increasingly attested since the 19th century—of this process, which has been judged dormant or extinct in French (Darmesteter [2d ed.] 1894, Meyer-Lübke 1895, Nyrop 1924) and in Spanish (Menéndez Pidal 1941). Students of Occitan (Rohlfs 1935 [1977], Ronjat 1937) and Catalan (Badia Margarit 1962) have more accurately gauged the vigor of this pattern, which must not be claimed to have disappeared from Western Romance.

It is less difficult to explain the success of a compound pattern than to account for its demise; no single factor alone ensures survival, but, rather, a number of interactive factors. Derivational patterns do not necessarily disappear in the course of shifts in basic word order. OV compounding continues to flourish in otherwise SVO-ordered Mod. English, for example, just as suffixation (concomitant with OV order; cf. Greenberg 1963:92–93) lives on in the Romance languages. Taken separately, internal or external evidence alone fails to account for the peculiar and in part self-contradictory distribution of N + V compounding in the four languages under consideration here, that is, for its retreat in literary French and Spanish as against its entrenchment in the respective *patois* and dialects.

No evidence of Greek influence, even in southeastern Gaul, or of other substratal support, has come to light. No N + V compounds are listed in von Wartburg's (1956) study of Massaliotic loanwords in the dialects of Southern France; the Iberian substratum of Aquitanian Latin offers a possible course of future investigation which has been noted here in passing. Three centuries of bilingualism in northern Gaul (5th to 8th century) could only have encouraged compounding, given the compositional proclivities of superstratal Germanic. Evidence of the Germanic overlay remains visible in OFr. *estanfique* 'slender column dividing a bay window' (*FEW* XII, s.v. "stare"), dial. Fr. (North) *banjointant* 'contiguous', etc., but contact with Germanic was minimal in those Pyrenean areas most conspicuously engaged in modern N + V compounding.

In each corpus, the multiple sources of N + V are visible. Some modern compounds have survived from the pre–17th-c. period, a number of these from spoken Latin itself; many have been freshly coined. The earliest survivors coalesced from OV-ordered syntactic phrases or appeared by back-formation from nominal or adjectival bases, transparently bipartite N + Adj compounds being of particular importance. Analogical processes account for the largest part of each corpus, both medieval and modern. The mintage of novel compounds is encouraged by the possibility of either nominal or verbal replacement within semantic notions (the medieval 'Lent' series; the modern 'tumble' series, and so on). Compounds also result from reinterpretation (Gasc. *pelleba (se)* 'to become angered' from *perlebar*; *plumomudar* 'to molt', cf. *pèl-, pel-mudar*); and from reinforcement, e.g., dial. Fr. *peaumuer* 'skin' + 'molt', Cat. *ullcegar* 'eye' + 'blind'. Along with calques, or loan translations, borrowing and diffusion complete the roster of potential sources.

N + V compounds, once formed, can themselves serve as derivational bases capable of generating new lexical items, through (i) single or double affixation, (ii) conversion, and (iii) back-formation: e.g., (i) parasynthetic Béar. *s'espernabate* 'to fall with one's legs in the air', *acabourrá/encabourrí* 'to be stubborn'; (ii) OBéar. *carn-bedar* 'Lent', lit. 'flesh, meat' + 'forbid'; (iii) Béar. *gay-hasén* 'pleasing' →

gayhasénce 'gracious quality, kindness'; or denominal Béar. *culhebeta* 'to kick' (of a horse), by means of nominal suffix *-èt* (*culhebèt* 'horse's kick') on the verb *cu-lhebà* 'to raise the tail or end'.

Within the overlaps between composition and derivation fall both: confusion between prefixal *pe(r)-* and nominal Occ. *pe(l)* 'hair' (e.g., Occ. *perlevar*), or between Occ.–Cat. adj. *cap* 'principal' and nominal *cap* 'head, end', both from L. *caput*; and similar, although less frequent, confusion of compound constituent with suffix, e.g., Cat. *capgirellar* 'to tumble', interpreted as *capgirell* 'somersault' + *-ar*, or Occ. *cabiroula* 'to tumble', which lends itself to analysis as suffixal *cabirole* 'somersault' + *-a[r]*. The blurring of the line separating compounds and syntactic phrases found in, e.g., Fr. *tasse à thé* 'teacup' is missing in OV-ordered examples; however, to OPr.–OBéar. *viandan(t)*, *biandant* 'pilgrim' corresponded OPr. (hap.) *anar via* 'to leave'; congealed Béar. *causse-ha* is balanced by the free group *ha causses*.

N + V compounding, including its ramifications in the area of affixation, must be accorded its rightful place in studies of Western Romance word formation. Emerging clearly from the study of L. *manūtenēre*, its reflexes, and its analogs is a sense of the ongoing vitality of the N + V compound pattern, in the face of word-order change, phonetic erosion, and morphological reshaping. The present study has sought to trace the origins and history of a compositional pattern amply attested in Med. Latin, known in the early Western Romance vernaculars, and surviving unexpectedly into modern times as a genuinely vernacular model, illustrating the multiple vicissitudes of the compositional process.

Appendix A

French Corpus

In preparing the alphabetically arranged Appendices to this monograph, I have not sought to assign primacy of nominal, adjectival, or verbal parts of speech on the basis of earliest recorded attestations. Written attestation need not faithfully reflect relative dating, and such documentation as is available at a given moment can never be considered exhaustive or definitive.

Wall. *abastorner* 'to beat someone with a stick'; *FEW* "tornare"; N:bâton 'stick' + V:tourner 'to turn'

MFr. (16th c.) *aile-porte* 'wing-bearing'; Marty-Laveaux; N:aile 'wing' + V:porter 'to bear'

Center *bafumer* 'to fumigate'; *embaufumé* 'ill, swollen'; *FEW* "balsamum," *FEW* "fumus," *FEW* "buff-, puff-"; N:BALSAMU(M) 'balsam' + V:fumer 'to smoke'

Meuse *banjointant* 'contiguous, abutting on' (of territories or communes); *FEW* "jungere"; N:ban 'edge' + V:joindre 'to (ad)join'

Wall. *bastorner* 'to beat (nut or fruit) trees'; *FEW* "tornare"; N:bâton 'stick' + V:tourner 'to turn'

Mos. *bècbassieu* [*sic*] 'to meander, twist'; *FEW* "*bottia"; N:bec 'beak' + V:bossuer 'to meander'

billebarré 'striped, variegated'; (16th c.) *billebarrer* 'to stripe, garnish with bands of color'; (Mod.) 'to mottle with various colors', (intr.) 'to be striped, variegated'; AD, *GRS* II §594 (N + V), KN §569 (N + V), *FEW* "*bilia," B-W, 4; N:bille 'wedge of wood; stripe' + V:barrer 'to draw a line'

125

blanc-poudré, -poudrer (pass.) '(to be) white with powder' (of face or hair), (active) 'poudrer à blanc'; AD, KN §569 (N + V), Littré, Robert "poudrer"; N:blanc 'white' + V:poudrer 'to powder'

MFr. (15th c.) *blanc-signé* (Mod. *blanc-seing*) 'signature to a blank document'; AD; N:blanc 'blank' + V:signer 'to sign'

MFr. (15th c.) *se boffumer* 'to be angered'; *FEW* "buff-, puff-"; N:buff- (onom.) 'blowing noise' + V:fumer 'to smoke out'

OFr. (Bourg.) *boranfler* 'to swell, be swollen'; MFr. *bourranflé* 'puffy'; (Mod.) *bourenfler* 'to swell'; *bourenfle* 'bladder'; Bourg. *bourrenfle* 'overly swollen'; Berry *boudifler* 'to blister'; Suisse Rom. *boudifflo* 'fat-cheeked'; *REW* §1182a "bod" (Fr. *boudenflé* is listed in Index only), *FEW* "inflare" (possibly a tautological compound, *bourrer* 'to stuff' + *enfler*); N:bod- 'round shape'/ bourre 'hair, stuffing' + V:enfler 'to swell'

Pic. *bornifiker* 'to slap in the face (across the eyes)'; Corblet; N:bornifle 'soufflet dans les yeux' (var. of *mornifle* 'slap on the nose' [q.v.]) + V:ficher 'to fix (to)', 'mettre'

OFr. *borsoflé* 'swollen'; (16th c.) *boursouf(f)ler* 'to swell, be swollen'; OFr. *borroflement* 'swelling'; (16th c.) *boursouflure*, (19th c.) *boursouflement*, (19th c.) *boursouflage* idem; Diez "bouder," AD, *FEW* "sufflare" (rejects bod- → bour- on chronological grounds), T-L, B-W, *TLF*; N:bourre 'hair, stuffing'/bod- 'round shape' + V:souffler 'to blow'

(16th c.) bouleverser 'to upset, turn over'; AD (N + V), KN §569 (N + V), *REW* §1239 "botellum" (N:OFr. *boele* 'bowels' + *verser*), *FEW* "versare" (N + V, although more likely a tautological compound, with V:*bouler* 'to spill, roll'), B-W "boule"; N:boule (?) 'ball' + V:verser 'to spill'

Maine-et-Loire *bournicher, bourniger* 'to work without accomplishing much'; *bournigeoter* idem; *bournigerie* 'useless activity, painstaking work'; Verrier, *FEW* "burra" + "nidicare"; N:bourre 'hair, stuffing' + V:(West) nicher, niger 'to be lazy, waste time' (lit. "to make a nest")

à bout portant, touchant 'point-blank'; *FEW* "tokk-"; N:bout 'end' + V:porter, V:toucher 'to touch'

West *bulleménaou* 'noisy'; *FEW* "minare"; N:bruit 'noise' + V:mener 'to lead' + Adv:haut 'high, loud'

OFr-Pr. (Bresse) *burdemeclia* 'to mix'; *FEW* "*borda," "burra"; N:borda 'fraud'/bourre 'stuffing' + V:mêler 'to mix'

Southwest *chère en caillmachâ* 'to fall to pieces, cave in'; *en cailmacherat* 'on top of each other'; *FEW* "makk-"; N:cail 'pebble', 'caillou' + V:mâcher 'to chew'

Fr.-Pr. *(é)camp(h)oussi* 'to chase out'; Pic. (19th c.) *campousser* 'to banish; chase'; *prendre la campousse* 'to take to one's heels'; Corblet, *FEW* "*pulsiare"; N:champ 'field' + V:pousser 'to push'

Norm. *canverser* 'to turn an object on its side, turn it partly over'; *FEW* "versare"; N:chant 'edge' + V:verser 'to pour, turn'

Fr.-Pr. *caraviri* 'to upset'; *FEW* "vibrare"; N:cara 'face' + V:virer 'to turn'

OFr.-Pr. (*Girart de Roussillon*, hap.) *carbon-fadere*, var. *charbofaziera* 'charcoal-maker, charcoal-merchant', 'charbonnier'; *FEW* "facere" (OPr. *fadere* 'maker'); N:c(h)arbon 'charcoal' + V:faire/far 'to make, do'

MPic. (16th–17th c.) *carême prenant*, (Mod.) Perche *caren-prenan, calimpernant* 'Mardi-Gras, mask worn on Mardi-Gras' (OFr. *quarem pernant* [q.v.]); *Trésor Percheron*; N:carême 'Lent' + V:prendre 'to seize (= begin)'

OFr. (13th c.) *caresmentran, quaresmentrant, caresmentré, quaramantrei*, Fr.-Pr. *carimentrant* 'beginning of Lent'; God, *FEW* "quadragesima," T-L; N:carême 'Lent' + V:entrer 'to enter'

(16th c.) *carnaval*, Pic. (16th–17th c.) *carnavaux, carnavailles*, Pic. (19th c.) *carnavieux* 'Carnival, Carnival amusements' (from Ital. *carnevale* 'Shrove Tuesday, Mardi Gras'); *carnavalesque* 'pertaining to Carnival'; Corblet, B-W (OFr. [13th c.] *quarnivalle*), Debrie; N:It. carne 'flesh' + V:It. levare 'to remove'

OFr. (13th c.) *chafresner* 'to restrain, tame' (hap.); (12th c.) *chanfrein* 'bit (of a bridle); (armor covering) front part of a horse's head from the ears to the nostrils, nose'; *REW* §1668 "caput" (deverbal *chanfrein* originates in Gaulish *cantofrin*), *FEW* "caput" (*chanfrein* is deverbal), B-W, Greimas (verb is denominal from *chanfrein*); N:chap 'head' + V:OFr. frener 'to restrain, bridle'

(19th c. slang, from Bourg.) *chambarder* 'to upset, turn over, agitate, break'; (19th c.) *chambardement* 'overturning, disorder, violence'; (19th c.) *chambard* 'noise, disorder'; (19th c.) *chambardeur* 'noise-maker'; B-W; N:chambe 'jambe' + V:barder 'to slide'

chambouler (from East dials.) 'to turn upside down, stumble, trip, cause unrest'; *FEW* "bulla"; N:chant 'edge' + V:bouler 'to spill, roll'

West *champbouter* 'to place an object upside down'; *FEW* "canthus"; N:chant 'edge' + V:bouter 'to strike'

champbrûler 'to frost' (of vines); *FEW* "pilare"; N:champ 'field' + V:brûler 'to burn'

OFr. (1278) *champcheü* 'fallen on the battlefield'; *GRS* II §556 (N + Adj/Ptc), Greimas; N:champ 'field' + V:ch(e)oir 'to fall'

Yonne *champler* 'to frost' (of vines); *FEW* "pilare" (*n*27 argues for direct composition, as against metathesis of the *champbrûler*-type favored by Gamillscheg); N:champ 'field' + V:peler 'to peel'

(18th c.) *champlever* (engraving term) 'to remove material around a pattern, leaving it raised'; *champlevage* 'action of removing material . . .'; AD, *GRS* II §594 (N + V), AThomas 1898, B-W "champ," *TLF*; N:champ 'field of an engraving' + V:lever 'to raise'

OFr. (14th c.) *chanfraindre*, (17th c.) *chamfrainer*, (Mod.) *chanfreiner*, denomin. *chanfrer* 'to bevel'; MFr. (15th c.) *chanfraint, -freint*, (Mod.) *chanfrein* 'small oblique surface, chamfer, bevelled edge'; (15th c.) *chanfrainter* idem ("Mémoire des constructions faites au collège de Fortet, à Paris, en 1409," Bibl. Nat. Franç. 8630, fol. 68); (20th c.) *chanfreinage* 'bevelling'; West *regarder en chanfrein* 'to look underneath', 'regarder en dessous'; Verrier, AThomas 1898, *FEW* "canthus," B-W (*chanfraindre* is primary), *TLF*; N:chant 'edge' + V:fraindre 'to break'

(17th c.) *chantourner* 'to meander'; (17th c., woodworking) *chantourner*, Mons *cantourner* 'to cut out along a pattern'; *chantournage* 'cutting out along a pattern'; *chantournement* 'sinuous movement'; Pic. (refl.) *décantourner* 'to turn aside, work around'; Corblet, AD, Littré, *GRS* II §594 (N + V), AThomas 1898, KN §569 (N + V), *REW* §8794 "tornare," *FEW* "tornare," *TLF*; N:chant 'edge' + V:tourner 'to turn'

OFr. (FrComté) *charboter* 'to swell'; MFr. *encharboter* 'to embarrass'; *FEW* "botan"; N:chair 'flesh' + V:bouter 'to strike'

Fr-Pr. (16th c.) *chateni* 'to stop a bull by the horns' (lit. 'by the head'); 'to dominate; restrain, prevent s.o. from doing'; *FEW* "tenere"; N:chap 'head' + V:tenir 'to hold'

OFr. (12th c.) *chatien* 'aid, support'; *FEW* "tenere"; N:chap 'head' + V:tenir 'to hold'

Norm. *chatourne* 'slap'; *FEW* "tornare"; N:chap 'head' + V:tourner 'to turn'

Manche *chaufumer* 'to douse a crop with lime'; *FEW* "fumus"; N:chaux 'lime' + V:fumer 'to smoke'

Suisse Rom. *chauspougna* 'to manipulate; patrol'; *FEW* "pugnus"; N:CALCEM 'heel' + V:pougner (empoigner) 'to grab'

(17th c.) *chavirer* 'to capsize' (from Occ. *capvira* 'to turn upside down'); (19th c.) *chavirement, chavirage, chavirade* 'capsizing, overturning'; (19th c.) *chavirable* 'capsizable'; dial. *faire le chavirâ* 'to capsize'; Diez, AD, Verrier, Littré, *REW* §1668 "caput," Benveniste 1966 (N Instr + V), Kuryłowicz 1976 (N Dir Obj + V), B-W, *TLF*; N:Occ. cap 'head' + V:virer 'to turn'

Fr-Pr. *chéuplâ* 'to step on'; *FEW* "pilare"; N:CALCEM 'heel' + V:PILĀRE 'to push in; pile up'

Norm. *chiffe-tirer* 'to disagree'; Perche (19th c.) *(être) à chiffes-tirées, (avoir des) chiques-tirées, des chipes-tirées* 'to be on bad terms with s.o.'; Norm. *chiffetirée* 'quarrel, dispute'; Moisy 1887, *FEW* "martyrium," *Trésor Percheron*; N:chiffe 'rag' + V:tirer 'to pull'

OFr. (12th c.) *clo(u)fermer* 'to attach (with a nail)'; Bos, *FEW* "clavo figere"; N:clou 'nail' + V:OFr. fermer 'to attach'

OFr. (11th c.) *clofichié*, (12th c.) *claufiiés* 'crucified'; (1260) *cloufire, claufir*, (14th c.) *cloufichier, cloufichir* 'to nail, drive in (a nail); crucify'; *clofichement* 'fabrication of nails; nails'; *cloficheure* 'mark of nails'; AD, AThomas 1898, God *Lex*, Bos, *GRS* II §594 (N + V), KN §569 (N + V), *REW* §1980 "clāvifīgĕre," *FEW* "clavo figere," Greimas; N:clou 'nail' + V:ficher 'to fix (to)'

Berry *se coderser* 'to stand up, stand stiffly'; *FEW* "directiare"; N:coq 'cock' + V:dresser 'to stand on end'

MFr. (16th c.) *cœur-rongeant* 'which gnaws at the heart'; Marty-Laveaux; N:cœur 'heart' + V:ronger 'to gnaw'

(14th c.) *colporteur*, (15th c.) *-euse, -eresse* 'vendor', 'marchand ambulant'; (16th c.); *colporter* 'to carry on the neck, peddle, hawk'; (18th c.) *colportage* 'hawking, peddling'; AD (N + V), *GRS* II §594 (N + V), KN §569 (N + V), *REW* §2104 "comportāre," *FEW* "comportare" (reinterpretation of *comporter* through influence of OFr. *porter a col*), "portare" (cf. MFr. *portacol* 'peddler'), B-W; N:col 'neck' + V:porter 'to carry'

Norm. *corbatre* 'to torment', Boul. *se corbattre* 'to fight'; *FEW* "battuere" (*corpus* + *battuĕre*); N:corps 'body' (by reinterpretation of *com-?*) + V:battre 'to strike, beat'

OFr. *corda toccar* [sic] 'to touch the strings of a lyre'; *FEW* "tokk-"; N:corda 'string' + V:toccar 'to touch'

Pic. *corni-, cornufiker* 'to butt with a horn'; Corblet; N:corne 'horn' + V:ficher 'to fix (to)'

sans coup férir 'without striking a blow'; Porteau; N:coup 'blow' + V:férir 'to strike'

A.-Norm. *croizficher* 'to crucify'; *A.-Norm. Dict.*; N:croix 'cross' + V:ficher 'to fix (to)'

West *croulever* 'to rise and separate from the crumb', 'grincher' (of the breadcrust); (16th c.) *crousteleveur* [n.g.]; AD, AThomas 1898, *FEW* "crusta"; N:croûte 'crust' + V:lever 'to raise'

Mos. *cubassieu* 'to distort, mix'; *FEW* "*bottia"; N:cul 'butt' + V:bossuer 'to distort with lumps (*bosses*)'

Metz (NE France) *cuboûlé*, Moselle *ka(n)bolé* 'to tumble, turn upside down'; *FEW* "bulla"; N:cul 'butt' + V:bouler 'to spill, roll'

OFr. *cuirpaner* 'to cover with leather'; God *Lex*; N:cuir 'leather' + V:paner 'to cover'

MFr. (16th c.) *cuisse-né* 'born from the thigh'; Marty-Laveaux; N:cuisse 'thigh' + V:naître 'to be born (*né*)'

West (Nantes) *culbonder* 'to tumble, turn upside down'; *FEW* "culus"; N:cul 'butt' +
   V:bonder (Fr. *bondir* 'to jump')

(15th c.) *culbute* 'a tumble', (16th c.) *culbuter* 'to take a tumble' (*culer* + *bouter*); AD
   (N + V compound), *GRS* II §594 (N + V), KN §569 (N + V), *FEW* "culus,"
   B-W; N:cul 'butt' + V:buter 'to strike'

Bret. *külpeta* 'to tumble, turn upside down'; *FEW* "culus"; N:cul 'butt' + V:peter 'to
   break'

Wall. *culvéchi* 'to tumble, fall'; *FEW* "versare"; N:cul 'butt' + V:verser 'to pour, turn'

Wall. *cusoter* 'to bounce an object around, bob it in the air'; *FEW* "saltare"; N:cul
   'butt' + V:sauter 'to jump'

Fr-Pr. *cutemelé* 'to tumble, fall'; *FEW* "*tûmôn"; N:cul 'butt' + V:OFr. tumer 'to
   tumble'

Wall. *ès cutoûrner* (refl.) 'to move, agitate'; *FEW* "tornare"; N:cul 'butt' + V:tourner
   'to turn'

Pic. *décafiker* 'to husk, hull (nuts and fruits)' (cf. *escalbotter* [q.v.]); Corblet; N:Gmc.
   *SKALA (Pic. *écafle* 'husk, shell') + V:ficher 'to fix (to)', 'mettre'

OFr. *dieulever* 'raising, elevation of the Host'; God (*sonner a-Dieu-lever*); N:Dieu
   'God' + V:lever 'to raise'

OFr. (10th c.) *dieumenti, deumentiz* 'one who betrays his solemn oath'; *FEW* "deus"
   + "mentiri" (OFr. [13th c., hap.] *mentir Deu*); N:Dieu 'God' + V:mentir 'to lie'

(18th c.) *eau donner* 'to soak before adding indigo' (step in dying process); *FEW*
   "donare"; N:eau 'water' + V:donner 'to give'

Provins *s'éboulancer* 'to get ready to jump'; *FEW* "lanceare"; N:boule 'ball' + V:lancer
   'to throw'

Norm. *embaufumer* 'to stink (out)'; *FEW* "balsamum"; N:BALSAMU(M) 'balsam' +
   V:fumer 'to smoke'

Norm. *encauchumer* 'to spread lime'; Moisy 1877; en + N:caux 'lime' + V:sumer 'to
   sow, spread'

OFr. (13th c.) *enchifrené* 'subjugated by love', 'asservi d'amour', (17th c.) '(suffering
   from a) stuffy nose'; *enchifrener* 'to cause a head cold with accompanying
   stuffy nose'; Vendôme *enchifarme* m. 'head cold', 'enchiffrènement'; B-W
   "enchifrené," "chanfrein"; N:chief (chap) 'head' + V:OFr. frener 'to restrain,
   bridle'

Poit. *encoubaissé* 'to tie up an animal with the end of the halter'; *FEW* "collum";
   N:cou 'neck' + V:baisser 'to lower'

MFr. *escalbotter* 'to shell peas'; *FEW* "*skala"; N:Gmc. *SKALA 'scale' + V:bouter 'to
   strike, beat'

OFr. (14th c.) *estanfique*, (Mod.) *étanfiche* 'slender column in the masonry of a bay
   window'; Pic. *s'estafiker* 'to settle into one spot'; Pic. *détafiker* 'to displace,

detach'; Corblet ("se statu figere"), *FEW* "stare" (either V:STĀRE + V:fiche <
* FĪGĬCĀRE, or Gamillscheg's N:*estan + V:fichier); N:*estan 'supporting
beam' + V:fichier 'to fix (to), make fast'

Champ. *faire dzarvolá* 'to spin a dancer, make her petticoats fly'; *FEW* "volare";
N:jarret 'calf (of the leg)' + V:voler 'to fly'

OFr. (12th c.) (*soi*) *ferarmer* 'to cover oneself in armor', (12th–13th c.) *ferarmé*
'warrior'; AD, Bos, *GRS* II §556 (N + Adj/Ptc), KN §569 (N + V), *FEW*
"ferrum"; N:fer '(iron) armor' + V:armer 'to arm'

OFr. (11th c.) *fervesti*, (12th c.) *fervestir*, (13th c.) *fervestu* 'armored, protected'; AD,
Bos, *GRS* II §556 (N + Adj/Ptc), KN §569 (N + V), *FEW* "ferrum" +
"vestire"; N:fer '(iron) armor' + V:vêtir 'to clothe'

MFr. (16th c.) *feu-soufflant* 'fire-breathing'; Marty-Laveaux; N:feu 'fire' + V:souffler
'to blow'

MFr. (16th c.) *feu-vomissant* 'fire-spewing'; Marty-Laveaux; N:feu 'fire' + V:vomir 'to
vomir, spew forth'

OFr. (12th c.) *foimenti, -mentif, -entu*, (12th c.) *-menteör* 'traitor'; *foimentie* f. 'perjury,
violation of an oath'; AD, Bos, *GRS* II §556 (N + Adj/Ptc), God *Lex*, *FEW*
"fides," "mentiri"; N:foi 'faith' + V:mentir 'to lie'

OFr. *foitenant* 'loyal, keeping faith'; Walker; N:foi 'faith' + V:tenir 'to hold'

(13th–17th c.) *go(u)rfoler* 'to beat, trample, damage'; Norm.–West–Poit. *gour-, gar-,
guerfouler* 'to press, bruise, damage, crush, sprain, mistreat'; MFr. *gourfoule-
ment* 'bruise, wound'; Center *garfoulure* 'sprain'; West *en gourfoule* 'in a
compact group'; Verrier, Bos (*gort* 'club' +), *REW* §3560 "*fullāre," *FEW*
"fullare," Greimas ("premier élément obscur"), *Trésor Percheron*; N:go(u)r(t)
'club'/'fat' + V:fouler 'to beat, damage'

Fr-Pr. *gormenó* 'to bother, worry, pester', 'tarabuster' = (orig.) 'to make noise'; *FEW*
"minare"; N:GORR- 'noise of swine' + V:mener 'to lead'

Manche *goulimacher* 'to chew slowly'; *FEW* "gula" (+ *MAKKARE); N:guêle 'mouth'
+ V:mâcher 'to chew'

Wall.-Norm. *gourmacher* 'to ruminate'; Perche *gourmacher* 'to masticate, chew
incompletely, eat sloppily'; *FEW* "gorr-" + "masticare," *Trésor Percheron*;
N:GORR- 'noise of swine' + V:mâcher 'to chew'

Poit. *gourmelai* 'to mutter'; *FEW* "misculare"; N:GORR- 'noise of swine' + V:mêler 'to
mix'

Norm. *gournâcher* 'to nibble at'; *FEW* "nasicare"; N:GŬRDUS 'fat'/GORR- 'noise of
swine' (cf. Norm. *gourmacher*) + V:NĀSICĀRE 'to sniff(le)'

OFr.-MFr. *gouteprenant* 'with dignified mien' (lit. "contracting gout"); God *Lex*;
N:goute 'gout' + V:prendre 'to seize'

MFr. (*se*) *graisse-fondre* 'to stifle (with heat)'; *FEW* "*crassia"; N:graisse 'fat, grease'
    + V:fondre 'to melt'

MFr. (14th c.) *etre grosse d'enfant sentant* 'to feel one's unborn child moving'; *FEW*
    "sentire"; N:enfant 'child' + V:sentir 'to feel'

Pic. (19th c.) *harlifiker* 'to beat with a *hart*'; Corblet; N:(arch.) hart 'band, binder' (for
    bundles of twigs) + V:ficher 'to fix (to)', 'mettre'

Suisse Rom. *jambälou* 'to waddle, roll from side to side'; *FEW* "camba"; N:jambe 'leg'
    + V:BALLĀRE 'to dance'

MFr. (16th c.) *jour-apporte* (L. *lūcifer*, Gr. *phōsphóros*) 'bringing light'; N:jour
    'day(light)' + V:apporter 'to bring'

Pic. *se keurpiller* 'to grab by the hair, fight'; *FEW* "pilleum"; N:cuir 'leather, scalp' +
    V:piller 'to steal'

Manche *konbrüšé(r)* 'to scratch with a horn'; *FEW* "cornu"; N:corne 'horn' + V:dial.
    brüše(r) 'to scratch'

OFr. (Bret.) *koñibote* 'to walk swinging the head to and fro'; *FEW* "cornu"; N:corne
    'horn' + V:bouter 'to strike'

une lance tenant 'a lance-throw away'; *FEW* "tenere"; N:lance + V:tenir 'to hold'

(16th c.) *lettre-féru* 'well-lettered, learnèd' (Montaigne, cf. 16th-c. Occ. *létroferit*); AD
    (N + V), *DECC* "lletra" ("ja devia estar en ús en el s. 16, no sols en terres
    occitanes"); N:lettre 'letter' + V:férir 'to strike'

MFr. (16th c.) *lierre-porte* 'ivy-bearing'; Marty-Laveaux; N:lierre 'ivy' + V:porter 'to
    bear'

OFr. (1287) *luetenant*, (13th c.) *lieu tenant* 'replacement, deputy, administrator', (17th
    c.) *lieutenant* 'lieutenant'; *lieutenant général du royaume* 'one invested with royal
    authority'; 'magistrate, administrator'; (from 15th c.) 'military rank'; (15th c.)
    lieutenance 'grade or function of lieutenant'; *lieutenancie, lieutenanderie*
    'lieutenancy' (Merovingian Lat. *locumtenentia* 'charge'); *lieutenandise* 'function
    of lieutenant'; (1690) *lieutenante* 'wife of a magistrate with that title';
    lieutenant-colonel; *premier-lieutenant*; *sous-lieutenant*; AD, AThomas 1898,
    FEW "tenere," B-W "lieu" (Romance reflexes are calqued on Med.L. *locum
    tenēns*), Robert; N:lieu 'position' + V:tenir 'to hold'

OFr. (12th c.) *mainbornir, -bournir* 'to govern, administer, defend', (Mod.) East dials.
    mamborner 'to direct a legal ward, govern, dominate; mistreat'; OFr. (13th
    c.)–MFr., MPic. (15th c.) *ma(i)nbour, mambour* 'administrator, legal guardian,
    governor'; (12th c.) *mainbournie, -nerie, mainbournixe, -nissement* 'guardian-
    ship'; *mainbourneur, -nisseör* 'guardian, governor'; Bos, God *Lex, FEW*
    "mundboro," Debrie; N:MUNDEBORO [MUND 'hand' + BERAN 'to carry,
    support'] 'protector', blended with *main* 'hand'

OFr. (feudal) *mainfait* 'loss of rights of lineage'; N:main 'hand' + V:faire 'to make, do'

(14th c.) *mainlevée* (law) 'withdrawal, release of mortgage, restoration of goods' (cf. apr. *manlevar* 'obtenir sous garantie la délivrance d'une personne arrêtée, d'une chose saisie, etc.'); AD ("N + Adj juxtaposé"), *FEW* "levare"; N:main 'hand' + V:lever 'to raise'

OFr. (14th c.) *mainmetre*, MFr. *manumetre, -metter* 'to free a slave'; OFr. (12th c.) *marmissio*, OFr.–MFr. *mainmission, manumission* 'emancipation'; (14th c.) *mainmise, misemain* 'legal confiscation, seizure; domination', (Mod.) 'confiscation'; DuC, God *Lex*, *FEW* "manumittere," Greimas, de Gorog, Robert; N:main 'hand' + V:mettre 'to place'

MFr.–Mod.Fr. *sans main mettre* 'without effort, physical or financial'; *FEW* "manus"; N:main 'hand' + V:mettre 'to place'

OFr.–MFr. (13th–14th c.) *mainmuable* 'serf who could change hands' (cf. OGasc. *maamudar* 'to change hands' [of property] [q.v.]); T-L; N:main 'hand' + V:muer 'to change'

OFr. *mainpast*, A.-Norm. *manupast* 'household, protégés of a lord, dependent, servant'; *REW* §5338 "*manūpāstus," *FEW* "*manu pastus," "pascere" (perhaps modeled on *mainbor*); N:main 'hand' + V:PĀSTU(M) 'nourished'

OFr. (14th c.)–MFr. *mainplant* 'plantation (by the hand of man)'; *FEW* "manus"; N:main 'hand' + V:planter 'to plant'

A.-Norm. (13th c.) *main-, meynprendre* 'to guarantee, accept a guarantee or caution'; *main-, meynpernor, -preneör* 'guarantor'; *mainpris, mainprise* 'guarantee, bail, act of posting bail'; (14th c.) *mainprenable* 'able to guarantee, post bail'; God *Lex*, *FEW* "manus" + "prehendere," Greimas; N:main 'hand' + V:prendre 'to seize'

(ca. 1130) *maintenir*, OFr. vars. *mantenoir, -toivre*, OPoit. *mantaire* 'to defend, protect, govern a land', (Mod.) 'to hold up, maintain'; A.-Norm. *maintenant* 'support, means of support'; *maintenement* 'conservation; support; conduct'; (1155) *maintenance, manutenance* 'protection, preservation; action of maintaining, of confirming'; A.-Norm. (12th c.) *maintenance, -tenant, -tenement* 'means of support'; (1953) (from Eng.) 'maintenance'; (13th c.) *maintien* '(action of) maintaining', (Mod.) 'keeping order', 'upholding (of an opinion)', 'carriage, countenance'; (15th c.) *maintenue* 'administration'; 'le fait de loger quelque part', 'conservation'; (16th c.) (law) 'jugement confirmant quelqu'un dans la possession d'un bien ou droit'; (1931) *maintenage* (tech.) '(re)forestation', (North) 'regulation width or height of a mine-shaft'; OFr. *mainteneor*, A.-Norm. (12th c.) *maintenere*, MFr. (1460) *manuteneur* 'protector, support(er)', (19th c.) *mainteneur* 'who maintains'; OFr. *parmantenir* 'to maintain fully'; OFr. *parmainteneur* 'who maintains, supports constantly'; OFr. (law) *faire admaintenance d'une requête* 'persister aux fins d'une requête, en maintenir les conclusions, les affirmer'; (1170) *maintenant* 'at once', (Mod.) 'now'; *demaintenant* idem, (nom.) 'the present moment'; OFr. *tres maintenant* 'as of now'; AD, AThomas 1898, God *Lex*, Moisy 1895, *GRS* II §594 (N + V), KN §569 (N + V), *REW* §5340 "manūtenēre," *FEW* "manu tenere," Malkiel 1945, T-L, Walker; N:main 'hand' + V:tenir 'to hold'

MFr. (15th c.) *maintien*, Belg. *mantagne*, Norm. *maintint* 'handle of a flail'; Fr-Pr. *manténa* 'balustrade' (cf. *tient-main* 'bannister' [q.v.]); Fr. *maintenant* m. 'end of the oar in a galley' (from Occ.); Moisy 1887 ("*manu tentus*"), *FEW* "manu tenere," *DECC* "mà"; N:main 'hand' + V:tenir 'to hold'

(17th c.) *à main-tourner* 'in a flash', 'en un tourne-main'; *FEW* "tornare"; N:main 'hand' + V:tourner 'to turn'

(18th c.) *malitouche* f. 'malady allegedly cured by the laying on of hands by Pierre de Lentivi and his descendants'; *FEW* "tokk-"; N:main 'hand' + V:toucher 'to touch'

OFr. (1112) *manaie, manaye* 'aid, power, possession, quarter', *manaide* 'pity'; (12th c.) *mana(i)ier* 'to protect, guarantee; take pity on'; *manaidier* 'to treat with mercy'; *en manaye* 'abundantly'; Diez "manaier," AD, Bos, *REW* §5339 "manus"; N:main 'hand' + V:aider 'to aid'

West (19th c.) *manifait* 'mischievous', 'qui aime à faire des niches'; Verrier (perhaps from *manu facit* 'qui se livre à des jeux de mains'); N:main 'hand' + V: faire 'to do'

Suisse Rom. *māpa, mēpá* 'third cowman', *mampat* 'suspicious-looking fellow'; Engad. *paschamaint* 'sustenance for Alpen herdsmen'; *REW* §5338 "*manūpāstus*," *REW* §6263 "pascĕre," *FEW* "*manu pastus*"; N:main 'hand' + V:PĀSTU(M) 'nourished'

Vosges *ma(n)toš* 'handle of a flail'; *FEW* "manu tenere"; N:main 'hand' + V:tenir 'to hold' × (dial.) toucher 'to strike'

OFr. (1248) *manuevre* 'corvée manuelle', 'quota of manual labor owed to the feudal lord', (Mod.) f. *manœuvre* 'maneuver'; m. *manœuvre* (15th c.) 'manual laborer', (Mod.) 'unskilled laborer'; (11th c.) *manuvrer* 'to work or put with one's hands', *manovrier*, (Mod.) *manœuvrer* 'to work, maneuver', dial. (West) *manoper* 'to handle carelessly'; *manopá, mani-, menoper* 'to caress'; (12th c.) *manouvrier* 'day laborer', (Mod.) *manœuvrier* 'first-class seaman, military tactician; skillful in maneuvering'; (1706) *main-d'œuvre* 'labor, manpower'; (19th c.) *manœuvrabilité* 'maneuverability'; *mainœuvrerie* 'dwelling of a manœuvre'; Diez, AD, *GRS* II §594 (N + V), AThomas 1898, *REW* §5336

"manūŏperāre," *FEW* "manuopera," *DCE[LC]* "mano"; N:main 'hand' +
V:œuvrer 'to work'

OFr. (13th c.) *mentevoir, -aveir, ment-, mantoivre, a-/re-mentevoir,* OPoit. *mantaire* 'to
remember, notice'; *amentevoir, amentoivre* idem; *amentevance* 'remembrance';
amenteveur 'one who remembers'; *ramentevoir* 'to recognize'; *ramentevable*
'deserving of remembrance'; *ramentevance, ramentoivement* 'remembrance';
AD (*mentoivre* by analogy with *recevoir/recoivre*), AThomas 1898, Bos, *GRS*
II §594 (N + V), *REW* §5507 "mĕnte habēre," *FEW* "mens"; N:MĔNTE(M)
'mind' + V:avoir 'to have'

(20th c.) *microchanter* 'to sing into a microphone'; Céline; N:micro 'microphone' +
V:chanter 'to sing'

MFr. (16th c.) *montagne-porte* 'mountain-bearing'; Marty-Laveaux; N:montagne
'mountain' + V:porter 'to bear'

(1320) *morfondre* (arch.) 'to catch cold' (of horses), (Mod.) 'to chill to the bone;
mope, fret, be dejected'; OFr. (13th c.) *morfondee* 'snot, nasal catarrh'; MFr.
(15th c.) *morfondure, morfonture* 'nasal catarrh' (of horses); *morfondement*
idem; *morfondu* 'dejected'; *morfondant* 'freezing'; AD, AThomas 1898, KN
§569 (N + V), *FEW* "fundere," B-W (from Occ. *mourre*); N:mourre 'snout' +
V:fondre 'to melt'

(16th c.) *mornifle* 'slap, swat on the nose' (with the back of the hand), (19th c., rare)
mornifler 'to slap'; *FEW* "niff-," B-W (probably deverbal, from **mournifler*);
N:mourre 'snout' + V:nifler 'to sniff(le)'

Belg. *mourmacher, -î* 'to chew, ruminate'; *FEW* "masticare"; N:mourre 'snout' +
V:mâcher 'to chew'

OFr. *nientdisant* 'insignificant, of which one can say naught, which tells one naught';
God; N:nient 'nothing' + V:dire 'to say'

OFr. *nongresachant* 'unthankful, ungrateful'; OFr. *nongrésachance* 'unthankfulness';
T-L, Greimas (*nonsachant* 'ignorant'), Walker; N:gré 'thankfulness' + V:(non)
savoir '(not) to know, be ignorant of'

MFr. (16th c.) *nuit-volant* 'flying by night'; Marty-Laveaux; N:nuit 'night' + V:voler
'to fly'

OFr. (1240) *orbatteur,* OFr. (1280)–MFr. *orbateör* 'goldsmith', 'batteur d'or'; (14th c.)
orbateresse 'batteuse d'or'; (14th c.) *orbatre* 'to work gold'; (14th c.) *orbaterie,
orbateüre* 'goldsmithing'; God *Lex, FEW* "aurum"; N:or 'gold' + V:battre 'to
beat'

OFr. (12th c.) *orfergié* 'embroidered with gold'; God (from a translation of Latin
psalms), Greimas; N:or 'gold' + V:fergier 'to chain'

OFr. *orpoignant* 'gold embroidery'; God (*auripictum*); N:or 'gold' + V:poindre 'to
embroider'

MFr. (16th c.) *Ourse-gardant* 'watching the heavens' (lit. the constellation Ursa);
Marty-Laveaux; N:Ourse '(Great/Little) Bear' + V:(re)garder 'to look at'

OFr. *painquerant* 'mendicant (friar)', lit. 'seeking [gifts of] bread'; Norm. (19th c.) *être
à son pain chercher* 'to be absolutely indigent'; Moisy 1887, T-L, Walker;
N:pain 'bread' + V:OFr. querre, (Mod.) chercher 'to search for'

Center *pallemener* 'to scrape soil around vines with a shovel'; *FEW* "pala"; N:pelle
'shovel' + V:mener 'to lead'

MFr. (Poit., 16th–18th c.) *part-prenant* 'legatee', 'personne ayant part dans un
héritage'; *FEW* "pars"; N:part 'part' + V:prendre 'to take, seize'

Fr-Pr. *patevôler* 'to flutter around in circles', East *pativoler* 'to flutter the wings and
push with the feet' (of chickens); Bourg. *(ils) s'épatvoulant* '(they) squawk and
flap their wings'; *FEW* "patt-," "volare"; N:patte 'leg, paw' + V:voler 'to fly'

Norm. (19th c.) *patte-fiche* (woodworking) 'large triangular nail with square shank and
flat head' (for mirrors, etc.); Moisy 1887, B-W; N:patte 'leg, paw, tongue' +
V:ficher 'to fix (to)'

(20th c.) *pattemouille* 'damp cloth for ironing'; Robert (Gmc. **paita* + *mouiller*);
N:(dial.) patte 'rag' + V:mouiller 'to dampen'

East *pauficher* 'to work clumsily'; West *paufichonner* 'to tear to shreds'; *FEW* "palus"
+ "*figicare"; N:PĀLU(M) 'stick' + V:ficher 'to fix (to)'

Center *peaumuer* 'to molt'; *FEW* "mutare"; N:peau 'skin' + V:muer 'to molt'

OFr. *pele-fouans* 'digging with a shovel'; DuC; N:pelle 'shovel' + V:OFr. foer (fouir)
'to shovel'

(19th c.) *pelleverser* 'to shovel'; *pelleversage* 'shoveling'; *pelleversoir* 'shovel'; AD,
AThomas 1898, M, *FEW* "pala" (from Lim. *palaversa* [q.v.], in which *versa(r)*
replaced nom. *bessa* 'square shovel'); N:pelle 'shovel' + V:verser 'to pour,
turn'

OFr. *pié estant*, MFr. *piez estant* 'immediately', Belg. *pî-stant, stant-pî* 'standing'; *FEW*
"stare"; N:pied 'foot' + V:être 'to be' ([e]stant)

(17th c.) *geler à pierre fendre, à pierre fendant* 'to freeze'; *FEW* "findere," Porteau
1961:45; N:pierre 'stone' + V:fendre 'to split'

MFr. (Bret.) (law) *poifait* 'negligence'; *poifaisant* 'negligent'; God; N:poi 'little' +
V:faire 'to make, do'

North *pore-levet* 'male midwife', 'accoucheur juré'; *FEW* "levare"; N:père 'father' +
V:lever 'to raise'

Vaud. *puoutirar* 'to pull by the hair'; *FEW* "martyrium"; N:poil 'hair' + V:tirer 'to pull'

OFr. (13th c.) *quaresmentrant, quaramantrei* 'beginning of Lent'; God, Bos, *FEW*
"quadragesima," T-L "caresme entrant"; N:carême 'Lent' + V:entrer 'to enter'

OFr. (12th c.) *quarem pernant, prenant* 'beginning of Lent'; God, *FEW* "quadragesima"; N:carême 'Lent' + V:prendre 'to seize (= begin)'

Suisse Rom. *quesauter* 'to hop about'; *FEW* "saltare"; N:queue 'tail' + V:sauter 'to jump'

OFr. (12th c.) *sancmesler, estre sanmellez* 'to catch cold from one's wounds; become upset or angry'; MFr. *se sangmeller*, (17th c.) *faire sang mesler* idem, 'to make one's blood boil'; (15th c.) *sancmesleure* 'trouble, emotion'; Center (Mod.) *sang-mêlure* (bot.) 'common name for the *fumeterre*'; *sancmelison* 'anger, trouble'; Norm.–Center *sang mêlai* 'illness said to be caused by a panic'; *sang-meslé* 'extraordinary, bloodcurdling' (of a fright); Norm. *ensangmêler* 'to be troubled'; God, *FEW* "sanguis," Greimas; N:sang 'blood' + V:mêler 'to mix'

Suisse Rom. *sādzevra, sanzayvrá* 'to catch cold'; *avé un sanggivre* 'be in a cold sweat'; *sadzevro* 'numbed with cold'; *sadzáivre* 'fever with chills'; *FEW* "sanguis"; N:sang 'blood' + V:givrer 'to freeze'

Center–West *se san(g)-glacer* 'to catch pleurisy, be hot and cold'; *sangglacé* 'pleurisy, chill'; *FEW* "sanguis"; N:sang 'blood' + V:glacer 'to freeze'

OFr. *sangmüer* 'to catch a cold'; *avoir le sang mué* 'to be troubled'; *sangmueçon* 'agitation', (13th c.) *sangmuçonner* 'be troubled'; MFr. *sangmeué* 'troubled, frightened', Bourg. *sanmu* '(emotionally) touched'; *FEW* "sanguis," T-L; N:sang 'blood' + V:mouvoir 'to move'

Center *santourner* 'to turn an object over and over'; *FEW* "tornare"; N:sens 'direction' + V:tourner 'to turn'

Fr-Pr. *sanveri* 'to upset'; *FEW* "vibrare"; N:sang 'blood' + V:virer 'to turn'

MFr. (15th c.) (law) *sauf-faisant* 'homme qui, demeurant dans l'étendue d'une justice seigneuriale, n'en était pas justiciable'; *FEW* "salvus"; N:sauf 'safe' + V:faire 'to make, do'

(14th c.) *saupiquet* 'spicy sauce or stew'; (Mod., since 1712) *salpicon* idem; MFr. *saupiquette* 'saupiquet'; MFr. (16th c.) *saupiqué* 'gamey' (of fish); MFr. *saupiqueter* 'to give a spicy taste'; *FEW* "sal"; B-W (from **saupiquer* 'piquer avec du sel'), Robert, Corominas–Pascual "sal" (OFr. *saupiquée*); N:sel 'salt' + V:piquer 'to strike'

(1398) *saupoudrer* 'to sprinkle (with salt)'; (1873) *saupoudrage* 'sprinkling'; (1825) *saupoudroir*, (1900) *saupoudreur* 'sprinkler, shaker'; (adj.) *saupoudrant*; *saupoudré* 'condiment of vinegar, salt, figs, and honey, cooked and pulverized'; AD, AThomas 1898, KN §569 (N + V), *REW* §7521 "sāl," *FEW* "sal"; N:sel 'salt' + V:poudrer 'to powder'

OFr. (12th c.) *signeportant* 'zodiac' (also *signiferant*; cf. L. *signifer*); Walker; N:signe 'sign' + V:porter 'to bear'

Bourg. *taneuser* 'to waste time'; *FEW* "tempus"; N:temps 'time' + V:user 'to use (up)'

Suisse rom. *tarabuta* 'to uncover the base of a wall or tree'; *FEW* "terra"; N:terre 'land' + V:bouter 'to strike'

Bourg. *taramatsíe* 'to chew'; *FEW* "masticare"; N:(onom.) TAR- 'noise' + V:mâcher
     'to chew'

Jura *tarmené* 'to rumble'; *FEW* "minare"; N:(onom.) TAR- 'noise' + V:mener 'to lead'

Morv. *tenduement* 'ennui, melancholy'; *FEW* "durare"; N:temps 'time' + V:durer 'to
     last' + -ment

West *terrebécher* 'to hoe with a *terrebéchet*'; *FEW* "*bissicare"; N:terre 'land' +
     V:bêcher 'to shovel'

MFr. (15th c.) *terreguarde* 'police' (cf. OPr. *terragarda* 'action of visiting an estate');
     God *Lex*, *FEW* "terra"; N:terre 'land' + V:garder 'to guard'

terrejeter 'to plant in rows', 'labourer par la culture en planches' (cf. OPr. *terragiet*
     'earth removed from a trench and thrown up along the sides'); *FEW* "terra";
     N:terre 'land' + V:jeter 'to throw'

(16th c.) *terre-né* 'earthborn'; *FEW* "terra"; N:terre 'land' + V:naître 'to be born (*né*)'

MFr. *terretenant* 'foot-soldier'; God, *FEW* "terra"; N:terre 'land' + V:tenir 'to hold

OFr. (12th c.) *torfait* 'wrongdoing'; *torfaire* 'to do a wrong'; (13th c.) *torfesor*
     'wrongdoer, enemy'; God, Greimas; N:tort 'wrong' + V:faire 'to make, do'

tranche-maçonné (heraldry) 'se dit d'un écu dont une division est en maçonnerie';
     AD, Littré; N:tranche 'slice, edge' + V:maçonner 'to construct of masonry'

OTHER COMPOUND STRUCTURES APPROXIMATING N + V

arcbouter 'to support with a flying buttress'; AD, *GRS* II §594; N:arc-boutant 'flying
     buttress' + V:-er

(13th c.) *caillebotter* 'to coagulate'; AD (N + V compound), KN §569 (N + V), B-W;
     V:cailler 'to coagulate' + (West) botter 'to gather into bunches'

Fr-Pr. *champihtar* 'to tread on someone's foot'; *FEW* "calcare"; V:CALCĀRE +
     V:PISTĀRE

OFr. (13th c.) *chapignier* 'to tear, rip'; Pic. (19th c.) *capeigner* (refl.) 'to grab by the
     hair'; OFr. *chapignement* 'struggle, blow'; Corblet (*caput* + *pigner*), God *Lex*;
     either N:chap 'head' or V:OFr. chapler 'to strike, split' + V:OFr. pigner 'to
     beat'

Jura *chôvanté* 'to dry out prematurely from warm winds' (of cereals); *FEW* "ventus";
     N:chaud vent 'warm wind' + V:-er

Fr-Pr. *corfoundut* '(emotionally) moved'; *FEW* "fundere"; N:cor 'heart' + V:fondre 'to
     melt'

(18th c.) *court-mancher* (culin.) 'to prepare a shoulder of lamb'; *Dictionnaire Général*
     (either N + V, or N + Adj + -er); Adj:court 'short' + N:manche 'sleeve' +
     V:-er

culberger 'to tumble, take a spill backwards'; *FEW* "culus"; N:cul 'butt' + berge 'edge (of a river, etc.)' + V:-er

(16th c.) *jouer au cul levé*, (18th c.) *jouer à lève-cul* 'to replace the loser, while playing'; (ornith.) MFr. *hausse-queue* 'wagtail'; *FEW* "culus"; N:cul 'butt' + V:lever 'to raise'

Loir-et-Cher *s'écalpatrer* 'to fall facedown, prone'; *FEW* "patt-"; N:Gmc. *skala 'scale' + patte 'leg, foot' + V:-er

(18th c.) *escalborder* 'to embark'; *FEW* "bord"; N:*skala 'scale' + bord '(ship)board' + V:-er

MFr. *escalventrer* 'to burst a stomach, by kicking'; *FEW* "venter"; N:Gmc. *skala 'scale' + ventre 'belly' + V:-er

faufiler 'to baste'; *GRS* II §594, Wartburg 1922, Barbier 1930; N:faux fil 'false thread' + V:-er

OFr. (12th c.) *ferlier* 'to bind tightly', OWall. *ferm lier*; AD (N + V), *GRS* II §594 (N + V), KN §569 (N + V), *REW* §3320 "fĭrmus," *FEW* "firmus"; Adj:fer(me) 'firm(ly)' + V:lier 'to bind'

OFr. *fernoer* 'to tie up tightly'; KN §569 (N + V), *REW* §3320 "fĭrmus," *FEW* "firmus"; Adj:fer(me) 'firm(ly)' + V:nouer 'to bind'

franc-tenant 'qui possède noblement et sans aucune charge roturière'; *FEW* "frank"; Adj:franc 'free' + V:tenir 'to hold'

Perche *frasibouiller* 'to speak inconsiderately'; *Trésor Percheron*; N:phrase 'sentence' + -bouiller (? cf. *gribouiller* 'to scribble)

MFr. *gras-fondure* '(equine) loss of weight, consequent on disease', (Mod.) *gras-fondu* 'emaciated'; *FEW* "crassus"; N:gras 'fat' + V:fondre 'to melt'

Fr-Pr. *graspilyi* 'to steal, ravage'; *FEW* "pilleum" 'rag'; N:gras 'fat' + V:piller 'to plunder'

OFr. (12th c.) *g(u)aimenter* 'to lament'; Diez, Bos, Greimas; N:guai 'alas' + V:(la)menter 'to lament' (cf. *lai* 'alas')

OFr. (13th c.) *houcepignier*, (Mod.) *houspiller* 'to scold'; *Dictionnaire Général* (N + V), *REW* §4229b "hultia," B-W "houx"; V:housser 'to sweep with a broom' + V:OFr. pigner 'to comb' + -iller

OFr. *jambaterrer*, OFr-Pr. *janbe terrat* 'to dismount'; *FEW* "terra," Walker; N:camba 'leg' + V:(?) terrata 'set on the ground', or N:jambe + a + terre 'foot on ground' + V:-er

OFr. *jointenant* 'joint tenant', *jointenanc(i)e* 'joint tenancy'; God *Lex*, Malkiel 1945; Adj:join(t) 'joint' + V:tenir 'to hold'

nerf failli 'tendon du cheval qui diminue vers le pli du genou'; *FEW* "nervus"; N:nerf 'muscle, nerve' + V:faillir 'to fail'

(17th c.) *nerf-féru* '(equine) inflammation of the tendon'; (17th c.) *nerf-férure* 'bruise of the tendon'; *nerférer* 'to bruise, inflame'; AThomas 1898, *FEW* "nervus" + "ferire"; N:nerf 'nerve' + V:férir 'to strike'

(19th c.) *nerf-foulure* 'equine sprain of the tendon'; *FEW* "fullare"; N:nerf 'muscle, nerve' + V:fouler 'to sprain'

(nom.) *nerfrē* 'limping, incapable of walking' (of an animal); *FEW* "nervus"; N:nerf 'muscle, nerve' + V:FRANGĔRE 'to fracture'

Fr. (19th c.) *palafitte* (archeol.) 'pile-dwelling' (from It. *palafitta*); *DECC* "pal"; N:It. palo 'stick' + V:It. figgere 'to fix (to)'

(12th c.) *pêle-mêle* 'in a mixed-up fashion', *peslemesler* 'to mix'; *GRS* II §594 (N + V), *REW* §5606 "misculāre," *FEW* "misculare," B-W (differentiation of *mesle-mesle* idem); V:mêler 'to mix'

Fr-Pr. *sampilli* 'to tear into rags'; *FEW* "pilleum"; N:cent 'hundred' + V:piller 'to plunder'

A.-Norm. *sancfuison* 'bloodshed, loss of blood' (FŪSIŌNEM); *FEW* "sanguis"; N:sang 'blood' + V:FŪSIŌNEM × FŬNDĔRE

A.-Norm. (13th c.) *sangterné* 'mixed with blood'; *FEW* "sanguis"; N:sang 'blood' + V:(?) tourner/ternir 'to (make) dull' (not att. before late 14th c.)

Nantes *avoir les sangs tournés* 'be upset'; Norm. *sang-tourné* 'illness said to be caused by a panic'; Le Havre *mourir d'un santourné* 'to die of apoplexy'; *FEW* "sanguis" + "tornare"; N:sang 'blood' + V:tourner 'to turn'

(16th c.) *saugrenu* 'preposterous' (from 16th-c. *saugrenée* 'fricassee of peas' by reinterpretation as *sel* + *grain*); nominal suffix of exaggeration *-u* < -ŪTU); AD (N + V), B-W "sel"; N:sel 'salt' + grain 'grain' + V:-er

solbatu 'footsore' (of cattle); *sole battue* 'wound on sole of horses's hoof'; *FEW* "solea"; N:sole 'foot' + V:battre 'to beat'

(15th c.) Fr. (West) *tient-main* 'handhold, protuberance that affords purchase'; *FEW* "tenere"; N:main 'hand' + V:tenir 'to hold'

OFr. *tourneboeler* 'to tumble, fall head over heels', from (12th c.) *'torneboele* 'a tumble'; *GRS* II §594, Greimas; V:tourner 'to turn' + N:OFr. boele 'bowels'

MFr. (16th c.) *tournevirer* 'to spin around'; *GRS* II §594; V:tourner 'to turn' + V:virer 'to turn' + V:-er

OFr. (13th c.) *vermoulu* 'worm-eaten', (13th c.) *vermoulure*, (16th c.) *vermolissure*; AD (N + V), *GRS* II §556 (N + Adj/Ptc), God, KN §569 (N + V), Orr 1951 (a likely reinterpretation of *vermelu, -elé* 'wormy'; cf. *motelé* 'spotty' → Eng. *motley*), B-W "moudre"; N:ver(m) 'worm' + V:moudre 'to grind'

DUBIOUS

FrComté *caboule* 'bump on the forehead'; *-er*, Doubs *camboulâ* 'to bump on the forehead'; *FEW* "bulla" (prefixal *ca(m)-*, with influence of AMPULLA); N:boule 'bump' + V:-er

FrComté *coulisbata* 'to slither'; *FEW* "colare"; V:couler 'to slide' + ?

(15th c.) *courbatu* 'beaten, stiff, aching all over'; B-W "battre"; Adj:court '(with) short(ened arms)' + V:battre 'to beat'

Norm. *culoiner* 'to tarry, dawdle in one's work'; Perche *culouâner*, *cultouâner* idem; Moisy 1877, *Trésor Percheron*; N:cul 'butt' + ?

Norm. *faim-vaillé*, *-vaillier* 'having a great appetite'; *Trésor Percheron*; N:faim 'hunger' + ?

Reims *fergouiller* 'to make a noise in the water with an instrument'; *FEW* "*gullja" 'pool'; N:(?) Gmc. ver- + (?) gouiller

Perche *ferlamper* 'to beat s.o.'; *Trésor Percheron*; N:(?) Gmc. ver- + (?) lamper

Lainsecq *se ferlicher* 'to lick one's lips'; *FEW* "*lekkon"; N:(?) Gmc. ver- + V:lécher 'to lick'

Perche *fernouiller* 'to make a noise by shaking a bunch of objects'; *défernouiller* 'to leave hurriedly'; *Trésor Percheron*; N:(?) Gmc. ver- + (?) nouiller

Cher *gangouiller* 'to splash about in the water'; *FEW* "*gullja" 'pool'; N:? + V:gouiller

St-Pol *mafouye(r)* 'to mistreat, handle roughly'; *FEW* "*fodiculare"; N:ma(i)n 'hand' + V:fouiller 'to handle', or pref. *mal* +

Perche *oulvasser* 'to buffet back and forth' (of an object in a river); *Trésor Percheron*; N:oules f.pl. 'cavities in a riverbed' + ?

Orléans *vertaper* 'to plug up'; *FEW* "tappôn" 'to plug, mend'; N:(?) + V:taper 'to plug'

MEDIEVAL AND RENAISSANCE FRENCH NOMINAL ELEMENTS

aile-porte	N:aile 'wing'	V:porter
billebarrer	N:bille 'wooden wedge, stripe'	V:barrer
blanc-signé	N:blanc 'white'	V:signer
bouleverser	N:boule 'ball'	V:verser
boranfler, bourranflé	N:bourre 'stuffing'/ BOD- 'round shape'	V:enfler

burdemeclia	N:bourre 'stuffing'/ BORDA 'fraud'	V:mêler
borsoflé, boursouffler	N:bourre	V:souffler
boffumer	N:BUFF- 'blowing noise'	V:fumer
caresmentré, -entrant	N:carème 'Lent'	V:entrer
quaresme prenant	N:carème	V:prendre
charboter, encharboter	N:chair 'flesh'	V:bouter
champcheü	N:champ 'field'	V:choir
chanfraindre	N:chant 'edge'	V:fraindre
chanfrein, chafresner	N:cha(p)- 'head'	V:OFr. frener
enchifrené	N:cha(p)-	V:OFr. frener
chatien, chateni	N:cha(p)-	V:tenir
carbon-fadere	N:c(h)arbon 'charcoal'	V:faire
clo(u)fermer	N:clou 'nail'	V:OFr. fermer
cloufichier, cloufir	N:clou	V:ficher
cœur-rongeant	N:cœur 'heart'	V:ronger
colporter	N:col 'neck'	V:porter
koñibote	N:corne 'horn'	V:bouter
croizficher	N:croiz 'cross'	V:ficher
cuirpaner	N:cuir 'leather'	V:paner
cuisse-né	N:cuisse 'thigh'	V:naître
dieulever	N:dieu 'God'	V:lever
dieu-menti, deumentiz	N:dieu	V:mentir
estanfique	N:*ESTAN 'supporting beam'	V:ficher
ferarmer	N:fer 'iron'	V:armer
fervestir	N:fer	V:vêtir
feu-soufflant	N:feu 'fire'	V:souffler
feu-vomissant	N:feu	V:vomir

foimenti, feimentie	N:foi 'faith'	V:mentir
foitenant	N:foi	V:tenir
gorfoler, gour-, garfoler	N:go(u)r(t) 'club; fat'	V:fouler
gouteprenant	N:goutte 'gout'	V:prendre
graisse-fondre	N:graisse 'grease, fat'	V:fondre
nongresachant	N:gré 'thankfulness'	V:non . . . savoir
jour-apporte	N:jour 'day'	V:apporter
lettre-féru	N:lettre 'letter'	V:férir 'to strike'
lierre-porte	N:lierre 'ivy'	V:porter
luetenant	N:lieu 'position'	V:tenir
manaidier, manaier	N:main 'hand'	V:aider
mainbor, mainbornir	N:MUNDEBORO 'protector'	
mainfait	N:main	V:faire
mainlevée	N:main	V:lever
main-, manumetre, marmissio	N:main	V:mettre
mainmuable	N:main	V:muer
manovier, manuvrer	N:main	V:œuvrer
mainpast	N:main	V:PĀSTU(M)
main-plant	N:main	V:planter
mainprendre, mainprise	N:main	V:prendre
maintenir, maintien	N:main	V:tenir
mentevoir, -oivre	N:MĔNTE(M) 'mind'	V:avoir
montagne-porte	N:montagne 'mountain'	V:porter
morfondre	N:mourre 'snout'	V:fondre
nientdisant	N:nient 'nothing'	V:dire
nuit-volant	N:nuit 'night'	V:voler
orbateör, orbatre	N:or 'gold'	V:battre
orfergié	N:or	V:fergier
orpoignant	N:or	V:poindre
Ourse-gardant	N:Ourse '(Great/ Little) Bear'	V:(re)garder

painquerant	N:pain 'bread'	V:OFr. querre
part-prenant	N:part 'part'	V:prendre
pele-fouans	N:pelle 'shovel'	V:fouir
poifaisant	N:peu 'little'	V:faire
saupiquet (*saupiquer) saupoudrer	N:sal 'salt' N:sal	V:piquer V:poudrer
sancmesler sancmuer	N:sang 'blood' N:sang	V:mêler V:muer
signeportant	N:signe 'sign'	V:porter
escalbotter	N:*SKALA 'scale, shell'	V:bouter
terreguarde terre-né terretenant	N:terre 'land' N:terre N:terre	V:garder V:naître V:tenir
torfaire, -fait, -fesor	N:tort 'wrong'	V:faire

MEDIEVAL AND RENAISSANCE FRENCH VERBAL ELEMENTS

manaide, manaidier	N:main	V:aider 'to aid'
jour-apporte	N:jour	V:apporter 'to carry'
ferarmer	N:fer	V:armer 'to arm'
mentevoir, mentoivre	N:MĔNTE(M)	V:avoir 'to have'
billebarrer	N:bille	V:barrer 'to draw a line'
orbateör, orbatre	N:or	V:battre 'to beat'
charboter, encharboter koñibote escalbotter	N:chair N:corne N:*SKALA	V:bouter 'to strike, beat' V:bouter V:bouter
champcheü nientdisant	N:champ N:nient	V:choir 'to fall' V:dire 'to say'
boranfler, bourranflé	N:bourre/BOD-	V:enfler 'to swell'
caresmentré, -entrant	N:carème	V:entrer 'to enter'

carbon-fadere	N:c(h)arbon	V:faire 'to make, do'
mainfait	N:main	V:faire
poifaisant	N:peu	V:faire
torfait, torfesor	N:tort	V:faire
orfergié	N:or	V:fergier 'to chain'
lettre-féru	N:lettre	V:férir 'to strike'
clofermer	N:clou	V:OFr. fermer 'to attach'
cloufichier, cloufir	N:clou	V:ficher 'to fix (to), make fast'
croizficher	N:croiz	V:ficher
estanfique	N:*ESTAN	V:ficher
graisse-fondre	N:graisse	V:fondre 'to melt'
morfondre	N:mourre	V:fondre
pele-fouans	N:pelle	V:fouir 'to dig'
gor-, gour-, garfoler	N:go(u)r(t)	V:fouler 'to beat, damage'
chanfraindre	N:chant	V:fraindre 'to break'
chanfrein, chafresner	N:cha(p)-	V:OFr. frener 'to restrain, bridle'
enchifrené	N:cha(p)-	V:OFr. frener
boffumer	N:BUFF-	V:fumer 'to smoke'
Ourse-gardant	N:Ourse	V:(re)garder 'to regard'
terreguarde	N:terre	V:garder 'to guard'
dieulever	N:dieu	V:lever 'to raise'
mainlevée	N:main	V:lever
mainbor, mainbornir	N:MUNDEBORO 'protector'	
burdemeclia	N:bourre/BORDA	V:mêler 'to mix'
sancmesler	N:sang	V:mêler
dieu-menti, deumentiz	N:dieu	V:mentir 'to lie'
foimenti, feimentie	N:foi	V:mentir
main-, manumetre, marmissio	N:main	V:mettre 'to place'
mainmuable	N:main	V:muer 'to change'
sangmuer	N:sang	V:muer

cuisse-né	N:cuisse	V:naître 'to be born'
terre-né	N:terre	V:naître
manovrier, manuvrer	N:main	V:œuvrer 'to work'
cuirpaner	N:cuir	V:paner 'to cover'
mainpast	N:main	V:PĀSTU(M) 'nourished'
saupiquet (*saupiquer)	N:sal	V:piquer 'to strike'
main-plant	N:main	V:planter 'to plant'
orpoignant	N:or	V:poindre 'to embroider'
aile-porte	N:aile	V:porter 'to bear'
colporter	N:col	V:porter
lierre-porte	N:lierre	V:porter
montagne-porte	N:montagne	V:porter
signeportant	N:signe	V:porter
saupoudrer	N:sal	V:poudrer 'to powder'
quaresme prenant	N:carème	V:prendre 'to begin'
gouteprenant	N:goutte	V:prendre 'to seize'
mainprendre, mainprise	N:main	V:prendre
part-prenant	N:part	V:prendre
painquerant	N:pain	V:OFr. querre 'to search for'
cœur-rongeant	N:cœur	V:ronger 'to gnaw'
nongresachant	N:gré	V:non . . . savoir '(not) to know, be ignorant of'
blanc-signé	N:blanc	V:signer 'to sign'
borsoflé, boursouffler	N:bourre	V:souffler 'to blow'
feu-soufflant	N:feu	V:souffler
chatien, chateni	N:cha(p)-	V:tenir 'to hold'
foitenant	N:foi	V:tenir
luetenent	N:lieu	V:tenir
maintenir, maintien	N:main	V:tenir
terretenant	N:terre	V:tenir
bouleverser	N:boule	V:verser 'to pour, turn'
fervestir	N:fer	V:vêtir 'to clothe'

nuit-volant	N:nuit	V:voler 'to fly'
feu-vomissant	N:feu	V:vomir 'to vomit, spew forth'

MODERN FRENCH NOMINAL ELEMENTS

bafumer	N:BALSAMU(M) 'balsam'	V:fumer
embaufumer	N:BALSAMU(M)	V:fumer
banjointant	N:ban 'edge'	V:joindre
(a)bastornar	N:bâton 'stick'	V:tourner
bècbassieu	N:bec 'beak'	V:bossuer
billebarrer	N:bille 'wooden wedge, stripe'	V:barrer
blanc-poudrer	N:blanc 'white'	V:poudrer
bornifiker	N:bornifle	V:ficher
s'éboulancer	N:boule 'ball'	V:lancer
bouleverser	N:boule	V:verser
bourenfler	N:BOD- 'round shape'/ bourre 'stuffing'	V:enfler
bourniger	N:bourre	V:nicher, niger
boursouffler	N:bourre	V:souffler
à bout portant	N:bout 'end'	V:porter
à bout touchant	N:bout	V:toucher
bulleménaou	N:bruit 'noise'	V:mener + haut
(en) caillmachâ	N:cail 'pebble'	V:mâcher
chéuplâ	N:CALCE(M) 'heel'	V:piler
chauspougna	N:CALCE(M)	V:pougner (empoigner)
caravirer, caraviri	N:cara 'face'	V:virer
champbrûler	N:champ 'field'	V:brûler
champlever	N:champ	V:lever
champler	N:champ	V:peler
(é)c(h)ampoussi	N:champ	V:pousser

chambouler	N:chant 'edge'	V:bouler
champbouter	N:chant	V:bouter
chanfreiner, chanfrer	N:chant	V:OFr. fraindre
c(h)antourner	N:chant	V:tourner
canverser	N:chant	V:verser
chanfrein, enchifrené	N:chap 'head'	V:OFr. frener
chateni	N:chap	V:tenir
chatourne	N:chap	V:tourner
chavirer	N:chap	V:virer
chaufumer	N:chaux 'lime'	V:fumer
encauchumer	N:chaux	V:sumer
à chiffe-tirer	N:chiffe 'rag'	V:tirer
se coderser	N:coq 'cock'	V:dresser
konbrüše(r)	N:corne 'horn'	V:brüšer
cornifiker	N:corne	V:ficher
se corbattre	N:corps 'body'	V:battre
encoubaissé	N:cou 'neck'	V:baisser
colporter	N:cou	V:porter
croulever	N:croûte 'crust'	V:lever
se keurpiller	N:cuir 'leather, scalp'	V:piller
culbonder	N:cul 'butt'	V:bonder
cubassieu	N:cul	V:bossuer
cuboûlé	N:cul	V:bouler
culbuter	N:cul	V:buter
külpeta	N:cul	V:péter
cusoter	N:cul	V:sauter
ès cutoûrner	N:cul	V:tourner
cutemelé	N:cul	V:tumer 'to turn'
culvéchi	N:cul	V:verser
estafiker, étanfiche	N:*ESTAN 'supporting beam'	V:ficher
gourmacher	N:GORR- 'noise of 'swine'	V:mâcher
gourmelai	N:GORR-	V:mêler
gormenó	N:GORR-	V:mener
gour-, garfouler	N:OFr. go(u)r(t) 'club'/ GŬRGE(M) 'throat'	V:fouler

graspilyi	N:gras 'fat'	V:piller
goulimacher	N:guêule 'mouth'	V:mâcher
gournacher	N:GŬRDU(M) 'fat'/ GORR 'noise of swine'	V:NĀSICĀRE
harlifiker	N:hart 'band'	V:ficher
jambälou	N:jambe 'leg'	V:BALLĀRE
chambarder	N:jambe	V:barder
faire dzarvolá	N:jarret 'calf'	V:voler
lieutenant	N:lieu 'position'	V:tenir
manifait	N:main 'hand'	V:faire
mainlevée	N:main	V:lever
mainmise	N:main	V:mettre
manœuvrer	N:main	V:œuvrer
mēpá, paschamaint	N:main	V:PĀSTU(M) (paître)
maintenir	N:main	V:tenir
maintint	N:main	V:tenir
malitouche, ma(n)toš	N:main	V:toucher
mamborner	N:MUNDEBORO 'protector'	
microchanter	N:micro 'microphone'	V:chanter
morfondre	N:mourre 'snout'	V:fondre
mourmacher	N:mourre	V:mâcher
mornifler	N:mourre	V:OFr. nifler
pauficher, paufichonner	N:PĀLU(M) 'stick'	V:ficher
part-prenant	N:part 'part'	V:prendre
pattefiche	N:patte 'tongue'	V:ficher
pattemouille	N:patte 'rag'	V:mouiller
patevôler, pativoler, épatvoulant	N:patte 'leg, paw'	V:voler
peaumuer	N:peau 'skin'	V:muer
pallemener	N:pelle 'shovel'	V:mener
pelleverser	N:pelle	V:verser

pore-levet	N:père 'father'	V:lever
pî-stant	N:pied 'foot'	V:être ([e]stant)
puoutirar	N:poil 'hair'	V:tirer
quesauter, cusoter	N:queue 'tail'	V:sauter
saupiquet	N:sal 'salt'	V:piquer
saupoudrer	N:sal	V:poudrer
sãnzevra	N:sang 'blood'	V:givrer
se san-glacer	N:sang	V:glacer
ensangmêler	N:sang	V:mêler
sangmuer	N:sang	V:muer
sanveri	N:sang	V:virer
santourner	N:sens 'direction'	V:tourner
dékafiker	N:*SKALA 'scale, shell'	V:ficher
taramatsíe	N:TAR- 'noise'	V:mâcher
tarmené	N:TAR-	V:mener
tenduement	N:temps 'time'	V:durer + -ment
taneuser	N:temps	V:user
terrebêcher	N:terre	V:bêcher
tarabuta	N:terre 'land'	V:bouter
terrejeter	N:terre	V:jeter
terre-né	N:terre	V:naître
tranche-maçonné	N:tranche 'slice, edge'	V:maçonner

MODERN FRENCH VERBAL ELEMENTS

encoubaissé	N:cou	V:baisser 'to lower'
jambälou	N:jambe	V:BALLĀRE 'to dance'
chambarder	N:jambe	V:barder 'to slide'
billebarrer	N:bille	V:barrer 'to draw a line'
(se) corbattre	N:corps	V:battre 'to beat'
terrebêcher	N:terre	V:bêcher 'to shovel'
culbonder	N:cul	V:bonder (Fr. -ir) 'to jump'

bècbassieu	N:bec	V:bossuer 'to disfigure with lumps'
cubassieu	N:cul	V:bossuer
chambouler	N:cant	V:bouler 'to spill, roll'
cuboûlé	N:cul	V:bouler
champbouter	N:chant	V:bouter 'to strike'
tarabuta	N:terre	V:bouter
champbrûler	N:champ	V:brûler 'to burn'
konbrüše(r)	N:corne	V:brüše(r) 'to scratch'
culbuter	N:cul	V:buter 'to bump into'
microchanter	N:micro	V:chanter 'to sing'
se coderser	N:coq	V:dresser 'to stand on end'
tenduement	N:temps	V:durer 'to last' (+ ment)
bourenfler	N:BOD-/bourre	V:enfler 'to swell'
pî-stant	N:pied	V:être 'to be' ([e]stant)
manifait	N:main	V:faire 'to make, do'
bornifiker	N:bornifle	V:ficher 'to fix (to)'
cornifiker	N:corne	V:ficher
estafiker, étanfiche	N:*ESTAN	V:ficher
harlifiker	N:hart	V:ficher
pauficher, paufichonner	N:PĀLU(M)	V:ficher
patte-fiche	N:patte	V:ficher
dékafiker	N:*SKALA	V:ficher
morfondre	N:mourre	V:fondre 'to melt'
gour-, garfouler	N:OFr. go(u)r(t)/ GǓRGE(M)	V:fouler 'to beat, damage'
chanfreiner, chanfrer	N:chant	V:OFr. fraindre 'to break'
chanfrein, enchifrené	N:chap	V:OFr. frener 'to restrain, bridle'
bafumer	N:BALSAMU(M)	V:fumer 'to smoke'
embaufumer	N:BALSAMU(M)	V:fumer
chaufumer	N:chaux	V:fumer
sādzevra	N:sang	V:givrer 'to freeze'

san-glacer (se)	N:sang	V:glacer 'to freeze'
terrejeter	N:terre	V:jeter 'to throw'
banjointant	N:ban	V:joindre 'to join'
(s') éboulancer	N:boule	V:lancer 'to throw'
champlever	N:champ	V:lever 'to raise'
croulever	N:croûte	V:lever
mainlevée	N:main	V:lever
pore-levet	N:père	V:lever
(en) caillmachâ	N:cail	V:mâcher 'to chew'
gourmacher	N:GORR-	V:mâcher
mourmacher	N:mourre	V:mâcher
taramatsíe	N:TAR-	V:mâcher
tranche-maçonné	N:tranche	V:maçonner 'to construct of masonry'
gourmelai	N:GORR-	V:mêler 'to mix'
ensangmêler	N:sang	V:mêler
bulleménaou	N:bruit	V:mener 'to lead'
gormeno	N:GORR-	V:mener
pallemener	N:pelle	V:mener
tarmené	N:TAR-	V:mener
mainmise	N:main	V:mettre 'to place'
pattemouille	N:patte	V:mouiller 'to dampen'
peaumuer	N:peau	V:muer 'to molt'
sangmuer	N:sang	V:muer
terre-né	N:terre	V:naître 'to be born'
gournacher	N:GŬRDU(M)/GORR-	V:NĀSICĀRE 'to sniff(le)'
bourniger	N:bourre	V:nicher, niger 'to be lazy, waste time'
mornifler	N:mourre	V:OFr. nifler 'to sniff(le)'
manœuvrer	N:main	V:œuvrer 'to work'
mẽpá, paschamaint	N:main	V:PĀSTU(M) (paître) 'to nourish'

champler	N:champ	V:peler 'to peel'
külpeta	N:cul	V:péter 'to break'
chéuplâ	N:CALCE(M)	V:piler 'to push in, pile up'
se keurpiller	N:cuir	V:piller 'to plunder'
saupiquet	N:sel	V:piquer 'to strike'
à bout portant	N:bout	V:porter 'to bear'
colporter	N:cou	V:porter
blanc-poudrer	N:blanc	V:poudrer 'to powder'
saupoudrer	N:sal	V:poudrer
chauspougna	N:CALCE(M)	V:pougner (empoigner) 'to grab'
(é)c(h)ampoussi	N:champ	V:pousser 'to push'
part-prenant	N:part	V:prendre 'to seize'
cusoter	N:cul?	V:sauter 'to jump'
quesauter	N:queue	V:sauter
boursouf(f)ler	N:bourre	V:souffler 'to blow'
encauchumer	N:chaux	V:sumer 'to sow, spread'
chateni	N:chap	V:tenir 'to hold'
lieutenant	N:lieu	V:tenir
maintenir	N:main	V:tenir
maintint	N:main	V:tenir
à chiffe-tirer	N:chiffe	V:tirer 'to pull'
puoutirar	N:poil	V:tirer
à bout touchant	N:bout	V:toucher 'to touch'
malitouche, ma(n)toš	N:main	V:toucher
bastorner	N:bâton	V:tourner 'to turn'
chantourner, cantourner	N:chant	V:tourner
chatourne	N:chap	V:tourner
cutoûrner (ès)	N:cul	V:tourner
santourner	N:sens	V:tourner
cutemelé	N:cul	V:OFr. tumer 'to tumble'

taneuser	N:temps	V:user 'to use (up)'
bouleverser	N:boule	V:verser 'to pour, turn'
canverser	N:chant	V:verser
culvechi	N:cul	V:verser
pelleverser	N:pelle	V:verser
chavirer	N:c(h)ap	V:virer 'to turn'
caraviri	N:cara	V:virer
sanveri	N:sang	V:virer
faire dzarvolá	N:jarret	V:voler 'to fly'
patevôler, pativoler, épatvoulant	N:patte	V:voler

Appendix B

Occitan Corpus

Gasc. *à barre-lùua* 'to raise with a lever'; Arnaudin; N:barre 'lever' + V:lùua (*levar*) 'to raise'

aboudenfli 'to bruise'; *FEW* "*bod-"; N:bod- 'round shape' + V:enflar 'to swell'

acabourrá-s 'to be stubborn' (*capbourrut* 'stubborn'); *FEW* "caput"; N:cap 'head' + V:borrar 'to stuff'

Quer., Béar. *acourbacha-s, s'acourbaissa* 'to lower oneself', 's'abaisser'; Pal; N:còr 'heart' + V:bachar (*baissar*) 'to lower'

aiga-, aigo-muda 'to change the water'; Piat, M, JR; N:aiga 'water' + V:mudar 'to change'

aiga-pich 'small waterfall'; Pal; N:aiga 'water' + V:pichar (*pissar*) 'to piss'

aiga-prene, aygue-préne 'to catch cold from humidity or sweat'; Pal; N:aiga 'water' + V:prene 'to take'

aigatrebolar 'to be agitated'; LA; N:aiga 'water' + V:trebolar 'to trouble'

aigo-, aigue-pendent 'slope of a hill'; M, Piat, JR; N:aiga 'water' + V:pendre 'to incline'

aigo-pico 'mineral water, sparkling water'; JR; N:aiga 'water' + V:picar 'to strike, sting'

OBéar. (14th c.) *ayguebees*, (Mod.) *aigo-bes*, Occ. (19th c.) *aigo-vers* 'water divide'; OPr. *aiga-versar* 'to divide waters'; M, Piat, *FEW*; (inf.) Levy, JR, *FEW*; N:aiga 'water'+ V:versar 'to pour'

Béar. *ale-bacha* 'to lower the wing, humiliate oneself'; *ala-, ale-bàt* 'sparrow, bird of passage'; M (*alo-baissat, -baichat*), Pal; N:ala 'wing' + V:bachar (*baissar*) 'to lower'

Béar. *ale-bate* 'to beat one's wings, not feel well' (cf. *s'eschalabatre* [q.v.]); Pal; N:ala 'wing' + V:batre 'to beat'

155

Béar. *amaligà* 'to assemble s.th. into a handful' (cf. *manouliâ* 'to bundle twigs'; *croustemaligà* 'to crisscross'; *entermaligà* 'to bind several sheaves' [q.v.]); *FEW* "ligare"; N:man 'hand' + V:ligar 'to tie'

l'annado (*la semano, lou meis*) *entrant* 'the coming year (week, month)'; Daniel "entrant"; N:annado 'year' + V:entrar 'to enter'

Lim. *banc-leva*, Périg. *banlevar*, Quer. *bonleva* 'to seesaw, topple, fall over, cause to fall, lose one's balance'; Lim. *banlèuo, bonlèvo* 'seesaw; blunder'; Pal; *faire banc-lèvo* 'to seesaw, topple'; *faire à la banc-lèvo* 'to play on a seesaw'; Azaïs, M, Piat, Daniel, *FEW* "*bank(s)"; N:banc 'bench' + V:levar 'to raise'

Gasc. *barbo-leca, -lequa* 'to lick one's chin, eat voraciously'; M, Piat, *FEW* "*lekkon," Pal; N:barba 'beard' + V:lecar 'to lick'

OPr. *bens-tenen* 'heir', (Mod.) *bèn-tenènt* 'landowner'; Levy 1973, M, Adams ('property-holding'); N:bèn '[inherited] goods' + V:tener 'to hold'

Béar. *bente-boueita, -boeytà* 'to disembowel, gore, purge'; Lespy 1877, Azaïs (*bente boèyt* 'starving'), Piat; N:bente 'belly' + V:boueitar (*voidar*) 'to empty'

OBéar. *biandant* 'traveller', OPr. *viandan(t)* (q.v.); Lespy; N:via 'way' + V:anar 'to go'

Béar. *bie-passà* 'to exceed, transcend the limits' (cf. Eng. *by-pass*); *à passe-bie* 'on the way'; Pal; N:via 'way' + V:passar 'to pass'

Périg. *blanc-signat* 'signature to a blank document'; Daniel; N:blanc 'white' + V:signar 'to sign'

blaugetar, -guela 'to incrust a fine strip of gold, silver, or copper on a metallic surface', 'damasquiner'; M, LA; N:blau 'blue' + V:getar 'to push, throw'

bordifalha, bourdufaillo, boustifaille 'flotsam and jetsam, nonsense'; *FEW* "borda" 'dust', LA; N:*borda 'dust' + V:FALLĔRE 'to fail' + -aille

borramesclar, bourro-mescla 'to upset, turn over, mix up'; *borramescla* 'mixture of grains or fodder'; Azaïs, M, Vayssier, *FEW* "*borda" 'fraud'/"burra" 'hair, stuffing' + "misculare," LA, R. Barthe; N:borda 'fraud'/bourre 'stuffing' + V:mesclar 'to mix'

OPr. *botenflat*, (Mod.) *bodenfle, boudoufle, -flas* 'swollen'; *botiflau* 'pot-bellied'; *boudouflét* 'chubby child'; *botifla, boudiflo* 'blister; bladder'; Gasc. *boudufle, boudoùflo* 'spinning-top; blister, swelling'; *boudenflitge* 'swelling'; Occ. *bodenflar, botiflar*, Gasc. *bauduf(l)a* 'to swell, be sad, cry; form blisters'; *boudenflejar* 'to begin to swell; be sad'; *aboudenfli* 'to cause to swell'; Pal, *DECC* II 171b, LA, Diez "boucher," M, *REW* §1182a "bod," *FEW* "*bod-"; N:bod- 'round shape' + V:enflar 'to swell' *boulouversá* (← Fr. *bouleverser*) 'to upset, turn over'; *FEW* "versare"; N:(?) boule 'ball' + V:versar 'to spill'

Gasc. *bouque-barrà* 'to remain silent'; *bouque-barrat* 'discreet'; Pal; N:boca 'mouth' + V:barrar 'to squeeze, tighten'

Périg. *bournifle* 'one who blows one's nose noisily', 'mournifle' (q.v.), Fr. 'qui se mouche salement'; *FEW* "niff-"; N:bourre 'stuffing' + V:niflar 'to sniffle'

Béar. *camalhègue, -lhèbe, -lhèute* 'new mother's prayer of thanks, made at church', 'relevailles de couches'; Lespy, Pal; N:cama 'bed' + V:levar (intr.) 'to arise'

H.-Alpes *camba-buou* 'to kick up one's heels while lying on the ground'; *FEW* "camba"; N:camba 'leg' + V:beure 'to drink'

cambalevar, comboleba 'to trip someone'; Vayssier "combolebá," M, LA; N:camba 'leg' + V:levar 'to raise'

OPr.–Mod.Occ. *camba-liga*, Lang. *-lié*, Gasc. *kamelinge* 'garter' (cf. OPr. *lia-camba* [q.v.]), Médoc 'association, coalition'; *camboligueto, cambaieireto* 'little garter'; Ambert *chambalho de la Santo Viarjo* 'rainbow'; Occ. *cambaligar, came- liga(-s), cambalia(-s)*, Aveyr. *combellá* 'to put on or wear garters, bind the legs', Médoc 'to group'; Béar. *ha la camaligue* 'to trip s.o.'; Lim. *faire cambo-ligueto* 'to hop along'; *descambaligar* 'to remove garters', (fig.) 'to get out of a bind'; Lespy, AThomas 1898, Azaïs, M, *REW* §5024 "ligāre," Pal, *FEW* "camba," LA; N:camba 'leg' + V:ligar 'to bind'

cambavirar, combobira, Béar. *came-bira(-s)* 'to trip, tumble, turn upside down', 'tourner les jambes en l'air'; Malvezin, Azaïs, Vayssier, M, Pal, *FEW* "camba" + "vibrare," LA, R. Barthe; N:camba 'leg' + V:virar 'to turn'

Béar. *cambira* 'to dig up (a field), upset, turn over'; *cambirade* 'plowing, action of *cambira*'; Pal, *FEW* "vibrare"; N:camp 'field' + V:virar 'to turn'

Toul. *cambotira* 'to trip someone'; *FEW* "camba"; N:camba 'leg' + V:tirar 'to pull'

cambo-viroula, Rouerg.–Aveyr. *combo-biroula*, Biterrois *cambiroula*, (*-virar, -virolar* rather than *-roular*) 'to trip, turn head over heels'; *cambirolo, cambo-virolo*, Rouerg. *cambo-birouolu* 'somersault'; Azaïs, M; N:camba 'leg' + V:virolar 'to turn'

Béar. *came-boutà* 'to place one's foot, straddle'; Pal; N:camba 'leg' + V:botar 'to place'

Béar. *came-, camipouda-s* 'to break one's leg'; Pal, *FEW* "putare" (*poude-cames* 'wearying task'); N:camba 'leg' + V:podar 'to break'

Béar. *came-tòrse* 'to break a leg or a plant stem'; Pal; N:camba 'leg' + V:torse (*tòrcer*) 'to twist'

Lang. *càmo-coupà* 'to break s.o.'s leg'; Moulis; N:camba 'leg' + V:copar 'to cut, break'

Béar. *càmo-malhà* 'to cross one's legs'; Pal; N:camba 'leg' + V:malhar 'to hit with a hammer'

can-lheba, -leuà, calleva, Gers *calleua,* Béar. *cantlhebá* 'to topple by one end or side'; *cant-lhèbe, canlèuo, calléuo* 'balancing-pole', 'poutre d'un système à bascule pour remonter l'eau d'un puits'; Lespy (*cant*), M (*cap*), Pal, *FEW* "levare" (*cap* +); N:cant 'edge' + V:levar 'to raise'

Béar. *cant-birà* 'to set edgewise'; Pal; N:cant 'edge' + V:virar 'to turn'

Béar. *cap-bacha, -baxa, cap-baissa, -beissa* 'to lower the head, be ashamed'; Quer. *l'aiga pren la cap-baissada* 'the water is beginning to subside'; Béar. *da u(n) cap-bach* 'to insult, cause a scandal'; Lespy, Piat, XdeF, *FEW* "bassiare"; N:cap 'head' + V:bachar (*baissar*) 'to lower'

Béar. *cap-barià(-s), -barreya* 'to be confused, lose one's head'; Pal; N:cap 'head' + V:barrejar 'to turn (a bar)'

cap-batre, Lim. *cha-, tso-batre* 'to shell (wheat, corn) with a stick; quarrel'; Piat, Vayssier, M, *FEW* "battuere," LA; N:cap 'head' + V:batre 'to beat'

Toul. *capbilhar,* Gers–Cév. *cap-bilha, capilha,* 'to tumble head first, trip; turn over; join two pieces of wood with dowels'; Gasc. *descabilhà, -lhoà, descalhiuà* 'to remove a peg or bolt', (fig.) 'to upset'; *descabilhade* 'action of *descabilhà*'; Azaïs, Pal, *FEW* "caput," LA; N:cap 'head' + V:bilhar 'to garrot', 'serrer un chargement avec le tortoir'

OGasc. *capbira* 'to train oxen to pull either to right or to left'; *FEW* "vibrare"; N:cap 'head' + V:virar 'to turn'

cap-bordelar, -bourdilha 'to roll a cask, pushing either end alternately'; (Quer.) 'to tumble'; Rouerg. *capbordar* 'to capsize, lean over'; Piat, M, LA, Mouly; N:cap 'head' + V:bord-elar, -olhar 'to roll'

Béar. *cap-enfla-s, -inla-s, -illà-s* 'to swell' (the head); *cap-enlàt, -eslàt, -inlàt* 'polliwog'; Pal; N:cap 'head' + V:enflar 'to swell'

Gasc. *cap-eschaureya-se* 'to get dishevelled' (in the wind) (Lespy *eschaurat* 'evaporated'); Pal; N:cap 'head' + V:eschaurejar 'to blow about' (of the wind)

capescodre, cap-escoudre 'to shell (wheat, corn, other cereals) with a flail, beat (nut trees)'; Vayssier, M, LA, *FEW* "excutere"; N:cap 'head' + V:escodre 'to beat, sweep'

cap(es)dressà 'to stand upright, raise the end in the air'; Pal; N:cap 'head' + V:dressar 'to straighten'

OPr.–Mod.Occ. *capgirar, -jira, cagirà* 'to turn around, twist one's neck, upset'; M, Piat, *FEW* "gyrare," LA; N:cap 'head' + V:girar 'to turn'

cap-haussà 'to stand upright', (woodworking) 'to raise'; Pal; N:cap 'head' + V:auçar 'to raise'

Béar. *cap-hautà* 'to stand upright, raise'; Pal; N:cap 'head' + V:hautà (*autar*) 'to raise'

Béar. *cap-hen(d)e* 'to split the head' (top or stalk); Pal; N:cap 'head' + V:fendre (Gasc. *héne*) 'to split'

Béar. *cap-herrà* 'to shoe one end of a stick'; Pal, *LeG*; N:cap 'head'+ V:ferrar 'to cover (with iron)'

Béar. *cap-houradà(-s)* 'to pierce' (the end); Pal; N:cap 'head' + V:foradar (*forar*) 'to pierce'

OPr.–Mod.Occ. *caplevar, -lheba, -leuà, callevá, calleua* 'to tumble, seesaw, raise the end or head; levy a tax', Gasc. 'to capsize'; OPr. *cap-lève,* (Mod.) *caplèu, cap-leveto* 'seesaw'; *caplèva,* Gasc. *cap-lhèbe* idem, 'fosse de puits à bascule pour capturer les loups et les renards'; *capleveta* 'seesaw'; Gasc. *cap-lhebàn, capilhebàn, cap-lhetàrou* 'who walks with head held high'; *faire à cap-leveto, fa callèvo, faire cap-lèvo* 'to seesaw'; M, AThomas 1898, Pal, *FEW* "levare," LA; N:cap 'head' + V:levar 'to raise'

Béar. *cap-lissà* 'to link, join' (ends); 'to sharpen'; Pal; N:cap 'head' + V:lissar 'to smooth, polish'

cap-maçar, -massar(-se) 'to stun' (cf. Cat. *capmassar-se* 'to worry'); LA; N:cap 'head' + V:maçar 'to hammer'

Béar. *cap-mounta* 'to get worried, raise the end'; JR, Pal, *LeG*; N:cap 'head' + V:montar 'to raise, excite' (cf. Fr. *le vin lui monte à la tete* 'wine goes to his head')

Béar. *cap-plegà* 'to bend or lower one end'; Pal, *LeG*; N:cap 'head' + V:plegar 'to bend'

Béar. *cap-pouda* 'to behead, knock off the head'; (grammar) *cap-poudat* 'apheresized'; JR; N:cap 'head' + V:podar 'to break'

Béar. *cap-pountà* (woodworking) 'to position and fasten together a scaffolding'; Pal; N:cap 'head' + V:pontar 'to make a bridge'

Béar. *cap-préne-s* 'to take hold of one's head, develop a headache'; Pal; N:cap 'head' + V:prene 'to take'

Béar. *cap-quilha(-s)* 'to raise the head, end'; (refl.) 'to straighten up'; *cap-quilhat, -quilhèt, -quilhoû* 'proud person'; Pal; N:cap 'head' + V:quilhar 'to stand on end'

Béar. *capseca-s* 'to dry from the top'; Pal; N:cap 'head' + V:secar 'to dry'

(12th c.) *captenir* 'to govern, support, protect'; *cap-téner, -teni,* Béar. *-tiene,* Gasc. *catténi* (17th c.) 'to behave', (Mod.)' 'to defend, master oneself, stand firm; hold the end'; M.Lat. *captennium,* OGasc. *captenh* 'payment for royal protection'; OPr. *cap-tenh, -tein* 'protection, aid; conduct', 'defender'; *captenemen* 'conduct, countenance'; *captenensa* idem, 'aid'(?), (Mod.) 'carriage of the head'; *captenedor* 'defender'; M, Piat, Levy, *REW* §1668 "caput," *FEW* "caput" + "tenere," LA; N:cap 'head' + V:tener 'to hold'

Béar. *captorse* 'to twist the neck'; Pal; N:cap 'head' + V:torse (tòrcer) 'to twist'

Lang. *captraire* 'to complete, conduct, examine'; M (OPr. *captraire*), *FEW* "trahere" (OPr. *traire a cap* 'to finish'), LA; N:cap 'head' + V:traire 'to pull'

OPr.–Occ. *capvirar*, Béar. *-bira, capira*, Lim. *chavira* 'to turn the head, upset, become crazy, die'; (Béar.) 'to reverse ends, turn upside down'; (refl.) 'to torment oneself'; Occ. *cap-virado* 'extremity of a field, where the oxen turn'; *capvirament* 'dizzy spell'; *recapvirar* 'to rear' (of horses) (q.v.); Gasc. 'to resist, react, turn around'; Gasc. *recapbiret* 'blow with the back of the hand'; M, AThomas 1898, Adams, Daniel, JA (N Dir Obj + V), *REW* §1668 "caput," Pal, *FEW* "vibrare," LA; N:cap 'head' + V:virar 'to turn'

Quer. *capvirolar, -biroulà*, Biterrois *cambiroula* 'to tumble, roll, fall headfirst; *capvirol* 'somersault', 'cabriole'; Guy. *cap-viroulic, cap-biroulic, capbiroulète* 'light-headed'; Rouerg. *pèrdre lo carabiròl* 'to lose one's head'; Azaïs, Vayssier, M, AThomas 1898, Piat, LA, Mouly, d'Estalenx; N:cap 'head' + V:virolar 'to turn'

Rouerg. *carabrina, calabrinar* 'to roast badly, scorch'; Vayssier, Piat, M; N:carn 'flesh' + V:rabinar 'to scorch'

(13th c.) *caramantrant*, (Mod.) *Careimentrant, Carmantran, Coreime-entran*, etc. 'first day of Lent, Mardi Gras, Carnival', (Mod.) idem, 'menstruation'; *carementreto* 'penultimate week of Carnival, or first Sunday of Lent; Carnival gift; Carnival reveler'; Périg. *careimentrâ*, Gers *couaramenta* 'to enter the period of Lent'; AThomas 1898, Piat, Daniel, *FEW* "quadragesima," Dhéralde; N:carèma 'Lent' + V:entrar 'to enter'

OPr. *caravirar* 'to change political party'; *se carabirá* 'to feel strong emotion'; Mod.Occ. *caravirar, caro-vira, coro-bira* 'to tumble, frighten, upset, disfigure'; (refl.) 'to become upset, pale'; *caravirado* 'sudden, violent emotion'; Occ. *caravirat, caravirolard* 'hideous, haggard, frightened'; Auv. *incorovira(t)* 'obstinate'; Levy, Azaïs, Piat, Pal, JR, *FEW* "cara" + "vibrare," LA, Becquevort; N:cara 'face' + V:virar 'to turn'

Gasc. *care-birà* 'to open new cuts on a pine tree'; Arnaudin; N:cara 'face' + V:virar 'to turn'

OPr. *carema prenens, caren-pernent* 'first day of Lent'; N:carèma 'Lent' + V:prene 'to seize (= begin)'

carfouladis 'sprain'; Robert; N:carn 'flesh' + V:folar 'to crush'

Dauph. *cariboussa* 'to be deformed, deform'; M; N:cara 'face' + V:OPr. bossar, Occ. boçar 'to form a lump'

carnaval (from It. *carnevale*) 'Carnival; Carnival mannequin; fallen woman; *carnavalas* 'grand carnaval; loose woman'; *carnavalet* 'petit carnaval'; *carnavalada* 'Carnival jest, mascarade, debauchery'; *carnavalenc* 'belonging to Carnival';

carnavalejà 'to debauch', 'faire le carnaval'; Gasc. *encarnabalà* 'to disguise;
  dress as for Carnival'; M, AThomas 1989; Pal; N:It. carne 'flesh' + V:It. levare
  'to remove'

OBéar. *carn-bedar* 'Lent'; Lespy, *FEW* "caro"; N:carn 'flesh' + V:vetar 'to forbid'

Gasc. *carnmatar* 'to bruise, damage'; LA; N:carn 'flesh' + V:matar 'to kill, bruise'

Gasc. *caso-heyt* 'homemade'; Pal; N:casa 'house' + V:ha (*far*) 'to make'

Gasc. *causse-ha* 'to knit stockings'; Pal; N:causse 'stocking' + V:ha (far) 'to make'

OPr. *cazatenen* 'house-owner'; Levy; N:casa 'house + V:tener 'to hold'

chan-, (Mars.) *cham-frenar*, Aveyr. *chonfriná* (from Fr. *chanfreiner* 'to bevel');
  chanfren, chamfrenat 'chamfer, bevelled edge'; Achard, M, Daniel, *FEW*
  "canthus" 'edge'; N:Fr. chant 'edge' + V:OFr. fraindre 'to break'

chanlevâ (from Fr. *champlever*) 'to remove material around a pattern, leaving it
  raised, before applying enamel'; Lim. (refl.) 'to crack open' (a walnut husk);
  M, Daniel; N:Fr. chant 'edge' + V:levar 'to raise'

chantournâ, Mars. *chantournar*, Lim. *tsantourná*, Béar. *cantourná* (from Fr.
  chantourner) (woodworking) 'to cut out along a given pattern'; M, Daniel,
  FEW "tornare"; N:Fr. chant 'edge' + V:tornar 'to turn'

OPr. (13th c.) *c(h)apfrenar* 'to repress, tame a passion'; Prov. *chanfrin* 'part of horse's
  nose from forehead to nostrils'; Prov. (17th–18th c.) *chi(f)farneou* 'blow to the
  head', 'chinfreneau' Lespy, *REW* §1668 "caput"; Puget, Achard, *FEW* "caput";
  N:cap 'head' + V:frenar 'to restrain, bridle'

Lim. *chaplavar* 'to raise one's voice' (MFr. *laver la tête à quelqu'un* 'to reprimand
  severely'); Béar. *labe-cap* 'reprimand'; Lespy, Pal, *FEW* "lavare"; N:cap 'head'
  + V:lavar 'to wash'

Périg. *charmenâ* 'to fight'; M, *FEW* "minare"; N:carn 'flesh' + V:menar 'to lead'

Périg. *charmountâ* 'to heal' (a wound); *charmounto* 'healing of a wound'; Daniel, *FEW*
  "*montare"; N:carn 'flesh' + V:montar (intr.) 'to rise'

Périg. *char-uflâ* 'to swell'; *FEW* "inflare"; N:carn 'flesh' + V:enflar 'to swell'

Périg. *chavirâ* (from Fr. *chavirer*, itself borrowed from Occ. *capvirar*) 'to capsize'; M,
  Daniel; N:cap 'head' + V:virar 'to turn'

OPr. *clauficar* 'to crucify'; *FEW* "clavo figere"; N:clau 'nail' + V:ficar 'to fix (to)'

Dauph.–Lang. *cla(u)fir, cl(i)afi* 'to fill (to the rim), cover'; *cloûfit* 'spirited'; *claufiment*
  'action of filling, covering'; M (from *caffiu[m]* 'measure'), *FEW* "clavo figere,"
  LA (no etymon indicated); N:clau 'nail' + V:FĪGĔRE 'to fix (to)'

Gasc. *clauhicà* 'to introduce a key; undertake a job; make overtures to s.o.'; *clauhicàn*
  'indiscreet'; Pal; N:clau 'key' + V:ficar 'to introduce'

OPr. *clauponh* '(action of) nailing'; *DECC* II 918a; N:clau 'nail' + V:PŬNCTU(M)
  'pricked'

coalevar, co-, couo-, coul-leva, Béar. *coude-lhebà* 'to raise the tail, (cause to) topple';
OPr. *coaleva* 'lever or pulley of a cross-bow'; (Mod.) *co-levo*, Montpellier
coulleu 'seesaw, lever'; Aveyr. *coullebéto* 'seesaw'; Nice *en coualeva* 'unstable';
fa lo collebéto 'to cause to seesaw'; (ornith.) *coueto-levo, coueto-lebet* 'wagtail';
Levy, Vayssier, M, AThomas 1898, Daniel, Pal, *FEW* "levare," LA, Blaquière;
N:coa 'tail' + V:levar 'to raise'

Béar. *co-bouri* 'to be troubled by a physical ailment, be carried away, boil';
co-bourimén 'malaise, indigestion'; Pal; N:còr 'heart' + V:bourir (*bolhir*) 'to
boil'

Béar. *co-clabà* 'to break the heart, stupify'; Pal; N:còr 'heart' + V:clavar 'to nail'

Béar. *coechipoudá-se* 'to break one's thigh (bone)'; Pal, *FEW* "coxa"; N:coech 'thigh'
+ V:podar 'to break'

còlcrebar 'to break the neck'; LA; N:còl 'neck' + V:crevar 'to break'

còlportar, còu-, coul-pourta (from Fr. *colporter*) 'to peddle, carry on the shoulders';
coupourtage 'peddling'; *coupourtaire* 'hawker, peddler'; M, AThomas 1898, Piat,
Daniel, LA; N:còl 'neck' + V:portar 'to carry'

colormudar 'to change color' (of wheat that is beginning to turn yellow); Lespy, M,
LeG, JR, *FEW* "color," LA; N:color 'color' + V:mudar 'to change'

còltòrcer, -torse, -turse 'to twist the neck, turn around' (with an effort); *cot-tourcùt,
-sude* 'having a twisted neck'; (ornith.) *cot-tor, cot-tourtùmi* 'torcol, oiseau
grimpereau'; Lespy, Azaïs, Pal, *FEW* "torquere," LA, Vigneau; N:còl 'neck' +
V:tòrcer, torse 'to twist'

Béar. *co-mourì* 'to faint, feel unwell'; Pal; N:còr 'heart' + V:morir 'to die'

OBéar. *conde-finar* 'to close out an account', Mod.Béar. *coùmpte-finà* idem, 'finish
paying a debt'; *conde-finat* 'payment of a debt'; Lespy, Pal, *FEW* "computus";
N:compte 'account' + V:finar 'to end'

OBéar. *coo-transi*, (Mod.) *co-transì* 'to pierce the heart', (refl.) 'to feel unwell';
co-transide 'failing of the heart'; Lespy, Pal, *FEW* "cor"; N:còr 'heart' +
V:transir 'to pierce'

Gasc. *co-passà* 'to be surprised, dismayed'; Arnaudin; N:còr 'heart' + V:passar 'to
feel, suffer'

còpténer 'to resist'; Périg. *còp tener* 'to support'; LA, Miremont; N:còp 'blow' +
V:tener 'to hold'

còrcachar 'to squeeze, press the heart'; *còrcachal* 'pressure on the heart, squeezing';
N:còr 'heart' + V:cachar 'to press, squeeze'

còrcrebar, Béar. *co-crebà* 'to break one's heart, become exhausted, die'; Piat, M, Pal,
LA; N:còr 'heart' + V:crevar 'to break'

Béar. *corde-lhebà* 'to excite'; Pal; N:corda 'heart(string)' + V:levar 'to raise'

Béar. *corde-mià* 'to lead'; Pal; N:corda 'heart(string)' + V:menar 'to lead' *còr-dòldre*, Béar. *co-dòle-s* 'to faint, be overcome with emotion, suffer in one's heart'; *cordouloû* 'heartbreak'; *còr-dolent* 'distressed'; Pal, *LeG*, LA; N:còr 'heart' + V:doldre 'to suffer, hurt'

còrfalir, *-fa(i)lhi* 'to faint, quiver with emotion', Périg. *esse corfalit* 'to be voraciously hungry'; Quer. *escarfalit, escorfalit* 'famished, exhausted'; Azaïs, Piat, Daniel, *FEW* "fallere," LA; N:còr 'heart' + V:falir 'to fail'

còrfendre, Béar. *co-héne* 'to break the heart, move'; M, *FEW* "findere," LA; N:còr 'heart' + V:fendre 'to split'

còrferir, Béar. *co-heri* 'to move, trouble, strike'; *co-heride* 'heartache'; M, Piat, Pal, *FEW* "ferire," LA; N:còr 'heart' + V:ferir 'to strike'

còrfondre 'to melt (the heart)', 'fondre le cœur'; M, Daniel, *FEW* "fundere," LA; N:còr 'heart' + V:fondre 'to melt'

còrmanar 'to spoil, rot' (of wood); M, *FEW* "manna," LA; N:còr 'heart' + V:manar 'to rot'

Béar. *corne-bachà* 'to lower the horns, pull on the yoke with lowered head' (of an ox), 'to give in'; Pal; N:corna 'horn' + V:bachar (*baissar*) 'to lower'

Béar. *corne-quilhà* 'to raise the horns, stand an object upright, stand up straight'; Pal; N:corna 'horn' + V:quilhar 'to stand on end'

Lang. *cor-*, *cour-quichar*, *escolquicha* 'to put one's feet on the throat (of an opponent), squeeze, oppress, bruise'; M, Piat, *FEW* "cor," JR, R. Barthe; N:còr 'heart' + V:quichar 'to squeeze, bruise'

còrsecar 'to dry thoroughly' (of chestnuts), (refl.) 'to languish, be despondent'; M, Pal, LA; N:còr 'heart' + V:secar 'to dry'

cors-passar, Gasc. *cospassa* 'to oppress, overpower (morally)'; M, Piat, *FEW* "corpus"; N:còrs 'body' + V:passar 'to perish', (intr.) 'to be spent'

còrvirar, Béar. *co-birá* 'to upset one's stomach, trouble'; M, Piat, Pal, JR, LA; N:còr 'heart' + V:virar 'to turn'

Gasc. *co-sarrà* 'to be surprised, dismayed'; Arnaudin; N:còr 'heart' + V:sarrar 'to squeeze'

Béar. *cos-préne* 'to solidify'; Pal; N:còrs 'body' + V:prene 'to take'

Béar. *cot-birà* 'to twist the neck, turn'; Pal; N:còl 'neck' + V:virar 'to turn'

Béar. *cot-crouchì* 'to twist (the neck), grind'; *cot-crouchide* f. 'twisting of the neck, strangling'; Pal; N:còl 'neck' + V:crouchir (*cruissir*) 'to grind, squeal'

Béar. *cot-juntà* 'to join two objects'; Pal; N:còl 'neck' + V:juntar (*jònher*) 'to join'

Béar. *cot-ligà* 'to bind the neck'; Pal, *LeG*; N:còl 'neck' + V:ligar 'to bind'

Gasc. *cot-panà* 'to twist a beast's head toward the shoulder, so as to tame it'; Pal; N:còl 'neck' + V:panar 'to wipe' *coubeissâ* 'to lower the head, deliver a blow on the neck so as to make the head drop'; Poitou *encoubaissà* 'to tie an animal's leg with one end of the halter'; Daniel, *FEW*; N:còl 'neck' + V:baissar 'to lower'

Béar. *coude-poudà* 'to crop the tail'; Pal; N:coa 'tail' + V:podar 'to break'

Aveyr. *coullebá*, Gasc. *cot-lhebà* 'to raise the head, cause to topple'; Azaïs, Pal, *FEW* "levare"; N:còl 'neck' + V:levar 'to raise'

Béar. *coùmpte-dà* 'debt' (*qu'ey de coùmpte-dà* 'it's due'); Pal; N:compte 'account' + V:dar 'to give'

cou-pouda, Béar. *cot-pouda(-s)* 'to break the neck, kill oneself'; *au poude-cot* 'au casse-cou'; Lespy, Piat, Pal, *FEW* "putare"; N:còl 'neck' + V:podar 'to break'

cour-bagna (hort.) 'to layer'; M (*courbagno, -bado* 'vine shoot'), Pal; N:(?) còr 'heart' + V:bagnar 'to bathe'

courcreva 'to press a man or an animal against a wall so as to flatten or stifle him/it'; Azaïs, M, *FEW* "cor"; N:còr 'heart' + V:crevar 'to break'

còutrenca, col-, Béar. *cot-trinca* 'to decapitate, cut the neck'; Cénac-Moncaut, Azaïs, M, Pal; N:còl 'neck' + V:trencar 'to slice, break'

Béar. *croustemaligà* 'crossroads'; Pal, *FEW* "ligare"; N:crotz 'cross' + man 'hand' + V:ligar 'to bind'

se crousto-leva, -lebá, Gasc. *crouste-lheba* 'to detach from the crumb' (of the breadcrust); *crousto-lèvo* 'se dit du pain dont la croûte s'est relevée seule'; Auv. *crèutalevado* 'action of *crousto-leva*; Gasc. *crouste-lhebèt* 'in a bad mood, grumpy'; Gasc. *crouste-lhèyte* f. 'se dit surtout de la mesture mal cuite dont la croûte n'est pas adhérente à la masse'; Vayssier, Azaïs, M, Piat, *FEW* "crusta," JR, Michalias ; N:crosta 'crust' + V:levar 'to rise'

Béar. *cu-agusà* 'to dwindle to a point; swing one's butt in walking'; Pal; N:cul 'butt' + V:agusar 'to sharpen'

Béar. *cu-, cuou-bacha* 'to tumble, trip, crouch, humiliate s.o.'; Roques, Pal; N:cul 'butt' + V:bachar (*baissar*) 'to lower'

Béar. (1317–1789, Bayonne) *cu-bagnadei* 'ordinance fixing punishment similar to the dunking stool', (Mod.) *cubagnader* 'bidet'; *Fables causides* ("réservé aux femmes querelleuses et calomnieuses"), d'Estalenx; N:cul 'butt' + V:bagnar 'to bathe'

cu-bagna 'to bathe', 'donner ou prendre un bain de siège'; Lespy, M (*cuou-bagna[t]* '[Marseille] fishermen's nickname', *Fables causides*, Pal; N:cul 'butt' + V:bagnar 'to bathe'

Béar. *cu-barrà* 'to be frightened, keep silent', 'serrer les fesses'; Pal; N:cul 'butt' + V:barra 'to squeeze, tighten'

Béar. *cu-baysà* 'to kiss the bottom of a pot' (loser's penalty in certain rural games); Pal ("en certains jeux, celui qui perd doit baiser le fond d'une poêle ou d'un chaudron"); N:cul 'butt' + V:baisar 'to kiss'

Béar. *cu-bouchà* 'to rub, clean the insides of a container'; *cu-bouch* 'dungeon'; Pal; N:cul 'butt' + V:bouchar 'to rub'

Béar. *cu-bouhà* 'to brag, incite against someone'; Pal; N:cul 'butt' + V:bouhà (*bufar*) 'to pant, wheeze, brag'

Béar. *cu-boussà* 'to stanch a leak, close up the bottom of a container'; *cu-boussàt* 'constipated, withdrawn, sullen'; Pal; N:cul 'butt' + V:boçar 'to form a lump; close up'

Béar. *cu-dà* 'to turn one's back'; Lespy, *FEW* "dare"; N:cul 'butt' + V:dar 'to give'

Béar. *cu-hourrà* 'to chase; to bother or speak ill of s.o.'; *cuhourrade* 'action of *cu-hourrà*, of pestering; pursuit'; *encuhourràt* 'enclosed, bashed in, bothered' ("*encuhournat* est un synonyme moins vigoureux"); Pal; N:cul 'butt' + V:forrar 'to stuff'

Béar. *cu-labà* 'to bathe', 'prendre un bain de siège'; Pal, *LeG*; N:cul 'butt' + V:lavar 'to bathe'

Béar. *cu-labadé* 'public baths in Bayonne', 'cu-bagnadei' (q.v.), (Mod.) *cuulavader* 'bidet'; Pal ("un emplacement de bains publics de Bayonne porte ce nom—il viendrait de ce qu'autrefois on plongeait là, après jugement, toutes nues, les filles publiques surprises en flagrant délit de racolage"), d'Estalenx; N:cul 'butt' + V:lavar 'to wash'

Béar. *cu-laurà* 'to drag oneself on one's butt', 'labourer avec le cul'; Pal; N:cul 'butt' + V:laurar (*laborar*) 'to plow, labor'

Béar. *cu-lhebà* 'to tumble; empty a bottle, get drunk', 'lever le cul'; *culhèbe* f. '(cross)beam'; *culhebét* 'horse's kick', der. *culhebetà* 'to jump'; Prov. *cuou-levo* 'movement of a seesaw or lever'; Nice *faire couha-leva* 'to tumble'; *jouer à lève-cu*, *jouer à cu-levé* 'to play, taking turns to replace the loser'; Lespy, Azaïs, Pal, *FEW* "culus," Castellana; N:cul 'butt' + V:levar 'to raise'

Béar. *cu-ligà* 'to bind up the bottom of a sack', 'relier les parties qui forment un fond'; Pal; N:cul 'butt' + V:ligar 'to bind'

cuolfregar, *cuou-frega*, Lang. *quieu-frega*, Béar. *cu-regà* 'to quiver, tremble, become agitated', 'traîner'; Pal, LA; N:cul 'butt' + V:(f)regar 'to rub'

Gasc. *cu-pédasà* 'to protect a ewe from the ram', 'mettre un chiffon au cul (pour préserver la brebis de la saillie du mouton)'; Schmitt, *FEW* "pittacium"; N:cul 'butt' + V:pedaçar 'to cover with rags'

Isère *cupela* 'to tumble'; *faire lou cuou-pela* 'to sit on the ground'; *cupelét*, *cupelié* 'headfirst tumble'; *cu-pelat* 'miser(ly)'; Ambert *seupeleto* 'tumble'; M, Pal; N:cul 'butt' + V:pelar 'to peel'

Béar. *cu-senti* 'to be indiscreet, spy on', 'aller sentir au derrière à la manière des chiens'; Lespy, Piat, Pal, *FEW* "sentire"; N:cul 'butt' + V:sentir 'to smell'

Gasc. *cu-toune* 'to shear a sheep around the anus'; Pal, *LeG*, Schmitt; Gasc. *cu-tounedéres* 'bits of wool removed during *cu-toùne*'; *cu-tounùt* 'miser(ly)'; N:cul 'butt' + V:toune (tondre) 'to shear'

Gasc. *dèbe-dà* 'debt'; Pal; N:débe 'debt' + V:dar 'to give'

OGasc. (14th c.) *deit-dizador* 'referee'; *Archives Gironde*; N:dit 'legal decision' + V:dire 'to say'

(12th c.) *descaptener* 'to abandon' (in a nonphysical sense); *FEW* "tenere"; N:cap 'head' + V:tener 'to hold'

(13th c.) *desmantener*, (Mod.) *-teni(r)*, Béar. *-tién(gu)e* 'to abandon'; (Mod.) idem, 'fall to pieces, let go of one's catch'; OPr. *desmantenensa*, *desmanteniment* 'relinquishment, dispossession'; Rayn, AThomas 1898, M, Pal, *FEW* "manu tenere," LA; N:man 'hand' + V:tener 'to hold'

Gasc. *ha déute-pague* 'to pay cash'; Pal, d'Estalenx; N:deute 'debt' + V:pagar 'to pay'

Dieu-Trouva, name of a hero in a folk story from Provence; M ('qui a trouvé Dieu'); N:Dieu 'God' + V:trovar 'to find'

Gasc. *dit-poustà* 'to position'; Pal; N:det 'finger' + V:postar 'to position'

Gasc. *diu-bedë* 'raising, elevation of the Host'; Arnaudin; N:Dieu 'God' + V:véser, veire 'to see'

Auv. *dza[m]bardzá* 'to stamp on, trample'; *FEW* "camba"; N:camba 'leg' + V:bregar (Gmc. *brekan*) 'to break'

Gasc. *èl-traire* 'to tear one's eyes away', 'fatiguer la vue'; *soun èl-trait* 'I've looked so hard that I no longer see anything'; N:uèlh 'eye' + V:traire 'to pull'

Pr. *embòufuma* (intr.) 'to stink'; (tr.) 'to mystify; stink out'; M, *FEW* "fumus"; N:BALSAMU(M) + V:fumar (tr.) 'to smoke (out)'

s'empalaficar 'to settle down in an armchair', Prov. 'to freeze in one's stracks'; Lim. *balafincar* 'to send off'; Puget, M, *FEW* "palum"; N:pala 'stick' + V:ficar 'to fix (to)' Gasc. *empataligà-s* 'to trip, get tangled in s.th.'; Pal; N:pata 'foot' + V:ligar 'to bind'

encabourrí-s 'to be stubborn' (*capbourrut* 'stubborn'); *desencabourrí* 'to correct s.o.'s stubbornness'; *FEW* "caput," Pal; N:cap 'head' + V:borrar 'to stuff'

enchifrenà, s'enchifrounà 'to have a stuffy nose' (cf. Fr. *enchifrené* [17th c.] 'stuffy nose' [q.v.]); M, Pal; N:cap 'head' + V:frenar 'to restrain, bridle'

Béar. *entermaligà* 'to bind several sheaves'; *FEW* "ligare"; N:man 'hand' + V:ligar 'to bind'

s'eschalabatre 'to beat the wings; feel unwell', 'ale-bate' (q.v.); *eschalabatejà* (freq.) idem; *eschalabàt, -ade* f. 'noise of wings beating' (in the air, on the water); *FEW* "battuere," Pal; N:ala 'wing' + V:batre 'to beat'

Gasc. *escù-goaytà* 'to watch from hiding'; *escù-gàytou* 'mystery'; Pal; N:escù 'night' + V:goaytà (*gaitar*) 'to watch'

Gasc. *esgautirà-s* 'to yawn'; *esgautirade* 'yawning', 'slap across the mouth'; Pal; N:gauta 'cheek' + V:tirar 'to pull'

Béar. *eslou-passà* 'to wither, lose its flowers' (of a plant); Pal; N:flor 'flower' + V:passar 'to perish, (intr.) be spent'

Lang. (Toulouse) *espelferi* 'to make one's hair stand on end'; *espelferido* 'action of *espelferi*; Rouerg. *espelofrit* 'hairy; puny'; *FEW* "martyrium," "ferire" (*pelférit* 'numbed'), Moulis, Mouly; N:pel 'hair' + V:ferir 'to strike'

Lang. (Toulouse) *espeltirá*, *espâoutira* 'to pull at from every side'; Azaïs, M; N:pel 'hair' + V:tirar 'to pull'

Béar. *s'espernabate* 'to fall with one's legs in the air'; Piat; N:perna 'leg' + V:batre 'to beat'

Gasc. *espernapicà* 'to fall with one's legs in the air', 'espernabate'; *espernapìco* 'tumble'; Pal; N:pèrna 'leg' + V:picar 'to strike'

Gasc. *espéuligà* 'to wind thread/yarn on a spindle'; *espeulìo* 'length of thread/yarn'; Pal; N:pel 'hair' + V:ligar 'to bind'

Béar. *estrem-birá* 'to overturn'; *estrembirade* 'tumble, overturning'; *FEW* "extremus" + "vibrare," Pal, JR; N:estrem 'end' + V:virar 'to turn'

OBéar. *fedessos* 'bail, relinquishing of a piece of property, seignorial jurisdiction'; *FEW* "fidejussor"; N:FIDĔIŪSSIŌ 'bail'

OBéar. *fedexor* 'local government agent'; *FEW* "fidejussor"; N:FIDĔIŪSSOR 'guarantor, executor'

Béar. *fee-hasent* 'trusting in justice' (cf. Sp. *fehaciente* 'authentic' [q.v.]); *FEW* "fides"; N:fe 'faith' + V:ha (*far*) 'to make, do'

OPr. *fementit* 'traitor', OBéar. *fee-mentit* 'renegade', OLim. *femendit*; Occ. *fe(e)-menti* 'to betray a trust'; Lespy, Piat, JA (N + V); *FEW* "fides"; N:fe 'faith' + V:mentir 'to lie'

OPr. *fervestit* '(armor-clad) warrior'; Adams (N + V Past Ptc), JA (N + V), *FEW* "ferrum"; N:fer 'iron (armor)' + V:vestir 'to clothe'

Tarn *fial-frexa*, Toul. *fiel-freja* 'to ravel, fray, be stringy' (of cloth or foods); Périg. *fialfros* 'stringy'; Lang. *desfialfrà* 'to fray', 'enlever les fils du bâti'; Piat, *FEW* "filum", Miremont, Moulis; N:fiel 'wire' + V:frechar (frachar) 'to break'

fiau-tirâ 'to stretch barbed wire'; Daniel; N:fiel 'wire' + V:tirar 'to pull'

Occ. *fi(e)l-*, *fi(é)u-bastar*, Aveyr. *fiolbosta*, Périg. *fialbartâ*, Rouerg. *fil-*, *fiu-gastar*, Auv. *fiougastâ*, *fiarhabastâ*; Gasc. *hiuvastá* 'to baste'; Occ. *fiéu-basto* 'basting'; Azaïs, Piat, M, Daniel, *FEW* "filum" + "*bastjan," LA, Miremont; N:fiel 'wire' + V:bastar 'to baste'

Rouerg. *florcurar* 'to wither', (hort.) 'to set'; M, LA; N:flor 'flower' + V:curar (colar) 'to remove flowers'

OGasc. *fort[s]-fasedor* 'wrongdoer'; Lespy; N:fòrça 'violence' + V:far 'to make, do'

Gasc. *frèbe-passà* 'to be shaken by fever'; Pal, d'Estalenx; N:fèbre 'fever' + V:passar 'to feel, suffer'

Lang. *gauto-bira* 'to slap'; Allanche; N:gauta 'cheek' + V:virar 'to turn'

Béar. *gay-hasén* 'pleasing'; *gayhasénce* 'gracious quality; kindness'; JR, Pal; N:gay 'pleasure' + V:ha (*far*) 'to make'

gòrja-, *gorjo-fendre* 'to slit the throat; scream'; M, Piat, LA; N:gorja 'throat' + V:fendre 'to split'

Aude *gorjo-bada* 'to open wide one's mouth; be left destitute'; *bâda-gorgi* 'gawking onlooker'; Azaïs, M, Piat, *FEW* "batare"; N:gorja 'throat' + V:badar 'to open'

gorjovira, Aveyr. *guourjo-bira*, Gasc. *gorye-bira* 'to kill by twisting the neck; eat gluttonously', Aveyr. 'to disfigure'; Lespy, Azaïs, M, Piat, LeG, *FEW* "gurges"; N:gorja 'throat' + V:virar 'to turn'

Béar. *gorre-*, *esgorro-bàte* 'to rampage, be delirious' (of a sick person); *gorrebàt* 'noisy', 'uproar, din'; Foix, Pal; N:gorre 'wooden ball; bad weather' + V:batre 'to beat'

Gasc. *goudeslat* 'swollen with pride'; Land. *goudeslà* 'to swell'; Arnaudin, Pal; N:(?) gòda 'show-off'/gauta 'cheek' (cf. Cat. *galt-* 'cheek' + *-inflat*) + V:enflar to swell'

Béar. *goute-herì(-s)* 'to be numb with cold, chilled to the bone'; Pal, *LeG*, *FEW* "gutta"; N:gota 'drop; gout' + V:ferir 'to strike'

Béar. *goute-préne* 'to develop gout'; *-prés* 'gout-stricken'; Pal; N:gota 'drop; gout' + V:prene 'to take, seize'

graisfondre (*se*) 'to become overheated, sweat profusely'; M, LA; N:grais 'fat' + V:fondre 'to melt'

Gasc. *hioupassa* 'to darn socks'; N:fil 'string, thread' + V:passar 'to feel, suffer; pass'

Béar. *hum-dà* 'to give off smoke, incense'; *humdade* 'action of smoking'; Pal; N:hum 'smoke' + V:dar 'to give'

lanaperdent 'losing its wool' (of a sheep); Alibert §117; N:lana 'wool' + V:perdre 'to lose'

Béar. *lenga-bira-s* 'to trip over one's tongue', 'fourcher la langue'; Lespy; N:lenga 'tongue' + V:virar 'to turn'

lengamanjar 'to tear into, speak ill of s.o.'; LA; N:lenga 'tongue' + V:manjar 'to eat'

Béar. *lengue-bourrà-s* 'to trip over one's tongue'; M (*lengo-bourra* 'stammerer'), Pal; N:lenga 'tongue' + V:borrar 'to stuff'

Béar. *lengue-passa* 'to speak ill of s.o.'; Lespy, *FEW* "lingua"; N:lenga 'tongue' + V:passar 'to pass, perish'

Béar. *lengue-plegà* 'to hold one's tongue, keep silent'; Pal; N:lenga 'tongue' +
    V:plegar 'to fold'

Béar. (16th c.) *letre-herit*, Lang. *létroferit* 'fond of letters, well-lettered, learnèd'; Pal,
    FEW "ferire," *DECC* "lletra" ("ja devia estar en ús sols en terres occitanes");
    N:letra 'letter(s)' + V:ferir 'to strike'

OPr. (13th c.) *loc-, loga-tenen*, OBéar. *leotenent, logtient* 'administrative replacement,
    second in command', *loctenensa(ria)* 'office'; (Mod.) *lòctenen* 'lieutenant';
    Lespy, Luchaire, Adams ('place-holding'), *FEW* "tenere," LA; N:lòc 'place' +
    V:tener 'to hold'

OGasc. *maamudar* 'to change hands' (of a property); *maamude* 'transfer (of
    property)' (cf. OFr. *mainmuable* 'capable of changing hands [q.v.]); *FEW*
    "mutare"; N:man 'hand' + V:mudar 'to change'

OPr. *ma-fa(i)t, -fach* 'handmade'; Levy *Supplement*; N:man 'hand' + V:FACTU(M)
    'made'

Gasc. *mahà, mâ-ha, -he* 'to have the lead' (in cards); N:man 'hand' + V:ha (*far*) 'to
    make, do'

Béar. *ma-ligà* 'to tie the hands', Périg. *manouliâ* 'to bundle twigs'; Béar. *ma-ligade* f.
    'action of *ma-ligá*, embarrassment'; *croustemaligá* 'to crisscross' (q.v.); Daniel,
    Pal; N:man 'hand' + V:ligar 'to bind'

OPr. *mamessor* 'servant'; DuC; N:MANŪMISSOR 'executor' ('emancipator')

OGasc. (14th c.) *manaobrar* 'to put with the hands'; Occ. *manobrar, -oubra, -oper* 'to
    maneuver; handle carelessly'; (13th c.) *man(a)obra* f. 'manual labor'; m.
    'laborer', (Mod.) 'hodman, day laborer'; *man(a)obrier* idem; *manobrer* 'foreman
    of a gang of workmen'; OGasc. (13th c.) *manobrar* 'servant', (Mod.) *manoubrè*
    'manual laborer, day laborer'; Gasc. *manoubrade* f. 'menial task, job; allowance
    from the commune'; Gasc. *manoubràdje* m. 'manual labor'; Luchaire, Vayssier,
    M, Pal, *FEW* "manus," LA; N:man 'hand' + V:obrar 'to work'

OPr. *manaya* 'protection'; Diez "manaier," Bos, *REW* §5339 "manus"; N:man 'hand'
    + V:ADIUTĀRE 'to aide'

16th c. *manbestir* 'to invest'; Millardet; N:man 'hand' + V:(in)vestir 'to invest'

OPr. *manbor* 'guardian; curatorship, administration', Auv. *ma(n)bour* 'complicated
    situation'; Diez "mainbour," *FEW* "mundboro"; N:MUNDEBORO 'protector'

man-estrena 'to tip, make a New Year's gift', 'donner l'étrenne'; M; N:man 'hand' +
    V:estrenar 'to make a gift; tip'

Lim. *mangroçar* 'to massacre a job of work'; Dhéralde; N:man 'hand' + V:grusar,
    grudar 'to crush'

manicouquear 'to handle, manipulate, fiddle with'; *FEW* "manus"; N:man 'hand' +
    V:coquelar 'to crumble, flake'

OPr. *manleu*, Béar. *mal(h)èu* m. 'loan, withdrawal; feudal tax'; OPr. *manleuta*, Béar. *malhèute* f. 'loan'; 'mainlevée' (= release of arrested person or goods; cf. *man-levada*, etc.); Levy 1973, Pal, R. Barthe; N:man 'hand' + V:LEVĬTA 'raised, removed'

OPr. (12th c.) *manlevar* 'to borrow, bail out, swear (on raised hand)', 'obtenir sous garantie la délivrance d'une personne arrêtée ou d'une chose saisie'; (Mod.) *manlevar*, Gasc. *malhebà* 'to borrow', Périg. 'to be guilty of extortion; tip over, seesaw'; Occ. *malhèbe*, Gasc. *manlhèbo* 'loan'; 'mainlevée' (= release of arrested person or goods); 'lever on the bucket of a well'; Nice *man-levada* (Castellana), Gasc. *ma(n)lhebade* 'mainlevée'; *manlèvement* 'loan'; *manlevaire*, *manlevador*, Gasc. *malhebadoù* 'borrower'; *ma(n)-levéto* 'ready with his fists'; Occ. *amanleu* 'loan', *amanlevaire* 'borrower'; *solta-manleuta* 'action of releasing an object pledged' (*FEW* "solvere"); Gasc. *sosmalhebar* 'to give or obtain *manlhébo*'; *sosmalheute* 'manlhébo'; Sauvages, Levy 1973, Lespy, Malvezin, Adams (N + V), Daniel, *REW* §5335 "manum levāre," M, Pal, *FEW* "levare," LA, D'Hombres; N:man 'hand' + V:levar 'to raise'

Béar. *mâ-ligà(-s)*, Périg. *manouliâ* 'to bind the hands, manacle; gather into a handful, bundle', (refl.) 'to engage o.s.'; Daniel, Pal, *FEW* "ligare" (*amaligà* [q.v.], *entermaligà* [q.v.]); N:man 'hand' + V:ligar 'to bind'

Béar. *mâ-méte* (law) 'to confiscate'; *FEW* "manus"; N:man 'hand' + V:met(r)e 'to put'

OPr. *mansaizir* 'to give s.th. to s.o.'; OGasc. *mansaysir de* 'to put s.o. in possession of'; Levy 1973, Adams (N + V), *FEW* "*sazjan"; N:man 'hand' + V:saisir 'to seize'

manstraire (se faire), Lim. *se fa monstraire* 'to be blessed at church' (of mothers after childbirth); M, *FEW* "trahere"; N:man 'hand' + V:traire 'to pull (out)'

Béar. *mantasta* 'to grope for; fish by hand', 'pêcher à tâtons avec la main'; Vivarais *amantasta* Gasc. *mâ-taste* f. 'action of feeling'; *à mantasto* 'gropingly', *a la mâ-taste* 'by hand'; XdeF, Pal, Seuzaret, *FEW* "taxitare"; N:man 'hand' + V:tastar 'to feel'

OPr. *mantenen* 'balustrade', Auv. *manteins* 'balustrade (of a bridge)'; Béar. *maa-tien* 'handle'; Gasc. *mantengadére* 'bannister, ramp'; Adams, *FEW* "tenere"; N:man 'hand' + V:tener 'to hold'

manténer, -tenir -tiene, -tenei, -chengue, etc., 'to maintain, affirm, continue, aid; place a bet for s.o.'; OPr. *mantenh*, (Mod.) *manten, mantenemen* 'support, aid'; OPr. *mantenensa*, (Mod.) *-tenença* f. 'act of maintaining, supporting'; *mantenguda* f. 'maintenue' (LA); (cult.) Gasc. *manuténce* (law) 'maintenue', 'act confirming possession'; OPr. *manteneire/-tenedor* 'supporter, protector'; (Mod.) 'croupier, one who bets'; *mantenent* 'one who supports or aids'; Gasc. *mantengadé* 'one who helps to maintain'; *mantenensial* 'de maintenance' (Piat); *desmantener* 'to abandon' (q.v.); OPr. *amantenir* 'to maintain, etc.'; *mantenen* 'immediately;

now'; Avril, Levy 1973, Azaïs, AThomas 1898, Adams, *REW* §5349 "manūtenēre," *FEW* "manu tenere," LA, Dhéralde; N:man 'hand' + V:tener 'to hold'

OPr. *mantersa* 'towel'; Levy *Supplement*; N:MANŪTERGIUM 'towel'

OGasc. *mantreyt* '(hand)work'; Morère; N:man 'hand' + V:trait 'movement'

OPr. *manumitar* 'to set free; take possession of' (Béar. *mâ-méte* [q.v.]); OPr.
manmesa, *-misa*, *manumission* 'confiscation'; Levy 1973, *Archives Gironde*;
N:MANU 'hand' + V:MITTĔRE 'to send'

OPr. (14th c., from French?) *mar-*, *morfondre* 'to catch a cold' (of horses); (15th–18th
c.) 'to catch cold'; (Mod.) *-fondre*, *-fondir*, etc., 'to catch cold; lose weight;
worry excessively'; OPr. *marfondemen* 'chill, equine illness', Lim. 'chill, cold',
Pr. 'loss of weight', Aurillac 'stiffness, aching'; *marfi* 'numbing of the fingers,
pallor caused by the cold'; Lim. *màrfie* 'chilled to the bone'; Gasc. *marfandide*
f. 'action of *marfandi(r)*, numbing'; 's.th. that chills or numbs'; Aurillac
morfièiro 'torpor'; *marfondum* '(equine) loss of weight'; *marfoundre la terro* 'to
plow out of season'; Avril, Malvezin, Levy 1973, M, Piat, Adams (N + V),
FEW "fundere," LA, Lhermet, Gonfroy; N:morre 'nose' + V:fondre 'to melt'

OPr. *marmetre* 'to abandon' (1240 *marmes*); *marmessió* 'action of abandoning';
Chambon, *DECC* "mà"; N:MANU 'hand' + V:MITTĔRE 'to send'

Rouerg. *matrifusar*, Aveyr. *motrifusá* 'to adulterate (merchandise)', 'mêler des denrées
de qualités diverses, pour débiter les médiocres à la faveur des bonnes';
matrifusa 'deceit, adulteration'; M, *FEW* "fundere," LA; N:matiera 'material'
+ V:fusar (FŬNDĔRE) 'to mix'

(12th–14th c.) *mentaver*, *mentaire*, (Mod.) *mentaure*, Béar. *mentábe(r)* 'to remember,
cite, mention, boast, accuse, call'; *rementabe* idem; *mentagos*, *-agut* 'mentioned';
mentevedor 'mentionnable'; OPr. (1285) *mentagudamen* 'expressly, especially';
Levy 1973, *Archives Gironde*, AThomas 1898, Adams, JA (N + V), M, Pal,
FEW "mente habere"; N:ment 'mind' + V:aver 'to have'

OPr. (12th c.) *misa-cantant*, *mesacantan*, OGasc. *missacantaa* 'priest', *missecandera*
'priest's housekeeper'; Béar. *misso-canta* 'to be a priest'; Lespy, Levy 1973,
Luchaire, Piat, Adams, *FEW* "missa"; N:missa 'Mass' + V:cantar 'to sing'

Béar. *moun-*, *moum-birà* 'to upset, cause to fall, tumble, lose one's balance';
desmoumbirà idem; Pal, *FEW* "vibrare"; N:monde 'world' + V:virar 'to turn'

Ariège *mourficá* (hort.) 'to layer'; *FEW* "mergus" 'diver; gull'; N:morre 'nose' +
V:ficar 'to fix (to)'

Toul. *mourlecá* 'to show off'; *morlecada* 'social pretensions'; *morlec* 'self-important,
coquet(te)'; *mourlèque* 'affected, dilettante'; *FEW* "*murr-," LA, Blaquière;
N:morre 'nose' + V:lecar 'to lick'

morlevar 'to show off, be vain; brag'; *morlevada* 'vanity, pretension'; LA; N:morre
'nose' + V:levar 'to raise'

Dauph. *morniflar* 'to sneak, snoop; strike on the nose'; *mornifla(t)* m. 'blow on the nose'; *esmourniflàt, -ade* 'blow', 'mornifle'; *morniflo* f. 'teasing', 'mornifle'; *mournifle* m., *-niflo* f. 'snot-nosed child'; *mourniflòus* 'teasing, mocking'; M, Piat, *FEW* "niff-," Pal, LA, D'Hombres; N:morre 'nose' + V:niflar 'to sniff'

mourre-finta 'to sniff hesitantly'; Lang. *-fintaire* 'curious'; M, Piat, *FEW* "*murr-"; N:morre 'nose' + V:fintar 'to pretend, hesitate'

mourre-senti 'to sniff'; *FEW* "*murr-"; N:morre 'nose' + V:sentir 'to smell'

Béar. *nas-lhebà* 'to be arrogant, raise one's nose', *-levat* 'insolent woman', (Ariège) *-lebat* 'bold'; M, Pal, *FEW* "levare"; N:nas 'nose' + V:levar 'to raise'

Béar. *nas-tapà* 'to catch cold'; Pal, *FEW* "tappôn"; N:nas 'nose' + V:tapar 'to seize'

Gasc. *obre-léche* 'ringing of church bells, signaling an end to work in the fields'; Arnaudin; N:òbra 'work' + V:laissar 'to quit'

Béar. *oélh-birà* 'to squint; die'; Pal; N:uèlh 'eye' + V:virar 'to turn'

Béar. *oélh-perì* 'to blind'; Pal; N:uèlh 'eye' + V:perir 'to perish'

Béar. *oélh-tirà* 'to blind; look at pointedly'; Pal; N:uèlh 'eye' + V:tirar 'to pull (off), remove'

Béar. *palabentà* 'to winnow with a shovel'; Pal, *FEW* "ventus" (OGasc. *pala bentadera* 'pelle à vanner'); N:pala 'stick' + V:bentar (ventar) 'to winnow'

(es)palaficar, paufica, -hicá, 'to plant in the earth, push with a pole, work clumsily'; (tr.) 'to overcome with surprise; rush, fall upon; waste, dissipate'; *palafica, paufich* 'stake, bar'; Périg. *paufich(o)* 'pole'; *palaficage* 'planting with a stake'; Gasc. *empauhicà* 'to set in, incrust'; *a palafi, a balafi* 'in profusion'; Azaïs, AThomas 1898, *REW* §3280 "fictus," Daniel, *FEW* "palus" + "*figicare," JR, LA; N:pala 'stick' + V:ficar 'to fix (to)'

pala-versar, -bessar 'to work with a shovel/hoe' (*pala-vèrs,* Fr. *pelle-versoir*); *palaversaire, palabessaire* 'one who shovels/hoes'; *palaversada* 'work done with a *pala-vèrs*', 'terrain bêché';*palavèrsa* 'upset, tumble'; *esparabissar* (n.g.); *REW,* M, AThomas 1898, Daniel, *FEW* "pala," JR, LA (as against M, distinguishes two primitives: *palavèrs* and *palabés*); N:pala 'shovel' + V:versar 'to spread'

pala-, pale-virar, Gasc. *pale-bira* 'to shovel, turn over with a shovel, upset'; Dauphiné *palavire* 'shovelful; blow, punch'; *à palavira, à viro-palados* 'in profusion', lit. 'by the shovelful'; Villa, Azaïs, M, AThomas 1898, Pal, *FEW* "vibrare," *FEW* "fundere" (N Abl + V); N:pala 'stick' + V:virar 'to turn'

panaussa 'to hike up one's skirt or petticoat'; *despanaussar* idem; M, *FEW* "pannus"; N:pan 'flap' + V:auçar 'to raise'

Gasc. *pa(n)hourrà* 'to gorge on bread or other food, satisfy in a gluttonous manner'; Bazas 'to drag the feet'; *espahourrà* 'to gorge on bread... '; M, Pal, *FEW* "panis"; N:pan 'bread' + V:forrar 'to stuff'

Lang. *pan-*, *pal-levar*, *pelleba* 'to raise a heavy object with a lever'; Azaïs, M, *FEW* "levare," JR, LA; N:pan 'flat surface' + V:levar 'to raise'

Béar. *panminjant* '[long-term] day-laborer', Landes 'celui qui travaille presque toujours pour la même personne'; M; N:pan 'bread' + V:manjar 'to eat'

B.-Alpes *panavelear* 'to float'; *FEW* "velum"; N:pan 'flap' + V:velejar 'to put to sail'

Béar. *part-birà* 'to upset, turn over, move'; *pale-birà* idem, 'upset, torment'; *part-birat, -ada* f. 'action of *part-birà*; upset, torment'; Pal, *FEW* "vibrare," d'Estalenx; N:part 'part' + V:virar to turn'

Béar. *part-mudà* 'turn over, move'; Pal; N:part 'part' + V:mudar 'to change'

pata-, *pato-vira*, Gasc. *pato-birá* 'to die'; Lang. *viropatá* idem, 'turn over'; M, Piat, *FEW* "vibrare," LA; N:pata 'leg, paw' + V:virar 'to turn'

H.-Alpes *pate tetiar* 'to caress'; *FEW* "patt-"; N:patte 'leg, paw' + N:(dial.) teste 'head' + -ar

Béar. *pè-bira(-s)* 'to turn one's ankle, walk with difficulty'; Pal, *FEW* "vibrare"; N:pè 'foot' + V:virar 'to turn'

Béar. *pè-branla* 'to move'; Piat; N:pè 'foot' + V:branlar 'to shake'

Auv.–Lang.–Gasc. *pè(d)batre* 'to shiver, become agitated, flee'; *repèbatre* 'agoniser en agitant les jambes'; *fa pè-batre* 'to put to flight'; Villa, Azaïs, M, *FEW* "pes," LA; N:pè 'foot' + V:batre 'to beat'

Gasc. *ped-descaussa (se)* 'to take off one's shoes'; M; N:pè 'foot' + V:des+caussar 'to unshoe'

Béar. *pè-hica* 'to stand fast; walk pigeon-toed', 'marcher avec les pieds en dedans'; Pal, *FEW* "pes"; *pè-ic* 'indiscreet; pigeon-toed'; *pè-hican* 'indiscreet, inoppor-tune'; N:pè 'foot' + V:ficar 'to fix'

Béar. *pè-hourè*, *-hourì*, *-hourà-s* 'to stamp on the ground, twist one's ankle, step on s.o.'s foot'; *pè-houràyre* 'maladroit'; Pal; N:pè 'foot' + V:foure (forar) 'to pierce'

pèira-, *pèyra-batre*, Gasc. *peiro-bate* 'to stone, shatter; hail'; 'whetstone'; *pèiro-batudo*, *pèyrebatude* 'blister on the foot'; *pèyrabatude* 'heavy fall of hail'; Lespy, Azaïs, Cénac-Moncaut, M, Pal, *FEW* "petra," LA; N:pèira 'stone' + V:batre 'to beat'

Rouerg. *pèiraficar*, *pèiro-fica* 'to pave'; *-ficaire* 'paver'; M, AThomas 1898, JR, LA, Gonfroy; *peirafis*, *-fic* 'vertically fissured ground'; N:pèira 'stone' + V:ficar 'to fix'

Béar. *(tourrà) a pèira-héner*, *a peyre hene* 'to freeze', 'geler à pierre fendre'; Pal, *FEW* "findere," Darrigrand; N:pşira 'stone' + V:fendre 'to split'

pè-jùgne, Béar. *pè-juntà* 'to join the feet; follow closely, catch up with someone running, gallop'; Pal, *FEW* "pes"; N:pè 'foot' + V:jugne, junta (jònher) 'to join'

pelbufar 'to have a dull coat' (of cattle); LA; N:pel 'hair' + V:bufar 'to pant, wheeze, blow'

Béar. *pè-lhebà* 'to raise the foot; to raise with a lever'; *pè-lhèbe* 'lever', *péne-lhèbe* idem; OPr. *pèe-lhèbe*, *pèd-levo* 'trap'; Lespy, M, Pal, *FEW*; N:pè 'foot' + V:levar 'to raise'

pellecar 'to spoil' (see "Dubious" below); Azaïs, *FEW* "*lekkon," LA; N:pèl 'skin' + V:lecar 'to lick'

pellevar (se), *pel-*, *peu-leba* 'to raise up by pulling the hair or ears; get riled, angry'; *pellevament* 'raising (by the hair)'; *pellebádo* 'flurry of blows to the ears'; Azaïs, Vayssier, M (péu 'hair'/per?), Piat, LA, R. Barthe; N:pel 'hair' + V:levar 'to raise'

pèlmudar, *pèu-mudá*, Béar. *pèt-mudà* 'to molt, change skin; fail, die'; *peu-mudage* 'molting'; Lespy, Vayssier, M, Pal, JR, *FEW* "fundere" (N Dir Obj + V), LA; N:pèl 'skin' + V:mudar 'to change'

OPr. (13th c.) *pelpartidura* 'part (in the hair)'; JR, *FEW* "pars"; N:pel 'hair' + V:partir 'to part'

pel-, *peu-*, *espel-tira* 'to pull the hair; pull s.o. by his hair or his clothes'; *pel-tirado*, *peu-tirage*, *peu-tiro* 'prise aux cheveux'; *peu-tiraire* 'one who pulls s.o.'s hair'; *peltirament* 'pulling, yanking'; *peltirat* 'type of material'; *peltrach* 'standing on end' (of the hair); Castres *peltiri* 'difficulty'; Périg. *fà a tiro-piaus* 'to grab by the hair'; Vayssier, Azaïs, M, Piat, *FEW* "martyrium," LA, R. Barthe; N:pel 'hair' + V:tirar 'to pull'

Béar. *pè-mudà* 'to move one's foot'; Pal, *FEW* "mutare"; N:pè 'foot' + V:mudar 'to move'

Béar. *pè-picà* 'to walk, striking one's heel; be impatient, stamp one's feet'; *pepic*, *-pique* 'clubfoot'; Pal, *FEW* "*pikkare"; N:pè 'foot' + V:picar 'to strike'

Gasc. (16th c.) *pernabatre* 'to fight (with the feet)', Toul. *pèrnabatre*, *pernabàter*, Gasc. *espernabate* 'to agitate the legs, fall with one's legs in the air, wriggle about'; Béar. 'to die'; Béar. *espernabatude* 'agitation of the legs and buttocks'; Azaïs, M, Piat, *FEW* "perna," LA; N:perna 'leg' + V:batre 'to beat'

Gasc. (18th c.) *perne-bira* 'to tumble, turn over'; *Fables causides*; N:perna 'leg' + V:virar 'to turn'

Béar. *pèt-eslà-s* 'to swell with pride'; Pal; N:pèl 'skin' + V:enflar 'to swell'

Béar. *pè-tirà-s* 'to run away'; Pal; N:pè 'foot' + V:tirar 'to remove'

Béar. *pè-tòrse* 'to twist the foot'; Gasc. *pè-tor* 'clubfoot'; *pè-toursut* 'lame'; Pal, *LeG*, *FEW* "torquere"; N:pè 'foot' + V:torse (tòrcer) 'to twist'

Béar. *pè-tournà* 'to revenge, give tit for tat'; *pè-tournét* m. 'revenge'; Pal, *FEW* "tornare"; N:pè 'foot' + V:tornar 'to return'

Béar. *pè-tourtejà* 'to limp; shilly-shally, look for a way out'; Pal, *FEW* "torquere"; N:pè 'foot' + V:tortejar 'to wiggle'

Béar. *pè-triscà* 'to walk with one's feet crossed'; Pal, *FEW* "threskan"; N:pè 'foot' + V:triscar (trescar) 'to plait'

Béar. *pè-troulhà* 'to stamp the feet'; Pal; N:pè 'foot' + V:trulhar 'to press'

pèu-bouli, Béar. *pèt-bouri* 'to scald'; Lespy, Piat; N:pèl 'skin' + V:bourir (*bolhir*) 'to boil'

(*se*) *pèu-lia*, Béar. *peu-*, *poulligá*, (Landes) *péulha* 'to tie the hair'; *peuliga* 'lock of hair'; *péulho, peoulio* 'hair ribbon'; *peulheto* 'small hair ribbon'; M, AThomas 1898, *FEW* "ligare," JR; N:pel 'hair' + V:ligar 'to bind'

Béar. *péulissà* 'to comb, smoothe the hair'; *péu-lìs* 'having smooth hair'; *péulissade* 'action of *péulissà*', (colloq.) 'drubbing'; Pal; N:pel 'hair' + V:lissar 'to smoothe'

péu-muda, Mars. *-mia* 'to molt'; *pelmudatge* 'molting'; Azaïs, M, *FEW* "mutare"; N:pel 'hair' + V:mudar 'to change'

Béar. *péu-passà* 'to lose one's hair'; Pal; N:pel 'hair' + V:passar 'to perish'

péu-tireja, Rhône dials. *poútireja* 'to pull at from every side' (cf. Fr. *tirer par les cheveux* 'to be far-fetched'); M; N:pel 'hair' + V:tirejar 'to jerk'

pèu-vira, Béar. *pétbira, petchibira* 'to tumble, trip, turn over, fall down'; *viro-pel* 'pest'; Lespy, Azaïs, M, Pal, *LeG*, *FEW* "vibrare"; N:pèl 'skin' + V:virar 'to turn'

pl(ó)u-, plumo-muda, plooumiar, plumya 'to molt, lose the feathers'; M, *LeG*, *FEW* "mutare"; N:pluma 'feather' + V:mudar 'to change'

Béar. *pot-birà* 'to turn up one's lip, sulk, grimace'; Pal; N:pot 'lip' + V:virar 'to turn'

potligà 'to bridle (a horse)', 'mettre la *potlìgo*'; Pal, *FEW* "pott-"; N:pot 'lip' + V:ligar 'to bind'

Gasc. *poú-herit* 'fear-stricken'; Cassagnau; N:páur 'fear' + V:ferir 'to strike'

OPr. *prestlevar* 'to lend, borrow'; Adams, *FEW* "prestare"; N:prest 'loan' + V:levar 'to remove'

Gasc. *prouhasent* 'comely'; Lespy; N:prou 'advantage, profit' + V:ha (far) 'to make, do'

Gasc. *quilhe-courneja* 'to walk, cross at an angle'; Pal; N:quilha (colloq.) 'leg' + V:cornejar 'to butt with horns' (of an animal)

recapvirar 'to rear' (of horses); LA; N:cap 'head' + V:virar 'to turn'

Gasc. *rementabe* 'to remember'; Lespy; N:ment 'mind' + V:aver 'to have'

salicar (*se*) 'to savor one's food'; M, *FEW* "*lekkon*"; N:sal; 'salt' + V:lecar 'to lick'

OPr. (13th c.) *salpicar* 'to spread with ashes'; Mars. *salpicar, saupicá* 'to sprinkle with salt; beat, give blows'; *saupi, salpic* 'splash'; *saupiquet* (from Fr.?) 'spicy sauce or stew'; Gasc. *saupìc, saupicoû* 'spicy sauce or stew', 'one with a difficult character'; *saupicado* 'amount sprinkled at one time, flurry of blows'; *saupicaduro* 'area sprinkled'; *saupicage* 'action of sprinkling'; *saupicaire* 'one who sprinkles'; Gasc. *faire un saupicoû* 'finish off one's soup with wine', 'faire chabrol'; *ressaupicar* 'to splash, spurt'; M, *REW* §7521 "sāl," Pal, *FEW* "sal," LA, R. Barthe; N:sal 'salt' + V:picar 'to strike'

salposcar, Gasc. *sal-*, *sau-pouscá* 'to sprinkle' (with salt); *saupousc* 'splashing (of waves); M, *FEW* "posca," LA; N:sal 'salt' + V:poscar 'to powder'

Lim. *salprene*, *saupren(dr)e* 'to absorb salt' (of meat); Azaïs, M, *FEW* "prehendere," LA; N:sal 'salt' + V:prene 'to take'

OPr. (14th c.) *salprés*, *saupres* 'salt pork'; (Mod.) *saupresado* 'cervelas, sausage'; *FEW* "prehendere"; N:sal 'salt' + V:PRĒNSU(M) 'seized'

Béar. *sang-barrejà* 'to spill blood, cut the throat, bleed'; Pal, *FEW* "sanguis"; N:sang 'blood' + V:barrejar 'to turn (a bar)'

sangbeure, Lang. *sangveure* 'to desire greatly, covet'; Azaïs, M, *FEW* "sanguis" (*sang-bégut* 'numbed with cold'), JR, LA; N:sang 'blood' + V:beure 'to drink'

Béar. *sang-birà* 'to upset (morally), be troubled'; *birá lou sang* idem; Pal, *FEW* "sanguis"; N:sang 'blood' + V:virar 'to turn'

Béar. *sang-bouri*, *-boure* 'to boil, overheat' (of the blood); 'to be impatient'; *-bourimen* 'overheating'; *-bourit* 'one whose blood has overheated'; Pal, *FEW* "sanguis"; N:sang 'blood' + V:bourir (bolhir) 'to boil'

Béar. *sang-cremà-s* 'to be troubled', 'se brûler le sang'; Pal; N:sang 'blood' + V:cremar 'to burn'

sang-dévorant 'restless person'; M; N:sang 'blood' + V:devorar 'to devour'

OPr. *sanc-foizó*, OLang. (12th c.) *-fois* 'bloodshed'; OLang. *sanc-foisonant*, OPr. *-foi(s)onat* 'wounded'; Levy 1973, *FEW* "sanguis"; N:sang 'blood' + FŪSIŌ, -IŌNE(M) × FŬNDĔRE

san(g)-glaçar, *-glassa*, *-glaceja*, *songloçá* 'to freeze the blood', (refl.) 'to feel one's heart stop cold'; *sang-glacéjà* idem; *sang-glaçamen* 'chill' (of the blood); *sanglaçat* 'pleurisy'; Vayssier, Azaïs, M, Piat, Daniel, *FEW* "glacies," LA; N:sang 'blood' + V:glaçar 'to freeze'

san-goula, *-gulha* 'to pierce and let the blood flow out, cut the throat, kill'; M; N:sang 'blood' + V:colar 'to flow'

Auv. *sangoulhá* 'to agitate an object in the water', Périg. 'to splash around in the water'; *FEW* "*gullja"; N:sang 'blood'/SANIĒS 'bloody matter, poison' + V:colar 'to flow'

sangpausa 'to calm'; Piat, *FEW* "sanguis" + "pausare"; N:sang 'blood' + V:pausar 'to place, rest'

Guy. *sangtradi* 'to surprise, render speechless'; M, Pal, *FEW* "sanguis" + "tradere"; N:sang 'blood' + V:tradir (transir) 'to pierce'

Béar. *sang-transi* 'to surprise'; Pal; N:sang 'blood' + V:transir 'to pierce'

Béar. *saupoudra* (var. of *saupousca*?) 'to sprinkle (with salt)', 'saupoudrer'; *saupoudrade, saupoudràdje* 'sprinkling'; *saupoudrìs* 'saltshaker'; *saupoudràyre* 'one who sprinkles'; Pal, *FEW* "sal"; N:sal 'salt' + V:poudrar 'to powder'

sengirar 'to return, upset'; LA; N:sens 'direction' + V:girar 'to turn'

Gasc. *sens-birà* 'to change direction, turn upside down'; Pal; N:sens 'direction' + V:virar 'to turn'

Béar. *sère-birà-s* 'to fall from horseback'; *sère-biràt, sère-biroû* 'reversed saddle'; (fig.) 'deranged'; Pal; N:selle 'saddle' + V:virar 'to turn'

Béar. *sole-bàte* 'to beat one's soles on the road'; Béar. *sole-batude, solibatud*, Prov. *solbatudo* 'bruising of the flesh under the sole'; *solebatut* 'footsore' (cattle); Achard, Dupleich, M, Pal, *FEW* "solea"; N:sol 'foot' + V:batre 'to beat'

Béar. *sou-coélhe* 'to harvest with the sun'; *sou-coélhude* 'harvest (under the sun)'; Pal, *FEW* "colligere"; N:solelh 'sun' + V:coelhe 'to gather'

Béar. *sòulhebà* 'to remove surface dirt', 'lever un sol'; Pal; N:sol 'soil' + V:levar 'to raise'

sucapelar, suco-pela, -pola, supela 'to become bald'; Vayssier, M (*su-pela*), Piat, LA; N:suco 'pate' + V:pelar 'to peel'

talafissâ, Lim. *tolofissa* 'to torment, goad'; M, Daniel, *FEW* "*talo-*" + "fixare"; N:talon 'heel' + V:fissar 'to pierce'

tal(h)-virá, Périg. *tai-virâ*, Gasc. *talbirá* 'to ruin the edge' (of a knifeblade); Gasc. *talh-birade* 'action of ruining a knifeblade', 'change of mood'; Azaïs, Malvezin, M, Piat, Daniel, *FEW* "taliare," Alibert; N:talh 'cutting edge' + V:virar 'to turn'

OPr. *terragardar* 'to make an inspection; police, function as game warden'; (13th c.) *terragarda* 'legal inspection of grounds', (Mod.) *terro-gardo* 'game warden'; Levy 1973, M, *FEW* "terra" + "wardôn"; N:terra 'land' + V:gardar 'to guard'

OPr. (15th c.) *terragiet* 'earth dug out of a moat and thrown up along the sides'; M, *FEW* "terra"; N:terra 'land' + V:getar 'to throw'

OGasc. (13th c.) *terratenen* 'tenant', Béar. *tèrratenent* 'landowner'; Périg. 'adjoining another property'; Lespy, *FEW* "terra," Alibert, Miremont; N:tèrra 'earth' + V:tener 'to hold'

(en) terre-estant 'during one's lifetime'; M; N:tèrra 'earth' + V:estar 'to be'

Béar. *terre-passà* 'to overstep a boundary, go beyond one's rights'; Pal; N:tèrra 'earth' + V:passar 'to pass'

Béar. *terre-pèrdre* 'to lose one's footing'; *terre-perdén* 'losing one's footing'; Pal; N:tèrra 'earth' + V:perdre 'to lose'

Béar. *terre-pouyrì* 'to rot in the ground'; Pal; N:tèrra 'earth' + V:porir 'to rot'

tèrre-tién 'adjoining land' (cf. Levy 1973: OPr. *a un tenen de* 'adjoining'(?), and Norm. *tenant* 'piece of land adjoining another owned by the same person'); N:tèrra 'earth' + V:tener 'to hold, adhere'

Lim. *trancho-daurâ* 'to gild the edges of books', 'dorer sur tranches'; Daniel; N:trancha 'slice, edge' + V:daurar 'to gild'

OPr. (14th c.) *viandant*, OGasc. *biandant* 'pilgrim'; *vianar* 'to travel'; (hap.) *anar via* 'to leave'; Lespy, Adams, JA (N + V), *FEW* "via" + "andare"; N:via 'way' + V:anar 'to go'

OTHER COMPOUNDS APPROXIMATING N + V STRUCTURE

aqueferar, -ir, Gasc. *enqueherì-s* 'to be worried, make an effort to find out s.th.'; Gasc. *aqueherit* 'diligent'; Cassagnau 1965 (*[a]quehè* 'busy' + *ferir* 'to strike'), LA (*a + que + fèr + -ar, -ir*; cf. Cat. *aqueferar*); N:que 'what' + fer (far? 'to make, do') + V:-ar, -ir; or N:que + V:ferir 'to strike'

cabiroulá 'to roll down'; *FEW* "rotella" 'little wheel'; N:cap 'head' + ROTELLA

OPr. *calpizar*, Occ. *-pisar, caupisa, choupisar* 'to crush underfoot'; Levy 1973, Adams (N + V), M, *FEW* "calcare" (from *calx* 'heel') + "*pinsiare"; V:CALCĀRE 'to tread (on)' + V:PI(N)SĀRE 'to pound'

OPr. *cambaterrar* 'to dismount'; Levy 1973, Adams (N + V?), M, *FEW* "camba"; N:camba 'leg' + a terra 'on the ground', or *CAMBA TERRATA?

cambavirotat m. 'poisonous mushroom, with a twisted foot'; M, LA; N:camba 'leg' + V:virotar 'to turn over, tumble'

cap-bordona 'to trip, tumble'; M, LA; N:cap bordon 'large stick' + V:-ar

Gasc. *cap-bourrut* 'stubborn'; Pal; N:cap 'head' + bourrut 'stuffed' (cf. *borra* 'stuffing')

capfinar 'to caress, cuddle'; LA; N:cap + fin 'delicate head' + V:-ar

cap-rodelar, Lang. *-roudela*, Rouerg. *car-rudela, -roudelá* 'to tumble, take a spill; roll on its wheels' (of furniture); Vayssier, M, *FEW* "rotulare," LA; N:caprodèla 'wheel' [of furniture] + V:-ar

Lim. *chafena* 'to put hay in s.o.'s hair'; M (through reinterpretation of *escafagna* 'to tousle'/*escarpena* 'to card [wool]')

chaupica 'to sprain one's ankle, fouler le pied'; *FEW* "calcare" (from *calx* 'heel'); V:CALCĀRE + V:*pikkāre 'to strike'

Lim.-Périg. *c(h)aus-fourna* 'to prepare lime'; M, Daniel; N:chaufour 'lime-oven' + V:-ar

chalibourdounâ 'to tumble, fall down'; *fa lous chalibourdons* idem; M, Daniel; N:? + bordon 'mountain walking stick' + V:-ar

cintra-basti 'to baste'; Piat; V:cintrar 'to baste' + bastir idem

Gasc. *cot-courre* (n.g.); Arnaudin; N:(?) còl 'neck' + V:(?) córrer 'to run'

Béar. *cu-herrà* 'to stabilize, affix firmly', '(être) de cul ferme'; Pal; N:cul ferm (cf. pè fèrm 'firm footing') + V:-ar *cu-plata-s* 'to fall on one's butt'; Pal; N:cul 'butt' + plat 'flat' + V:-ar

Prov. *desfaufilar* 'to remove basting'; Achard; N: faux fil 'false thread' + V:-ar

Gasc. *(à) galhcantàn* 'at cock-crow, dawn' (cf. *hasâ-cantàn* 'dawn'; and Sp. [*Laguna de*] *Gallocanta*); Pal; N:gal 'rooster' + V:cantar 'to sing'

mourfina, moufida 'to sniff hesitantly'; M, Piat; N:morre fin 'delicate nose' + V:-ar, or N:morre 'nose' + V:(?) funa 'to search for'

Lang. *ner-ferodure* '(equine) inflammation of the tendon'; Seuzaret; N:nerf 'nerve' + V:ferir 'to strike'

Lang. *ner-fouladuro* '(equine) sprain of the tendon'; Seuzaret; N: nerf 'musce, nerve' + V:folar 'to crush'

Gasc. *queha* 'business'; *queharam* idem (lit. "what shall we do?"); Lespy; N:que 'what' + V:ha (far) 'to make, do'

Béar. *palagrilha* 'to dig with a shovel'; Lespy (*palagrilh* = Roman *rastrum*), Pal, LA; N:(arch.) palagrilh 'shovel' + V:-ar

OPr. *palferre* 'heavy iron bar'; *palahèr* 'short-handled [iron] shovel', 'pelle-bêche'; *palaherrà* 'to dig with a *palahèr*'; *palaherrade, palaherràt* 'movement of the *palahèr*'; *palaherràyre* 'one who handles a *palahèr*'; AThomas, Pal, *FEW* "pala," "palus"; N:palahèr 'short-handled [iron] shovel' + V:-ar

Gasc. *pè-(h)rémà, pè-herrà* 'to stand one's ground', '(être) de pied ferme'; *pè-rém* 'action of standing one's ground'; *pè-remade* 'action of pressing one's foot to the ground; footprint, print of a shoe'; *pè-remàyre* adj. 'bête de trait qui fait effort habituellement sur les pieds de derrière'; Pal, *FEW* "pes"; N:pè fèrm 'firm footing' + V:-ar

Gasc. *péne-lhèbe* f. 'lever' (cf. *pè-lhèbe* idem); Pal; V:péne (*pendre*) 'to hang' + V:levar 'to raise'

peyraherrà, Béar. *peyrahemà* 'to set up a lever', 'prendre un point d'appui sur une pierre et jouer d'un levier'; Pal; N:peira ferma 'firm ground' (lit. 'stone') + V:-ar

pèyrecayrà 'to place dressed stones in a corner of a piece of masonry'; M, Piat, Pal, LA; N:pèyre de càyre 'cornerstone' + V:-ar

pifourc 'pitchfork'; *pifourcà* 'to strike or pierce with the *pifourc*'; Gasc. *empihourcà, entihourcà* 'to pierce with the *pifourc*' (cf. Gasc. *tihòurc* 'pike, hunting spear, sharpened stake'), (refl.) 'to get astride'; Pal; N:*pifourc* 'pitchfork' + V:-ar

Gasc. *que-ha, quehà* m. 'affair, occupation' (cf. *aqueferar* [q.v.]); Pal; N:que 'what' + V:ha (far) 'to make, do'

soul-funa, -fina, foul-fina, -sina 'to scent' (like a dog); M, Piat; N:sol 'soil' + V:(?) funa 'to search for', or N:sol + fin + V:-ar

DUBIOUS

Landes *amourlicá* 'to curl up in a ball', akin to Toul. *mourlecá* 'to show off'; *FEW* "*murr-"; N:(?) morre 'nose' + V:(?) lecar 'to lick'

Lang. *ca-*, *char-pigna* 'to look for trouble, cause a fight'; D'Hombres (*cap* +); either prefixal *ca-*, or N:cap 'head' + V:pignar 'to comb', or capler (see OFr. *chapignier* 'to tear, rip')

OPr. *corcolar* 'to be worm-eaten'; Levy 1973; N:(?) caca 'insect, type of cricket' (cf. Cat. *corc* 'woodworm'?) + V:(?)

coudasquejar, coudiquejà 'to flutter the tail'; Azaïs, Pal; N:coa 'tail' + V:(?)

Lim. *s'emarlicá* 'to develop', 'prendre bonne façon', akin to Toul. *mourlecá* 'to show off'; *FEW* "*lekkon"; N:(?) morre 'nose' + V:lecar 'to lick'

Quer. *jangoutá* 'to drip'; *FEW* "gutta"; prefixal *con-* + *goutte* + V:-ar

Aveyr. *jon-gibrá*, Rouerg. *joungira* 'to freeze, frost over, penetrate with cold'; M, *FEW* "*gevero" 'wintery'; prefixal *con* is likely

OPr. *mantuzar* 'to handle, take in the hand'; Mod.Occ. idem, Gasc. 'to continue'; Azaïs, M, LA; N:(?) manutigium; or (?) manu + V:(?) *tusiāre (from *tundĕre* 'to strike, beat'), (?) *trusiāre 'to push with the hand')

(se) pelleba 'to remove, raise'; Azaïs, M, Piat; prefixal *per*, or N:pel 'hair' + levar

Gasc. *pellecar* 'to spoil' (a child or pet); *FEW* "*lekkon" (*per* + *lecar*, with later reinterpretation as *pel*)

MEDIEVAL AND RENAISSANCE OCCITAN NOMINAL ELEMENTS

aigaversar	N:aiga 'water'	V:versar
benstenen	N:bèn '[inherited] goods'	V:tener
botenflat	N:BOD- 'round shape'	V:enflar
cambalia	N:camba 'leg'	V:ligar
capfrenar	N:cap 'head'	V:frenar
capgirar	N:cap	V:girar
caplheba	N:cap	V:levar
captenir	N:cap	V:tenir
capvirar, capbira	N:cap	V:virar

caravirar	N:cara 'face'	V:virar
caramantrant	N:carèma 'Lent'	V:entrar
carema prenens	N:carèma	V:prendre
carn-bedar	N:carn 'flesh'	V:vetar
cazatenen	N:casa 'house'	V:tener
clauficar	N:clau 'nail'	V:ficar
clauponh	N:clau	V:PŬNCTU(M)
coa-leva	N:coa 'tail'	V:levar
conde-finar	N:conde 'account'	V:finar
coo-transi	N:cor 'heart'	V:transir
cubagnadei	N:cul 'butt'	V:banhar
culabadé	N:cul	V:lavar
fedessos	N:FIDEIŪSSIŌ 'bail'	
fedexor	N:FIDEIŪSSOR 'guarantor, executor'	
fementit	N:fe 'faith'	V:mentir
fervestit	N:fer 'iron (armor)'	V:vestir
etre-herit	N:letra 'letter(s)'	V:ferir
loctenent	N:loc 'position'	V:tener
manaya	N:man 'hand'	V:ADIŪTĀRE
mafa(i)t, -fach	N:man	V:FACTU(M)
manbestir	N:man	V:(in)vestir
manlevar	N:man	V:levar
manleu(ta)	N:man	V:LEVĬTA
marmetre, manumitar, marmessia	N:man	V:metre
maamudar	N:man	V:mudar
manobrar	N:man	V:obrar
mansaysir	N:man	V:saisir
mantenen	N:man	V:tener
mantener	N:man	V:tener
mamessor	N:MANŪMISSOR 'executor' ('emancipator')	

mantersa	N:MANŪTERGIUM 'towel'	
manbor	N:MUNDEBORO 'protector'	
menthaver, mentaure	N:ment 'mind'	V:haber
misacantant	N:misa 'Mass'	V:cantar
morfondre	N:morre 'nose'	V:fondre
pèe-lhèbe	N:pè 'foot'	V:levar
pelpartidura	N:pel 'hair'	V:partir
pernabatre	N:perna 'leg'	V:batre
prestlevar	N:prest 'loan'	V:levar
salpicar	N:sal 'salt'	V:picar
salpres	N:sal	V:PRĒ(N)SU(M)
sancfois, -foizó	N:sang 'blood'	V:FŪSIŌ, -IŌNE(M) × FŬNDĔRE
terragardar	N:terra 'land'	V:gardar
terragiet	N:terra	V:getar
terratenen	N:terra	V:tener
viandant, biandant, vianar	N:via	V:anar

MEDIEVAL AND RENAISSANCE OCCITAN VERBAL ELEMENTS

manaya	N:man	V:ADIŪTĀRE 'to aid'
viandant, biandant, vianar	N:via	V:anar 'to go'
cu-bagnadei	N:cul	V:banhar 'to bathe'
pernabatre	N:perna	V:batre 'to beat'
manbor	N:MUNDEBORO 'protector'	
misacantant	N:misa	V:cantar 'to sing'
botenflat	N:BOD-	V:enflar 'to swell'

caramantrant	N:carèma	V:entrar 'to enter'
mafa(i)t, -fach	N:man	V:FACTU(M) 'made'
letre-herit	N:letra	V:ferir 'to strike'
claufIcar	N:clau	V:ficar 'to fix (to)'
conde-finar	N:conde	V:finar 'to end'
morfondre	N:morre	V:fondre 'to melt'
sancfois, -foizó	N:sang	V:FŪSIŌ, -IŌNE(M) × FŬNDĔRE
capfrenar	N:cap	V:frenar 'to restrain, bridle'
terragardar	N:terra	V:gardar 'to guard'
terragiet	N:terra	V:getar 'to throw'
capgirar	N:cap	V:girar 'to turn'
mentaver, mentaure	N:ment	V:haber 'to have'
manbestir	N:man	V:(in)vestir 'to invest'
fedessos	N:FIDEIŪSSIŌ	(V:IUBĒRE 'to command')
fedexor	N:FIDEIŪSSOR	
culabadé	N:cul	V:lavar 'to wash'
caplheba	N:cap	V:levar 'to raise'
coa-leva	N:coa	V:levar
manlevar	N:man	V:levar
pèe-lhèbe	N:pè	V:levar
prestlevar	N:prest	V:levar
manleu(ta)	N:man	V:LEVĬTA 'raised'
cambalia	N:camba	V:ligar 'to bind'
fementit	N:fe	V:mentir 'to lie'
marmetre, manumitar, marmessia	N:man	V:metre 'to send'
maamudar	N:man	V:mudar 'to change'
manobrar	N:man	V:obrar 'to work'
pelpartidura	N:pel	V:partir 'to part'

salpicar	N:sal	V:picar 'to strike'
carema prenens	N:carèma	V:prendre 'to take, seize'
salpres	N:sal	V:PRĒ(N)SU(M)
clauponh	N:clau	V:PŬNCTU(M) 'pricked'
mansaysir	N:man	V:saisir 'to seize'
benstenen	N:bèn	V:tener 'to hold'
captenir	N:cap	V:tener
cazatenen	N:casa	V:tener
loctenent	N:loc	V:tener
mantenen	N:man	V:tener
mantener	N:man	V:tener
terratenen	N:terra	V:tener
mantersa	N:MANŪTERGIUM	(V:TERGĔRE 'to wipe')
coo-transi	N:cor	V:transir
aigaversar	N:aiga	V:versar
fervestit	N:fer	V:vestir 'to clothe'
carn-bedar	N:carn	V:vetar
capvirar, capbira	N:cap	V:virar
caravirar	N:cara	V:virar

MODERN OCCITAN NOMINAL ELEMENTS

aiga-, aigo-muda	N:aiga 'water'	V:mudar
aigo-pendent	N:aiga	V:pendre
aigo-pico	N:aiga	V:picar
àga-pich	N:aiga	V:pichar (pissar)
aiga-, aygue-prene	N:aiga	V:prene
aigatrebolar	N:aiga	V:trebolar
aiga-vers	N:aiga	V:versar
ale-bacha	N:ala 'wing'	V:bachar (baissar)
ale-bate	N:ala	V:bate
embòufuma	N:BALSAMU(M) 'balsam'	V:fumar
banc-, bonleva	N:banc 'bench'	V:levar

barbo-leca, -lequa	N:barba 'beard'	V:lecar
bèn-tenènt	N:bèn '(inherited) goods'	V:tener
bente-bo(u)eita	N:bente 'belly'	V:boueitar (voidar)
blanc-signat	N:blanc 'white'	V:signar
blaugetar	N:blau 'blue'	V:getar
boud-enfla, -ifla, bauduf(l)a	N:BOD- 'round shape'	V:enflar
bourdufaillo, boustifaille	N:*BORDA 'dust'	V:FALLĔRE + -aille
borramesclar, bourro-mescla	N:borra 'stuffing' /BORDA 'fraud'	V:mesclar
bournifle	N:borra	V:niflar
boulouversa	N:Fr. boule 'ball'	V:versar
camalhègue	N:cama 'bed'	V:levar
camba-buou	N:camba 'leg'	V:beure
came-boutà	N:camba	V:botar
dza[m]bardzá	N:camba	V:bregar (brekan)
camba-levar, comboleba	N:camba	V:levar
cambaligar, cambalia-s	N:camba	V:ligar
càmo-malhà	N:camba	V:malhar 'to hit with a hammer'
came-pouda-s	N:camba	V:podar
cambo-tira	N:camba	V:tirar
camba-torse	N:camba	V:torse (tòrcer)
camba-vira, combobira	N:camba	V:virar
cam(bo)-biroula	N:camba	V:virolar
cambira	N:camp 'field'	V:virar
chan-, chamfrenar	N:Fr. chant 'edge'	V:OFr. fraindre
can(t)lheba	N:cant	V:levar
chan-leva	N:Fr. chant	V:levar
chan-tourna	N:Fr. chant	V:tornar
cant-bira	N:cant	V:virar
cap-haussa	N:cap 'head'	V:auçar
cap-bacha, -baxa, -baissa	N:cap	V:bachar (baissar)
cap-baria, -barreja	N:cap	V:barrejar

capbatre	N:cap	V:batre
cap-bilha(r)	N:cap	V:bilhar
cap-bordelar, -bourdilha	N:cap	V:bord-elar, -olhar
acabourrá, encabourrí	N:cap	V:borrar
cap-(es)dressa	N:cap	V:dressar
cap-enfla-s, -inla-s	N:cap	V:enflar
cap-eschaureya-se	N:cap	V:eschaurejar
capescodre	N:cap	V:escodre
cap-hen(d)e	N:cap	V:fendre
cap-herrà	N:cap	V:ferrar
cap-hourada	N:cap	V:foradar (forar)
enchifrenà	N:cap	V:frenar
capgirar	N:cap	V:girar
cap-hautà	N:cap	V:hautà (autar)
chap-lavar	N:cap	V:lavar
cap-leva, -lheba	N:cap	V:levar
cap-lissa	N:cap	V:lissar
cap-maçar, -massar	N:cap	V:maçar
cap-mounta	N:cap	V:montar
cap-plega	N:cap	V:plegar
cap-pouda	N:cap	V:podar
cap-pounta	N:cap	V:pontar
cap-préne-s	N:cap	V:prene
cap-quilha(-s)	N:cap	V:quilhar
capseca-s	N:cap	V:secar
captener, -teni	N:cap	V:tenir
cap-torse	N:cap	V:torse (tòrcer)
cap-traire	N:cap	V:traire
cap-vira, -bira-s, chavirâ	N:cap	V:virar
capvirolar, cambiroula	N:cap	V:virolar
car-iboussa	N:cara 'face'	V:OPr. bossar, Occ. boçar
caravirar, corobira	N:cara	V:virar
careime-entra, careimentrant	N:carèma 'Lent'	V:entrar
char-ufla	N:carn 'flesh'	V:enflar
carnmatar	N:carn	V:matar
char-menâ	N:carn	V:menar
char-mounta	N:carn	V:montar
car+(r)abrina, calabrinar	N:carn	V:rabinar
casoheyt	N:casa 'house'	V:ha (far)
causse-ha	N:causse 'stocking'	V:ha (far)

clauhicà	N:clau 'key'	V:ficar 'to fix (to)'
cl(i)afi	N:clau 'nail'	V:ficar
coalevar, coude-lheba	N:coa 'tail'	V:levar
coude-poudà	N:coa	V:podar
coechipouda	N:coech 'thigh'	V:podar
cou-beissâ	N:còl 'neck'	V:baissar
còlcrebar	N:còl	V:crevar
cot-crouchi	N:còl	V:crouchir (cruissir)
cot-junta	N:còl	V:juntar (jònher)
coullebà, cot-lheba	N:còl	V:levar
cot-liga	N:còl	V:ligar
cot-pana	N:còl	V:panar
cou-pouda, cot-pouda-s	N:còl	V:podar
colportar	N:còl	V:portar
còltòrcer, cot-torse	N:còl	V:tòrcer, torse
cou-trenca, cot-trenca	N:còl	V:trencar
cot-bira	N:còl	V:virar
color-, couloumuda	N:color 'color'	V:mudar
coùmpte-da	N:compte 'account'	V:dar
coùmpte-finà	N:compte	V:finar
còp-téner	N:còp 'blow'	V:tener
acourbacha	N:còr 'heart'	V:bachar (baissar)
cour-bagna	N:còr	V:bagnar
co-bouri	N:còr	V:bourir (bolhir)
còrcachar	N:còr	V:cachar
co-claba	N:còr	V:clavar
co(r)-creba, courcreva	N:còr	V:crevar
còr-dòldre, co-dole-s	N:còr	V:doldre
còrfalir, cor-fal(h)i	N:còr	V:falir
còrfendre, co-hene	N:còr	V:fendre
còrferir, co-heri	N:còr	V:ferir
còrfondre	N:còr	V:fondre
cormanar	N:còr	V:manar
co-mouri	N:còr	V:morir
co(u)r-quicha, escolquicha	N:còr	V:quichar
còr-seca(r)	N:còr	V:secar
co-transi, coo-transi	N:còr	V:transir
cor-vira(r)	N:còr	V:virar
corde-lheba	N:corda '(heart)string'	V:levar
corde-mia	N:corda	V:menar

corne-quilha	N:corna 'horn'	V:quilhar
corne-bacha	N:corna	V:bachar (baissar)
cors-passar	N:còrs 'body'	V:passar
cos-prene	N:còrs	V:prene
crouste-lheba, se crousto-leva	N:crosta 'crust'	V:levar
croustemaligà	N:crotz 'cross' + man	V:ligar
cu-agusa	N:cul 'butt'	V:agusar
cu-bacha, cuou-bacha	N:cul	V:bachar (baissar)
cu-bagna, cuou-bagna	N:cul	V:bagnar
cu-baysà	N:cul	V:baisar
cu-barrà	N:cul	V:barrar
cu-boussà	N:cul	V:boçar
cu-bouchà	N:cul	V:bouchar
cu-bouhà	N:cul	V:bufar
cu-dà	N:cul	V:dar
cu-hourrà	N:cul	V:forrar
cuolfregar, cu-rega	N:cul	V:(f)regar
cu-laurà	N:cul	V:laurar (laborar)
cu-labà	N:cul	V:lavar
cu-lhebà	N:cul	V:levar
cu-ligà	N:cul	V:ligar
cu-pédasà	N:cul	V:pedaçar
cu(ou)-pela	N:cul	V:pelar
cu-senti	N:cul	V:sentir
cu-toune	N:cul	V:toune (tondre)
débe-dà	N:débe 'obligation'	V:dar
dit-poustà	N:det 'finger'	V:postar
Dieu-trova	N:Dieu 'God'	V:trovar
escù-goaytà	N:escù 'night'	V:goaytà (gaitar)
estrem-bira	N:estrem 'end'	V:virar
fee-hasen	N:fe 'to lie'	V:ha (far)
fe-menti	N:fe	V:mentir
fi(e)lbasta(r)	N:fiel 'string'	V:bastar
fial-frexa	N:fiel	V:frechar (frachar)
fiau-tirâ	N:fiel	V:tirar
florcurar, flourcura	N:flor 'flower'	V:curar (colar)

eslou-passà	N:flor	V:passar
esgautirà	N:gauta 'cheek'	V:tirar
gay-hasén	N:gay 'joy'	V:ha (far)
goudeslat	N:gòda 'show-off'/gauta 'cheek'	V:enflar
gorjo-bada	N:gorja 'throat'	V:badar
gorjo-, gorja-fendre	N:gorja	V:fendre
gorje-, gorye-bira, gorjovira	N:gorja	V:virar
gorre-, esgorrobate	N:gorre 'wooden ball; bad weather'	V:batre
gouto-heri	N:gota 'gout'	V:ferir
goute-préne	N:gota	V:prene
grais-fondre	N:grais 'fat'	V:fondre
hum-dà, humda	N:hum 'smoke'	V:dar
lanaperdén	N:lana 'wool'	V:perdre
lengue-bourrà-s	N:lenga 'tongue'	V:borrar
lenga-manjar	N:lenga	V:manjar
lenga-, lengue-passa	N:lenga	V:passar
lenga-, lengue-plega	N:lenga	V:plegar
lenga-bira-s	N:lenga	V:virar
létroferit	N:letra 'letter(s)'	V:ferir
lòctenent	N:lòc 'position'	V:tenir
man-icouquear	N:man 'hand'	V:coquelar
man-estrena	N:man	V:estrenar
mangroçar	N:man	V:grusar, grudar
mahà	N:man	V:ha (far)
man-leva, malheba	N:man	V:levar
(a)ma-ligá, manou-lia	N:man	V:ligar
entermaligá	N:man	V:ligar
mâ-méte	N:man	V:met(r)e
manobrar	N:man	V:obrar
man-tasta	N:man	V:tastar
maa-tien, manteins	N:man	V:tenir
man-teni, -tener	N:man	V:tenir
man-straire	N:man	V:traire

ma(n)bour	N:MUNDEBORO 'protector'	
matrifusa, motrifusa	N:matiera 'matter'	V:fusar (FŬNDĔRE)
mentaure, mentábe(r)	N:ment 'mind'	V:aver
misso-canta	N:missa 'Mass'	V:cantar
moun(de)-, moumbira	N:monde 'world'	V:virar
m(o)ur-fica	N:morre 'nose'	V:ficar
mourre-finta, morre-	N:morre	V:fintar
mar-foundre, morfondre	N:morre	V:fondre
mourleca	N:morre	V:lecar
morlevar	N:morre	V:levar
mour-nifla, mournifla	N:morre	V:niflar
mour(re)-senti	N:morre	V:sentir
nas-lhebà	N:nas 'nose'	V:levar
nas-tapà	N:nas	V:tapar
palabentà	N:pala 'shovel'	V:bentar (ventar)
pala-, pau-fica(r)	N:pala 'stick'	V:ficar
palaversar	N:pala 'shovel'	V:versar
palavirar	N:pala	V:virar
pahourra	N:pan 'bread'	V:forar
panminjant	N:pan	V:manjar
panaussa	N:pan 'flap'	V:auçar
panlevar, pallevar, pelleba	N:pan	V:levar
panavelear	N:pan	V:velejar
part-mudà	N:part 'part'	V:mudar
part-birà	N:part	V:virar
empataligà-s	N:pata 'foot'	V:ligar
pato-, pata-vira	N:pata	V:virar
póu-herit	N:páur 'fear'	V:ferir
pè-batre	N:pè 'foot'	V:batre
pè-branla	N:pè	V:branlar
ped-descaussa (se)	N:pè	V:des+caussar
pé-hica	N:pè	V:ficar
pé-hourè, -hourra-s	N:pè	V:foure (forar)

pé-jugne, pe-junta	N:pè	V:jugne, junta (jònher)
pé-lhebà	N:pè	V:levar
pé-mudà	N:pè	V:mudar
pé-picà	N:pè	V:picar
pé-tirà-s	N:pè	V:tirar
pé-tournà	N:pè	V:tornar
pé-torse	N:pè	V:torse (tòrcer)
pé-tourteja	N:pè	V:tortejar
pé-trisca	N:pè	V:triscar (trescar)
pé-troulha	N:pè	V:trulhar
pè-bira	N:pè	V:virar
peyra-, peiro-bate	N:pèira 'stone'	V:batre
peira-hener (torra a)	N:pèira	V:fendre
peiro-, peira-ficar	N:pèira	V:ficar
pet-bouri, peu-bouli	N:pèl 'skin'	V:bourir (bolhir)
pet-esla-s	N:pèl	V:enflar
pellecar	N:pèl	V:lecar
pèu-muda	N:pèl	V:mudar
pèu-vira, petchibira	N:pèl	V:virar
pel-bufar	N:pel 'hair'	V:bufar
espelferi, pelferit	N:pel	V:ferir 'to strike'
pel-, peu-leba	N:pel	V:levar
péu-lia, se peulha	N:pel	V:liar
péulissa	N:pel	V:lissar
péu-muda	N:pel	V:mudar
péu-passa	N:pel	V:passar
(es)pel-, peu-tira	N:pel	V:tirar
péu-tireja	N:pel	V:tirejar
(es)perna-batre	N:pèrna 'leg'	V:batre
espernapicà	N:pèrna	V:picar
perne-bira	N:pèrna	V:virar
plu(mo)mudar	N:pluma 'feather'	V:mudar
potligà	N:pot 'lip'	V:ligar
pot-birà	N:pot	V:virar
salicar	N:sal 'salt'	V:lecar
salpicar, saupica	N:sal	V:picar
salposcar, -poudra	N:sal	V:poscar 'to powder'
saupoudra	N:sal	V:poudrar
sal-, sau-prene	N:sal	V:prene

sang-barreja	N:sang 'blood'	V:barrejar
sang-beure	N:sang	V:beure
sang-bouri	N:sang	V:bourir (bolhir)
sang(o)ul(h)a	N:sang/SANIĒS	V:colar
sang-crema-s	N:sang	V:cremar
sang-dévorant	N:sang	V:devorar
sangglaçar, songlaça	N:sang	V:glaçar
sang-pausa	N:sang	V:pausar
sangtradi	N:sang	V:trahir
sang-transi, -tradi	N:sang	V:transir
sang-birà	N:sang	V:virar
sère-birà-s	N:sèla 'saddle'	V:virar
sengirar	N:sens 'direction'	V:girar
sens-birà	N:sens	V:virar
sole-bàte	N:sol 'foot'	V:batre
soulheba	N:sol 'soil'	V:levar
sou-coélhe	N:solelh 'sun'	V:coelhe
sucopola, sucapelar	N:suco 'pate'	V:pelar
tal-vira	N:talh 'cutting edge'	V:virar
tala-, tolo-fissa	N:talon 'heel'	V:fissar
(en) terre-estant	N:tèrra 'land'	V:estar
terro-gardo	N:tèrra	V:gardar
terre-passà	N:tèrra	V:passar
terre-pèrdre	N:tèrra	V:perdre
terre pouyri	N:tèrra	V:pourir
tèrratenent, tèrretién	N:tèrra	V:tenir
trancho-daura	N:trancha 'slice, edge'	V:daurar
oélh-perí	N:uèlh 'eye'	V:perir
oélh-tirà	N:uèlh	V:tirar
èl-traire	N:uèlh	V:traire
oélh-birà	N:uèlh	V:virar
viandant, biandant	N:via 'way'	V:anar
bie-passà	N:via	V:passar

MODERN OCCITAN VERBAL ELEMENTS

cu-agusà	N:cul	V:agusar 'to sharpen'
vianant, biandant	N:via	V:anar 'to go'
panaussa	N:pan	V:auçar 'to raise'
cap-haussa	N:cap	V:auçar
mentaure, (re)mentábe(r)	N:ment	V:aver 'to have'
ale-bacha	N:ala	V:bachar (baissar) 'to lower'
cap-bacha, cap-baxa	N:cap	V:bachar (baissar)
coubeissâ	N:còl	V:baissar
acourbacha	N:còr	V:bachar (baissar)
corne-bacha	N:còrne	V:bachar (baissar)
cu(ou)bacha	N:cul	V:bachar (baissar)
gorjo-bada	N:gorja	V:badar 'to open'
cu-baysa	N:cul	V:baisar 'to kiss'
cour-bagna	N:còr	V:banhar 'to bathe'
cu(ou)bagna	N:cul	V:banhar
cu-barra	N:cul	V:barrar 'to squeeze, tighten'
cap-baria, -barreja	N:cap	V:barrejar 'to turn (a bar)'
sang-barreja	N:sang	V:barrejar
fi(e)l-basta(r)	N:fiel	V:bastar 'to baste'
ale-bate, eschalabatre	N:ale	V:batre 'to beat'
cap-batre	N:cap	V:batre
gorre-, esgorrobate	N:gorre	V:batre
pè-batre	N:pè	V:batre
peyra-bate	N:pèira	V:batre
(es)pernabatre	N:pèrna	V:batre
sole-bàte	N:sòl	V:batre
palabenta	N:pala	V:bentar (ventar) 'to winnow'
camba-buou	N:camba	V:beure 'to drink'
sang-beure	N:sang	V:beure
cap-bilha(r)	N:cap	V:bilhar 'to garrot', 'serrer un chargement avec le tortoir'

car-iboussa, cariboussa	N:cara	V:OPr. bossar, Occ. boçar 'to form a lump, close up'
cu-boussa	N:cul	V:boçar
capbourdelar, -bourdilha	N:cap	V:bord-elar, -olhar 'to roll'
acabourra, encabourri	N:cap	V:borrar 'to stuff'
lengue-bourrà-s	N:lenga	V:borrar
came-bouta	N:camba	V:botar 'to place'
cu-boucha	N:cul	V:bouchar 'to rub'
bente-bo(u)eita	N:bente	V:boueitar (voidar) 'to empty'
co-bouri	N:còr	V:bourir (bolhir) 'to boil'
pèt-bouri, pèu-bouli	N:pèl	V:bourir (bolhir)
sang-bouri	N:sang	V:bourir (bolhir)
pè-branla	N:pè	V:branlar (brandar) 'to shake'
dza(m)bardzá	N:camba	V:bregar (brekan) 'to break'
cu-bouhà	N:cul	V:bufar 'to pant, wheeze, brag'
pel-bufar	N:pel	V:bufar
còrcachar	N:còr	V:cachar 'to press, squeeze'
misso-canta	N:messa	V:cantar 'to sing'
co-clabà	N:còr	V:clavar 'to nail'
sou-coélhe	N:solelh	V:coelhe 'to gather'
sang(o)ulha	N:sang/SANIĒS	V:colar 'to flow'
manicouquear	N:man	V:coquelar 'to crumble, flake'
còlcrebar	N:còl	V:crebar 'to break'
còrcrebar, courcreva	N:còr	V:crebar
sang-cremà-s	N:sang	V:cremar 'to burn'
cot-crouchi	N:còl	V:crouchir (cruissir) 'to squeal'
flo(u)rcura(r)	N:flor	V:curar (colar) 'to remove flowers)'

coùmpte-da	N:compte	V:dar 'to give'
cu-da	N:cul	V:dar
débe-dà	N:débe	V:dar
hum-dà	N:hum	V:dar
trancho-daura	N:trancha	V:daurar 'to gild'
ped-descaussa (se)	N:pè	V:des + caussar 'to unshoe'
sang-dévorant	N:sang	V:devorar 'to devour'
cor-doldre, co-dole-s	N:còr	V:doldre (dòler) 'to hurt'
cap-(es)dressa	N:cap	V:dressar 'to raise'
boud-enfla, -ifla, bauduf(l)a	N:BOD-	V:enflar 'to swell'
cap-enfla-s, -inla-s	N:cap	V:enflar
char-ufla	N:carn	V:enflar
goudeslat	N:gòda/gauta	V:enflar
pèt-eslà-s	N:pèl	V:enflar
careime-entra, couarmenta	N:carèma	V:entrar 'to enter'
cap-eschaureya-se	N:cap	V:eschaurejar 'to blow about' (of the wind)
capescodre	N:cap	V:escodre 'to sweep'
(en) terre-estant	N:tèrra	V:estar 'to be'
man-estrena	N:man	V:estrenar 'to make a gift, tip'
cor-fali	N:còr	V:falir 'to fail'
bourdufaillo, boustifaille	N:*BORDA	V:FALLĔRE + -aille
cap-hen(d)e	N:cap	V:fendre, héne 'to split'
cor-fendre, co-héne	N:còr	V:fendre, héne
gorjo-, gorja-fendre	N:gorja	V:fendre
peira-hener (torra a)	N:pèira	V:fendre, héne
corferir, co-heri	N:còr	V:ferir 'to strike'
gouto-heri	N:gota	V:ferir
létroferit	N:letra	V:ferir
poú-herit	N:páur	V:ferir
pelférit, espelferi	N:pel	V:ferir

cap-herra	N:cap	V:ferrar 'to shoe (with iron)'
clauhicà	N:clau	V:ficar 'to fix (to)'
cl(i)afi	N:clau	V:ficar
m(o)urfica	N:morre	V:ficar
pala-, paufica(r)	N:pala	V:ficar
pè-hica	N:pè	V:ficar
peiro-, peira-ficar	N:pèira	V:ficar
coùmpte-finà	N:compte	V:finar 'to end'
mo(u)rre-finta	N:morre	V:fintar 'to pretend, hesitate'
tala-, tolo-fissa	N:talon	V:fissar 'to pierce'
cor-fo(u)ndre	N:còr	V:fondre 'to melt'
grais-fondre	N:graissa	V:fondre
marfoundre, morfondre	N:morre	V:fondre
cap-hourada	N:cap	V:foradar (forar) 'to pierce'
cu-hourra	N:cul	V:forrar 'to stuff'
pa-hourra, pahourra	N:pan	V:forrar
pe-houre, pe-hourra-s	N:pè	V:foure (forrar)
chan-, chamfrenar	N:Fr. chant	V:OFr. fraindre 'to break'
fialfrexa	N:fiel	V:frechar (frachar) 'to break'
cuolfregar, cu-rega	N:cul	V:(f)regar 'to rub'
enchifrenà	N:cap	V:OFr. frener 'to restrain, bridle'
embòufuma	N:BALSAMU(M)	V:fumar 'to smoke (out)'
matri-, motri-fusa	N:matiera	V:fusar (FŬNDĔRE) 'to mix'
terro-gardo	N:tèrra	V:gardar 'to guard'
blaugetar	N:blau	V:getar 'to throw'
capgirar	N:cap	V:girar 'to turn'
sengirar	N:sens	V:girar
sanglaçar, songloça	N:sang	V:glaçar 'to freeze'
escù-goaytà	N:escù	V:goaytà (gaitar) 'to watch'
mangroçar	N:man	V:grusar, grudar 'to crush'

casoheyt	N:casa	V:ha (far) 'to make, do'
causse-ha	N:causse	V:ha (far)
fee-hasen	N:fe	V:ha (far)
gay-hasén	N:gay	V:ha (far)
mahà	N:man	V:ha (far)
cap-hauta	N:cap	V:hautà (autar) 'to raise'
pe-jugne, pe-junta	N:pè	V:jugne, juntar (jónher) 'to join'
cot-junta	N:còl	V:juntar (jónher)
cu-laura	N:cul	V:laurar (laborar) 'to labor'
chap-lavar	N:cap	V:lavar 'to wash'
cu-laba	N:cul	V:lavar
barbo-leca, -lequa	N:barba	V:lecar 'to lick'
mourleca	N:morre	V:lecar
pellecar	N:pèl	V:lecar
salicar	N:sal	V:lecar
banc-leva, bonleva	N:banc	V:levar 'to raise'
camalhègue	N:cama	V:levar
camba-levar,	N:camba	V:levar
comboleba		
cant-lheba, canlheba	N:cant	V:levar
cap-leva, -lheba, -leua	N:cap	V:levar
chan-leva	N:Fr. chant	V:levar
coalevar, coudelhebà	N:coa	V:levar
coullebà, cot-lheba	N:còl	V:levar
corde-lheba	N:corda	V:levar
crouste-lheba	N:crosta	V:levar
cu-lheba	N:cul	V:levar
man-leva(r)	N:man	V:levar
morrelevar	N:morre	V:levar
nas-lhebà	N:nas	V:levar
panlevar, pallevar	N:pan	V:levar
pè-lhebà	N:pè	V:levar
pel-, peu-leba	N:pel	V:levar
soulheba	N:sòl	V:levar
cambaligar, came-liga-s	N:camba	V:ligar 'to bind'
cot-liga	N:còl	V:ligar
croustemaliga	N:crotz + man	V:ligar
cu-liga	N:cul	V:ligar
(a)ma-liga, entermaligà	N:man	V:ligar
empataligà-s	N:pata	V:ligar

pèu-lia, se peulha	N:pel	V:ligar
potligà	N:pot	V:ligar
cap-lissa	N:cap	V:lissar 'to smooth, polish'
péulissa	N:pel	V:lissar
camo-malha	N:camba	V:malhar 'to hit with a hammer'
cormanar	N:còr	V:manar 'to rot'
lengamanjar	N:lenga	V:manjar 'to eat'
panminjant	N:pan	V:manjar
cap-maçar, -massar	N:cap	V:maçar 'to hammer'
carn-matar	N:carn	V:matar 'to kill'
char-mena	N:carn	V:menar 'to lead'
corde-mia	N:corda	V:menar
fe-menti	N:fe	V:mentir 'to lie'
borramesclar, bourro-mescla	N:borra/BORDA	V:mesclar 'to mix'
mâ-méte	N:man	V:metre 'to put'
cap-mounta	N:cap	V:montar 'to raise'
char-mounta	N:carn	V:montar
co-mourî	N:còr	V:morir 'to die'
aiga-muda, aigo-muda	N:aiga	V:mudar 'to change'
color-, couloumuda	N:color	V:mudar
part-muda	N:part	V:mudar
pè-mudà	N:pè	V:mudar
pèu-muda	N:pèl	V:mudar
péu-muda	N:pel	V:mudar
plu(mo)muda	N:pluma	V:mudar
bournifle	N:borra	V:niflar 'to sniffle'
mournifla	N:morre	V:niflar
manobrar	N:man	V:obrar 'to work'
cot-pana	N:còl	V:panar 'to wipe'
cors-passar	N:còrs	V:passar 'to perish'; (intr.) 'to be spent'

eslou-passa	N:flor	V:passar
lenga-, lengue-passa	N:lenga	V:passar
péu-passà	N:pel	V:passar
terre-passà	N:tèrra	V:passar
bie-passà	N:via	V:passar
sang-pausa	N:sang	V:pausar 'to place, rest'
cu-pédasá	N:cul	V:pedaçar 'to cover with rags'
cu(uo)pela	N:cul	V:pelar 'to peel'
suco-pela, sucopola	N:suca	V:pelar
aigo-pendent	N:aiga	V:pendre 'to incline'
lanaperdén	N:lana	V:perdre 'to lose'
terre-pèrdre	N:tèrra	V:perdre
oélh-peri	N:uèlh	V:perir 'to perish'
aigo-pico	N:aiga	V:picar 'to strike'
pè-picà	N:pè	V:picar
espernapicà	N:pèrna	V:picar
salpicar, saupica	N:sal	V:picar
àga-pich	N:aiga	V:pichar (pissar) 'to piss'
cap-plega	N:cap	V:plegar 'to fold'
léngue-plegà	N:lenga	V:plegar
cap-pounta	N:cap	V:pontar 'to make a bridge'
colpourta, colportar	N:còl	V:portar 'to carry'
sal-poscar, -poudra	N:sal	V:poscar 'to powder'
came-pouda-s	N:camba	V:podar 'to break'
cap-pouda	N:cap	V:podar
coech-ipouda	N:cuèissa	V:podar
coude-pouda	N:coa	V:podar
cou-pouda, cot-pouda-s	N:col	V:podar
terre-pouyri	N:tèrra	V:porir 'to rot'
dit-poustà	N:det	V:postar 'to position'
saupoudra	N:sal	V:poudrar 'to powder'

aiga-prene (aygue-prene)	N:aiga	V:prene 'to take'
cap-prene-s	N:cap	V:prene
co(r)s-prene	N:còrs	V:prene
goute-préne	N:gota	V:prene
sal-prene, sauprene	N:sal	V:prene
co(u)r-quicha, escolquicha	N:còr	V:quichar 'to squeeze, bruise'
cap-quilha(-s)	N:cap	V:quilhar 'to stand on end'
corne-quilha	N:còrna	V:quilhar
car+(r)abrina, calabrinar	N:carn	V:rabinar 'to scorch'
capseca-s	N:cap	V:secar 'to dry'
còr-seca(r)	N:còr	V:secar
cu-senti	N:cul	V:sentir 'to feel'
mour(re)-senti	N:morre	V:sentir
blanc-signat	N:blanc	V:signar 'to sign'
nas-tapà	N:nas	V:tapar 'to seize'
man-tasta	N:man	V:tastar 'to feel'
bèn-tenènt	N:bèn	V:tener 'to hold'
cap-tener, -teni, -tiene	N:cap	V:tener
còp-téner	N:còp	V:tener
maa-tien, manteins	N:man	V:tener
man-tener, -teni, -tiene	N:man	V:tener
tèrratenent, tèrre-tién	N:tèrra	V:tener
cambo-tira	N:camba	V:tirar 'to pull (off), remove'
fiau-tira	N:fiel	V:tirar
esgautirà	N:gauta	V:tirar
pè-tira-s	N:pè	V:tirar
pel-, peu-tira	N:pel	V:tirar
oélh-tira	N:uèlh	V:tirar
peu-tireja	N:pel	V:tirejar 'to jerk'
cu-toune	N:cul	V:toune (tondre) 'to shear'
chantournâ	N:cam	V:tornar 'to turn'
pè-tourna	N:pè	V:tornar

came-torse	N:camba	V:torse (tòrcer) 'to twist'
cap-torse	N:cap	V:torse (tòrcer)
còltòrcer, cot-torse	N:còl	V:torse (tòrcer)
pè-torse	N:pè	V:torse (tòrcer)
pè-tourteja	N:pè	V:tortejar 'to wiggle'
sang-tradi	N:sang	V:trair 'to betray'
captraire	N:cap	V:traire 'to pull'
manstraire	N:man	V:traire
èl-traire	N:uèlh	V:traire
co-transi	N:còr	V:transir 'to pierce'
sang-transi, sang-tradi	N:sang	V:transir
aiga-trebolar	N:aiga	V:trebolar 'to trouble'
cou-trenca, cot-trenca	N:col	V:trencar 'to slice, break'
pè-triscà	N:pè	V:triscar (trescar) 'to plait'
Dieu-trova	N:Dieu	V:trovar 'to find'
pè-troulha	N:pè	V:trulhar 'to press'
panavelear	N:pan	V:velejar 'to put to sail'
boulouversa	N:Fr. boule	V:versar 'to spread, pour'
palaversar, -bessar	N:pala	V:versar
camba-vira, came-bira-s	N:camba	V:virar 'to turn'
cambira	N:camp	V:virar
cant-bira	N:cant	V:virar
cap-vira, -bira-s, chavirâ	N:cap	V:virar
caravirar, corobira	N:cara	V:virar
cot-bira	N:còl	V:virar
còrvirar	N:còr	V:virar
estrem-birá	N:estrèm	V:virar
gorje-bira, gorye-vira	N:gorja	V:virar
lenga-bira-s	N:lenga	V:virar
moun(de)-, moum-bira	N:mond	V:virar
palavira(r)	N:pala	V:virar
part-bira	N:part	V:virar
pato-, pata-vira	N:pata	V:virar
pè-bira	N:pè	V:virar
pèu-vira, pel-, pet-bira	N:pèl	V:virar
perne-bira	N:pèrna	V:virar

pot-bira	N:pot	V:virar
sang-birà	N:sang	V:virar
sère-birà-s	N:sèla	V:virar
sens-birà	N:sens	V:virar
tal-vira	N:talh	V:virar
oelh-bira	N:uèlh	V:virar
cam(bo)-biroula	N:camba	V:virolar 'to turn'
capvirolar,cambiroula	N:cap	V:virolar

Appendix C

Catalan Corpus

(late 19th c.) *aiguabarrejar-se* 'to merge' (of two or more rivers); (late 19th–early 20th c.) *aiguabarreig* 'fork' (made by two streams); BM §352 (N Dir Obj + V), Torrellas, *DECC* "aigua" (perhaps denominal?); N:aigua 'water' + V:barrejar 'to mix'

aiguabatre 'to run, beat down' (of water), 'to rain', 'ruixar amb aigua batent'; *aigua-batent* 'surface or slope exposed to rain'; *-batut* 'rain-soaked field'; *DECC* "aigua," AM, *Tresor*, PF; N:aigua 'water' + V:batre 'to beat (down)'

aiguadeix 'alluvium, alluvial deposit'; *Dicc* 1982; N:aigua 'water' + V:deixar 'to leave'

aigualleix, m.pl. *aigualeixos* 'alluvium, alluvial deposit'; AM, *Dicc* 1982; N:aigua 'water' + V:lleixar 'to leave'

aiguaneix 'source of a spring' (cf. Occ. *aiganaissent* idem); *Dicc* 1982; N:aigua 'water' + V:néixer 'to be born'

OCat. (15th c.) *aigua-toldre* (J. Esteve) 'to defecate'; AM, *DECC* "aigua"; N:aigua 'water' + V:toldre 'to empty'

(14th c.) *aigua-vers, -vés*, (16th c.) *-vessant*, Mod. (Andorra) *aiguavertent* 'slope' (of mountain, terrain, or roof); AM (AQUAE VERSU 'girada de la aygua'), Torrellas, *DECC* "aigua"; N:aigua 'water' + V:VERSUS (vessar 'to pour')

(19th c.) *aire-, ayre-ferir-se* 'to suffer an attack of apoplexy, be incapacitated'; *aireferit* 'incapacitated, lamed, suffering from apoplexy'; *DECC* I 103 (cf. *llampferit* 'struck by lightning', stemming from primitive Pyrenean phraseology, and Basque *aire-gaizto* ["mal aire"] 'thunderbolt, lightning'); N:aire 'air' + V:ferir 'to strike'

(18th c.) *aygua-regant* 'irrigable (land)'; AM; N:aigua 'water' + V:regar 'to irrigate'

barba-punta, -punyent 'starting to have a beard', Cast. 'barbiponiente', 'barbipungente'; *Tresor*, Torrellas, *DECC* "barba"; N:barba 'beard' + V:pondre × PŬNCTUM 'to put (on)'

botinflar-se 'to swell'; Valencia *bot-inflat*, Mallorca *-iflat* 'swollen', 'inflat com un bot'; *botinflament* 'swelling'; AM, *DECC* II 171b (cf. OPr. *botenflat*), Albertí; N:bot 'gourd' + V:inflar 'to swell with air'

(14th c.) *camalliga*, *camalligues* 'garter', 'lligacama, lligacames' (q.v.); *DECC* "cama"; N:cama 'leg' + V:lligar 'to bind'

(19th c.) *camatrencar* 'to break a[n animal's] leg[s]' (Cast. *perniquebrar, -at*); AM, PF, Torrellas, *DECC* "cama" ("frequently refl."), Ruaix; N:cama 'leg' + V:trencar 'to break'

OCat. (15th c.) *camptinent* 'corporal'; AM, *DECC* II 462b; N:camp 'field' + V:tenir 'to hold'

capalçar 'to raise the head, raise one end of an object', (refl.) 'to move at one end'; (regional) 'to plough sideways'; (17th c.) *cap(i)alçat* (archit.) 'top of a door frame'; *capalça, capalçada* 'act of raising the head'; *descabalsar* 'to change s.o.'s mind'; AM, PF, *Tresor*, BM §352 (N Dir Obj + V), Torrellas, Vallès, *DECC* "cap"; N:cap 'head, end' + V:alçar 'to raise'

capbaixar-se 'to cower, abase oneself; lower one end of an object'; *-baix* 'crestfallen', Cast. *cabizbajo*; *capbaixenc* 'rustic'; AM, PF, *Tresor*, Torrellas, *DECC* "cap"; N:cap 'head, end' + V:baixar 'to lower'

capbatre (n.g.); cf. Occ. *cap-batre* 'to shell (wheat, corn) with a stick, quarrel(?)'; *DECC* "cap"; N:cap 'head, end' + V:batre 'to beat'

capfermar (naut.) 'to attach a cord (to a fixed point inside or outside a boat)'; *Tresor*, Torrellas, Vallès; N:cap 'head, end' + V:fermar 'to fasten'

OCat. (15th c.) *capfic* 'worried, with hanging head'; (17th c.) *capficar* (tr.) 'to vex; cause s.o. to fall headlong to the ground'; (intr.) 'to sink or drive the end of one object inside another'; (hort.) 'to layer, fix a vine shoot in the ground so as to create a new vinestock'; (refl.) 'to dive; worry too much'; *cap-ficat, -ficadet* 'preoccupied, worried'; (hort.) *cap-ficat, -ficada* 'layered vine'; *capficó* (hort.) 'layering'; *capficall* 'downward movement of the head'; *capficament* 'worry'; *capficador* 'worrying'; *capficadament* 'in a worried way'; Aladern, AM, PF, *Tresor*, BM §352 (N Dir Obj + V), Torrellas, Vallès, *DECC* "cap"; N:cap 'head, end' + V:ficar 'to fix (to)'

capfilar 'to ponder over'; AM ("filar amb el cap"); N:cap 'head, end' + V:filar 'to conjecture, reveal'

(15th c.) *capgirar* (*-girant*, J. Roig), Moz./Mallorca *capyirare, fer capirú* 'to turn upside down; bother, upset; spin a bowling ball'; (refl.) 'to change one's mind'; (19th c.) *capgirada, cap-girament, -giradura* 'act of upsetting; confusion, dismay, tergiversation'; *capgiro* 'act of turning over' (esp. a vehicle); *capgira, capgireta* 'tumble, somersault'; *capgires* m. 'one who habitually inverses words'; *capgiró* m., *capgirolla* f. 'tumble, somersault'; *capgirador* 'that tumbles'; *capgirell* 'tumble, somersault'; (19th c.) *capgirellar, fer capgirells* 'to tumble'; *anar/caure a capgirells* idem; Aladern, AM, *Tresor*, BM §352 (N Dir Obj + V), *DCE[LC]* "cap," Torrellas, *DECC* "cap" + "girar"; N:cap 'head, end' + V:girar 'to turn'

capguardar-se 'to foresee or prevent a mishap; realize, notice; set one's mind on something'; AM, *Tresor*, Vallès, *DECC* "guardar"; N:cap 'head, end' + V:guardar 'to guard, watch'

capitombar, captombar 'to fall headlong, tumble; make s.o. fall'; *capitomb, capitomba, capitonda* 'tumble, somersault'; AM, Albertí, *DECC* "cap"; N:cap 'head, end' + V:tombar 'to knock down, fall'

OCat. (14th c.) *capl(l)euta* 'bail, [object left as] pledge; legal evidence', (15th c.) 'bond, bail, guarantee'; *caplleutador* 'guarantor'; Aladern, *DCE[LC]* "capleuta," *DECC* "cap" + "lleu"; N:cap 'head, end' + V:LEVĬTA 'raised'

(13th–14th c.) *capllevar* 'to post bond or bail for s.o.'; (Mod.) 'to get someone out of a jam; pull up plants'; (intr.) 'to raise one's head; be, live; disappear secretly'; (dial.) *fer catlleva* 'to seesaw, raise the end'; (15th c.) *capllevador* 'one who posts bond', (Mod.) 'wide pillow'; AM, *Tresor*, *DECC* "cap" + "lleu" ("es podria explicar el mot a base simplement del valor prefixal que té *cap-* en *captenir-se, -guardar*, pero no és segur que no hi hagi *cap* amb un sentit més substantiu (*caplletra*) o intermedi (*capbatre, -girar*); entre altres coses es pot suggerir que hi hagi la idea d'alçar el cap fent act de presència, acord o solidaritat"); N:cap 'head, end' + V:llevar 'to raise'

caplliga 'oarlock'; AM ('el bedoll que serveix per lligar el rem a les remenes'), *DECC* "cap"; N:cap 'head, end' + V:lligar 'to bind'

cappelar 'to lose one's hair', *-pela(t)* 'bald (head)'; AM, *DECC* "cap"; N:cap 'head, end' + V:pelar 'to peel'

(13th c.) *captenir(-se)* 'to behave; work'; *capteniment, captener* 'behavior, conduct, comportment'; (arch.) *captenença, captinença* idem; (13th c.) *capteny* '(outward) appearance'; *captenidor* 'custodian'; Aladern (*cap-* "idea de contenir" + *tenirse*), AM, Torrellas, Vallès, *DECC* "cap"; N:cap 'head, end' + V:tenir 'to hold'

capterrar 'to cover a haystack's thatch with dirt, against the wind'; 'place stones atop a dry-wall for reinforcement'; *capterrera* 'bundles of rushes mixed with earth, set against exterior walls to protect from damp, rain, etc.', 'thatch', 'wall protected with thatch'; *capterreres* 'thatch'; *capterrarar* 'to thatch'; *Tresor*, Torrellas; N:cap 'head, end' + V:terrar 'to cover with earth'

captrencar 'to strike, hit (in the head)'; (refl.) 'turn sour' (of wine); *Tresor*, AM ('ferir de mort'), PF, Torrellas, *DECC* "cap"; N:cap 'head, end' + V:trencar 'to break'

capvirar 'to turn around' (of peasants, while plowing; or fishermen); *cap-virada, -virament* 'turning around'; Aladern; N:cap 'head' + V:virar 'to turn'

capxafar 'to crack s.o's head', der. (Catalonia) *capxifollar* 'to destroy' (*capxafar* ×
  follar); AM; N:cap 'head, end' + V:xafar 'to wrinkle, rumple, flatten'

OCat. (14th c.) *carafaxada*, (15th c.) *cara-xafat* 'split'; (19th c.) *carafeixar*, -*fexat* 'to
  split, slice something partially; breach'; Aguiló, AM, *Tresor*; N:cara 'face' +
  V:feixar 'to wrap'

(1898) *caragirar-se* 'to change one's mind'; (16th c.) *caragirat* 'turn-coat, traitor' (in
  18th–19th c. anent Catalans who went over to the French during the
  Revolution and Napoleonic Wars); (16th c.) *caragirats* m.pl. (bot.) 'black-eyed
  beans'; AM, PF, Torrellas, *DECC* "cara," Albertí; N:cara 'face' + V:girar 'to
  turn'

(16th c.) *caravirat* 'turn-coat'; *DECC* "cara"; N:cara 'face' + V:virar 'to turn'

(19th c.) *carnaval* 'the three days before Lent' (from It. *carnevale*); *carnavalada*
  'Carnival amusement'; *carnavalenc* 'pertaining to carnaval'; *carnavalaç* 'un gran
  carnaval'; Aladern, Albertí; N:It. carne 'flesh' + V:It. levare 'to remove'

(12th c.) *carnes-*, *carnistoltes* f.pl. 'the last (three) day(s) to eat meat before Lent';
  (Mod.) 'three days preceding Ash Wednesday; grotesque Carnival figure'; m.
  'bizarre costume; scatterbrain'; *carnestoltada* 'Carnival escapade, orgy';
  carnestoltesc 'relating to Carnival'; (16th c.) *fer carnestoltes* 'to abstain from
  meat'; *REW* §1706 "carō," PF, *Tresor*, *DECC* "carn," Torrellas, Albertí; N:carn
  'flesh' + V:*TOLLĬTAS 'removed'

(17th c.) *casatinent* 'householder'; Aladern, AM, *DECC* "casa"; N:casa 'house' +
  V:tenir 'to hold'

clau-passar 'to pierce with nails; sew the edges of a shoe to hide stitches'; -*passat*
  'exhausted, weakened by disease'; PF, AM, *DECC* "clau"; N:clau 'nail' +
  V:passar 'to pass, undergo'

(arch.) *claupresó* 'imprisonment'; *DECC* II 918a (citing an archaic popular song "La
  Presó de Lleida"); deverbal from *claupendre 'to capture'; N:clau 'nail' +
  V:prendre 'to seize'

OCat. *clavificat* 'crucified', (13th c.) *clauficar* 'to crucify'; (Mod.) -*ficat* 'pierced, fixed
  with nails'; *Tresor*, *DECC* II 745a (*crozficar* [q.v.], crou-, clou-, clau-ficar listed
  as phonetic and morphological vars. of CRŬCI-FĪGĔRE, -*FICARE and CLĀVO
  FĪGĔRE, -*FICARE); N:clau/creu 'nail' + V:ficar 'to fix (to)'

collgirar 'to twist the neck, turn around'; *collgirada* 'sprain, dislocation of the neck';
  Tresor, AM; N:coll 'neck' + V:girar 'to turn'

collportar 'to carry on one's shoulders' (from Fr. *colporter*); AM, Torrellas, Vallès,
  DECC "coll"; N:coll 'neck' + V:portar 'to carry'

colltombar 'to fall from the neck', 'tombar del coll'; AM; N:coll 'neck' + V:tombar
  'to fall'

(19th c.) *coll-torçar, -tòrcer* 'to wither, spoil, bend under its own weight' (of wheat); 'twist the neck, faint, die'; *-tort* 'wry-necked; hypocrite', (ornith.) 'wryneck'; *colltorçament* 'twisted neck'; *colltorçable* 'that can *colltòrcer*'; Aladern, *DECC* "coll"; N:coll 'neck' + V:tòrcer, torçar 'to twist'

colltrencar(-se) 'to dislocate, break the back of the neck by a blow', (Pyrenees) 'to die a violent death'; *colltrencat* 'sour wine'; *Tresor*, AM, Torrellas, *DECC* "coll"; N:coll 'neck' + V:trencar 'to break'

collvinclar-se 'to bend over onto the stem' (of a flower), 'colltorçar-se'; PF, Torrellas, Vallès; N:coll 'neck' + V:vinclar 'to sway, bend'

copbatre 'to beat violently'; AM, *DECC* "cop"; N:cop 'blow' + V:batre 'to beat'

corbategar 'to beat, palpitate' (of the heart); AM; N:cor 'heart' + V:bategar 'to beat'

corcaure 'to lose one's nerve', 'caure de cor'; AM; N:cor 'heart' + V:caure 'to fall'

corcorcar-se 'to be consumed with worry or anguish'; AM, *DECC* "cor"; N:cor 'heart' + V:corcar-se 'to pine', 'sofrir l'acció del corc ('woodborer') = pensament dolorós'

fer corcruix 'to be compassionate', 'fer compassió'; AM; N:cor 'heart' + V:cruixir 'to crackle, creak'

cordoldre's 'to suffer in one's heart, feel sorrow or pity'; *cordol* 'sorrow, affliction, pity'; *cor-dolença, -dolencia* 'heartache'; Aladern; N:cor 'heart' + V:doldre 'to hurt'

coresforçar-se 'to make an effort'; *coresforç* m. '(moral) effort'; Ruaix, *DECC* "cor"; N:cor 'heart' + V:esforçar 'to make an effort'

corferir 'to afflict, cause pain; knock down'; *-ferit* 'afflicted'; *corferidor* 'afflictive', 'that causes pain'; PF, AM ("és vocable literari"), Torrellas, Albertí, *DECC* "cor"; N:cor 'heart' + V:ferir 'to strike'

(19th–20th c.) *corfondre* 'to have the same thoughts and feelings as another person; become confused, feel faint; covet; melt, even in the innermost parts'; *corfòs* 'confused, faint'; AM, *Tresor*, Torrellas, *DECC* "cor"; N:cor 'heart' + V:fondre 'to melt'

(18th c.) *corgelar(-se)* 'to freeze through or harden from the cold' (of a piece of fruit); *corgelador* 'freezing'; PF 'congelar-se', *Tresor*, *DECC* "cor"; N:cor 'heart' + V:gelar 'to freeze'

corglaçar-se 'to be frightened, frighten'; AM, PF, Vallès; N:cor 'heart' + V:glaçar 'to freeze'

(late 19th c.) *corlligar-se* 'to bind one's heart, fail in one's nerve', 'nuar el cor'; *corlligament* 'loss of one's nerve'; AM, *Tresor*, *DECC* "cor" + "lligar"; N:cor 'heart' + V:lligar 'to bind'

cornuar-se 'to have a fainting spell, feel one's heart stop', 'nuar-se-li a algú el cor';
    cornuament 'fainting spell'; PF, AM, Albertí, *DECC* "cor"; N:cor 'heart' +
    V:nuar 'to knot, tie'

(19th c.) *corprendre* 'to stir one's heart, be moved to pity'; (20th c.) *corprès* '(emotion-
    ally) moved'; *corprenedor* 'surprising'; AM ("not frequent in the vernacular"),
    DECC II "cor" (probably from older *comprès* (Llull), by analogical attraction
    into a series, e.g., *corferit, -glaçat, -lligat, -migrat, -nuat*, and especially *-secat*);
    N:cor 'heart' + V:prendre 'to seize'

(mid-19th c.) *corsecar* 'to dry out from the cold' (of fruit); refl. 'to lose one's vigor,
    worry, fade away'; *cor-secament, -secadura* 'action of drying out'; *corsecador,
    corsecant* 'that causes to dry out'; *corsec* m. 'dried area on a treetrunk';
    Aladern, AM, PF, *Tresor*, Albertí, *DECC* "cor"; N:cor 'heart' + V:secar 'to dry
    (out)'

cortrencar 'to suffer, cause pain'; *cortrencat* 'much pained'; AM; N:cor 'heart' +
    V:trencar 'to break'

(14th–15th c.) *creuclavat* 'nailed to the cross'; *DECC* "creu"; N:creu 'nail' + V:clavar
    'to nail'

(15th c.) *creuposar* 'to crucify'; *DECC* "creu"; N:creu 'nail' + V:posar 'to place'

OCat. *crozficar* 'to crucify'; *DECC* II 1050a; N:creu 'cross' + V:ficar 'to fix (to)'

cuixapenjant 'becoming poor'; *DECC* "cuixa"; N:cuixa 'thigh' + V:penjar 'to hang'

cuixatrencar 'to break one's leg', Cast. *perniquebrar, -at*; PF, AM; N:cuixa 'thigh' +
    V:trencar 'to break'

culbufar 'to give bad advice'; AM, *DECC* II 1100a; N:cul 'butt' + V:bufar 'to blow,
    breathe'

culmenejar 'to busy oneself in others' business, snoop around'; AM; N:cul 'butt' +
    V:menejar (Sp. *menear* 'to wiggle')

culremena m., f. 'one whose hips sway while walking' (= *remenar el cul* 'to wiggle
    one's hips', refl. 'to toss and turn'); AM; N:cul 'butt' + V:remenar 'to shake'

OCat. *desmantenir* 'to remove protection from s.o.'; *GMLCat* VII 889 (found only in
    vernacular translations of *Usatges*); N:man 'hand' + V:tenir 'to hold'

Roussillon *espeltirar* 'to pull by the hair' (cf. Occ. *espeltirar*); *DECC* "pèl"; N:pèl 'hair'
    + V:tirar 'to pull'

fe(e)-faent, -facient 'authentic'; AM, BM §352 (N Dir Obj + V); N:fe 'faith' + V:fer
    'to make, do'

feina-fuig 'lazy'; AM; N:feina 'work' + V:fuir 'to flee'

(arch.) *fementit* 'traitor'; *DCE[LC]* II 507a; N:fe 'faith' + V:mentir 'to lie'

filbastar 'to baste'; *filbast, filbasta* 'basting'; AM, *DECC* III 1027; N:fil 'string' +
    V:bastar 'to baste'

firandant 'merchant at fairs' (Cast. *feriante*); AM, *Tresor*, Torrellas, *DECC* "fira"; N:fira 'fair' + V:anar 'to go'

greixfondre 'to lose weight, be much worried', 'fer-se mala sang'; AM, *DECC* "gras"; N:greix 'fat' + V:fondre 'to melt'

llampferit 'struck by lightning'; *DECC* "aire"; N:llamp 'ray' + V:ferir 'to strike'

(16th c.) *lletraferit* 'fond of letters, well-lettered'; *Tresor*, AM, Vallès, *DECC* "lletra" ("ja devia estar en ús en el s. 16, no sols en terres occ."); N:lletra 'letter' + V:ferir 'to strike'

lloctinent 'lieutenant', 'tinentlloc' (q.v.); (15th–18th c.) 'royal deputy/substitute in Aragon–Catalonia', (Mod. dial.) *llautinent* 'bailiff'; *lloctinència*, (arch.) *lloctinentatge* 'profession of lieutenant, lieutenancy'; Malkiel 1945:159, BM §352 (N Dir Obj + V), *Dicc* 1982, Albertí, *DECC* "lloc"; N:lloc 'position' + V:tenir 'to hold'

mampara 'inner door; folding screen' (cf. Cast. *mampara*); *mamparo* 'bulkhead' (cf. Cast. *mamparo*); Aguiló, Albertí, *DECC* "parar"; N:man(o) 'hand' + V:Cast. amparar 'to protect'

(14th c.) *mampendre*, (Mod.) *mamprendre* 'to begin'; Valencia *mampresa* f. 'undertaking'; *Tresor*, AM, *DECC* "prendre"; N:man 'hand' + V:(em)prendre 'to undertake'

mamposteria 'dry-wall, stonework' (from Castilian); *mam-, mompost* 'alluvium, alluvial deposit'; Aguiló, AM, *Tresor*, *DECC* "mà" (*mompost* suggesting MONTEM POSĬTUM); N:Cast. mampuesto 'rubble' (< MANŪ POSĬTU[M])

(13th c.) *manlleuta* 'bail; loan, act of borrowing'; OCat. *manuleutes* 'bail'; (13th–14th c.) *manlleutar* 'to guarantee, post bail'; (17th c.) *amanlleutar* 'vadari aliquem'; *REW* §5335 "manum levāre," *Tresor*, AM, Vallès, *Dicc* 1982, *DECC* "mà"; N:man 'hand' + V:LEVĬTA 'removed'

(12th c., today arch.) *manllevar* 'to post bail, put in hock'; (Mod.) 'to borrow'; (15th c.) *-llevat* 'false, out of place'; *manlleu* m. 'borrowing, loan'; (13th c.) *manllevador* 'borrower'; *manllevadís* 'loanable; that can be lifted and placed'; *REW* §5335 "manum levāre," *Tresor*, AM, *DCE[LC]* I 559a, Albertí, *DECC* "mà" (not MANUM LEVĀRE 'to raise the hand [so as to swear an oath]', but Ā MANŪ LEVĀRE 'to remove from s.o.'s power'); N:man 'hand' + V:llevar 'to raise'

(13th c.) *man(i)-, mar-messor* 'executor testimentari per tal com li solien encarregar la manumissió dels serfs fidels per després de la mort del possessor', (17th c.) *manimasor*; (cult.) *manumitir* 'to emancipate'; (cult.) *manumissor* 'executor'; *comarmessor*; (cult.) *manumissió* 'manumission'; (1340) *marmessoria* 'career of manumissor'; *DCE[LC]* "mano," *DECC* "mà," *Dicc* 1982; N:MANŪMISSOR 'executor' ('emancipator') (< MANŪMITTĔRE)

manobra (14th c.) 'labor force'; (16th c.) 'feudal obligation to contribute to certain works of public interest'; (Mod.) 'construction materials'; *manobre, manobrer* 'laborer, day worker'; *maniobrar* (from French, through Castilian) 'to work with the hands, manipulate, maneuver'; *maniobra* 'handling, maneuver'; *maniobrable* 'maneuverable'; (mil.) *maniobrer* '(skilled in) maneuvering'; *fer maniobres* 'to maneuver'; (15th c.) *manobrejar, fer de manobre* 'to toil as a day worker'; *Tresor*, AM, Albertí, *DECC* "mà"; N:man(o) 'hand' + V:obrar 'to work'

(13th c.) *mantenir* 'to protect, support', (Mod.) 'to maintain'; (13th–14th c.) *man-tenidor, -tenedor* 'guardian', (Mod.) 'champion, president of a contest'; OCat. *mantinença* 'support'; *manteniment* 'maintenance, sustenance'; (dial.) *mantega* 'handle of the scourge'; *mantenents* (heraldry) 'two lions or other animals supporting an object'; (cult.) (arch.) *manutenència* 'protection'; (cult.) *manutenció* 'maintenance, board, shelter'; adv. *(de) mantinent* 'immediately, constantly'; *a manteniente* 'incessantly, strongly; reciprocally'; *Tresor*, Aladern, AM, Torrellas, Albertí, *DECC* "mà" (*mantenedor* due to copyist's error); N:man 'hand' + V:tenir 'to hold'

(17th c.) West Cat. *mantornar* 'to plough again'; (dial.) 'to patch clothing'; *man-tornada* 'second plowing'; *Tresor*, AM, Torrellas, Vallès, Albertí, *DECC* "mà"; N:man 'hand' + V:tornar 'to turn'

(13th c.) *missacantant* 'newly ordained priest', Cast. *misacantano*; AM, BM §352 (N Dir Obj + V), *DECC* "metre"; N:missa 'Mass' + V:cantar 'to sing'

(arch.) *missadient* 'newly ordained priest'; AM, *DECC* "metre"; N:missa 'Mass' + V:dir 'to say'

mor-, mar-fondre-se, morfondir-se, marfús 'to waste away, lose one's strength; die of consumption; be constipated'; *marfondiment* 'chill; deception'; *marfús* 'constipated'; *Tresor*, Aladern, AM, Torrellas, *DECC* "marfondre" (from Med. Gallo-Romance); N:murr- 'snout' + V:fondre 'to melt'

(14th c.) *palafanga* 'three-pronged spade'; *palafangar* 'to dig with a *palafanga*'; *palafanguer* 'worker using a *palafanga*'; AM, *DECC* "pala" (offers three possible etymologies: (i) nominal compound *pala* + *fanga*, L. VANGA; (ii) *palus-fabrica*; (iii) *palus* + *vangā(re)* 'to dig'); N:pala 'shovel' + V:fangar 'to dig'

palafit (archeol.) 'pile-dwelling', (archit.) 'pile (of wood, metal, or concrete)', from It. *palafitta* through Fr. (19th c.) *palafitte*; (15th c.) *palafic* 'driving in, placing a nail'; *DECC* "pal"; N:pal(o) 'stick' + V:It. figgere/Cat. ficar 'to fix (to)'

palplantar 'to stand tall and immobile'; *Tresor*, AM, PF, Torrellas; N:pal 'stick' + V:plantar 'to stand on end' *paltrigar, peltrigar* 'to tread'; *paltriga* 'footstep'; *paltrigada, paltrigament* 'trampling'; *paltrigadissa* 'effect of trampling'; *paltrigador* 'one who tramples'; AM, *DECC* "peu" (*peutridar* [q.v.] × *calcigar*, ca. 15th c.); N:peu 'foot' + V:trigar 'to delay, be slow'/TRĪTĀRĪ 'to rub, grind' × calcigar 'to trample'

pellforadar 'to pierce the skin', 'foradar la pell'; AM; N:pell 'skin' + V:foradar 'to pierce'

pellobrir-se 'to split open' (of fruit), Cast. 'abrirse una fruta'; *Tresor*, AM, Torrellas, Vallès; N:pell 'skin' + V:obrir 'to open'

pellpartir-se 'to split open' (of fruit), 'pellobrir-se'; AM, Torrellas, Vallès; N:pell 'skin' + V:partir 'to divide'

pelltrencar-se 'to excoriate'; AM, BM §352 (N Dir Obj + V), Torrellas, Vallès; N:pell 'skin' + V:trencar 'to break'

pèl-mudar 'to molt, change the hair or feathers'; *pelmuda* f. 'molting'; *fer la pelmuda* 'to molt'; *Tresor*, AM, *DECC* "pèl"; N:pèl 'hair' + V:mudar 'to change'

pernabatre 'to agitate the legs violently, bother'; *-batent* '(one) who hurries; death jerks'; *Tresor*, AM, Torrellas; N:perna 'leg' + V:batre 'to beat'

(15th c.) *peucalcigar* 'to trample under foot, press'; AM, Ruaix; N:peu 'foot' + V:calcigar 'to stamp (with the feet)'

peulligar 'to bind the feet'; *DECC* "peu"; N:peu 'foot' + V:lligar 'to bind'

(dial.) *peutridar* 'to tread, walk on', 'peutrigar' (q.v.), 'paltrigar, peltrigar' (q.v.); AM, *DECC* "peu"; N:peu 'foot' + V:TRĪTĀRĪ 'to rub, grind' (= 'to reduce to powder')

peutrigar 'to tread, walk on'; AM (*paltrigar* × *peu*, or simple phonetic var. of *paltrigar*); N:peu 'foot' + V:trigar 'to delay, be slow'/TRĪTĀRĪ 'to rub, grind' × calcigar 'to trample'

salpassar (eccles.) 'sprinkler for holy (= salted) water', (bot.) 'hyssop'; vars. *sal-passer, -pacer, -pisser*; *salpassa* f., *salpàs* m. 'Easter blessing of homes with the *salpassar*'; *sal-passada, -passerada* 'movement of the sprinkler'; *salpasset* m. [n.g.]; AM, *DCE[LC]* "sal," Albertí; N:sal 'salt' + V:passar 'to pass' × SPARSUS 'sprinkled'

(14th c.) *salpicar* 'to preserve with salt', (Mod. dial.) *-piscar* 'to sprinkle with salt, spatter'; (arch.) *salpicó* 'sprinkling; chopped mixture'; *salpiquet* 'chopped mixture, minced garlic, vegetable stew'; *salpicament* 'sprinkling'; *DCE[LC]*, *BDE[LC]* (Corominas arguing for underlying Gothic *salbôn* 'to anoint', through OCat. *salbuscar* 'to refresh with splashes of water'), Albertí; N:sal 'salt' + V:picar 'to strike'

(14th c.) *salprès, salp(r)endre*, 'to preserve with salt, conserve'; AM (denom. *salprémer* idem); N:sal 'salt' + V:p(r)endre 'to seize'

sangcremar-se 'to become impatient', 'cremar la sang, corsecar-se'; AM, PF, BM §352 (N Dir Obj + V); N:sang 'blood' + V:cremar 'to burn'

OCat. *sangfondre* 'to flush, overeat'; (veterinary medicine) *sangfús* (Llull) 'flushed, having overeaten'; (arch.) *sangfoniment* m., *sangfonió* f. 'excessive fullness of belly', 'act of flushing'; Corominas (*DECC*) rejected Moll's *sanguifundere, preferring to it a reinterpretation of prefixal L. *sūffusiō*; AM, *DECC* "fondre"; N:sang 'blood' + V:fondre 'to melt' (L. FŪSU[M] 'melted')

sang-girar 'to irritate, become irritated'; AM; N:sang 'blood' + V:girar 'to turn'

sangglaçar-se 'to take fright', Cast. 'helarse la sangre a uno', *sang-glaçat* 'indecisive'; *Tresor*, AM, BM §352 (N Dir Obj + V), *FEW* "sanguis," Torrellas, Vallès; N:sang 'blood' + V:glaçar 'to freeze'

sangtrair 'to turn black-and-blue, bruise'; *sangtrait* 'bruise'; AM; N:sang 'blood' + V:trair 'to pull'

solprès 'sunburned'; *Tresor*; N:sol 'sun' + V:PRĒNSU(M) (prendre) 'to seize'

tallgirar-se 'to become dull' (of a knife blade); Ruaix; N:tall 'cutting edge' + V:girar 'to turn'

terra-batut 'fallen on bad times (financially)'; AM; N:terra 'land' + V:batre 'to beat'

Ribes *terra-lleva* f. 'land for growing fruit'; AM; N:terra + V:llevar

terramanejar (fig.) 'to meddle, interfere'; AM; N:terra + V:manejar 'to handle'

(13th c.) *terra-*, (14th c.) *terres-tinent* 'landowner'; *Tresor*, AM, PF, BM §352 (N Dir Obj + V), Torrellas, Vallès; N:terra 'land' + V:tenir 'to hold'

testavirar 'to twist one's head around, make s.o. dizzy'; *Tresor*, AM, PF, Torrellas; N:testa 'head, pot' + V:virar 'to turn'

ullcegar 'to blind'; AM; N:ull 'eye' + V:cegar 'to blind'

ullferir 'to strike one's eye'; AM; N:ull 'eye' + V:ferir 'to strike'

(15th c.) *ullprendre* 'to bewitch, fascinate' (with one's eyes); *ullprès* 'disliked, inconsiderate'; *ullprenedor* 'bewitching'; *ullprenement* 'fascination'; *GRS* II §594, *Tresor*, AM, PF, BM §352 (N Dir Obj + V), Torrellas, Albertí; N:ull 'eye' + V:prendre 'to seize'

(13th c.) *vian(d)ant* 'traveller, pilgrim, pedestrian'; *Tresor*, AM, PF, BM §352 (N Dir Obj + V), *FEW* "via," *DCE[LC]* "via" (through popular reinterpretation of Lat. VIĀNS, -ĀNTIS after loss of the verb's finite forms); N:via 'way' + V:anar 'to go'

OTHER COMPOUNDS APPROXIMATING N + V STRUCTURE

aigües-juntes 'confluence of two rivers'; *DECC* I 96a; N:aigua 'water' + V:junyir 'to flow together'

(16th c.) *aygua-baxant*; Aguiló ("tal pessa de terra que està aigua baixant"); N:aigua 'water' + V:baixar 'to drop'

(14th c.) *capbrevar* 'to compile a legal inventory or contract, survey; annul'; Vallès, *DECC* "cap"; N:capbreu 'legal inventory of names, places' + V:-ar

(19th c.) *capgirellar* 'to turn a somersault'; *Tresor*, AM, Torrellas, *DECC* "cap"; N:capgirell 'somersault' + V:-ar

capllaçar 'to tie a bull by the horns with a rope'; AM, *DECC* "cap"; N:capllaç 'halter, rope' + V:-ar

(14th c.) *caplletrar* 'to illuminate a ms.'; *Tresor*, AM, *DECC* "cap" + "lletra"; N:caplletra 'decorated capital' + V:-ar

capmallolar 'to prune the first offshoots of a vine'; *Tresor*, AM; N:capmallol 'vine shoot' + V:-ar

capmartellar 'to wield a hammer'; AM, *DECC* "cap"; N:capmartell '(heavy) hammer' + V:-ar

(15th c.) *capsalmar* 'to illuminate a psalm'; Griera; N:capsalm 'decorated capital letter' + V:-ar

cap-serrar (n.g.), *-serrat* 'angle of two walls; protractor' (instrument); Ruaix (N + V); N:cap 'head, end' + V:serrar 'to saw, tighten'

carn-esqueixat 'torn muscle'; *Dicc* Vox 1983; N:carn 'flesh' + V:esqueixar 'to tear off', (intr.) 'come loose'

carnfu(g)it 'bruised flesh'; AM; N:carn 'flesh' + V:fugir 'to flee'

corfallit 'having lost one's nerve, lacking in courage'; *DECC* "cor"; N:cor 'heart' + V:fallir 'to fail'

cormigrat 'very worried'; AM; N:cor 'heart' + V:migrar 'to worry'

(20th c.) *cornafrat* 'wounded in the heart'; AM; N:cor 'heart' + V:nafrar 'to wound'

cor-robat 'seduced'; *Tresor*, Torrellas; N:cor 'heart' + V:robar 'to steal'

cultiparlar 'to speak affectedly, using Latin words and phrases to excess' (Sp. *cultiparlar* [q.v.]); *cultiparlista*, *cultiparlant* 'one who uses Latin words and phrases excessively'; AM; Adj:culto 'learnèd' + V:parlar 'to speak'

galta-inflat 'swollen'; Moreu-Rey; N:galta 'cheek' + V:inflar 'to swell with air'

giravoltar 'to take a tumble'; *DECC* "girar"; N:giravolt 'tumble' + V:-ar

gordinfleta 'corpulent', 'galta-inflat' (q.v.); Cast. 'gordi(n)flón'; *Tresor*; N:gord 'fat' + V:inflar 'to swell with air'

(14th c.) *lliga-cama, -cames* 'garter', 'camalliga, camalligues' (q.v.); *DECC* "lligar" (*ligacames* substituted for *camalligues* in an early printed version of Eiximenis); V:lligar 'to bind' + N:cama 'leg'

(19th c.) *morroaterrat* 'with nose to the ground'; AM; N:murr- 'snout, nose' + a terra 'to the ground' + V:-ar

pernagirat 'having the front legs toward flanks'; AM; N:perna 'leg' + V:girar 'to turn' *pernatrencat* 'having a broken leg', 'camatrencat'; *Tresor*; N:perna 'leg' + V:trencar 'to break'

potaferit 'wounded in one leg'; AM; N:pota 'leg' + V:ferir 'to strike'

Puigpunyent; AM (PODIUM PŬNGENTEM), *DECC* "puig" (not PODIUM PŬNGENTEM, but 'una mera etimologia notarial')

salpebrar 'to conserve meat with salt and pepper'; *Tresor*, AM, PF; N:salpebre 'salt and pepper mixture' + V:-ar

sangfluix 'hemorrhage'; Albertí; N:sang 'blood' + N:fluix 'flow'

sangprés 'coagulation'; Torrellas; N:sang 'blood' + V:PRĒNSU(M) (*prendre*) 'to seize'

(13th c., today arch.) *solabatut* 'tired, worn out'; *Tresor*, AM; N:sola 'foot' + V:batre 'to beat'

terraguixar 'to repair walls with *terraguix*'; *Tresor*; N:terraguix 'gypsum and sand mixture' + V:-ar

terraplenar 'to embank, fill', 'omplir de terra un fondal'; *Tresor*; denom. from *terraplè* '(land)fill'

(19th c.) *terratrémer* 'to quake' (of the earth); denom. from *terratrèmol*); *Tresor*, AM, PF, Torrellas; N:terra 'land' + V:trémer 'to shake'

(14th c.) *tinentlloc* 'lieutenant', 'lloctinent' (q.v.); Huber §393.3, AM; N:lloc 'position' + V:tenir 'to hold'

DUBIOUS

capmassar-se 'to worry', 'capficar-se'; AM, Torrellas; N:cap 'head, end' + V:(?) massar (cf. Occ. *capmaçar-se* 'to stun, worry')

(15th c.) *capvivar* 'to illuminate a ms.'; *Tresor*, AM; N:cap- + ?

carnxancar-se 'to feel bruised (after riding a horse)'; AM 'aixafat', 'pounded'; N:carn 'flesh' + V:(?) xancar

salobrejar 'to lead baby goats toward salt-covered stones, lick', 'fer salobre' ('to exude salt' [of stone, limestone walls]); N:salobre 'saline exflorescence' + V:-ar

MEDIEVAL AND RENAISSANCE CATALAN NOMINAL ELEMENTS

aiguatoldre	N:aigua 'water'	V:toldre
aiguavers	N:aigua	V:VERSUS
aiguavessant	N:aigua	V:vessar
camalliga	N:cama 'leg'	V:lligar
camptinent	N:camp 'field'	V:tenir

capfic	N:cap 'head, end'	V:ficar
capgirant	N:cap	V:girar
caplleuta	N:cap	V:LEVĬTA
capllevar	N:cap	V:llevar
captenir, captenir-se	N:cap	V:tenir
carafeixar	N:cara 'face'	V:faixar
caragirat	N:cara	V:girar
caravirat	N:cara	V:virar
carnes-, carnistoltes	N:carn(es) 'flesh'	V:*TOLLĬTAS
clavificat, clauficar	N:clau 'nail'	V:ficar
claupresó	N:clau	V:prendre
creuclavat	N:creu 'cross'	V:clavar
crozficar	N:creu	V:ficar
creuposar	N:creu	V:posar
fementit	N:fe 'faith'	V:mentir
lloctinent, tinentlloc	N:lloc 'position'	V:tenir
mampendre	N:man 'hand'	V:(em)pendre
manlleuta	N:man	V:LEVĬTA
manlevar, manllevar	N:man	V:llevar
mantenir, desmantenir	N:man	V:tener, -ir
marmessor	N:MANŪMISSOR 'executor' ('emancipator')	
missacantant	N:missa 'Mass'	V:cantar
missadient	N:missa	V:dir
morfondre	N:murr- 'snout'	V:fondre
palafangar	N:pala 'shovel'	V:fangar
peucalcigar	N:peu 'foot'	V:calcigar
salpicar	N:sal 'salt'	V:picar
salp(r)endre	N:sal	V:prendre
salprès	N:sal	V:PRĒ(N)SU(M)
sangfondre, -fús	N:sang 'blood'	V:fondre (FŪSU[M])
terratinent	N:terra 'land'	V:tenir
ullprendre	N:ull 'eye'	V:prendre

vian(d)ant	N:via 'way'	V:anar

MEDIEVAL AND RENAISSANCE CATALAN VERBAL ELEMENTS

vian(d)ant	N:via	V:anar 'to go'
peucalcigar	N:peu	V:calcigar 'to stamp (on)'
missacantant	N:missa	V:cantar 'to sing'
creuclavat	N:creu	V:clavar 'to nail'
missadient	N:missa	V:dir 'to say'
carafeixar	N:cara	V:faixar 'to wrap'
palafangar	N:pala	V:fangar 'to dig'
capfic	N:cap	V:ficar 'to fix (to)'
clauficar	N:clau	V:ficar
crozficar	N:croz	V:ficar
morfondre	N:murr-	V:fondre 'to melt'
sangfondre, -fús	N:sang	V:fondre (FŪSU[M])
capgirant	N:cap	V:girar 'to turn'
caragirar	N:cara	V:girar
caplleuta	N:cap	V:LEVĬTA 'raised'
manlleuta	N:man	V:LEVĬTA
capllevar	N:cap	V:llevar 'to raise'
manllevar	N:man	V:llevar
camalliga	N:camba	V:lligar 'to bind'
fementit	N:fe	V:mentir 'to lie'
salpicar	N:sal	V:picar 'to strike'
creuposar	N:creu	V:posar 'to place'
claupresó (*clauprendre)	N:*clau	V:prendre 'to seize'
mampendre	N:man	V:(em)prendre
salp(r)endre	N:sal	V:prendre
ullprendre	N:ull	V:prendre
salprès	N:sal	V:PRĒ(N)SU(M)
camp-tinent	N:camp	V:tener, -ir 'to hold'

cap-tenir(-se)	N:cap	V:tener, -ir
lloctinent, tinentlloc	N:lloc	V:tener, -ir
mantenir, desmantenir	N:man	V:tener, -ir
terra-tinent	N:terra	V:tener, -ir
aiguatoldre	N:aigua	V:toldre 'to remove'
carnestoltes	N:carn(es)	V:*TOLLĬTAS 'removed'
aigavers	N:aigua	V:VERSUS (vessar) 'to pour'
aigavessant	N:aigua	V:vessar
caravirat	N:cara	V:virar 'to turn'

MODERN CATALAN NOMINAL ELEMENTS

aiguabarrejar-se	N:aigua 'water'	V:barrejar
aigua-batre, -batent	N:aigua	V:batre
aiguadeix	N:aigua	V:deixar
aigualleix	N:aigua	V:lleixar
aiguaneix	N:aigua	V:néixer
aygua-regant	N:aigua	V:regar
aiguavés, -vertent	N:aigua	V:VERSUS (vessar)
ayreferir-se	N:aire 'air'	V:ferir
barbapunta, -punyent	N:barba 'beard'	V:pondre × PŬNCTU(M)
botinflar-se	N:bot 'gourd'	V:inflar
camalliga	N:camba 'leg'	V:lligar
camatrencar	N:camba	V:trencar
capalçar	N:cap 'head'	V:alçar
capbaixar-se	N:cap	V:baixar
capbatre	N:cap	V:batre
capfermar	N:cap	V:fermar
capficar, capficar-se	N:cap	V:ficar
capfilar	N:cap	V:filar
capgirar	N:cap	V:girar
capguardar-se	N:cap	V:guardar
caplleuta	N:cap	V:LEVĬTA
capllevar	N:cap	V:llevar
caplliga	N:cap	V:lligar
cappelar	N:cap	V:pelar
captenir, captenir-se	N:cap	V:tenir
capterrar	N:cap	V:terrar
capitombar	N:cap	V:tombar
captrencar(-se)	N:cap	V:trencar
capvirar	N:cap	V:virar

capxafar	N:cap	V:xafar
carafeixar	N:cara 'face'	V:feixar
caragirar	N:cara	V:girar
carnestoltes	N:carn(es) 'flesh'	V:*TOLLĬTA(S)
casatinent	N:casa 'house'	V:tenir 'to hold'
clauficat	N:clau 'nail'	V:ficar
claupassar	N:clau	V:passar
claupresó	N:clau	V:pendre
collgirar	N:coll 'neck'	V:girar
collportar	N:coll	V:portar
colltombar	N:coll	V:tombar
colltorçar, -tòrcer	N:coll	V:torçar, tòrcer
colltrencar-se	N:coll	V:trencar
collvinclar-se	N:coll	V:vinclar
copbatre	N:cop 'blow'	V:batre
corbategar	N:cor 'heart'	V:bategar
corcaure	N:cor	V:caure
corcorcar-se	N:cor	V:corcar
(fer) corcruix	N:cor	V:cruixir
cordoldre's	N:cor	V:doldre
coresforçar-se	N:cor	V:esforçar
corferir	N:cor	V:ferir
corfondre	N:cor	V:fondre
corgelar	N:cor	V:gelar
corglaçar-se	N:cor	V:glaçar
corlligar	N:cor	V:lligar
cornuar-se	N:cor	V:nuar
corprendre	N:cor	V:prendre
corsecar	N:cor	V:secar
cortrencar	N:cor	V:trencar
creuclavat	N:creu 'cross'	V:clavar
cuixapenjant	N:cuixa 'thigh'	V:penjar
cuixatrencar	N:cuixa	V:trencar
culbufar	N:cul 'butt'	V:bufar
culmenejar	N:cul	V:menejar
culremena	N:cul	V:remenar
fe-faent	N:fe 'faith'	V:fer
fementit	N:fe	V:mentir

feina-fuig	N:feina 'work'	V:fugir
filbastar	N:fil 'string'	V:bastar
firandant	N:fira 'fair'	V:anar
greixfondre	N:greix 'fat'	V:fondre
llampferit	N:llamp 'ray'	V:ferir
lletraferit	N:lletra 'letter'	V:ferir
lloctinent	N:lloc 'position'	V:tenir
mampara	N:Cast. mano 'hand'	V:Cast. amparar
mamprendre	N:mà (mano)	V:(em)p(r)endre
mamposteria	N:Cast. mano	V:Cast. poner
manllevar	N:mà	V:llevar
maniobrar	N:mà	V:obrar
mantenir	N:mà	V:tener
mantornar	N:mà	V:tornar
missacantant	N:missa 'Mass'	V:cantar
missadient	N:missa	V:dir
morfondre	N:murr- 'snout'	V:fondre
palafic	N:pal 'stick'	V:ficar
palplantar	N:pal	V:plantar
palafangar	N:pala 'shovel'	V:fangar
pèl-mudar	N:pèl 'hair'	V:mudar
espeltirar	N:pèl	V:tirar
pellforadar	N:pell 'skin'	V:foradar
pellobrir-se	N:pell	V:obrir
pellpartir-se	N:pell	V:partir
pelltrencar-se	N:pell	V:trencar
pernabatre	N:perna 'leg'	V:batre
peucalcigar	N:peu 'foot'	V:calcigar
peulligar	N:peu	V:lligar
peutridar, paltrigar	N:peu	V:tridar/trigar
salpassar	N:sal 'sal'	V:passar × SPARSU(M)
salpicar, -piscar	N:sal	V:picar
salp(r)endre	N:sal	V:prendre
sangcremar-se	N:sang 'blood'	V:cremar

sangfondre	N:sang	V:fondre
sang-girar	N:sang	V:girar
sangglaçar-se	N:sang	V:glaçar
sangtrair	N:sang	V:trair
solprès	N:sol 'sun'	V:PRĒ(N)SU(M)
tallgirar-se	N:tall 'cutting edge'	V:girar
terrabatut	N:terra 'land'	V:batre
terra-lleva	N:terra	V:llevar
terramanejar	N:terra	V:manejar
terratinent	N:terra	V:tener
testavirar	N:testa 'head, pot'	V:virar
ullcegar	N:ull 'eye'	V:cegar
ullferir	N:ull	V:ferir
ullprendre	N:ull	V:prendre
vian(d)ant	N:via 'way'	V:anar

MODERN CATALAN VERBAL ELEMENTS

capalçar	N:cap	V:alçar 'to raise'
mampara	N:mano	V:Cast. amparar 'to protect'
firandant	N:fira	V:anar 'to go'
vian(d)ant	N:via	V:anar
capbaixar-se	N:cap	V:baixar 'to lower'
aiguabarrejar	N:aigua	V:barrejar 'to mix'
filbastar	N:fil	V:bastar 'to baste'
corbategar	N:cor	V:bategar 'to beat'
aiguabatre, -batent	N:aigua	V:batre 'to beat'
capbatre	N:cap	V:batre
copbatre	N:cop	V:batre
pernabatre	N:perna	V:batre
terrabatut	N:terra	V:batre
culbufar	N:cul	V:bufar 'to blow, breathe'
peucalcigar	N:peu	V:calcigar 'to stamp (on)'

missacantant	N:missa	V:cantar 'to sing'
corcaure	N:cor	V:caure 'to fall'
ullcegar	N:ull	V:cegar 'to blind'
creuclavat	N:creu	V:clavar 'to nail'
corcorcar	N:cor	V:corcar 'to pine'
sangcremar	N:sang	V:cremar 'to burn'
(fer) corcruix	N:cor	V:cruixir 'to creak'
aiguadeix	N:aigua	V:deixar 'to leave'
missadient	N:missa	V:dir 'to say'
cordoldre's	N:cor	V:doldre 'to hurt'
coresforçar-se	N:cor	V:esforçar 'to make an effort'
palafangar	N:pala	V:fangar 'to dig'
carafeixar	N:cara	V:feixar 'to wrap'
fefaent	N:fe	V:fer 'to make, do'
ayreferir-se	N:aire	V:ferir 'to strike'
corferir	N:cor	V:ferir
llampferit	N:llamp	V:ferir
lletraferit	N:lletra	V:ferir
ullferir	N:ull	V:ferir
capfermar	N:cap	V:fermar 'to fasten'
capficar	N:cap	V:ficar 'to fix (to)'
clauficat	N:clau	V:ficar
palafic	N:pal	V:ficar
capfilar	N:cap	V:filar 'to conjecture, reveal'
corfondre	N:cor	V:fondre 'to melt'
greixfondre	N:greix	V:fondre
morfondre	N:mor	V:fondre
sangfondre	N:sang	V:fondre
pellforadar	N:pell	V:foradar 'to pierce'

feina-fuig	N:feina	V:fugir 'to flee'
corgelar	N:cor	V:gelar 'to freeze'
capgirar	N:cap	V:girar 'to turn'
caragirar	N:cara	V:girar
collgirar	N:coll	V:girar
sanggirar	N:sang	V:girar
tallgirar	N:tall	V:girar
corglaçar-se	N:cor	V:glaçar 'to freeze'
sangglaçar	N:sang	V:glaçar
capguardar-se	N:cap	V:guardar 'to guard'
botinflar	N:bot	V:inflar 'to swell with air'
aigualleix	N:aigua	V:lleixar 'to leave'
caplleuta	N:cap	V:LEVĬTA 'raised'
capllevar	N:cap	V:llevar 'to raise'
manllevar	N:mà	V:llevar
terra-lleva	N:terra	V:llevar
camalliga	N:camba	V:lligar 'to bind'
caplliga	N:cap	V:lligar
corlligar	N:cor	V:lligar
peulligar	N:peu	V:lligar
terramanejar	N:terra	V:manejar 'to handle'
culmenejar	N:cul	V:menejar 'to wiggle'
fementit	N:fe	V:mentir 'to lie'
pèl-mudar	N:pèl	V:mudar 'to change'
aiguaneix	N:aigua	V:néixer 'to be born'
cornuar	N:cor	V:nuar 'to knot, tie'
maniobrar	N:mà	V:obrar 'to work'
pellobrir	N:pell	V:obrir 'to open'
pellpartir	N:pell	V:partir 'to divide'
claupassar	N:clau	V:passar 'to pass, undergo'
salpassar	N:sal	V:passar × SPARSU(M) 'sprinkled'

cappelar	N:cap	V:pelar 'to peel'
cuixapenjant	N:cuixa	V:penjar 'to hang'
salpicar, -piscar	N:sal	V:picar 'to strike'
palplantar	N:pal	V:plantar 'to stand on end'
barbapunyent	N:barba	V:poner × PŬNCTU(M)
mamposteria	N:Cast. mano	V:Cast. poner 'to put'
collportar	N:coll	V:portar 'to carry'
claupresó	N:clau	V:prendre 'to seize'
corprendre	N:cor	V:prendre
mamprendre	N:mà (mano)	V:(em)p(r)endre 'to undertake'
salprendre	N:sal	V:prendre
solprès	N:sola	V:PRĒ(N)SUM)
ullprendre	N:ull	V:prendre
aygua-regant	N:aigua	V:regar 'to irrigate'
culremena	N:cul	V:remenar 'to wiggle'
corsecar	N:cor	V:secar 'to dry'
cap-tenir(-se)	N:cap	V:tener, -ir 'to hold'
casatinent	N:casa	V:tener, -ir
lloctinent	N:lloc	V:tener, -ir
mantenir	N:man	V:tener, -ir
terratinent	N:terra	V:tener, -ir
capterrar	N:cap	V:terrar 'to cover with earth'
espeltirar	N:pèl	V:tirar 'to pull'
carnestoltes	N:carn(es)	V:*TOLLĬTA(S) 'removed'
capitombar	N:cap	V:tombar 'to fall'
colltombar	N:coll	V:tombar
colltorçar, -tòrcer	N:coll	V:torçar, tòrcer 'to twist'
mantornar	N:man	V:tornar 'to turn'
sangtrair	N:sang	V:trair 'to pull'
camatrencar	N:cama	V:trencar 'to break'
captrencar	N:cap	V:trencar

colltrencar	N:coll	V:trencar
cortrencar	N:cor	V:trencar
cuixatrencar	N:cuixa	V:trencar
pelltrencar	N:pell	V:trencar
peutridar, paltrigar	N:peu	V:tridar 'to rub, grind'/
		trigar 'to delay, be slow'
aigavés, -vertent	N:aiga	V:VERSUS (versar 'to pour')
collvinclar	N:coll	V:vinclar 'to bend'
capvirar	N:cap	V:virar 'to turn'
testavirar	N:testa	V:virar
capxafar	N:cap	V:xafar 'to wrinkle'

Appendix D

Spanish Corpus

Arag. *aguallevado* 'dredging (of a riverbed)'; Nav. 'mountain gorge'; Iribarren, PA;
N:agua 'water' + V:llevar 'to raise, remove', (Mod.) 'to carry, take'

alicortar, -corto 'to cut the wings off; to wing, wound'; MzP (N + V), *Acad* 1984;
N:ala 'wing' + V:cortar 'to cut (off)'

(16th c.) *barbiponiente* 'starting to grow a beard; gullible; young man'; Cejador, AH;
N:barba 'beard'+ V:poner 'to put' × PŬNGENTE(M)

(15th c.) *botalima* 'inefficient bootblack'; Cejador; N:bota 'boot' + V:limar 'to polish'

Arag. *botinchau* 'swollen'; PA, Andolz; N:bota 'leather winebag' + V:hinchar 'to
swell'

botinflón, Arag. *-inflao* 'swollen'; PA, Andolz; N:bota 'leather winebag' + V:inflar 'to
swell with air'

(arch.) *cablieva* 'bail, pledge, guarantee' (from OCat. *caplleuta* through OArag.
caple[u]ta); Boggs, Oelschläger, *DCE[LC]* "cablieva," *Acad* 1984 (from
caplevāre); N:cabo 'head, end' + V:LEVĬTA 'raised'

OSp. (13th c.) *caboprender* 'to understand' (Ayala 1693 "en una sola palabra, es
comprender; voz muy antigua y desusada"); Gili y Gaya; N:cabo 'head, end'
+ V:(com?)prender 'to take'

cachipegar 'to copulate' (of dogs); *DCE[LC]* "cacha" (compound); N:cach[orr]o
'puppy' + V:pegar 'to stick'

cachipodar 'to prune'; GdeD 1985 (**capodar* × *chapodar*); N:cacho 'bit, slice' +
V:podar 'to prune'

Ast. (refl.) *caltener* 'to hold up, stand firm, maintain oneself; watch one's expenditures
closely'; *REW* §1668 "caput"; *DCE[LC]* "tener" (labeled this a "préstamo
occitano"); N:cabo 'head, end' + V:tener 'to hold'

Arag. (arch.) *camajuste* 'ladder for picking olives'; PA; N:camal (from *caminal* 'fat
branch at bottom of hearth') + V:ajustar 'to adapt'

Arag. *camaliga* 'garter', Cast. *ligagamba* (from Catalan); *REW* §5024 "ligāre," PA,
　　Andolz; N:Cat. cama 'leg' + V:ligar 'to bind'

(16th c.) *capialzar* (archit.) 'to splay, bend the face of an arch or lintel into an
　　outward slope'; *capialzado* 'curve or bend of an arch; flashing over a door or
　　window'; *capialzo* m. 'splay' (from Cat. *capalçar*); *DCE[LC]* "cabo"; N:cap
　　'head, end' + V:alzar 'to raise'

Arag. (arch.) *caple(u)ta, ca(b)lieuta* 'bail, pledge, guarantee' (from OCat. *caplleuta*);
　　(13th c.) *capletar* 'to jail for debt'; PA; N:cabo 'head, end' + V:LEVĬTA
　　'removed/raised'

OArag. (14th c.) *cap-, cab-levar* 'to deliver a pledge' (from 13th-c. Cat. *capllevar*
　　idem); *cap-, cab-levadura* 'bail'; *caplebador* 'guarantor'; Gili y Gaya, Andolz;
　　N:cabo 'head, end' + V:llevar 'to raise, remove', (Mod.) 'to carry, take'

OSp. (13th c.) *cap-, cabtener*, OArag. *captener* 'to protect, maintain; represent; retain'
　　(from OCat. *captenir*); (arch.) *captenencia* (13th c.) 'conduct; appearance',
　　(arch.) 'conservation, protection'; Ast. *caltener* 'to stand firm' (q.v.); *REW*
　　§11668 "caput," Oelschläger, Hanssen, *Acad* 1970, Andolz, Alvar 1976; N:cap
　　'head' + V:tener 'to hold'

Arag. *carabirar* 'to disfigure, disguise, distort'; Andolz (from Occ.); N:cara 'face' +
　　V:virar 'to turn'

carnaval 'the three days before Ash Wednesday' (from It. *carnevale*); *carnavalada* f.
　　'action or joke proper to Carnival'; *carna-valesco, -válico* 'pertaining to
　　Carnival'; *Acad* 1984; N:It. carne 'flesh' + V:It. levare 'to remove'

(13th c.) *carnes-, carnis-, garras-tolendas* f.pl. 'Lent, the three meat days that precede
　　Lent', (Mod.) 'Carnival, Shrovetide'; Nav. *carrastolendas* 'Carnival masquer-
　　ades'; Arag. *carnistoltas* (arch.) 'one who is odd'; *REW* §1706 "carō," PA,
　　Fontecha, *DCE[LC]* "carne," Andolz; N:carnes 'flesh' + V:TOLLENDAS
　　'removed'

(17th c.) *caulevar* (arch.) 'to raise up, support', 'soubsleuer'; *caulevador* 'supporting';
　　Gili y Gaya; N:cap 'head, end' + V:llevar 'to raise', (Mod.) 'to carry, take'

(17th c.) *cornicantano* 'cuckold' (Quevedo); AH; N:CORNU 'horn' + V:cantar 'to
　　sing'

Arag. *croceficar* 'to crucify', Ast. *crocheficar*; Novo Mier; N:CRŬCI- 'cross' + V:ficar
　　'to fix (to)'

Arag. *culmené* 'snoopy, meddlesome, intrusive' (cf. Cat. *culmenejar*); Andolz; N:culo
　　'butt' + V:(Cat.) menar 'to lead, bring'

(14th c.) *desmamparar*, (Mod.) *desamparar* 'to abandon'; *DCE[LC]* "parar"; N:mano
　　'hand' + V:amparar 'to protect'

OSp. *faz-, façferir* → *çaherir* 'to wrong, offend', lit. 'to slap'; (Mod.) *zaherir* (q.v.) 'to
　　reproach'; AlemB, Oelschläger; N:faz 'face' + V:herir 'to strike'

fefaciente, (Mod.) *fehaciente* (law) 'authentic'; Hanssen, *DCE[LC]* "fe"; N:fe 'faith' +
    V:hacer 'to make, do'

(13th c.) *fementido* 'false'; *fementidamente* 'falsely, perfidiously'; Oelschläger,
    DCE[LC] "fe," *EDAF*; N:fe 'faith' + V:mentir 'to lie'

(Laguna de) Gallocanta lit. '[the] cock sings'; cf. *gallicinio* 'cock-crow' (*DCE[LC]*
    "gallo": GALLICINIUM, from *canĕre*), and Occ. *galh-cantàn* 'dawn'; Vaño-Cerdá;
    N:gallo 'cock' + V:cantar 'to sing'

Arag. *gulli-baixar* 'to keep one's glance lowered', *-baixo* 'with lowered eyes'; Andolz;
    N:güello (Cast. *ojo*) 'eye' + V:baixar (Cast. *bajar*) 'to lower'

OArag. *lugartinient* 'advisor' (one of five at the Justicia Mayor de Aragón); (1590) Sp.
    lugarteniente 'lieutenant, deputy'; *lugartenencia* 'lieutenancy'; PA, *DCE[LC]*
    "lugar" (a loan translation from Med. Latin), *EDAF*; N:lugar 'position' +
    V:tener, -ir 'to hold'

maherir (older *manferir* [q.v.]), 'to signal with the hand, touch, shake, look for', (arch.)
    'to designate for military service (by a touch of the hand on the shoulder)', 'to
    protect, shelter'; *maherimiento* m. 'indication, pointing out'; (17th c.) *maherido*
    'trained, skilled'; Fontecha, *Acad* 1970, *DCE[LC]* "mano," J. Barthe 1979,
    EDAF; N:mano 'hand' + V:herir 'to strike'

(13th c., today arch.) *mam-, man-parar* 'to protect, defend, support, shelter'; (Mod.)
    mampara 'protection; fire screen; small door'; *mamparo* (naut.) 'bulkhead';
    Diez, *REW* §500a "anteparāre," §5337 "manū parāre"; *DCE[LC]* "parar,"
    "guardar" (*mam-* through popular alternation of ANTE-, attested elsewhere in
    OSp. *amampiés* as against OFr. *avantpiés*), Williams; N:mano 'hand' +
    V:amparar 'to protect'

OSp. *mampastor* 'household dependent', and cf. OFr. *mainpast* (q.v.); J. Barthe 1979;
    N:MANU 'hand' + V:PĀSTU(M) 'nourished'

mam-postear, Ast. *-postiar*, (16th–17th c.) 'to build a dry-wall of rubble or stones', 'to
    cement with mortar'; *mampuesto* 'rubble, rough stone; parapet', Amer. 'support
    for a gun'; *mampuesta* 'course of bricks'; *mampostería* 'rubblework, covered
    battery'; *mampostero* 'rubble mason'; adj. *mampuesto* 'overlapping'; *de
    mampuesto* 'spare, emergency; under cover'; AlemB (N Compl + V), Williams,
    BDE[LC], Novo Mier, *Acad* 1984; N:mano 'hand' + V:poner 'to place'

Murcia, Valencia *mamprender* 'to subdue by hand' (cf. Sp. *mampresar* [q.v.]); GdeD
    1985; N:mano 'hand' + V:prender 'to seize'

OSp. (12th c.) *mampuesta, manpuesta, manuposito, mano postas* 'protection'; OSp.
    mampostor, -postero 'protector; tax collector', (Mod.) 'collector of alms for
    certain hospitals'; *mam-postoría*, (Mod.) *-postería* 'office of tax collector,
    collection of alms for certain hospitals'; Cejador, Oelschläger, J. Barthe 1979,
    EDAF; N:MANU 'hand' + V:POSĬTU(M) 'placed'

OSp. *manbor* 'protector, guardian'; Diez "mainbour"; N:MUNDEBORO 'protector'

Arag. *mancuspir* 'to spit into one's hands and rub them together before taking hold
of a tool'; Novo Mier; N:mano 'hand' + V:Arag. cuspir 'to spit'

OSp. (13th c.) *mane(n)trar* 'to attack, assault, undertake'; Boggs, Oelschläger; N:mano
'hand' + V:entrar 'to attack'

manferir 'to designate (by a blow of the hand on the shoulder) for military service';
(Mod.) 'to signal with the hand; touch, shake; anticipate', 'maherir' (q.v.);
manferidor 'resistance' [*sic*], 'one who signals'; *DCE[LC]* "mano," *EDAF*;
N:mano 'hand' + V:herir 'to strike'

Ast. *manferir*, Cast. *malherir* 'to injure badly', through reinterpretation of *ma-* +
V:ferir/herir; Novo Mier; N:mano (*mal*) + V:ferir/herir 'to strike'

(17th c.) *maniatar, -ado*, Nav. (18th c.) *manatar* 'to manacle, shackle, tie the hands,
handcuff'; Ecuador *maniate* 'shackles'; MzP (N + V), Iribarren, *Acad* 1970,
BDE[LC], *EDAF*; N:mano 'hand' + V:atar 'to bind'

OSp. (1140) *man(i)-, malfestar*, (Mod.) *manifestar* 'to reveal, state, confess, make
public admission of a debt or crime'; *REW* §5304 "manifestare," Cejador,
Boggs, *DCE[LC]* "mano"; *mal-* through reinterpretation of V:MANIFESTĀRE
'to reveal'

OArag. *manifestar* 'to liberate', (*sacar*) *manifestada* 'to free a young woman of legal
age from her home and father's power so that she may contract marriage'; PA,
Andolz; V:MAN(I)FESTĀRE 'to reveal'

manobrar 'to work with the hands'; *man-obre* 'hod carrier'; *manobra* Arag. 'worker,
peasant', Murcia 'building materials'; *manobrero* 'keeper of irrigation ditches';
(18th c.) *maniobrar* 'to maneuver, work with the hands' (from Fr. *manoeuvrer*);
maniobra 'handling, maneuver'; (naut.) 'gear, tackle'; Arag. 'bricklayer's
materials'; *maniobrista* (naut.) 'skillful maneuverer'; *maniobrero* (mil.) 'skilled
in maneuvering'; *maniobrabilidad* 'maneuverability'; *maniobrable* 'maneuverable'; AD, *REW* §5336 "manŭŏperāre," PA, Williams, Andolz,
Corominas–Pascual III 819b, *DECC* "mà"; N:mano 'hand' + V:obrar 'to work'

OSp., OArag. *maleuar*, (Mod.) *man-lebar, -levar* 'to borrow, contract, guarantee a
debt, leave (an object as) a pledge against a sum of money' (lit. "to raise the
hand [so as to swear an oath]"); (Mod.) 'to contract or assume a debt'; Arag.
manlevator 'guarantor'; AD, *DCE[LC]* "mano," *Acad* 1970, Andolz; N:mano
'hand' + V:llevar 'to raise', (Mod.) 'to carry, take'

(13th c.) *mansessor*, (14th c.) *marmessor, manumisor*, (Mod.) *mansesor*, Murcia
marmesor 'executor, executrix'; *Acad* 1970, *DCE[LC]* "mano," *BDE[LC]*
(*manumitir* 'enviar los esclavos lejos del poder del dueno'), *EDAF*;
N:MANŪMISSOR 'executor' ('emancipator')

(13th c.) *mantener*, Arag. *mantení, mantinre*, OPtg. *manteer*, Mod.Ptg. *manter* 'to maintain, provide with food, support, keep, stay'; OArag. *manteniença* 'financial management', (Mod.) *mantenencia, mantención* 'maintenance, support; conservation'; *mantenida* 'concubine'; *mantenedor* 'president of a contest or tournament'; (arch.) (*a*) *mantiniente* 'now; with all one's might, with both hands'; (cult.) *manutener* (law) 'to maintain, support'; *manu-tención* 'conservation, aid'; *-tenencia* 'protection'; *REW* §5340, Boggs, Oelschläger, *DCE[LC]* "mano," Andolz, *EDAF*; N:man(o) 'hand' + V:tener 'to hold'

Arag. *mantorn(i)ar* 'to plow a second time'; AlemB (N Compl + V), *DCE[LC]* "mano," PA, Andolz; N:man(o) 'hand' + V:tornar 'to turn (under)'

OArag. *manuleuta* 'relinquishing of a piece of property'; OArag. (12th c.) *man-lieva, -lieve* 'act of posting bail or bond; trick, deception', (Mod.) 'loan, bail, ancient tax'; Maigne, *Acad* 1970, Boggs, Oelschläger, AH, *EDAF, Acad* 1984; N:MANU 'hand' + V:LEVĬTA 'raised'

(16th c.) *menteca(p)to* 'foolish, simple (weak in the head)'; *mente-catada, -catería, -catez* 'simpleness, folly, absurdity'; *DCE[LC]* "mente"; N:miente 'mind' + V:ca(p)tar 'to seize'

OSp. (13th c.) *mientesmetudo* 'prudent, sane'; *DCE[LC]* "mente"; N:miente(s) 'mind' + V:meter 'to put' (cf. *meter mientes* 'to consider')

(11th c.) *misacantano* 'priest who says Mass for the first time', 'cantamisano' (q.v.); Nav. 'feast celebrating a priest's first Mass'; AlemB, Cejador, Iribarren, *DCE[LC]* "meter"; N:misa 'Mass' + V:cantar 'to sing, say', with intrusion of *-ano*

(late 15th c.) *pelechar* 'to shed, molt; get or grow new hair, fledge', (colloq.) 'to keep in food and clothing', (fig.) 'to take a turn for the better'; *pelecho, pelecha* 'molting, molting season'; Amer. 'shedded snake-skin'; AlemB (N Compl + V), *DCE[LC]* "pelo," AH, *EDAF*; N:piel 'skin'/pelo 'hair' + V:echar 'to throw off'

Arag. *pelmudar* 'to molt'; Arag. *pelmuda* 'molting of skin or feathers'; PA, Andolz; N:piel 'skin'/pelo 'hair' + V:mudar 'to change'

perniabrir (Lope de Vega: "perniabrir la razón y se tiene a desvergüenza"), *perniabierto* 'bow-legged'; Rodríguez Marín, Williams; N:pierna 'leg' + V:abrir 'to open'

perniquebrar, -ado 'to break one's leg(s)'; MzP (N + V), Williams; N:pierna 'leg' + V:quebrar 'to break'

poderdante (law) 'constituent'; *DCE[LC]* "poder"; N:poder 'power' + V:dar 'to give'

poderhabiente (law) 'attorney, proxy'; *DCE[LC]* "poder"; N:poder 'power' + V:haber 'to have'

(19th c.) *reivindicar, revindicar* (law) 'to replevy; claim one's rights'; AlemB (N Compl + V; from either *rēm vindicāre or *rei vindicātiōnem*), *DCE[LC]* "real" (from *rei vindicātiōnem*); N:RĒ(M) 'object' + V:vindicar 'to avenge'

salpicar 'to sprinkle (with salt), splash; skip through'; *salpicón* 'dish of chopped or mixed ingredients; splash, splatter'; *salpicadura* idem, f.pl. 'indirect results'; *salpique* 'action of splashing'; *salpicadero* 'splasher'; (1570) *salpicado* 'in grains', (Mod.) 'splotchy, flea-bitten'; *REW* §7521 "sāl," *BDE[LC]* 522a (ultimately from Gothic *salb(isk)ôn* 'to anoint'), ACAD 1984, *EDAF*; N:sal 'salt' + V:picar 'to chop up, poke'

OSp. (13th c.) *salpreso* 'preserved with salt'; (17th c.) *salpresar* 'to preserve or season with salt'; *salpresamiento* 'preservation with salt'; *DCE[LC]* "sal" (underlying *salpres identified with Low Lat. *salspersus* 'sprinkled with salt' [Cl.L. *sparsus*]), *Acad* 1984 (*sal pressāre*); N:sal 'salt' + V:PRĒ(N)SU(M) 'seized'

OArag. *terrastenentes* 'tenants', Sp. *terrateniente* 'landowner, -holder', probably from 15th-c. Cat. *terratinent*; DuC, *DCE[LC]* "tierra," "tenēre"; N:Cat. terra 'land' + V:tener 'to hold'

(13th c.) *viandante* 'pilgrim', (Mod.) 'itinerant, stroller, tramp'; *REW* §9296 "vians"; *DCE[LC]* "via" (13th-c. OCat., OPtg., OPr., Ital. *viandant* through popular reinterpretation of L. VIĀNS, -ANTIS after loss of the verb's finite forms); Battisti–Alessio "viandante" (*viante* × *andare*); N:via 'way' + V:andar 'to go'

zaherir 'to reproach, criticize' (earlier *fazferir* 'to wrong' [q.v.]); *zaherimiento* 'upbraiding, reproach'; *zaherío* m. 'action of censuring'; *zaheridor* 'upbraider, fault-finder'; *zaherible* 'blamable, censurable'; MzP (N + V), *DCE[LC]* "herir," Williams, *EDAF*; N:faz 'face' + V:herir 'to strike'

OTHER COMPOUNDS APPROXIMATING N + V STRUCTURE

aguamelar 'to sweeten (water)', *aguamelado* 'washed with honey and water'; *EDAF*; N:aguamiel 'hydromel, mead' + V:-ar

Arag.-Nav. *aguas vertientes* 'watershed, water running downhill'; PA, Andolz; N:agua 'water' + V:verter 'to pour'

Andal., Mex. *cantamisano* 'newly ordained priest', 'misacantano' (q.v.); Andal., Mex. *cantamisa* 'act of singing one's first Mass'; *DCE[LC]* "meter," Williams, *Acad* 1984; N:misa 'Mass' + V:cantar 'to sing, say'

Argen. *culancharse* 'to be frightened'; *DECC*, Corominas–Pascual "culo"; N:cul(o) ancho 'scaredy-cat' (lit. 'wide butt') + V:-ar

(17th c.) *cultalatiniparla* (Quevedo, *La Culta Latiniparla*, 1629) 'macaronic or euphistic speech, excessive use of Latin words and phrases' (cf. *cultiparlar*,

latiniparla); Bolufer, *DCE[LC]* "culto," Corominas–Pascual "culto," Williams;
    N:culto 'learnèd' + latín 'Latin' + V:parlar 'to speak'

cultiparlar 'to speak with affected elegance'; *cultiparlista* 'affected in speech';
    Corominas–Pascual "culto," *EDAF*; Adj:culto 'learnèd' + V:parlar 'to speak'

gordi(n)flón, Arag.–Nav. *-inflas* 'chubby' (cf. Cat. *gordillón*); PA, Andolz,
    Corominas–Pascual; Adj:gord(o) 'fat' + V:inflar 'to swell with air'

(17th c.) *latiniparla* f. 'excessive use of Latin words and phrases', 'cultalatiniparla'
    (Quevedo, *La Culta Latiniparla*, 1629); *EDAF*; N:latino 'Latin' + V:parlar 'to
    speak'

(arch., from 17th c.) *mam-pesada, -pesadilla* 'nightmare'; Covarrubias, *REW* §6391
    "pe(n)sare" (OSp. *mampesad[ill]a* 'Alpdrücken'), *BDE[LC]*, Corominas-Pascual
    "peso," *DECC* "mà," *EDAF*; N:mano 'hand' + N:pesadilla 'nightmare' (from
    pesar [intr.] 'to weigh')

mamporro 'bump, contusion'; Williams, *DCE[LC]* "mano"; N:man(o) 'hand' +
    N:porro 'slap, cuff'

mampresar 'to catch, to begin to break in (horses)' (cf. *mamprender* 'to subdue by
    hand' [q.v.]); *GRS* II §594, AlemB (N Compl + V), *EDAF*; N:*manpres
    'caught by hand' + V:-ar

mampurra 'tip'; Novo Mier; N:man(o) 'hand' V:(?) poner 'to put'

Ast. *mancordiar* 'to tie a cow to a pole, with one end of the rope in one's hand'; Novo
    Mier; N:man(o) 'hand' + N:cuerda 'cord'

(19th c.) *man-cornar*, Ast. *-corniar* 'to rope a steer and hold its horns on the ground,
    rope together a horn and a foreleg of a steer'; 'to tie (two beasts or other
    objects) together (by the horns)', Ast. *-curniar* 'tie one leg of a cow before
    milking it'; *mancuerna* 'pair tied together, yoke of oxen; thong for tying two
    steers'; Amer. *mancornera* 'stirrup strap'; Amer. *mancuernas, mancornillas*
    'cufflinks'; MzP (§331, denominal from *mancuerno*), *Acad* 1970, *DCE[LC]*
    "mano," Novo Mier, *EDAF*; N:man(o) 'hand' + N:cuerno 'horn' + V:-ar

Amer. *salcocho* 'food boiled or cooked in salted water'; *salcochar* 'to boil or cook in
    salted water'; *EDAF*, GdeD 1985 (= *mal cocho*, cf. L. *semicoctus*); N:salcocho
    'cooked in salt' + V:-ar

salpimentar 'to season with salt and pepper; make pleasant'; *EDAF*; N:salpimienta
    'mixture of salt and pepper' + V:-ar

(17th c.) *sietedoblar* (Quevedo) 'to double repeatedly' (cf. OSp. *cincodoblar* 'contestar
    a la cuarta réplica'); Fontecha; N:siete (veces) 'seven (times)' + V:doblar 'to
    double'

sietelevar 'to raise seven points' (in a card game), 'siete puntos llevar'; AlemB (N
    Compl + V); N:siete (puntos) 'seven' + V:llevar 'to raise'

(16th c.) *terraplenar* 'to embank, fill in, terrace' (*pl-* points to Nav-Arag., and cf. Cat. *terraplenar* idem; *DCE[LC]* "tierra"; N:It. terrapieno 'embankment, fortification' + V:-ar

OSp. (13th c.) *tiestherido* 'de mala cabeza'; *DCE[LC]* "tiesto"; N:OSp. tiesta 'head' + V:herir 'to strike'

DUBIOUS

capuzar (naut.) 'to sink (a ship) at the bow', 'to duck, throw into the water'; *DCE[LC]* (from Cat. *capbussar* through blending of *cap* 'head' with *cabussar* 'to put one's head in the water'), *Acad* 1984 (*cabo* + **puteāre* 'to submerge'), GdeD 1985 (*cabo* + **puteāre* 'to submerge'); N:cabo 'head' + V:-ussar

(16th c.) *carcomer* 'to be worm-eaten'; AlemB (N Compl + V); Diez (*carne* 'wood' + *comedĕre*), *REW* §1692 (*cariēs* 'decay'), *DCE[LC]* "carcoma" (**corcona* > *carcoma* 'wood-borer, type of worm' × *comer* 'to eat' (cf. OPr. *corcolar* 'to be worm-eaten')

culcusido 'rough darn or patch'; *EDAF*, *Acad* 1984 (*cul-* = *corcusido* 'sewing with poorly formed stitches'), GdeD 1985 s.v. "constāre"; N:culo 'butt' + V:*(con)consuĕre 'to sew'

(es)camochar 'to prune'; MzP ("ēscam + mutilāre"), *DCE[LC]* "escamocho" (*camochar* as a der. of *escamochar* 'to leave untouched (food and drink)', from *esqui[l]mar* 'to harvest' through *esquimocho[n]* 'leavings of food and drink'), *Acad* 1984 (*caput* + *mutilāre*), GdeD 1985 (id.; *escamochar* as a der. of *camochar*); V:(?) OSp. esquirar 'to shear' + V:MUTILĀRE 'to mutilate'

(16th c.) *escamondar* 'to prune or trim a tree'; m. *escamondo*, f. *escamonda* 'pruning'; *escamondadura* 'pruned branches'; *BDE[LC]* "escamocho" (*escamoch[e]ar* × *mondar*, rejecting ĒSCAM 'scale' + MUNDĀRE 'to clean'), *Acad* 1984 (*ex* + *caput* + mundāre), GdeD 1985 (*caput* + *mundāre*, rejecting Corominas' derivation); V:(?) OSp. esquirar 'to shear' + V:mondar 'to prune'

escamujar 'to prune' (especially olive trees), 'to clear out branches'; Williams, *DCE[LC]* "escamocho" (from *esquimujar*, or from *escamochar* × **desmujar*), *Acad* 1984 (*ex* + *caput* + *mutilāre*); V:(?) OSp. esquirar 'to shear' + V:MUTILĀRE 'to mutilate'

escarapelar 'to quarrel' (said of women), 'to make someone's hair stand on end; peel' (of the skin); *BDE[LC]* "escarapela" (from EX-CARPĔRE, through Ptg. *escar[a]pelar-se*: "claro que luego se entendió como compuesto de *cara* ['face'] + *pelar* ['to peel']")

East León *mastronzar* (n.g.); *REW* §5400 "masturbāre"; N:MANU 'hand' +
    V:TURBĀRE 'to mix up'

Arag. *permudar, premudar* 'to molt (of mammals and birds)', var. of *pelmudar* (q.v.);
    PA; N:piel 'skin'/pelo 'hair' + V:mudar 'to change'

MEDIEVAL AND RENAISSANCE SPANISH NOMINAL ELEMENTS

barbiponiente	N:barba 'beard'	V:poner ✕ PŬNGENTE(M)
botalima	N:bota 'boot'	V:limar
capialzar	N:cabo 'head, end'	V:alzar
caple(u)ta, cablieva	N:cabo	V:LEVĬTA
cablevar	N:cabo	V:llevar
caboprender	N:cabo	V:(com?)prender
cabtener	N:cabo	V:tener, -ir
camajuste	N:cam(in)al 'branch'	V:ajustar
carnes tolendas	N:carne(s) 'flesh'	V:TOLLENDAS
croceficar	N:CRŬCI- 'cross'	V:ficar
fazferir (zaherir)	N:faz 'face'	V:herir
fementido	N:fe 'faith'	V:mentir
lugartinient	N:lugar 'position'	V:tener, -ir
mamparar, desmamparar	N:mano 'hand'	V:amparar
manbor	N:MUNDEBORO 'protector'	
mane(n)trar	N:mano	V:entrar
manfestar	N:mano	V:MAN(I)FESTĀRE
manferir, -herir	N:mano	V:herir
manlieva	N:mano	V:LEVĬTA
manlevar	N:mano	V:llevar
mansessor, marmessor	N:MANŪMISSOR 'executor' ('emancipator')	
mampastor	N:mano	V:PĀSTU(M)
mampuesta, mano postas	N:mano	V:POSĬTU(M)
mantener, manteniente	N:mano	V:tener
mentecapto	N:miente 'mind'	V:catar
mientesmetudo	N:miente(s)	V:meter

misacantano	N:misa 'Mass'	V:cantar
pelechar	N:piel 'skin'/pelo 'hair'	V:echar
pelmudar	N:piel/pelo	V:mudar
salpicado	N:sal 'salt'	V:picar
salpreso	N:sal	V:PRĒ(N)SU(M)
terrateniente	N:tierra 'land'	V:tener
viandante	N:via 'way'	V:andar

MEDIEVAL AND RENAISSANCE SPANISH VERBAL ELEMENTS

camajuste	N:cam(in)al	V:ajustar 'to adapt'
capialzar	N:cabo	V:alzar 'to raise'
mamparar, desmamparar	N:mano	V:amparar 'to protect'
viandante	N:via	V:andar 'to go'
misacantano	N:misa	V:cantar 'to sing'
mentecapto	N:mente	V:catar 'to capture'
pelechar	N:piel/pelo	V:echar 'to throw (off)'
mane(n)trar	N:mano	V:entrar 'to invade'
croceficar	N:CRŬCI-	V:ficar 'to fix (to)'
fazferir (zaherir)	N:faz	V:herir 'to strike'
manferir, -herir	N:mano	V:herir
caple(u)ta, cablieva	N:cabo	V:LEVĬTA 'removed'
manlieva	N:mano	V:LEVĬTA 'raised'
capllevar	N:cabo	V:llevar 'to raise, remove'
manlevar	N:mano	V:llevar
botalima	N:bota	V:limar 'to polish'
manfestar	N:mano	V:MAN(I)FESTĀRE 'to reveal'
fementido	N:fe	V:mentir 'to lie'
mansessor, marmessor	N:MANŪMISSOR 'executor' ('emancipator')	

mientesmetudo	N:miente(s)	V:meter 'to put'
pelmudar	N:piel/pelo	V:mudar 'to change'
mampastor	N:mano	V:PĀSTU(M) 'nourished'
salpicado	N:sal	V:picar 'to pierce'
barbiponiente	N:barba	V:poner × PŬNGENTE(M) 'to put'
mampuesta, mano postas	N:mano	V:POSĬTU(M)
caboprender	N:cabo	V:(com?)prender 'to seize'
salpreso	N:sal	V:PRĒ(N)SU(M) 'seize'
cabtener	N:cabo	V:tener 'to hold'
lugartinient	N:lugar	V:tener, -ir
manteniente, mantener	N:mano	V:tener
terrateniente	N:tierra	V:tener
carnes tolendas	N:carne(s)	V:TOLLENDAS 'to be removed'

MODERN SPANISH NOMINAL ELEMENTS

aguallevado	N:agua 'water'	V:llevar
alicortar	N:ala 'wing'	V:cortar
barbiponiente	N:barba 'beard'	V:poner × PŬNGENTE(M)
botinchau	N:bota 'gourd'	V:hinchar
botinflón	N:bota	V:inflar 'to swell with air'
botalima	N:bota	V:limar
camaliga	N:Cat. cama 'leg'	V:ligar
camajuste	N:cam(in)al 'branch'	V:ajustar
capialzar	N:cabo 'head, end'	V:alzar
cablieva	N:cabo	V:LEVĬTA
caulevar	N:cabo	V:llevar
caltener	N:cabo	V:tener
cachipegar	N:cach[orr]o 'pup'	V:pegar
cachipodar	N:cacho 'bit'	V:podar
carabirar	N:cara 'face'	V:virar

carnestolendas	N:carne(s) 'flesh'	V:TOLLENDAS
cornicantano	N:CORNU 'horn'	V:cantar
croceficar	N:CRŬCI- 'cross'	V:ficar (*FĪGĬCĀRE)
culmené	N:culo 'butt'	V:Cat. menar
zaherir	N:faz	V:herir
fehaciente	N:fe 'faith'	V:hacer
gallocanta	N:gallo 'cock'	V:cantar
gullibaixar	N:güello (Cast. ojo) 'eye'	V:bajar
lugarteniente	N:lugar 'position'	V:tener
mampara, -o	N:mano 'hand'	V:amparar
maniatar	N:mano	V:atar
mancuspir	N:mano	V:Arag. cuspir 'to spit'
maherir	N:mano	V:herir
manlebar	N:mano	V:llevar
maniobrar, manobrar	N:mano	V:obrar
mampostear, mampuesto	N:mano	V:poner
mamprender	N:mano	V:prender
mantener	N:mano	V:tener
mantorn(i)ar	N:mano	V:tornar
mansesor, marmessor	N:MANŪMISSOR 'executor' ('emancipator')	
mentecato	N:miente 'mind'	V:catar
misacantano, cantamisano	N:misa 'Mass'	V:cantar
pelechar	N:piel 'skin'/ pelo 'hair'	V:echar
pelmudar	N:piel/pelo	V:mudar
perniabrir	N:pierna 'leg'	V:abrir
perniquebrar	N:pierna	V:quebrar
poderdante	N:poder 'power'	V:dar
poderhabiente	N:poder	V:haber
reivindicar	N:RĒ(M) 'object'	V:vindicar

salpicar	N:sal 'salt'	V:picar
terrateniente	N:tierra 'land'	V:tener
viandante	N:vía 'way'	V:andar

MODERN SPANISH VERBAL ELEMENTS

perniabrir	N:pierna	V:abrir 'to open'
camajuste	N:cam(in)al	V:ajustar 'to adapt'
capialzar	N:cabo	V:alzar 'to raise'
mampara, -o	N:mano	V:amparar 'to protect'
viandante	N:vía	V:andar 'to go'
maniatar	N:mano	V:atar 'to bind'
gullibaixar	N:güello	V:bajar 'to lower'
cornicantano	N:CORNU	V:cantar 'to sing'
gallocanta	N:gallo	V:cantar
misacantano	N:misa	V:cantar
mentecato	N:miente	V:catar 'to capture'
alicortar	N:ala	V:cortar 'to cut (off)'
mancuspir	N:mano	V:Arag. cuspir 'to spit'
poderdante	N:poder	V:dar 'to give'
pelechar	N:piel/pelo	V:echar 'to throw (off)'
croceficar	N:CRŬCI-	V:ficar (*FĪGĬCĀRE) 'to fix (to)'
poderhabiente	N:poder	V:haber 'to have'
fehaciente	N:fe	V:hacer 'to do'
zaherir	N:faz	V:herir 'to strike'
maherir	N:mano	V:herir
botinchau	N:bota	V:hinchar 'to swell'

botinflón	N:bota	V:inflar 'to swell with air'
camaliga	N:Cat. cama	V:ligar 'to bind'
botalima	N:bota	V:limar 'to polish'
aguallevado	N:agua	V:llevar (Mod.) 'to carry, take'
capleta	N:cabo	V:LEVĬTA 'raised'
caulevar	N:cabo	V:llevar
manlebar	N:mano	V:llevar
culmené	N:culo	V:Cat. menar 'to lead, bring'
pelmudar	N:piel/pelo	V:mudar 'to change'
maniobrar, manobrar	N:mano	V:obrar 'to work'
cachipegar	N:cach[orr]o	V:pegar 'to stick'
salpicar	N:sal	V:picar 'to chop up, poke'
cachipodar	N:cacho	V:podar 'to prune'
barbiponiente	N:barba	V:poner × PŬNGENTE(M) 'to place'
mampostear, -puesto	N:mano	V:poner
mamprender	N:mano	V:prender 'to grasp'
perniquebrar	N:pierna	V:quebrar 'to break'
caltener	N:cabo	V:tener 'to hold'
lugarteniente	N:lugar	V:tener
mantener	N:mano	V:tener
terrateniente	N:tierra	V:tener
carnestolendas	N:carne(s)	V:TOLLENDAS 'removed'
mantorn(i)ar	N:mano	V:tornar 'to turn'
reivindicar	N:RĒ(M)	V:vindicar 'to avenge'
carabirar	N:cara	V:virar 'to turn'

Appendix E

Medieval Latin Corpus

Vernacular items from Latin glossaries, here enclosed in double square brackets, are fully analyzed in Appendices A–D.

aquifluis 'currents'; *GMLCat*; N:aqua 'water' + V:fluĕre 'flow'

aquivergium 'declivity into which water flows'; *aqua-, aqu(a)e-, aquis-versus* 'slope'; Forcellini, DuC, Maigne; N:aqua 'water' + V:versus 'poured'

canĕre missam 'to sing Mass'; *GMLCat*; N:missa 'Mass' + V:canĕre 'to sing'

cantāre missam, -as 'cantare ecclesiam, to sing Mass'; (1119) *missecantania* 'ecclesiastical gift offered for celebration of Mass'; *NGML, GMLCat*; N:mĭssam 'Mass' + V:cantāre 'to sing'

capitilavium 'lotion for anointing the head'; Alvar–Pottier 1983; N:caput 'head' + V:lavāre 'to wash'

cap(ut) tenēre, captenēre 'to maintain, protect'; *capitennium* '(payment for royal) protection'; *in capite tenēre* 'to hold a fief from the king'; DuC, Maigne; N:caput 'head, end' + V:tenēre 'to hold'

carementrannus 'Mardi Gras, or first Sunday of Lent'; [[OFr. *caresmentrant, caramantrant* 'Tuesday before Ash Wednesday']]; DuC; N:quadragesima 'period of 40 days' + V:Gallo-Romance entrer/entrar 'to enter'

[[OFr. *caresmeprenant*]]; DuC; N:quādragēsima 'period of 40 days' + V:Gallo-Romance prendre 'to take, begin'

Milan (1130) *carne-levale; -levarium,* (1195) *-levamine* 'first Sunday of Lent'; Diez "carnevale," DuC; N:carō 'flesh' + V:levāre 'to remove'

carnemlaxāre 'carnaval'; Maigne; N:carō 'flesh' + V:laxāre 'to release'

carni(s)privium, carnisbrevium, -brevii 'Lent, Shrove Tuesday'; Diez "carnevale," Forcellini, Maigne, B-L; N:carō 'flesh' + V:privārī 'to deprive'

[[OSp. *carnestolendas* 'Lent, the three days that precede Lent', from the L. phrase *dominica ante carnes tollendas*]]; *GMLCat*; N:carō 'flesh' + V:TOLLENDAS 'removed'

carnestoltas 'abstinencia de carne', [[OCat. *carnestoltas* 'first day of Lent']]; *GMLCat*; N:carō 'flesh' + V:*TOLLĬTAS 'removed'

car(r)ŏpera, carriŏpera 'cart-service'; *carŏperāre* 'to provide cart-service'; DuC, Maigne, B-L, *NGML*; N:carrus 'cart' + N:ŏpera 'work'/V:ŏperāre 'to work'

Cl.L. *clavifixus* '(crucified) Christ'; Forcellini; N:clavus 'nail' + V:fixus 'fixed (to)'

crucem fīgere 'to crucify'; *crucifīxus* '(crucified) Christ'; DuC; N:crux 'cross' + V:fīgere 'to fix (to)'

crucissignatio 'sign of the cross'; *crucesignati* 'Crusaders'; DuC, *GMLCat* "crucis signum"; N:crux 'cross' + V:signāre, signus 'to sign, mark'

(10th c.) *dĕōdicāta (femina)* 'nun, woman consecrated to God'; *GMLCat*; N:dĕus 'God' + V:(dē)dicātus 'dedicated'

dīcere missam 'to say Mass'; *GMLCat*; N:mĭssa 'Mass' + V:dīcere 'to say'

Late L. *fidedictor* (St. Augustine, hap.) 'surety, bail'; *fidedicĕre* 'to go bail for'; Forcellini, Maigne, L-S; N:fidēs 'faith' + V:dīcere 'to say'

Cl.L. *fidĕicommissum* 'feoffment in trust, testator's request that his heir convey a specified part of the estate to another person, or permit another person to enjoy such a part', *fidĕicommittĕre* 'to bequeath in trust' (lit. 'to entrust s.th. to s.o.'s good faith'); Forcellini, Webster's (2d ed.), *FEW* "fideicommissum," L-S; N:fidēs 'faith' + V:committĕre 'to commit'

fidefragus, fidefragium 'traitor'; Maigne; N:fidēs 'faith' + V:fractus 'broken'

Late L. *fidejubēre* 'to go bail for'; *fidejussiō*, Brit.L. *fedejusseo* 'giving surety or bail', Eng. (arch.) *fidejussion* 'bail, guarantee'; Late L. *fidĕ(i)jussor, fidejutrīx* (fem.) 'sponsor', Eng. (arch.) *fidejussor* 'one who enters into or authorizes a fidejussion'; Forcellini, *FEW* "fidejussor," B-J; N:fidēs 'faith' + V:iubēre 'to command'

fidejūrāre 'to swear'; Maigne; N:fidēs 'faith' + V:iūrāre 'to swear'

fidem levāre 'to swear an oath (with raised hand)'; DuC; N:fidēs 'faith' + V:levāre 'to raise'

(794) *fidementūtus, -mentirosus* 'oathbreaker, traitor'; *fidementūta, fidēs mentūta* 'breach of faith, treachery'; DuC, Maigne, Latham; N:fidēs 'faith' + V:Cl.L. mentītus '(having) lied' (cf. Sp. *mentira* 'lie')

fideprōmittĕre 'to go bail for'; Maigne; N:fidēs 'faith' + V:prōmittĕre 'to promise'

Gmc. *fidesfacta* (from Teutonic Law) (n.g.); Webster's (2d ed.); N:fidēs 'faith' + V:factus 'made, done'

lociservātor 'replacement, lieutenant', *locumservāns*; DuC, Maigne; N:locus 'position' + V:servāre 'to keep, reserve'

(10th c.) *locoposĭtus* 'replacement, lociservator'; Maigne; N:locus 'position' +
V:posĭtus 'placed'

locum tenēre 'to replace'; *locumtenēns* 'governor', *locumtenen[tē]s, locatenentēs*
'lieutenants'; *locumtenentia* 'charge, administrator', 'curate's vicar (substitute)';
Brit.Eng. *locum* '(professional) substitute'; DuC, Maigne; N:locus 'position' +
V:tenēre 'to hold'

mamposta (via OSp. *manpuesta*, from L. *manūpos[ĭ]ta*), *mampostarium* 'tax'; *NGML*;
N:manus 'hand' + V:posĭtus 'placed'

manaida, manaheda 'cash payment' (?) (identifiable with OFr. *manaye*, OPr. *manaya*
'power, possession'; or with 'household'?); *NGML*; N:manus 'hand' +
V:adiūtāre 'to aid'

Padua (1187) *manpresus, manupresum* 'detainee', 'arrêté'; *NGML*; N:manus 'hand'
+ V:prē(n)sus 'seized'

(1181) *manucapĕre* 'to go bail for', (1293) 'to undertake, decide'; *capio in manum, ad
manum* 'to take into the lord's possession'; *manu-captus* 'captive'; (1306)
-captio 'bail, mainprise, fidejussio'; *-captor* 'guarantor'; DuC, Maigne, B-J, B-L,
NGML; N:manus 'hand' + V:capere 'to take'

man(u)ducō, -ductō 'to lead, trace, dig'; *-ductus* 'led by the hand'; *-ductiō* 'leading by
the hand; safe passage'; Latham, *NGML*; N:manus 'hand' + V:dūcĕre 'to lead'

manū factus, manefactus 'handmade', *manufactum* 'product of family industry, paid
to one's lord'; [[OPr. *mafat*]]; *NGML*; N:manus 'hand' + V:factus 'made'

manulavium 'lavatory'; DuC; N:manus 'hand' + V:lavāre 'to wash'

manūlevāre ('to raise the hand to swear to an oath', and cf. *fidem levāre* [q.v.] and
manū fidem dare) 'to raise or levy money, go bail for', (1125) 'to borrow';
manulevatum, -levatio 'bail'; *manulevatio*, [[OArag. *manuleuta, manleuta*
'abandon, relinquishing of a property']], [[Mid.Fr. *mainlevée* 'restoration of
goods']]; (1131) *manleita* 'requisition'; DuC, Maigne, *NGML*; N:manus 'hand'
+ V:levāre 'to raise'

manum dare 'to swear allegiance'; DuC; N:manus 'hand' + V:dare 'to give'

Cl.L. *manū mittō, manūmittō*, Late L. *manūmittĕre* 'to release from one's power, set
free'; Cl.L. *manū missiō, manūmissiō*, Med.L. *manmessio* 'act of freeing,
emancipation'; (1154) *marmissio* 'freed (slave)'; *manūmissor* 'testamentary
executor'; Forcellini, DuC, *NGML*; N:manus 'hand' + V:mittĕre 'to send'

(800) *manūŏpera* 'manual work-service', 'corvée manuelle', vars.: *man-, mane-*, (1080)
manuum-, mann-opera, mannwerch; *manū ŏperāre, manuoperor*, Brit.L.
manuoperāre 'to work land'; Maigne, Latham, *NGML*; N:manus 'hand' +
V:ŏpera 'work'

(1124) *manūpāstus, mani-,* Brit.L. *mainpastus* 'household, protégés of a lord, servant';
Eng. (arch.) *mainpast* 'man's household'; Maigne, Latham, Webster's (2d ed.),
NGML; N:manus 'hand' + V:pāstus 'nourished'

(1080) *manūprisum* 'handing-over, transfer of a slave to a buyer'; Brit.L. (1295)
manuprisa, (1346) *meinprisa* 'bail, (arch.) mainprise' (Webster's [2d ed.]:
'undertaking of suretyship'; "the exact distinction between mainprise and bail
is not now known"); Latham, *NGML*; N:manus 'hand' + V:prae-, prē(he)ndere
'to seize'

Cl.L. *manū tenēre* 'to have personal knowledge of, know for certain'; *manibus teneri*
'to be certain'; Med.L. *manūteneo, mantineo,* (1015) *mantengo, maniteneo,*
manū-tenēre, -tere 'to support, maintain, defend; preserve; furnish'; Brit.L.
(1408) 'to take an oath'; *man-, mayntenementum* 'support, maintenance';
manūtenēns 'protector; powerful personnage'; *dēmanūtenēre,* [[OCat.
desmantenir]] 'to remove protection'; Forcellini, Maigne, Castro, L-S, *NGML,*
GMLCat; N:manus 'hand' + V:tenēre 'to hold'

(1128) *manūtrādĕre* 'to deliver, transfer'; Maigne; N:manus 'hand' + V:trādĕre 'to
hand over'

(693)   *mundeboro, mundiburdus* 'protector', vars.: *mandeburda, mainburnus,*
mamburnos, mamburditor, [[OFr. *mainbour*]], [[OPr. *manbor*]], [[OSp.
manbor]]; *mundi-, munde-burdium, maniburnia, mamburnia, -bornia* (from
[[OFr. *mainbournie*]]) 'protection (of king, church, Holy See)'; *mam-,*
mun-burnīre, -burnāre (←[[OFr. *mainbornir, -burnir*]]) 'to govern'; DuC,
NGML; N:OHG mundeboro 'protector' (N:Gmc. mund 'hand' + V:Gmc.
beran 'to protect'), cf. also Gmc. *mund* 'protection', G. *Vormund* 'guardian'

salpresa 'preserved with salt'; DuC (*salpresa* 'piscis genus'), *DCE[LC]* "sal" (-*pres[o]*
via Late L. **spersus,* from Cl.L. *sparsus* 'sprinkled'); N:sāl 'salt' + V:prē(n)sus
'seized'

Brit.L. *terram tenēns, terre-tenēns, -tenents, -tenant,* [[OArag. *terrastenentes*]]
'land-holder'; Latham; N:terra 'land' + V:tenēre 'to hold'

terrigenae 'indigenous', [[MFr. *terre-né* 'earthborn']]; DuC; N:terra 'land' + V:genus
'born'

Bibliography

The bibliography is divided into the following sections:
1. Indo-European and Latin
2. General Romance
3. French
4. Occitan
5. Catalan
6. Spanish
7. Italian and Other Romance
8. General Linguistics

1.1 INDO-EUROPEAN AND LATIN DICTIONARIES/GRAMMARS

Blatt, Franz, ed. 1957–. *Novum Glossarium Mediae Latinitatis (800–1200)*. Hafniae: Munksgaard. L–N; O–.

Brugmann, K., & B. Delbrück. 1897–1916 (2d ed.). *Grundriss der vergleichenden Grammatik der indogermanischen Sprachen*. II: *Allgemeines. Zusammensetzung (Komposita)*. Strasbourg: Karl Trübner. *A Comparative Grammar of the Indo-Germanic Languages*. II: *Morphology*, trans. from 1st ed. (1888) by R. S. Conway & W. H. D. Rouse. New York: Westermann & Co., 1891.

Buck, Carl Darling. 1933; 1969 (repr.). *Comparative Grammar of Greek and Latin*. Chicago: University of Chicago Press.

Burrow, Thomas. 1965 (2d ed.); 1973 (3d ed.). *The Sanskrit Language*. London: Faber & Faber.

Debrunner, Albert. 1917. *Griechische Wortbildungslehre*. Heidelberg: Winter.

Du Cange, Dominus. 1845. *Glossarium Mediae et Infimae Latinitatis*. Paris: Firmin-Didot.

Ernout, Alfred, & Antoine Meillet. 1979 (rev. 4th ed., 3d printing). *Dictionnaire étymologique de la langue latine*. Paris: Klincksieck.

Glare, P. G. W. 1982. *Oxford Latin Dictionary*. Oxford: At the Clarendon Press.

Glossarium Mediae Latinitatis Cataloniae. 1960–79. Vols. 1, 2 (A–Dotalis). Barcelona: Universidad de Barcelona, Escuela de Filología.

Hofmann, J. B. 1964–65. *Lateinische Syntax und Stilistik.* Rev. by A. Szantyr. Handbuch der Altertumswissenschaft, II:2:ii. Munich: C. H. Beck.

Latham, Ronald E. 1965. *Revised Medieval Latin Word List from British and Irish Sources.* London. Rev. of J.-H. Baxter & C. Johnson, *Medieval Latin Word List from British and Irish Sources*; Oxford: Oxford University Press, 1934.

———. 1975, 1981. *Dictionary of Medieval Latin from British Sources.* Fasc. I–II: A–C. London: Oxford University Press.

Lewis, Charlton, & Charles Short. 1969 (1st ed. 1897). *A Latin Dictionary.* Oxford: At the Clarendon Press.

Liddell, Henry George, & Robert Scott, rev. by Sir Henry Stuart Jones. 1968 (9th ed.). *A Greek-English Lexicon, with a Supplement.* Oxford: At the Clarendon Press.

Maigne d'Arnis, W.-H. 1890. *Lexicon manuale ad scriptores mediae et infimae Latinitatis.* Paris: Garnier.

Niermeyer, J. F. 1976. *Mediae Latinitatis Lexicon Minus.* Leiden: Brill.

Risch, Ernst. 1937; 1974 (rev. 2d ed.). *Wortbildung der homerischen Sprache.* Berlin & Leipzig: W. de Gruyter.

Souter, A. 1949. *A Glossary of Later Latin to 600 A.D.* Oxford: At the Clarendon Press.

Stolz, Friedrich, & J. H. Schmalz. 1926–28; 1977 (5th ed., rev. by Manu Leumann and J. B. Hofmann). *Lateinische Grammatik.* I: *Laut- und Formenlehre.* Handbuch der Altertumswissenschaft, II:2:i. Munich: C. H. Beck.

Walde, A., & J. B. Hofmann. 1938–56 (3d ed.). *Lateinisches etymologisches Wörterbuch.* 3 vols. Heidelberg: Winter.

1.2 INDO-EUROPEAN AND LATIN SECONDARY SOURCES

Adams, D. Q. 1983. "Latin *mas* and *masturbārī*." *Glotta* 63:241–47.

Bader, Françoise. 1962. *La Formation des composés nominaux du latin.* Ann. Littéraires de Besançon, 64. Paris: Les Belles Lettres.

Juret, A.-C. 1937. *Formation des noms et des verbes en latin et en grec.* Paris: Les Belles Lettres.

Lehmann, W. P. 1969. "Proto-Indo-European Compounds in Relation to Other PIE Syntactic Patterns." *Acta Linguistica Hafniensia* 12:1–20.

———. 1974; 1980 (2d printing). *Proto-Indo-European Syntax.* Austin: University of Texas Press.

Meillet, Antoine. 1934 (7th ed.). *Introduction à l'étude des langues indo-européennes.* Paris: Hachette. (Repr. 1964, with Introduction by George C. Buck, Univ. of Alabama Press).

Meunier, Louis-Francis. 1872. *Les Composés syntactiques en grec, latin, français et subsidiairement en zend et en indien.* Paris: L. Durand & Pédone Lauriel.

Salus, Peter. 1965. "The Types of Nominal Compound of Indo-European." *Orbis* 14:38–62.

Saussure, Ferdinand de. 1909. "Sur les composés latins du type *agricola.*" *Mélanges Havet*, 459–71. Paris: Hachette.

Staal, J.F. 1966. "Room at the Top in Sanskrit. Ancient and Modern Descriptions of Nominal Composition." *Indo-Iranian Journal* 9:165–98.

2.1 GENERAL ROMANCE DICTIONARIES/GRAMMARS

Diez, Friedrich. 1887 (5th ed). *Etymologisches Wörterbuch der romanischen Sprachen,* with Supplement by A. Scheler. Bonn: Adolph Marcus.

Körting, Gustav. 1891; 1907 (rev. 3d ed.). *Lateinisch-romanisches Wörterbuch.* Paderborn: F. Schöningh.

Malkiel, Yakov. 1960. "A Tentative Typology of Romance Historical Grammars." *Lingua* 9:321–416. (Repr. in *Essays on Linguistic Themes*, 71–164. Oxford: Blackwell; Berkeley & Los Angeles: University of California Press, 1968.)

Meyer-Lübke, Wilhelm. 1895. *Grammatik der romanischen Sprachen.* Vol. 2: *Formenlehre.* Leipzig: Reisland.

———. 1911[–20]; 1930–35 (3d ed.). *Romanisches etymologisches Wörterbuch.* Heidelberg: Winter.

2.2 GENERAL ROMANCE SECONDARY SOURCES

Bambeck, Manfred. 1959. *Lateinisch-Romanische Wortstudien.* Wiesbaden: Steiner Verlag.

Fernández González, J. Ramón. 1981. "Topónimos compuestos románicos: la estructura 'determinado + determinante'/'determinante + determinado'." *Verba* 9:229–45.

Giurescu, Anca. 1970. "Osservazioni sulla categoria dei composti romanzi." *RRL* 15:261–66.

———. 1975. *Les Mots composés dans les langues romanes.* Janua Linguarum: Series Practica, 228. The Hague & Paris: Mouton.

Lloyd, Paul M. 1964. "An Analytical Survey of Studies in Romance Word Formation." *RPh* 17/4:736–70.

Malkiel, Yakov. 1945. *Development of the Latin Suffixes '-antia' and '-entia' in the Romance Languages, with Special Regard to Ibero-Romance. UCPL* Vol. I:4, 41–188. Berkeley & Los Angeles: University of California Press.

———. 1976. "Contacts between BLASPHEMĀRE and AESTIMĀRE (With an Excursus on the Etymology of Hisp. *tomar*)." *RPh* 30/1:102–17.

———. 1984. "El engranaje de las peripecias románicas de *ferre* y *ferīre* (con particular atención a *reyerta* y *zaherir*)." *MR* 9:161–81.

Wright, Roger. 1982. *Late Latin and Early Romance in Spain and Carolingian France.* Liverpool: Cairns.

3.1 FRENCH DICTIONARIES/GRAMMARS

Baldinger, Kurt, J.D. Gendron, & G. Straka. 1971–. *Dictionnaire étymologique de l'ancien français.* Tübingen: Niemeyer; Québec: Presses de l'Université Laval.

Bloch, Oscar, & W. von Wartburg. 1932; 1968 (5th ed.). *Dictionnaire étymologique de la langue française.* Paris: PUF.

Bos, A. 1891. *Glossaire de la langue d'oïl.* Paris: Maisonneuve.

Corblet, Jules. 1851. *Glossaire étymologique et comparatif du patois picard, ancien et moderne.* Paris: Dumoulin, V. Didron & Techener. Repr. Geneva: Slatkine, 1978.

Creore, A. E. 1972. *A Word Index to the Poetic Works of Ronsard.* Leeds: W. S. Maney & Son.

Darmesteter, Arsène, A. Hatzfeld, & Antoine Thomas. 1889–1901; 1932 (9th ed.). *Dictionnaire général de la langue française du commencement du XVIIe siècle jusqu'à nos jours.* Paris: Delagrave.

Dauzat, Albert, J. Dubois, & H. Mitterand. 1964. *Nouveau dictionnaire étymologique et historique.* Paris: Larousse.

Debrie, René. 1984. *Glossaire du moyen picard.* Amiens: Université de Picardie.

de Gorog, Ralph. 1973. *Lexique français moderne–ancien français.* Athens: University of Georgia Press.

Dud'huit, Albert, Alain Morin, & Marie-Rose Simoni-Aurembou. 1979. *Trésor du parler percheron.* Mortagnes sur Perche: Association des Amis du Perche.

Gamillscheg, Ernst. 1926–28; 1966–68 (rev. 2d ed.). *Etymologisches Wörterbuch der französischen Sprache.* Heidelberg: Winter.

Godefroy, Frédéric. 1880–92; 1937–38 (repr.). *Dictionnaire de l'ancienne langue française et de tous ses dialectes du IXe au XVe siècle.* 10 vols. Paris: Libr. des Sciences et des Arts.

———. 1901; 1982 (repr.). *Lexique de l'ancien français.* Paris: Champion.

Greimas, A. J. 1969. *Dictionnaire de l'ancien français jusqu'au milieu du 14e siècle.* Paris: Larousse.

Haigneré, Daniel. 1903. *Le Patois boulonnais comparé avec les patois du Nord de la France*. Vol 2: *Vocabulaire*. Boulogne-sur-Mer. (Repr. Geneva: Slatkine, 1969.)

Littré, Emile. 1873–83. *Dictionnaire de la langue française*. 5 vols. Paris: Hachette.

Mineau, Robert, & Lucien Racinoux. 1975. *Glossaire des vieux parlers du département de la Vienne*. Poitiers: Le Bouquiniste.

——. 1981. *Glossaire des vieux parlers poitevins*. Poitiers: Brissaud.

Moisy, Henri. 1887. *Dictionnaire du patois normand*. Caen: Henri Delesques.

——. 1895. *Glossaire comparatif anglo-normand*. Caen: Libr. E. Brunet.

Nyrop, Kristoffer. 1908; 1924 (2d ed.), 1936 (repr.). *Grammaire historique de la langue française*. Vol. 3: *Formation des mots*. Copenhagen: Gyldendalske Boghandel, Nordisk Forlag.

Robert, Paul. 1958–64. *Dictionnaire alphabétique et analogique de la langue française*. Paris: Société du Nouveau Littré.

Stone, Louise W., W. Rothwell, & T. B. W. Reid. 1977–81. *Anglo-Norman Dictionary*. Fasc. 1–2, A–E. London: Modern Humanities Research Association.

Tobler, Adolf, & Ernst Lommatzsch. 1925–. *Altfranzösisches Wörterbuch*. Vol. 10: *Temeleor–tympanistes*. Wiesbaden: F. Steiner, 1976.

Trésor de la langue française. 1977–86. *Dictionnaire de la langue du XIXe et du XXe siècles (1789–1960)*. 12 vols., A–Pénétrer. Paris: CNRS.

Verrier, A.-J., & R. Onillon. 1908. *Glossaire étymologique et historique des patois et parlers de l'Anjou*. 2 vols. in 1. Angers. (Repr. Geneva: Slatkine, 1970).

Walker, Douglas C. 1982. *Dictionnaire inverse de l'ancien français*. Ottawa: Editions de l'Université d'Ottawa.

Wartburg, Walther von. 1922–. *Französisches etymologisches Wörterbuch. Eine Darstellung des galloromanischen Sprachschatzes*. Vol. 1, Leipzig: Klopp; later volumes, Basel: Helbing & Lichtenhahn, then Druck und Verlag Zbinden.

Wartburg, Walther von, H. E. Keller, & Robert Geuljans. 1969 (2d ed.). *Bibliographie des dictionnaires patois gallo-romains*. Geneva: Droz. (1st ed. *Bibliographie des dictionnaires patois gallo-romains*. Geneva: Droz, 1934. *Supplément*, by H.-E. Keller: Geneva: Droz; Lille: Giard, 1955.)

3.2 FRENCH SECONDARY SOURCES

Akeret, Walter. 1953. *Le concept 'gifle' dans les parlers gallo-romans. Etude sémantique*. St-Gall: Eirene M. Pfändler.

Barbier, P. 1930. "A Contribution to the History of a Germanic Prefix in French and the French Dialects." *RLiR* 6:210–305.

Bennett, W. A. 1977. "Predicate Binomials in French." *Lingua* 41:331–42.

Bierbach, Mechtild. 1982. *Die Verbindung von Verbal- und Nominalelement im Französischen: Beitrag zur Geschichte eines Wortbildungsmusters*. Tübingen: Narr.

———. 1983. "Les Composés du type *porte-feuille* : essai d'analyse historique." *TLL* 21:137–55.

Chamard, Henri. 1939. *Histoire de la Pléiade*. Paris: H. Didier.

Darmesteter, Arsène. 1874, 1894 (2d ed.). *Traité de la formation des mots composés dans la langue française comparée aux autres langues romanes et au latin*. Paris: A. Franck. (Repr. Paris: Champion, 1967.)

———. 1877. *De la création actuelle des mots nouveaux dans la langue française*. Paris: F. Vieweg.

Guiraud, Pierre. 1961. "Le Champ morpho-sémantique des composés tautologiques." *ZRPh* 77:444–69.

Harris, M. Roy. 1972. "Words and Word Criteria in French." *History and Structure of French: Essays in Honor of Prof. T. B. W. Reid*, 117–33, Oxford: Oxford University Press.

Klingebiel, Kathryn. 1983. "Arsène Darmesteter's *Traité de la formation des mots composés*: 1874, 1894, and Beyond." *RPh* 36/3:386–90.

———. 1986a. "Transformational vs. Structural Morphology, with an Excursus on Compounding." *RPh* 39:323–35.

Kuryłowicz, Jerzy. 1976. "Les Composés du type fr. *maintenir*." *KN* 23:163–65.

Marty-Laveaux, Charles. 1896–98. *La Langue de la Pléiade*. Paris: A. Lemerre.

Orr, John. 1951. "Quelques Mises au point étymologiques. I. Mots à redoublement synonymique: *bousculer, culbuter, bouleverser, houspiller*. II. Autres composés ou dérivés: *colporter* et *courbature, vermoulu, saupoudrer, morfondu*." *Mélanges Dauzat*, 245–56. Paris: d'Artrey.

Porteau, Paul. 1961. "Fossiles linguistiques en français moderne." *Deux Etudes de sémantique française*, 41–88, Paris: PUF.

Rickard, Peter. 1968. *La Langue française au XVIe siècle*. Cambridge, England: Cambridge University Press.

Sainéan, Lazare. 1922–23. *La Langue de Rabelais*. Paris: E. de Bocard.

Spence, N. C. W. 1969. "Composé nominal, locution et syntagme libre." *La Linguistique* 1969/2:5–26.

Spitzer, Leo. 1910. *Die Wortbildung als stilistisches Mittel, exemplifiziert an Rabelais. Nebst einem Anhang über die Wortbildung bei Balzac in seinen "Contes drolatiques."* Halle: Niemeyer.

Thiele, Johannes. 1978. "Zum Verhältnis von Theorie und Methode in A. Darmesteters lexikologischen Arbeiten unter besonderer Berücksichtigung der Wortbildung." *ZPhon* 31:613–18.

———. 1981. *Wortbildung der französischen Gegenwartssprache: ein Abriss.* Leipzig: Verlag Enzyklopädie.

Thomas, Antoine. 1895. "Les Noms composés et la dérivation en français et en provençal." *Romania* 24:339–56. (Repr. in *Essais de philologie française*, 50–73. Paris: E. Bouillon, 1898.)

Wartburg, W. von. 1922. "Neuschöpfung von Präfixen im Neufranzösischen." *Miscellanea Schuchardt dedicata a Hugo Schuchardt per il suo 80o anniversario*, 116ff. Geneva: L.S. Olschki, 1922.

4.1 OCCITAN DICTIONARIES/GRAMMARS

Achard, Claude François. 1785. *Vocabulaire françois-provençal. (Dictionnaire de la Provence et du Comté Venaissin*, vol. 1) 2 vols. Marseilles: J. Mossy. (Repr. Geneva: Slatkine, 1971.)

Alibert, Louis. 1966; 1977 (2d ed.); 1981 (repr.). *Dictionnaire occitan-français d'après les parlers languedociens.* Toulouse: IEO.

———. 1976 (2d ed.). *Gramatica occitana segon los parlars lengadocians.* Montpellier: CEO.

Allanche, Louis. 1941. *Eléments de grammaire du dialecte quercynol, suivis de proverbes et dictions.* Montauban: Imprimerie G. Forestié.

Anglade, Joseph. 1921; 1977 (repr.). *Grammaire de l'ancien provençal.* Paris: Klincksieck.

Arnaudin, Félix. (n.d.) *Glossaire du parler de Labouheyre.* A–T. Files in keeping of Jacques Boisgontier, C.N.R.S., Toulouse.

Avril, J.-T. 1839–40. *Dictionnaire provençal-français, suivi d'un Vocabulaire français-provençal, et enrichi de notes historiques et curieuses.* Apt: Cartier. (Repr. Geneva: Slatkine; Marseilles: Laffitte, 1970.)

Azaïs, Gabriel. 1877–78. *Dictionnaire des idiomes romans du Midi de la France.* 3 vols. Paris: Maisonneuve; Montpellier: Publications de la Société pour l'Etude des Langues Romanes.

Baldinger, Kurt. 1975a, 1977, 1980, 1982. *Dictionnaire onomasiologique de l'ancien gascon*, rédigé avec le concours de Inge Popelar. 5 fascs. in 4 vols. Tübingen: Niemeyer.

———. 1975b, 1980, 1982, 1984, 1986. *Dictionnaire onomasiologique de l'ancien occitan*, rédigé avec le concours de Inge Popelar. 4 fascs.; *Supplément*, 2 fasc. Tübingen: Niemeyer.

Barthe, Roger. 1970; 1973 (2d ed.). *Lexique français-occitan.* Paris: Les Amis de la Langue d'Oc.

———. 1972; 1980 (2d ed.). *Lexique occitan-français.* Paris: Les Amis de la Langue d'Oc.

Becquevort, Raymond. (n.d.) *Le parler d'Arconsat (Puy-de-Dôme): Recherches sur un lexique des confins arverno-foréziens.* Clermont-Ferrand: Cercle Occitan d'Auvergne–Auvèrnha Tarà d'Oc.

Béronie, Nicolas. 1823. *Dictionnaire du Bas-Limousin (Corrèze) et plus particulièrement des environs de Tulle, mis en ordre, augmenté et publié par Joseph-Anne Vialle.* Tulle: Imprimerie J.-M. Drapeau. (Repr. Geneva: Slatkine; Marseilles: Laffitte, 1971.)

Bonnaud, Pierre. 1975. *Vocabulaire du Cantal du Nord et de la Margeride Auvergnate.* Clermont-Ferrand: Cercle Occitan d'Auvergne–Auvèrnha Tarà d'Oc.

———. 1976. "Lexique français-auvergnat de base." *Petit manuel de base de l'auvergnat,* 1–30. Clermont-Ferrand: CRRDP.

———. 1978, 1979, 1980. *Grand Dictionnaire français-auvergnat.* 3 vols.: A–D, E–N, O–Z. Beaumont: Auvernhà, Tarà d'Oc (chez l'auteur).

Castellana, Georges. 1947. *Dictionnaire français-niçois.* Nice: Editions Ludographiques Françaises. (Repr. Nice: Serre, 1978.)

———. 1952; 1977 (repr.). *Dictionnare niçois-français.* Nice: Serre.

Cénac-Moncaut, Justin-Edouard. 1863. *Dictionnaire gascon-français, dialecte du département du Gers, suivi d'un abrégé de grammaire gasconne.* Paris: Aubry. (Repr. Geneva: Slatkine; Marseilles: Laffitte, 1971.)

Daniel, Jean. 1914. *Dictionnaire périgourdin.* I: *Dictionnaire français-périgourdin.* Périgueux: Imprimerie Ribes. (Repr., with preface by Marcel Fournier, Geneva: Slatkine; Marseilles: Laffitte, 1978.)

Darrigrand, Robert. 1974; 1984 (4th ed.) *Initiation au gascon.* Orthez: Per Noste.

Dhéralde, Léon. 1969. *Dictionnaire de la langue limousine (diciounari de lo lingo limousino).* Publié et augmenté selon l'œuvre inédite de Dom L. Duclou (1774), par Maurice Robert. 2 vols. Limoges: Société d'Ethnographie du Limousin, de la Marche et des Régions Voisines.

D'Hombres, Maximin. 1884. *Dictionnaire languedocien-français contenant les définitions, radicaux et étymologies des mots . . .* Alais: Imprimerie A. Brugueirolle.

Dupleich. 1843. *Dictionnaire patois-français. Ou choix intéressant de mots patois rendus en français, suivis de remarques pour la plupart de ceux qui y donnent lieu.* St-Gaudens: Imprimerie de J.-M. Tajan.

d'Estalenx, Jean-François. 1968. "Dictionnaire idéologique gascon-français." MS, Toulouse.

Foix, Vincent, l'abbé. 1907. "Les Termes injurieux du gascon des Landes." MS.

Fourvières, Xavier de [Rodolph Rieux]. 1973. *Lou pichot trésor.* Dictionnaire provençal-français et français-provençal. Avignon: Aubanel. (1st ed. [n.p.], 1902.)

Gary, Léger, l'abbé. 1845. *Dictionnaire patois-français à l'usage du département du Tarn et des départements circonvoisins.* Castres: Imprimerie J.-L. Pujol. (Repr. Geneva: Slatkine; Marseilles: Laffitte, 1969.)

Gonfroy, Gérard. 1975. *Dictionnaire normatif limousin-français.* Tulle: Editions "Lemouzi."

de Grateloup [*sic*]. 1886; 1887. "Grammaire gasconne et française." *Revue des Langues Romanes* 30:5–52; 31:15–48.

Honnorat, Samuel-Jude. 1846, 1848. *Dictionnaire de la langue d'oc ancienne et moderne. Vocabulaire français-provençal.* 3 vols.: A–D, E–O, P–Z. Digne: Repos. (Repr. Geneva: Slatkine; Marseilles: Laffitte, 1972.)

Lagarda, Andrieu. 1975. *Vocabulaire occitan; Mots, locutions, e expressions idiomaticas recampats par centres d'interès.* Toulouse: IEO.

Lespy, Jean-Désiré (dit Vastin). 1880 (2d ed.). *Grammaire béarnaise, suivi d'un vocabulaire béarnais-français.* Paris: Maisonneuve. (Repr. Geneva: Slatkine; Marseilles: Laffitte, 1978. 1st ed. Pau: Veronese, 1858)

Lespy, Jean-Désiré, & Paul Raymond. 1877. *Dictionnaire béarnais ancien et moderne.* 2 vols. in 1. Montpellier: Hamelin. (Repr. Geneva: Slatkine, 1970.)

Levy, Emil. 1894–1924. *Provenzalisches Supplement Wörterbuch.* 8 vols. Leipzig: Reisland. (Repr. Geneva: Slatkine, 1973.)

——. 1973 (5th ed.). *Petit Dictionnaire provençal-français.* Heidelberg: Winter. (Repr. Raphèle-lès-Arles: Marcel Petit C. P. M., 1980. 1st ed., 1909.)

Lhermet, Jean. 1931. *Contribution à la lexicologie du dialecte aurillacois.* Paris: Droz. (Repr., with preface by Jean-Claude Potte, Geneva: Slatkine; Marseilles: Laffitte, 1978.)

Malvezin, Pierre. 1908–9. *Glossaire de la langue d'Oc.* Paris: Imprimerie Coudert. (Repr. Geneva: Slatkine; Marseilles: Laffitte, 1973.)

Michalias, Régis. 1912. *Glossaire des mots particuliers du dialecte d'Oc de la commune d'Ambert (Puy-de-Dôme).* Paris: Champion. (Repr. Geneva: Slatkine; Marseilles: Laffitte, 1978.

Miremont, Pierre. 1974. *Glossari del Perigord negre.* Rodez: Carrère.

Mistral, Frédéric. 1932 (2d ed.); 1979 (repr.). *Lou Tresor dóu Felibrige, ou Dictionnaire provençal-français embrassant les divers dialectes de la langue d'oc moderne.* 2 vols. A–F, G–Z. Raphèle-lès-Arles: Marcel Petit C. P. M. (1st ed., Aix-en-Provence: Veuve Remondet-Aubin, 1879–1886.)

Morère, Maurice. 1980. *Glosari gascon dels fonemes juridics arcaics dam anotacions e remarcas.* Pau: "La Garbure étudiante."

Moulis, Adelin. 1978. *Dicciunari lengodoucian-français. Dictionnaire languedocien-français.* Vergniolle: Chez l'auteur.

Moureau, Pierre. 1870. *Dictionnaire du patois de La Teste*. La Teste: Imprimerie P. Moureau.

Palay, Simin. 1980 (3d ed.). *Dictionnaire du béarnais et du gascon modernes*. Paris: CNRS. (1st ed. Pau: Marrimpouey, 1932–34.)

Piat, Louis. 1893–94. *Dictionnaire français-occitanien, donnant l'équivalent des mots français dans tous les dialectes de la langue d'oc moderne*. 2 vols. in 1. Montpellier: Hamelin. (Repr. Aix-en-Provence: Editions R. Berenguié, 1970.)

Puget, Pierre. 18th century. *Dictionnaire provençal et français*. MS. 158, Bibl. Méjanes, Aix-en-Provence. (Repr. Geneva: Slatkine, 1978.)

Rapin, Cristian. 1971. *Diccionnari francés-occitan*. Agen: CAP e CAP.

Raynouard, François. 1838–44. *Lexique roman, ou Dictionnaire de la langue des troubadours comparée avec les autres langues de l'Europe latine*. 6 vols. Paris: Silvestre. (Repr. Geneva: Slatkine, 1977.)

Rohlfs, Gerhard. 1935; 1977 (3d ed.). *Le Gascon*. Beihefte zur ZRPh, 85. Halle: Niemeyer; Pau: Marrimpouey.

Ronjat, Jules. 1937; 1980 (repr.). *Grammaire [h]istorique des parlers provençaux modernes*. III. *Morphologie et formation des mots*. 4 vols., 1930–41. Montpellier: Société des Langues Romanes. (Repr. Geneva: Slatkine; Marseilles: Laffitte, 1980.)

Sauvages, Pierre Boissier de. 1785 (3d ed.). *Dictionnaire languedocien-français*. 2 vols. Nîmes: Michel Gaude. (Repr. Geneva: Slatkine; Marseilles: Laffitte, 1971.)

Schmitt, Alfons Theo. 1934. *La Terminologie pastorale dans les Pyrénées centrales*. Paris: Droz.

Seuzaret, Jules. 1947. "Dictionnaire patois-français du dialecte du Vivarais et de la région d'Aubenas (Ardèche)." MS.

Taupiac, Jacme. 1977. *Pichon diccionari francés-occitan*. Toulouse: IEO (CREO de Tolosa).

Vayssier, l'abbé. 1879. *Dictionnaire patois-français du département de l'Aveyron*. Rodez: Imprimerie Carrère.

Vigneau, Jean-Bernard. 1982. *Lexique du gascon parlé dans le Bazadais*. B.M. Bordeaux, MS. 2077, 1879, ed. Jacques Boisgontier & J.-Bernard Marquette. Bazas: Les Cahiers du Bazadais.

Villa, Etienne. 1802. *Nouveaux Gasconismes corrigés*. Montpellier: Izar & A. Ricard.

4.2 OCCITAN SECONDARY SOURCES

Adams, Edward L. 1913. *Word-Formation in Provençal*. New York: Macmillan.

Cassagnau, Marcel. 1965. "Notes de philologie gasconne." *BSGers* 66:222–28.

Chambon, J.-Pierre. 1978. "Notes lexicographiques d'ancien provençal." *RLiR* 42:75–80.

Klingebiel, Kathryn. 1986b. "Two Ventures in Occitan Lexicography (and Their Background), with Bibliographic Supplement." *RPh* 39:448–61.

Rohlfs, Gerhard. 1931. "Beiträge zur Kenntnis der Pyrenäenmundarten (Die Suffixbildung)." *RLiR* 7:120–69.

Schwegler, Armin. 1986. "The Chanson de Sainte Foy: Etymology of *cabdorn*." *RPh* 39:285–304.

Séguy, Jean. 1953. *Les Noms populaires des plantes dans les Pyrénées centrales*. Barcelona: IEP.

———. 1954–73. *Atlas linguistique et ethnographique de la Gascogne*. 6 vols. Toulouse: Institut des Etudes Méridionales de la Faculté des Lettres; Paris: CNRS.

Wartburg, W. von. 1956. "Die griechische Kolonisation in Südgallien und ihre sprachlichen Zeugen im Westromanischen." Rev. text. *Von Sprache und Mensch*, 61–126. Bern: Francke.

4.3 OCCITAN PRIMARY SOURCES

Abbadie, François, ed. 1892. *Livre noir de Dax* (cartulaire); *Livre rouge de Dax* (cartulaire); *Etablissements de Dax*. Paris: Picard; Bordeaux: Ferret. Glossaire; pp. 529–66. Also printed as *Le Livre noir et les Etablissements de Dax*, ed. François Abbadie, in *Archives historiques de la Gironde* 37:1–594. Bordeaux: Gounouilhou, 1902.

Archives historiques du Département de la Gironde. Glossaires gascons, vols. XI (1873), XXXVI, XLV (1910). Vol. XI printed separately as *Glossaire des mots des divers dialectes gascons, béarnais, bordelais, etc. employés dans les dix premiers vols. publiés par la Société des Archives Historiques du Département de la Gironde*. Bordeaux: Gounouilhou, 1873. Vol. XLV contains "Chartes gasconnes," ed. G. Millardet, 1–270.

Ducamin, J., ed. 1908. *Disciplines de clergie et de moralités, de Petrus Alphonsus, traduites en gascon girondin du XIV–XVe siècle*. Toulouse: Privat.

Fables causides de La Fontaine en bers gascouns. 1776. Bayonne: P. F. Duhard. (Repr. Bayonne: Editions Librairie "Limarc," 1980.)

Lafont, Robert. 1974. *Anthologie des baroques occitans*. Avignon: Aubanel.

Luchaire, Achille. 1881. *Recueil de textes de l'ancien dialecte gascon*. Paris.

Millardet, Georges. 1910. *Recueil de textes des anciens dialectes landais*. Paris: Champion.

Mouly, Enric. 1970. *Kathleen*. Rodez: Subervie.

5.1 CATALAN DICTIONARIES/GRAMMARS

Aguiló, M. 1925. *Diccionari català*. Barcelona: Instituto IEO.

Aladern, Joseph. 1905. *Diccionari popular de la llengua catalana*. 3 vols. Barcelona: Francisco Baxarias.

Albertí, S. 1983 (13th ed.). *Diccionario castellà-català, català-castellà*. Barcelona: Albertí.

Alcover, A. M., & F. de B. Moll. 1930–62. *Diccionari català-valencià-balear*. Palma de Majorca: Imprimeria Alcover.

Badía Margarit, Antoni. 1962. *Gramática catalana*. 2 vols. Madrid: Gredos.

Coromines, Joan. 1980–86. *Diccionari etimològic i complementari de la llengua catalana*. Vols. 1–6, A–Qu. Barcelona: Curial Ed. Catalanes, Caixa de Pensiones La Caixa.

Diccionari de la llengua catalana. 1982. Barcelona: Encliclopèdia Catalana.

Diccionari manual castellà-català, català-castellà. 1983 (7th ed.). Barcelona: Vox.

Fabra, Pompeu. 1966 (4th ed.). *Diccionari general de la llengua catalana*. Barcelona: A. López-Llausàs.

Griera, Antoni. 1935–47. *Tresor de la llengua, de les tradicions i de la cultura popular de la Catalunya*. 14 vols. Barcelona: Edicions Catalunyas.

Huber, Joseph. 1929. *Katalanische Grammatik*. Heidelberg: Winter.

Torrellas, Albert. 1959. *Diccionari català-castellà*. Barcelona: Ed. Miquel.

Vallès, E. 1962. *Pal.las. Diccionari català il.lustrat*. Barcelona: Massanés.

5.2 CATALAN SECONDARY SOURCES

Moreu-Rey, Enric. 1981. *Renoms, Motius, Malnoms i Noms de Casa*. Barcelona: Edicions Millà.

Ruaix i Vinyet, Josep. 1979. *El Català en fitxes*. Vol. 3: *Lèxic i estilística*. Barcelona: Homedes, Consell de Cent.

6.1 SPANISH DICTIONARIES/GRAMMARS

Alonso Hernández, José Luis. 1976. *Léxico del marginalismo del Siglo de Oro*. Salamanca: Universidad de Salamanca.

Alvar, Manuel, & Bernard Pottier. 1983. *Morfología histórica del español*. Madrid: Gredos.

Andolz, Rafael. 1977. *Diccionario aragonés: Aragonés-castellano; castellano-aragonés*. Zaragoza: Ediciónes Libreria General.

Barthe, Julio. 1979. *Prontuario medieval*. Murcia: Secretariado de Publicaciones, Universidad de Murcia.

Boggs, R. S., Lloyd Kasten, Hayward Keniston, & H. B. Richardson. 1946. *Tentative Dictionary of Medieval Spanish*. Chapel Hill: University of North Carolina Press.

Castro, Américo. 1936. *Glosarios latino-españoles de la Edad Media*. Madrid: Centro de Estudios Históricos.

Cejador y Frauca, Julio. 1929. *Vocabulario medieval castellano*. Madrid: Librería y Casa Editorial Hernando.

Corominas, Joan. 1954–57. *Diccionario crítico etimológico de la lengua castellana*. 4 vols. Bern: Francke; Madrid: Gredos.

——. 1961; 1967 (2d ed.). *Breve diccionario etimológico de la lengua castellana*: Madrid: Gredos.

Corominas, Joan, & José A. Pascual. 1980–85. *Diccionario crítico etimológico castellano e hispánico*. 5 vols: A–T. Madrid: Gredos.

Fontecha, Carmen. 1941. *Glosario de voces comentadas en ediciones de textos clásicos*. Madrid: CSIC.

García de Diego, Vicente. 1985. *Diccionario etimológico español e hispánico*. Madrid: Espasa-Calpe. (1st ed. Madrid: SAETA, 1955.)

Gili y Gaya, Samuel. 1947. *Tesoro lexicográfico 1492–1726*. A–G. Madrid: CSIC.

Hanssen, Federico. 1913; 1945 (repr.). *Gramática histórica de la lengua castellana*. Buenos Aires: El Ateneo.

Iribarren, José María. 1952. *Vocabulario navarro*. Pamplona: Diputación Foral de Navarra, Instituto "Príncipe de Viana."

Kasten, Lloyd, & John Nitti. 1978. *Concordances and Texts of the Royal Scriptorium Manuscripts of Alfonso X el Sabio*. Madison: Hispanic Seminary, University of Wisconsin.

Lanchetas, Rufino. 1900. *Gramática y vocabulario de las obras de Gonzalo de Berceo*. Madrid: "Sucesores de Rivadeneyra."

Menéndez Pidal, Ramón. 1911. *Cantar de mio Cid*. Vol. 2, 3d part: *Vocabulario*. Madrid: Bailly-Bailliere. (Rev. 2d ed. in *Obras completas*, vol. 4. Madrid: Espasa-Calpe, 1944–46.)

——. 1941 (6th ed.). *Manual de gramática histórica española*. Madrid: Espasa-Calpe.

Nitti, John, & Lloyd Kasten. 1982. *Concordances and Texts of the Fourteenth-Century Aragonese Manuscripts of Juan Fernández de Heredia*. Madison: Hispanic Seminar, University of Wisconsin.

Oelschläger, Victor R. B. 1940. *A Medieval Spanish Word-List*. Madison: University of Wisconsin Press.

Novo Mier, Lorenzo. 1979. *Dicionariu xeneral de la llingua asturiana*. Oviedo: Asturlibros.

Nuevo diccionario general español-inglés EDAF; New Comprehensive Spanish-English Dictionary EDAF. 1977. Madrid: EDAF.

Pardo Asso, José. 1938. *Nuevo Diccionario etimológico aragonés (voces, frases y modismos usados en el habla de Aragón)*. Zaragoza: Imprimeria del Hogar Pignatelli.

Ramsey, M. M., & Robert K. Spaulding. 1956 (3d ed.). *A Textbook of Modern Spanish*. New York: Holt, Rinehart & Winston.

Real Academia Española. 1970 (19th ed); 1984 (20th ed.). *Diccionario de la lengua española*. 2 vols. Madrid: Gredos.

Rodríguez Marín, Francisco. 1922. *Dos mil quinientas voces castizas y bien autorizadas que piden lugar en nuestro léxico*. Madrid: Tipografía de la "Revista de Archivos, Bibliotecas y Museos."

Romera-Navarro, Miguel. 1951. *Registro de lexicografía hispánica*. Madrid: Aguirre.

Spitzer, Leo. 1938. Review of *Glosarios latino-españoles de la Edad Media*, by Américo Castro. *MLN* 53:122–46

Williams, Edwin B. 1962 (rev. ed.). *Spanish and English Dictionary; Diccionario inglés y español*. New York: Holt, Rinehart & Winston.

6.2 SPANISH SECONDARY SOURCES

Alemany Bolufer, J. 1920. *Tratado de la formación de palabras en la lengua castellana: La derivación y la composición, estudio de los sufijos y prefijos empleados en una y otra*. Madrid: V. Suárez. (Repr. from *Boletín de la Real Academia Española* 4–6 [1917–19].)

Alvar, Manuel. 1976. "Nota sobre *captenencia*." *RFE* 58:231–35.

Giurescu, Anca. 1972. "El método transformacional en el análisis de los nombres compuestos del español moderno." *RRL* 17:407–14.

Lloyd, Paul M. 1960. "A Linguistic Analysis of Old Spanish Occupational Terms". Diss., University of California, Berkeley.

——. 1968. *Verb-Complement Compounds in Spanish*. Beihefte zur *ZRPh*, 116. Tübingen: Niemeyer.

Malkiel, Yakov. 1951. "The Hispanic Suffix *-(i)ego*." *UCPL* 4/3:111–213.

——. 1958. "Español antiguo *cuer* y *coraçón*." *BH* 60:180–207; 327–63.

Sandru-Olteanu, Tudora. 1972. "Bibliografía de los trabajos relativos a la formación de palabras en los idiomas iberorrománicos (1920–1970)." *BFE* 12:13–35.

Vaño-Cerdá, Antonio. 1984. "Sobre el tipo de composición romance *porta-plumas*." *Caligrama* 1:181–221.

7.1 ITALIAN AND OTHER ROMANCE: DICTIONARIES/GRAMMARS

Battisti, Carlo, & Giovanni Alessio. 1950–57. *Dizionario etimologico italiano*. 5 vols. Firenze: G. Barbèra.

Devoto, G. 1966; 1968 (2d printing). *Avviamento alla etimologia italiana. Dizionario etimologico*. Florence: F. Le Monnier.

Pfister, Max. 1979–84. *Lessico etimologico italiano*. Vol. I, Fasc. 1–8; Vol. II, Fasc. 9–10. Wiesbaden: L. Reichert.

7.2 ITALIAN AND OTHER ROMANCE: SECONDARY SOURCES

Giurescu, Anca. 1965. "Contributi al modo di definire i sostantivi composti della lingua italiana." *RRL* 10:395–400. (Rumanian version in *SCL* 16 [1965], 829–34.)

———. 1968. "I composti italiani del tipo verbo-nome, risultati di una trasformazione di frase." *RRL* 13:421–26.

———. 1973. "Les Noms composés dans le portugais contemporain." *RRL* 18/5:415–24.

[H]asan, Finuţa, & Fulvia Ciobanu. 1967. "Cuvintele compuse şi grupurile sintatice stabile." *Studii şi Materiale Privitoare la Formarea Cuvintelor în Limba Română*, vol. 4, 235–52. Bucharest: Ed. Acad. RSR.

Tollemache, Federico. 1945. *Le parole composte nella lingua italiana*. Roma: Rores di Nicola Ruffolo.

8.2 GENERAL LINGUISTICS SECONDARY SOURCES

Benveniste, Emile. 1966. "Convergences typologiques." *L'Homme* 6/2:5–12. (Repr. in *Problèmes de linguistique générale*, vol. 2, 103–12. Paris: Gallimard, 1974.)

———. 1967. "Fondements syntaxiques de la composition nominale." *BSLP* 62:15–31. (Repr. in *Problèmes de linguistique générale*, vol. 2, 145–62. Paris: Gallimard, 1974.)

Chomsky, Noam. 1970. "Remarks on Nominalization." *Readings in English Transformational Grammar*, ed. Roderick Jacobs & Peter Rosenbaum, 184–221. Waltham, Mass.: Ginn.

Greenberg, Joseph H. 1963. "Some Universals of Grammar with Particular Reference to the Order of Meaningful Elements." *Universals of Language*, ed. J. H. Greenberg, 58–90. Cambridge, Mass.: MIT Press.

Kastovsky, Dieter. 1982. "Word Formation: A Functional View." *Folia Linguistica* 16:181–98.

Malkiel, Yakov. 1966. "Genetic Analysis of Word Formation." *Current Trends in Linguistics*. Vol. 3: *Theoretical Foundations*, 305–64. The Hague: Mouton.

———. 1978. "Derivational Categories." *Universals of Human Language*. Vol. 3: *Word Structure*, ed. Joseph H. Greenberg et al., 125–49. Stanford: Stanford University Press.

Marchand, Hans. 1960. *The Categories and Types of Present-Day English Word-Formation*. Wiesbaden: O. Harrasowitz. (2d ed., completely revised and enlarged, Munich: C. H. Beck, 1969.)

Marouzeau, J. 1961 (3d ed.). *Lexique de la terminologie linguistique*. Paris: Librairie Orientaliste Paul Geuthner.

Mithun, Marianne. 1984. "The Evolution of Noun Incorporation." *Language* 60:847–94.

Pennanen, Esko. 1966. *Contributions to the Study of Back-Formation in English*. Tampere: Publications of the School of Social Sciences.

Index of Authors
in Bibliography and Notes

Index of Subjects